Kirklees
COUNCIL

Library and Information Centres

Red doles Lane

Huddersfield, West Yorkshire

KT-470-927

This book should be returned on or before
Fines are charged if the item is late.

16 Apr '18.

0 7 DEC 2018

You may renew this loan for a further period by phone, personal visit or at
www.kirklees.gov.uk/libraries, provided that the book is not required by
another reader.

NO MORE THAN THREE RENEWALS ARE PERMITTED

Making a Noise

Making a Noise

Getting it Right, Getting it Wrong in Life,
Broadcasting and the Arts

JOHN TUSA

WEIDENFELD & NICOLSON

First published in Great Britain in 2018
by Weidenfeld & Nicolson

1 3 5 7 9 10 8 6 4 2

A CIP catalogue record for this book
is available from the British Library.

ISBN 978 1 4746 0708 7

Typeset by Input Data Services Ltd, Somerset

Printed and bound by CPI Group (UK) Ltd, Croydon, CR0 4YY

Weidenfeld & Nicolson

The Orion Publishing Group Ltd
Carmelite House
50 Victoria Embankment
London
EC4Y 0DZ
An Hachette UK Company
www.orionbooks.co.uk

This book is dedicated to my wife Annie, who has lived through, experienced, endured, enriched, entered, enhanced – and I hope sometimes enjoyed – almost everything described in these pages. For her understanding, acceptance, kindness, common sense, relish, curiosity and sense of humour, thanks are inadequate.

Contents

1

Being Czech

Czechoslovakia and England 1936–49

The company town of Bata, the Czechoslovak shoe company, was built in the small south Moravian town of Zlín from 1906. Moravia, with Bohemia, was one of the two Czech provinces which united with Slovakia to form the new state of Czecho-Slovakia after the First World War. To the south and west of the town lie some of the glorious centres of Moravian baroque: Olomouc, the seat of archbishops and once the capital of Moravia; Kroměříž, the archbishops' summer residence, whose palace was the site of the failed attempt to secure Czech and Slovak independence after the 1848 revolutions against the Habsburg rulers. The palace houses a magnificent art gallery including Titian's *The Flaying of Marsyas*. Nearby is the provincial capital, Brno, with its squares, castle, cathedral, monasteries and churches.

The Hussite Wars of the fifteenth century raged in this area, inspired by Jan Hus, the Protestant revolutionary later adored as a national hero. Kroměříž Cathedral was burnt down in the fighting. During the Thirty Years War, 1618–48, the cathedral burned yet again. After their 1620 defeat in the Battle of White Mountain, the Protestant leaders who had precipitated the Thirty Years War were returned to Brno for trial; twenty-seven were executed as a dreadful example to all such rebels. (History mattered to my family; my mother came from a long line of Hussites and often muttered darkly about 'seven hundred years of persecution' – inaccurate, perhaps, but passionately felt. Very few Sunday lunches passed without my father referring with equal passion to the 'slaughter of the flower of Czech nobility at the White Mountain'. He was born Catholic but converted to Protestantism at my grandfather's insistence. All he had to do was to fill in a form from the post office!)

To the west of Zlín lies the village of Slavkov, historically known as Austerlitz, site of Napoleon's great victory in 1805. Southern Moravia had been wracked with war and turmoil, its gently rolling fields and meadows forming the backdrop for set-piece battles, but also for the war of manoeuvre, for cavalry, for massed ranks of uniformed infantry. This, not Belgium, was surely the true 'Cockpit of Europe'.

Of all this the newly established Bata company town of Zlín was mightily unaware, and probably indifferent too. It created and lived in a self-contained world remote from history. The firm was about the new, the modern, the future, the socially enlightened, the paternally directed. What did the past matter when you were building the future? Tomas Bata – 'The Founder', as he was always called – had no doubts; he would produce affordable shoes for the unshod millions of the world using the new system of conveyor-belt mass production. Modern well-lit factory buildings housing scores of production lines were built in the austere modernist style first conceived by the Bauhaus School in Dessau in Germany. The workers would – and did – live in similar Bauhaus-influenced houses: plain-fronted, flat-roofed, with private gardens, schools, clinics, shops and restaurants clustered around the factory buildings.

There was one architectural and social model for Bata communities anywhere in the world, whether in Czechoslovakia, England, Holland, France or even India – as Vikram Seth's great novel *A Suitable Boy* bears graphic witness. In this brave new Bata world, Seth's hero chooses the efficient modernity of the Bata factory, its management style, its work habits as representing the future rather than traditional India. Wherever they were established, Bata companies had no time or place for the cosy, the rustic, the vernacular, the local, the traditional. As for the past, it had bare feet. Where was the attraction in that?

This was the physical, social and cultural environment into which I was born. I learned only slowly how odd, on so many levels, such surroundings were, but I have never underestimated the cumulative effect of Zlín's strangeness on me. After all, to be born in a planned town, an ideological town, an authoritarian town, a town with but a single purpose and activity – making shoes – was mighty strange, fascinating, and in the end constricting. My father was a lifelong 'Bataman', chose Bata as his company, adopted Zlín as his town. He was proudly Czech, he who had been patted on the head as a young boy by the Emperor Franz Josef when he passed through on the 'Hofzug' – the imperial train! He who had been educated in German at school, in preparation for life and work in the Habsburg empire. But now Bata was to be my father's family, a Czech family, his own family having little bearing on his or our lives. System and order were essential elements of the company make-up; perhaps conformism too. It was one part of my own inherited background.

There was another part close by. Across the Hostýnské Vrchy, to the north-west, lay the country town of Bystřice pod Hostýnem. The 600-metre-high wooded hill of Hostýn played its role in the area's crowded history. For it was here in 1241 that the Virgin Mary halted the seemingly irresistible advance of the Tartars into Central Europe by sending lightning bolts to destroy their encampments. The town had a quiet sense of standing on the redoubts of threatened European civilisation. Ever since it has been a major centre of Marian pilgrimage. Bystřice was my mother's town and remains the home of some of her family today.

Belonging to a Protestant Hussite family dating back to the 1630s, they had always proudly asserted their religious identity in a predominantly Catholic area. Such need for self-awareness, for individual definition, for vigilance against external threat, for personal independence made up the inheritance from my mother's side. Grandfather, 'Deda', was a foreman in the famous Thonet bentwood furniture factory, then the chief employer in the town, still in business today. Much respected, he was the first Protestant to be buried in the town cemetery. Deda also kept animals, owned land, cultivated strips, tended extensive orchards. Such traditional individualism and confident variety were very different from the modern outlook, the organised sense of purpose of my father's background.

My own temperament and outlook has oscillated between these two poles, the worlds of Zlín and Bystřice, two towns on different sides of the Hostyn Heights: the modern, conformist, managerial world of Bata and the individualistic, traditionalist, familial world of the Sklenar – 'Glazier' – family of Bystrice. How have these contrasts, contradictions perhaps, resolved themselves in me and my life? Which of them is dominant in whatever exists or remains of my Czech identity? How has this Czech identity interacted with my subsequent need to become English, or British? And when it came to being British, what kind of Briton would I become? I have wrestled with these questions, sought an understanding, aimed to strike a balance between them all my life.

At the start, for a Bata baby born in a Bata clinic to a Bata man and woman from a Bata house in a Bata town, the Zlín effect was uppermost. I could not have ignored it even though I could not yet understand it. The daily family chatter of Zlín life, our family oral history, created and maintained a set of strongly implanted folk stories of the life taking place all around me as a baby and as a toddler. My early world was made by those words.

I heard how my father, a talented accountant, good with numbers, left school at sixteen, was spotted by the Founder and promoted in his early twenties to manage the Bata tannery at nearby Otrokovice. I heard how my father had to ask the Founder's permission to get married. Who was he marrying?

Did she come from a good family? Did he have enough money in his company bank account? How the company reserved part of every worker's salary in order to pay for any business losses for which they were responsible. How Tomas Bata's office was built in a huge lift on the outside of the main building so that he could and did appear on any floor at any time. (It exists to this day.) How the toilet cubicles in the company buildings were made extra narrow so that no one would linger there. How Tomas Bata fatally ordered the pilot of his private plane to take off in thick fog and was killed in the crash that followed minutes later.

These and many other stories formed the stuff of family life. Some were funny. Not knowing that there might be a different way of living and behaving, many of them seemed quite normal. How could a child tell? Some were very personal. I do not remember being addicted to my dummy. I don't recall and cannot resent my brother George asking indignantly: 'Why has Johnny not stopped sucking a dummy?' and promptly cutting it in half. Photographs of blond baby me surrounded by female relatives show rooms bathed in bright summer light, the early mornings of life's innocence. Striking any kind of balance between these images, remembered or taught, real or created, would only begin years later and take many years to achieve.

Then actual recollection or imagined memory begins to play its part. After the 1938 Munich Agreement, Nazi forces were gradually stationed throughout Czechoslovakia. Some were undoubtedly based in Zlín. Elder brother George recalls that the local kindergarten playground had an exercise wheel in it. On more than one occasion, a few German soldiers would pass by and ask if they could 'have a go' on the wheel. They wanted to play. It all seemed perfectly normal to him, aged six; quite unthreatening.

My own 'memory' of Nazi soldiers is as vivid as it is contested. I 'remember' two soldiers patrolling our residential street on a motorcycle and sidecar. Do I see their 'coal-scuttle' helmets too? I believe I do. As they passed our house – or

did they pull in? – George squirted them with a water pistol.
Nothing followed. George recalls nothing of the incident but
is too brotherly to dismiss it. Why should I think I remember it if the incident never took place? Why should I – or my
memory – make it up when I stood to gain nothing from doing
so? There is no answer to these riddles. The 'memory' will not
vanish as part of the life I lived in Zlín before the Second World
War. More reliable was the incident of a distressed neighbour
coming to our house, weeping that the Germans had come
to 'take away our land'. What', I was said to have cried, 'am I
going to stand on?'

Two other incidents in the run-up to world war were both
real, frightening and reliably witnessed. In June 1939, with
war only months away, Mother took George and me on a
Bata-company package holiday to Crikvenica on Yugoslavia's
Adriatic coast. Father was already in England as the newly
appointed General Manager of the British Bata shoe factory
near Tilbury in Essex. On the return journey we were stopped
at the Czechoslovak frontier by a German border guard who
insisted we did not have the correct documents to enter the
country. It was not clear what was wrong with them. The
only place that could issue valid documents, he insisted, was
Berlin. How we were supposed to get to Berlin to acquire
valid documents for our homeland posed a nightmarish problem for us but was a matter of profound indifference to the
German guards.

My brother George, aged seven, recalls a huge argument
between the guard, the train conductor (who took our side)
and the leader of the Bata holiday group. The German was
adamant: no entry without the correct documents. 'Get off
the train! Remove your bags! Go to Berlin! Get the correct
papers!' It was late evening; the train was seriously held up. We
started to get our bags together. The train conductor and the
Bata group leader hatched a desperate plot. We would appear
to agree to leave the train. They would get the German guard
off and onto the platform. The moment he had dismounted,

the train conductor would slam the carriage door, blow his whistle and the train would pull away. It worked.

I completely trust this detailed version of what happened. I can only add a single embellishment from the perspective of a three-year-old child. At one stage, as my mother stood on the platform, engaged in a heated argument with the German official, I howled so loudly at the terrifying prospect of losing my mother that she was told to get back on the train and shut the child up. This memory is not confirmed by George. He does not deny it. But my mother confirmed it more than once to Annie. How can this happen? There is no contradiction. George recalls what he believes happened. I remember how I felt. Fact, feeling – the two are wholly compatible. Memories, in all their layers, involve both. We had a very close call for sure.

For Father, a young man freshly installed in the newly built Bata company town on the Thames marshes, life was tricky too. It was 13 June 1939 when the Home Office in London finally wrote to say he could apply for a permanent visa to work in England. He arrived on 24 June to find no sign of a British visa for the rest of the family. Time was running short as the European crisis deepened. In near-despair, Father turned to the Chairman of the British Bata Shoe Company, a distinguished former general and politician, Sir Edward Spears. Unless the company could get visas for his family to join him in England, my father would return to Czechoslovakia immediately and not come back.

Spears, phenomenally well connected, pulled every one of his many Whitehall strings. Our visas materialised out of the Whitehall shadows and we reached England on 26 July 1939. War was just weeks away. I owe a huge debt to Edward Spears. That is one reason why his portrait hangs in our house to this day.

Our train journey from Czechoslovakia to England in July 1939, with war just weeks away, had its own moment of crisis. Shortly before reaching the frontier with Holland, a woman in our carriage approached Mother. She explained that she and her two children were Jewish. As they were almost certain to be removed from the train at the German border, would Mother take care of the children and get them into Holland as part of her family? My mother, as she told the story, decided that the ruse of passing those children off as part of our family would be seen through at once. Trying to smuggle children of a Jewish family out of Germany without papers would lead to our own detention as well. The chances of success were nil. She refused. It cannot have been an easy moment and stayed with her all her life.

My mother retold this story several times, especially to Annie once we were married. She felt she had had no alternative but to say 'no'. It lay on her conscience and lived on in her memory. What else could she have done? I would be amazed if her own recent trauma of being denied re-entry into Czechoslovakia on returning from Yugoslavia hadn't weighed with her. How could she risk going through that again? Sadly, I never asked her directly why she acted as she did. Perhaps because the exchanges between Mother and the German woman would have been discreet, muttered, sotto voce, neither I nor George knew anything of it until many years later. Children are sheltered from some of the worst moments. Innocence permits being oblivious to reality, which crowds in later but lacks explanations.

I never thanked my parents for bringing us out of Czechoslovakia and into a land of wondrous opportunities where foreigners could flourish. You don't when you are only three, but I should have been more openly grateful as I grew up. I never speculated what life would have been like had we remained in Czechoslovakia. An explanation for such failure of generosity towards them, though not a justification, might lie in my later life and experiences.

Father chartered a light aircraft to come and meet us off the train at Hook of Holland. No doubt he wanted to escort us off the Continent in person. We crossed together on the night ferry to Harwich and drove through the picturesque country-side of rural Essex to the very different estuarial Essex. Was this the best England had to offer? No hills, no pine forests, no rich meadows, no character, no personality, just flat, featureless fields. At last we saw it, our new home, the community that would shape us for a couple of decades, the British Bata Company estate of East Tilbury.

What did we find? Nothing English, nothing strange, nothing new but a reincarnation of the 'mother ship of Bata', Zlín, down to the last detail. Identical rectangular factory blocks, identical workers' and managers' square houses, identical social and sporting amenities of the enlightened 1930s kind. Instead of the lush surroundings of the Hostyn Heights cradling the shoemakers' community, there was only the flat, featureless, desolate marshes that line the north bank of the Thames estuary. We had left Zlín, Moravia, and ended up in proto-Zlín, Essex. The full humour of it only dawned years later. You can't see the joke when you are three. In July 1939, we considered ourselves lucky to be out of Czechoslovakia, luckier still to be in England, lucky to be employed, lucky to be in a friendly Czech community. Any complications surrounding identity, who I was, who I might become, these would have to wait.

Why were we on the Bata Estate, East Tilbury, Essex at all? As part of Tomas Bata's relentless global expansion, England, with its imperial, colonial trading links and connections, was an obvious site for a major shoe-manufacturing plant. Czechoslovakia was not the hub of a worldwide empire. Just as the British Empire had spanned the globe with its trade, its connections and its values, so would Tomas Bata's shoes.

The Founder's reputation must have spread fast, for it was a Tilbury-based clergyman, Canon Bown, who suggested that Bata might build a factory in south-east Essex where unemployment was high. A local farmer, Mr W. W. Wilson, was very keen to get rid of acres of potato fields bordering the Thames.

I met both Canon Bown and 'Farmer' Wilson some years later. No one bothered to tell me about their key parts in creating the Bata world that would shape so much of me. What would I have made of it? Maybe very little. Yet I feel a lingering resentment at not having this part of my own history opened to me.

By 1933, the first factory buildings had been built on the muddy empty wastes of the Thames marshes. The social centre of the Bata Estate, the very consciously Czech-named 'Community House', was finished a year later, as was the first row of houses in Bata Avenue. Building a company estate was an integral part of the Bata vision, the Bata way of life. It was a practical necessity too. There was nowhere nearby in sparsely peopled south-east Essex for the workers to live. By the outbreak of war, another street had been built – Queen Mary Avenue – and the swimming pool and tennis courts were ready for use. Healthy bodies were part of the enlightened paternalism of the times. The basic shape of 'Zlín-upon-Thames', as it was never called but as it was in reality, had been put into place. The very speed of its construction could not conceal the strangeness of the basic conception. From estuarial potato fields to model community in under a decade: that was Bata vision, Bata practicality in action.

We were now physically in England, Czechoslovakia left far behind. But how could I ever become English when my Czech base seemed to be pursuing me? One part of my Czech roots would not give up its hold – the ordered, planned, directed, Bata way of life. It took away nourishment from my other Czech roots, the instinctive, individualistic ways of my mother's family from rural Bystrice.

Father recognised at least part of the dilemma and declared, 'We speak English at home!' Mother continued to use Czech for talking to her many friends. Once, when she slipped into Czech as she spoke to me, I told her off: 'Don't talk like that in front of my friends.' Recognising the tensions and contradictions involved in living in England but being surrounded by Czechs, my parents bought an old farmhouse in the nearby village of Horndon-on-the-Hill in the autumn of 1940. The process of rebalancing identity could begin. Yet the Czech influence remained inevitably heavy when all life revolved around work and that work was Czech in nature and character.

The Bata Estate, East Tilbury, always represented a massive disruption, an intrusion of Central European modernism, Central European paternalism, Central European radicalism into the impoverished flatlands of south-east Essex. Here a few dozen Czech managers, speaking with a funny accent in broken English, applying a Czech system of making and working, organised, ran and managed a workforce of up to 3,000 English workers. If the English thought it was all a bit odd, they also appreciated good jobs in an area otherwise very short of them. This was valued even if the source of the new prosperity was what people called, in a perfectly friendly way, 'bloody foreigners'. For them it was not a judgement, still less a rejection, just a description.

But the Czechs knew that they were in a sense intruders. They wanted to be British; they tried to be British. The company's name proclaimed it to be the 'British Bata Shoe Company'. New streets were proudly and loyally named 'Coronation Avenue' and 'Queen Elizabeth Avenue'. In work practices and behaviour, however, it never ceased to be Czech. The estate, with its Bata Hotel, Bata School, Bata Technical College, Bata Farm, Bata Cinema, Bata Shoe Shop and Bata Garage, proclaimed its foreignness. There was no attempt to merge quietly into something more English, to ape some English ways. For not only was it Czech, the newcomers believed that the way they behaved and worked was very advanced, very modern. They were industrial colonisers bringing a better way of working and living to people who needed instruction. For the local English population, this was the experience of colonialism in reverse.

Many of Bata's practices – such as objective-setting, management by performance and payment by results – still sound radical today. It was a very forward-looking organisation. Eighty years ago, it had a brand image and a brand slogan – 'Our Customer Our Master'. It had a Mission Statement: 'Our service to the communities where we live and work is to produce good shoes and sell them at the lowest possible price. To make shoes available to everyone and, in so doing, be a partner with the rest of the people who are trying so hard to build up their communities.' There is something rather touching about the evident sincerity of the ideals in that Mission Statement, as well as a sense that the gaucheness of the language betrays the company's fundamental Czech-ness. Yet there was nothing sentimental about Bata's management style.

As a child and young boy, I took it all for granted – that was how they behaved at 'The Factory'. When he came home for lunch and over supper, my father would keep us informed with a running commentary on daily events at the workplace in vivid detail. The travails of work, of setting up a new factory, of building a nationwide network of retail shops, of initially collecting cash from the high-street shops at the week's end to pay the factory workers' wages, these matters were never left behind at the factory gate. They could not be.

He spent one day a week 'walking the factory floor'. Father must have known the names of between a third and half of the 3,000-strong workforce, and recognised the faces of even more. Today's 'advanced' management cant terms it MBWA – 'management by walking about' – as if it was a huge discovery. 'Batamen' were practising it half a century ago. Father had a legendary ability to open the one box of shoes waiting to be dispatched which contained one black and one brown shoe. The rumpus that followed the discovery of such a failure of quality control depended on the scale of the error. The management response was covered by the all-too-familiar phrase, 'playing hell'; mistakes were not treated kindly in the Bata organisation.

The previous Managing Director of the company had been notorious for the way he 'played hell'. On his regular visits to the Sample Room – where current and future shoe styles were displayed with all the costings, production and sales figures attached to each – the MD would invariably launch into a tirade of abuse and criticism, punctuated by volleys of shoes hurled in all directions. Cannier managers took to occupying strategic positions close to tables, taking shelter underneath them when the footwear started to fly. This form of 'Management by Throwing Around' ended with the old MD's departure.

The Friday Luncheon Conference was a key meeting during which production targets and sales figures were reviewed. If a production target had been missed or something had run over budget, those responsible would have to answer for their failings; the worse the failure, the more hell would be played. How anyone managed to eat their lunch while this was going on was a source of amazement to me. I lost count of the times that my father returned from work on a Friday evening and reported that he had played hell over some issue. He was often very angry. Afterwards, my mother would say: 'I thought he would have hard attack' (always pronounced 'hard attack'). He never did. It did nothing for his digestion or, I guess, that of his managers. And just in case his 'playing hell' didn't drive home the point about personal responsibility for performance, the portion of their salary liable to be forfeit in case of a loss in their area – not just an underperformance – would be duly deducted from their pay.

When it came to Christmas, the company really sailed in its Central European colours. Senior managers and their wives gathered in the Company Hospitality Flat in the Bata Hotel and received Christmas presents from Father in his capacity as Managing Director. The managers in turn clubbed together and gave my parents a present. We are not talking handkerchiefs here, hostess trolleys more like, on one occasion a walnut-veneered stereophonic radiogram. As a child, I was puzzled. Who paid for these gifts? Was it a kind of company Christmas bonus? Did my father pay from his own pocket? I couldn't bring myself to ask; as a result I remained faintly uncomfortable, and probably unnecessarily so.

Our own Czech/Bata identity reached its apogee on Christmas Eve. For all Central Europeans this is the high point of the Christmas season. My mother hated the muddy taste of the traditional dish of carp; good old turkey was just the thing to add English authenticity to an otherwise Czech occasion. A regular guest was the company's retail sales manager. Around nine-thirty, with the turkey dispatched and the flaming pudding waiting, complete with concealed sixpenny coins, the phone would ring. The retail manager, Norman Dover, would immediately get up from the table to take it in the corridor outside, returning a few minutes later with the retail sales numbers from Bata shops for the all-important Christmas fortnight. If targets had been met or exceeded, thanks were given all round. If missed, we had to settle for relief that they were not worse.

The whole ritual struck me as oddly, even uncomfortably confused; pagan, even. What was really going on? Were we celebrating the birth of Christ or the achievement of good retail sales? I never asked. The answer should have been 'both'. Without retail sales, who would pay for the turkey? And it was no odder than the Anglican Church's celebration of Harvest Thanksgiving. Here too, being Czech and being Bata were in the ascendant.

From the autumn of 1940, we lived in Horndon-on-the-Hill in a comfortable, rambling, wattle-and-daubed, wood-panelled, perhaps Tudor farmhouse that had at one time been the local post office. It had a large garden surrounded by trees and fencing, giving us privacy and seclusion. We had little contact with our English neighbours or the local community. Life continued to revolve for the most part around Czech friends on the Bata Estate three miles away. Having fled the suffocating intimacy of that imported Czech neighbourhood, we had in truth no other community to turn to. Home stood on the edge of this rather pretty English village with traditional cottages, small shops, pubs, church, instantly recognisable for what they were. This was how and where the English lived. Yet we largely turned our back on it all because we did not know how to live like the English.

The physical contrast between Horndon-on-the-Hill and the Bata Estate could not have been more pronounced. At East Tilbury there were no cottages, no crooked lanes, no pub, no church, no variety, nothing that showed signs of age. The houses were stuccoed, some fronted in red brick, flat-roofed, uniformly spaced along straight streets. The estate lacked surprise, the unexpected. The two basic types of house were modelled on those found in Zlín: the basic box (the majority), and the 'extended managerial' (which boasted a first-floor balcony). Designed to offer respite from Central Europe's stifling summers, in the more temperate climate of Tilbury the balconies seemed forlorn and pointless, and saw little use. The characteristic flat roofs of these Bata dwellings seemed hilariously unsuitable faced with English winter rain.

Set back from the street, each had a front garden, usually a patch of grass enclosing a flower bed. A path by the side of the house, wide enough to bounce balls against the house wall, led to a small, well-used back garden containing the essentials. Space for a coal box, a tool shed, the clothes line, a vegetable plot, flower beds, and of course, being Czech, some soft fruit bushes. The fruit trees, where they existed, were apples, pears, damsons and much-cherished Czech plum. Czech-owned gardens could often be distinguished from the rest by the muslin bag of *tvaroch* – a curd made from soured milk, which is an essential ingredient in many traditional dishes – hanging from the washing line. If there was modernist uniformity – conformity? – in the housing design, the gardens came from a peasant era.

The internal layout of the houses was standard throughout: a decent-sized front room for receiving visitors, an inner corridor leading to the dining room. The kitchen next door was small, with a sink, some cupboards, small gas stove and later a fridge. One person could cook in it, two children might wash the dishes – dishwashers were a generation away, freezers and microwaves two generations distant.

Yet within this constricted space, many Czech wives conjured miracles of cooking. 'Cuisine' is not the word for these traditional delights; such fare was never sufficiently refined to deserve the word. To say this is not to diminish the results; it was home cooking at its considerable best. Mrs Cermak ('Bozena') believed in tasty food; her specialities were roast duck and magically light walnut sponge cakes with cream topping seldom using – it was rumoured – fewer than twenty-four eggs. Mrs Soucek (always referred to as 'Sister') was renowned for her star- and crescent-shaped almond and hazelnut biscuits. Both ladies were mistresses of the plum dumpling, both took pride in their plum slice topped with sweet cheese. Each made wonderful apple strudel, the paper-thin pastry rolled, pulled and stretched out on a white cloth before the pre-cooked apple slices flavoured with cinnamon were folded in. For such magical activities, the entire dining-room table would be pressed into service. Conviviality centred on home cooking. No wonder many Czech managers returned home for lunch. Why trust the English-run company canteen?

But foreignness really erupted with the furnishings of the Czech houses. Almost universal was the long wooden integrated sideboard, glossily walnut-veneered, with cupboards for storage, shelves for books, curved doors, and cabinets with sliding glass doors to display treasured objects. Bohemian cut-glass vases, cigarette ashtrays and sweet boxes were dotted around in profusion, along with crystal bowls filled with hand-painted Easter eggs, the prevailing style a bourgeois version of folk-inspired art. My sister Vicky recalls ruby-red glass and figurines of devils chasing young girls, my brother George bulky armchairs with rounded wooden arms. I remember an ashtray with a hand-carved bear looming at one side. Hardly a plate existed that was not painted in cheerful, folksy, floral patterns.

To add to the wildly decorated effect, every piece of cut glass stood on a hand-crocheted lace mat of great intricacy. Most tables had lace runners. The windows had lace curtains. It was all very comfortable but at the same time contradictory: severe modernist exteriors concealing interiors decked out with the aesthetics of an age and a culture the architects would have abhorred. But the austere simplicity of the external forms accommodated these conventional yet alien aesthetics cheerfully enough. Such were my Czech-dominated surroundings as a child and young person.

I have one key, vivid but unverifiable memory of the year we lived on the Bata Estate. Does this make it unreliable? The German aerial blitz of London was on; the Battle of Britain was in full swing. The sense of threat and imminent danger was acute, sited as we were on the eastern approaches of the Thames estuary, providing Luftwaffe bombers an early landfall on their approach to London. Security was highly sensitive. One Bata employee was banished west of London when his wife was heard speaking German. One summer night I stood with my father at the window of my bedroom looking out towards the rear elevation of the Bata Hotel, a hostel for single workers. The rooms faced due east to the mouth of the Thames estuary and the Nazi-held Continent. Why was Father up? Was he looking for something? For my part, I recall seeing a large white signal lamp clearly sending Morse code flashes from one of those hotel windows. To whom? For what?

I never asked my father about it. George, who usually shared the bedroom, was away at boarding school. I know for sure that the room faced directly on to the back of the hotel. I have checked. I could have seen those clear, bright, white flashing signals – if they existed. I can't prove that they did. But why should my memory have made it up?

Life was confusing. We had moved to Horndon-on-the-Hill to escape the confines of the Bata Estate. My father wanted us to speak English at home. He spoke correct but heavily accented English all his life; he also retained his Czech and spoke immaculate Hochdeutsch, classical German, to his dying day. He had a penchant for German proverbs such as the obscure *'Vorsicht ist die Mutter der Porzellankiste'* – 'Care is the Mother of the Porcelain Vase', no doubt used as a frequent rebuke to slapdash children. Mother too occasionally resorted to a German saying, a warning to the idle: *'Morgen, morgen nur nicht heute, sagen alle faule Leute!'* – 'Tomorrow, tomorrow but not today, that is what lazy people say.' This was usually shortened to *'Morgen, morgen'*, which sometimes proved sufficient as a goad to action.

Mother spoke a vivid and rather personal form of English peppered with charmingly incorrect usages. When Annie had her first child by Caesarean section, Mother greeted this joyful event by telling friends that 'Annie had baby on Caesarewitch', then a well-known event in the horse-racing calendar. On another occasion, going upstairs carrying a new pot of face cream from Elisabeth Arden, she announced that she was going to 're-juvenile myself'. On another, she reported that her doctor had diagnosed her as having 'high blood pleasure'. A gall bladder problem was refashioned as a 'gold bladder'. Even in those days I found these versions of English very endearing.

Mother's own colourful vocabulary could not have been helped by her close friendship with 'Bozena' Cermak, whose fractured English was littered with gems such as 'I am going to Southend on artillery road' rather than 'arterial road'. We all knew what she meant.

Coming from a rural background, Mother's favourite sayings tended to be earthy. Anyone failing to close a door behind them would be greeted with the cry *'Mas oje v zadnice'*, 'Is a pole sticking out of your arse?' The response to remarks peppered with 'ifs' was 'If arseholes had fish in them, we would not need fishponds!' Asking for the impossible was invariably dismissed with *'Hodinky s vodotryskem!'* – 'What are you asking for, a wrist-watch with a water fountain?' Acts of extravagance would be greeted with the rueful yet resigned, *'Ak jede crava, tak jede tele'* – 'If the cow has gone, why bother about the calf?'

It felt very natural to live in a world filled with these words, these sayings. For this sound environment was a comforting part of my emerging and complex awareness of identity. Officially, we did not speak Czech at home. At least not to one another. But with visitors, whether business friends, old friends, or the regular groups of Czech pilots serving in the RAF during the Second World War, the conversation was entirely in Czech. On those occasions the air was filled with the sounds of laughter, jokes, friendship and conviviality. And the language used was Czech, those sounds were Czech. For me, it was the language of friendship. How could I reconcile that with being English? Did I need to learn how to laugh in English? I did not speak much Czech but its sounds, its surrounding atmosphere, held me in thrall. We lived in a babble of broken English, intermittent Czech, German proverbs and Czech farmyard slang. It was a rich linguistic loam.

In later years, the second high point of Christmas was Boxing Day, when the entire Bata Czech community would turn up at our house. After a very few drinks, the men decamped to the billiard room and sang the old Czech songs in flawless harmony. It was very touching and rather sad. This was their annual moment of shared identity. Most of them remained 'Czecho' exiles at heart to their dying day.

The wartime years could not resolve the identity question. We were English in spirit though not yet British citizens. We were intensely patriotic. The company prided itself on its title, the British Bata Shoe Company. We were part of the national war effort, with the factory supplying combat boots, wellingtons and gym shoes for the British armed services. (The mothership of Zlín was equally busy making boots for the Wehrmacht. After the war, Zlín shod the Soviet Red Army.) Yet despite my parents' best efforts, the family atmosphere was more Czech than English, the social environment more Czech than English, the actual and psychological family soundscape tuned to the sounds of Czech. When English was spoken, it was as a foreign language.

And in my own (as yet unrecognised) oscillation of identity between 'authoritarian Bata' and 'familial Bystřice', the scales weighed heavily in favour of the Bata influences. I suspect, though I do not know, that my parents had some sense of the need to rebalance our lives by sending George and myself on long holidays to Bystřice pod Hostýnem in 1946 and 1947. Perhaps they wanted to reconnect us with our homeland. Perhaps they wanted us to experience an extended family of grand-parents, aunts, uncles and cousins galore. This had been lost to us in the move to England in 1939 and it has always felt like a loss. I very much doubt if restoring us to my mother's family in Bystrice for a few weeks was seen as a conscious antidote to the dominating shadow of Bata. The 'Bata/Bystřice' polarity is my own, quite recent construct. Yet it has an emotional truth for me and life in the Sklenář grandparental household in 1946 and 1947 had its own precious essences.

There was 'Děda' (Grandpa), who shaved once a week and whose cold, wet, bristly kiss was dreaded all the way on the train from Prague at each visit. There was 'Babička' (Grannie), lovely, warm, round, with an incredibly tame Alsatian, Nero (diminutive 'Nerošku') who seemed to understand her every word. She endeared herself to me by being the only person to call me by a diminutive of a diminutive, indicating a deep tenderness. In my case, 'Jan' (John) was usually softened into 'Jenda' (probably Johnny), but in her mouth became 'Jenicku' (perhaps 'little Johnny'). Slav languages are very good at affec-tionate diminutives.

I reinforced my dormant baby Czech with something more formal and grown up. Given the volume of slang, local usage and the attraction of colourful swear-words in my speech, I did not dare use my Czech in polite company for years afterwards, but it served well enough during these mid-forties visits to the family environment of the single-storey house at Novosady 516, Bystřice pod Hostýnem, Moravia.

The backyard had a wooden outside loo adjacent to the dung heap, sometimes alarming as a wasp patrolled and occasionally settled on my penis; I would sit frozen with anxiety until it flew away. There was the cow, never named, used for hauling the farm cart which returned piled with Victoria plums from Deda's orchard, and sleep-inducing piles of clover and lucerne grass from his fields. Ferda the pig recognised only Uncle Jozka as a person worth paying attention to, especially when tempted with a branch laden with damsons. Peta, the tame fawn with a broken leg, had been rescued by Jozka on his farm in northern Moravia at Blahotovice. Once healed, Peta tried to escape, broke its leg again and Jozka, the gentlest of men, had to shoot it.

The main excitement in Bystrice itself was Josef Zrubek's ice cream parlour. Joe's *zmrzlina* (ice cream) – one Czech word impossible to forget – enlivened many a long summer country afternoon. As did 'helping' in the soda-bottling workshop opposite Deda and Babicka's house where two of Uncle Ota's chums pretended to work and tolerated us. I suspect that they were unemployed in the post-war doldrums, but no one was complaining. The Nazis had gone – they had been hated; the Red Army had come and gone – for the moment; they had been ridiculed as stupid and ignorant. The 'Ivans', it was said, stole wristwatches and wore them from wrist to elbow on both arms. One commandeered a bike from a Czech boy seen riding on it with his arms folded. The 'Ivan' took it, climbed on, pedalled off, folded his arms and fell in the ditch. He thought the bicycle would work on its own. Such were the small revenges of the defeated.

In 1946 and 1947, the country roads were dotted with khaki army three-ton lorries labelled *Dodala UNRRA* ('Donated by the United Nations Relief and Rehabilitation Organisation'). There was hope in the air, but it was to be short-lived. The following year, the communists seized power in Prague, Czechoslovakia was forced by Moscow to refuse the offer of US-funded Marshall Aid for European economic reconstruction.

The country vanished behind the Iron Curtain. So did our families. Their years of misery would last a generation.

Uncle Jozka stormed into the local party office, seized a microphone and called for resistance to the communist putsch of 1948. His doctor called an ambulance and got him put into an asylum for a few weeks to avoid a lengthy jail sentence. Cousin Luba, a vet at the national stud in Odry, was sent to the uranium mines on charges of sabotage after an alleged outbreak of equine fever. Acquitted by a local court, his case was referred to a higher court in Prague which duly convicted him as a saboteur. When Luba was released early, it was a sign that he would soon die of radiation sickness. Officially, according to the Czechoslovak government, 'nobody' died in the uranium mines themselves.

Second cousin Lydie used to wear Vicky's cast-off clothes sent by Mother. Condemned for her 'hooligan appearance', she was denied a local higher-education place. She had to find one in a remote school for mining engineering instead. My godfather was jailed for 'being consulted on farming questions by peasants'. He observed later that he slept very well in prison and preferred the company of the 'cream of Czech intellectual society'.

I never found it strange that there was more than a decade of virtual silence between us and our families in Czechoslovakia. Contacts were difficult, communication complicated, travel virtually impossible. We felt remote, estranged and impotent to help. Did they regard us as indifferent and heartless? When we returned en famille in 1961, the depth of their personal and political anguish was almost too much to bear. 'When will the West come to free us?' begged our cousin Luba. There was no reply because we knew what the true answer was.

There is a further explanation for the emotional distance of those years. I was very busy learning how to be English. It was a process that would take me on a kind of forced march through strange English educational institutions, adding further identity problems along the way. Becoming English involved putting

real distance between myself and my Czech origins. More profound questions, such as the tension between 'Company Zlín'
and 'Family Bystřice', were pushed into the background. There
were only so many directions in which my identity could be
tugged. Time spent in a distant English public school would
override everything else. It had to, however uncomfortable it
would prove to be.

2

Distance Learning

Boarding School During the Second World War 1942–45

Once my parents had dealt with the immediate problems of setting up home in a foreign country and adapting to life in a foreign tongue, they faced another knotty dilemma: how to educate their two sons. I was only three and a half when we arrived in England, my brother George some four years older. In my case, the solution was simple: the local primary school was just up the hill from our house. The building stands to this day, the construction typical of its time: brick-built, pitched roof, separate entrances for boys and girls. It had two classrooms – the larger one with several age year groups in it; the smaller one for older pupils. For fresh air and exercise and chaotic running around we had to make do with a playground with a rough asphalt surface.

I found lessons hard, especially writing. Forcing my seemingly uncontrollable hand to shape cursive letters neatly between parallel guidelines was a painful affair. Writing was in pencil; little children like us could not be trusted with inkwells and unruly pen-nibs. Rather than deal with desks covered in spatters of spilled ink, smeared exercise books, inky fingers, ink on clothes and general staining, the school had decided that pencil it had to be. Whatever the medium, writing did not come easy to me and to this day I have filthy handwriting – which is not my teachers' fault. There must be some problem of mind/hand coordination that I have never been able to understand or overcome.

Given that almost all the children came from the village or

nearby, given that we lived in the 'big house' at the foot of the hill, given that my parents spoke strange, broken English, I do not recall being treated as strange, let alone being bullied. If I felt uncomfortable at this, my first school, it must have reflected a more general unease at strangeness piled upon strangeness – foreign country, new language, peculiar people. Add to this the overriding discomfort of being taught at all, being taught things that were strange and which I found difficult to execute. I must have learned something, but the learning was painfully acquired, brought small understanding and little joy.

Although I must have been almost five when I first attended Horndon-on-the-Hill Village School and it was scarcely two years since I had set foot in England, I do not recall ever speaking broken English or speaking with a foreign accent. I find this odd now. The only possible explanation must be that I moved rapidly from the baby Czech of the three-year-old to the persuasive attraction of the new sounds around me. Besides, I had never learned to write in Czech, its spelling and sounds were not anchored in my mind by writing and speaking, so my ears may have been more able to adopt the prevailing sounds and cadences of English.

My elder brother George was not so lucky. He started his first English school aged eight, before he even spoke English. But which school was it to be? For my parents this was an awful problem. How did you educate children in this new country where there was no easy comparison or connection with the education found in Czechoslovakia or the remnant territories of the Austro-Hungarian Empire? It was so simple and straightforward there. Schools were run by the state and everyone went to them. Our parents asked for advice from acquaintances and new business colleagues. The answer came back loud and clear: 'If you want your sons to become "proper English gentlemen", you must send them to boarding school!' The prospect of a private education in a boarding school with the child removed from home must have been a colossal and painful shock to my parents. If so, they never spoke of it or complained about it. Our mother simply said: 'That was what we were told to do.' Having been told, they simply got on with it. We never questioned them about it – as children, it never occurred to us that our parents might have had feelings on the matter. Devoted as they both were to 'doing the best for the boys', if boarding school was what it took, then that was what they must do. And they did it without a word of complaint. Knowing I had no choice in the matter, I accepted it as inevitable, though that acceptance was mixed with puzzlement and resignation. Subsequent gratitude to my parents for a tough decision painfully taken would not have been expected and, perhaps shamefully, was never offered or expressed. Looking back on it, this was not nice on my part.

Before boarding school loomed for me I was struck down with double pneumonia, i.e. pneumonia in both lungs. Its cause was assumed to be too many nights in a modified Anderson shelter in our back garden, seeking refuge from the Luftwaffe's Blitz. A crude affair made of corrugated iron sheets, sunk a few feet into the ground, its curved tin roof was covered with a couple of feet of earth. Useless against a direct hit or near miss, it presumably offered some protection against blast.

Later, we installed a Morrison shelter inside the house. This was a massive steel table beneath which the family huddled. Even if the house were to suffer a direct hit, the steel lid was supposed to protect us from being crushed by masonry. Filled with pillows and blankets, it was oddly cosy, warm and reassuring, especially when nearby Tilbury Docks was getting a pasting from the Luftwaffe in 1940 and 1941. The anti-aircraft fire sounded terrifyingly close and the explosions as the bombs went off were deafening. With the sky overhead filled with flashes and the flicker of distant flames, I was frightened. One night, Horndon-on-the-Hill itself was bombed and we watched the flames from our bathroom window.

Aside from its dubious effectiveness against enemy bombs, the corrugated-iron Anderson shelter had no insulation and only rudimentary heating; it was very cold and constantly damp, with condensation dripping off the walls during the winter nights of 1940–41. I do not know how many nights or parts of nights we spent there. It must have been a lot. George doubts if the conditions in the Anderson shelter alone can be blamed for what happened; school and general austerity may have played their part. What is certain is that at the age of five I developed pneumonia then doubled it for good measure. It nearly did for me.

I was very ill, very ill indeed. There were no antibiotics or penicillin. I was clad in little red thermal wool waistcoats designed to dry up the fluids in my lungs. They were hot, scratchy and very uncomfortable. If they were doing any good, it never felt like it. I remember a local doctor trying to give me an injection in my upper thigh, and when I wriggled in protest his jab struck home and delivered the injection but left a scar that took twenty years to heal. Was his jab really so rough that blood spurted out? That is what I see, what I think I remember. The doctor must have been clumsy. I was undoubtedly an uncooperative patient. But I was a frightened one.

Once, or more than once, my temperature rose to 104 degrees Fahrenheit. I remember exactly how it felt to be that ill; it was like tasting the surface of a hard, dry bone with a concave surface and absolutely no life on it. I can still recapture that precise sensation, can still conjure up the precise image of that dry bone. I also remember turning my face to the wall. That Biblical notion of people turning their faces to the wall and dying makes perfect sense to me. Not that I think I was close to dying – or if I was, nobody told me, at the time or later – but I was extremely ill.

With the local GP at a loss, I was sent to hospital. Ironically, they sent me to what was then still known as 'the German Hospital' near Liverpool Street station. Perhaps my parents were comforted by the thought of treatment from the safe(r), more familiar hands of *mittel-europaische* medicine. This at least was more like home. George remembers staying with Mother at the Great Eastern Hotel nearby and visiting me in hospital every day for some weeks.

I recall nothing of the treatment, but the German Hospital did the trick and after an illness lasting eight weeks I returned home. My present for recovering was a splendid model electric railway set from the famous German firm, Marklin. It was bought at Hamley's in Regent Street, apparently unfazed by selling historic German toys in war-torn Britain. No one seemed to think this odd or unpatriotic. Perhaps my parents knew nothing of domestic English brands such as Hornby. It was all part of still being essentially foreigners in a foreign country.

Back home at The Gables, my convalescence involved regular exposure to ultraviolet and infra-red rays, delivered from what was undoubtedly a very fancy piece of equipment with twin paraboloid reflectors. Convalescence also involved sewing buttons randomly onto my sheets, an odd and totally inexplicable piece of compulsive behaviour.

As I recovered, I put on weight. I saw myself as fat, I looked fat. I was never bullied over it, but my young self-perception was of being fat, pudgy in the face, often feeling slothful. It took years to overcome. Looking at photographs of myself from that time, I cannot recognise the person I see, I cannot feel the physical being possessing those limbs, wearing those features. I look at a stranger. I feel rather sorry for him.

And so it was time for the English boarding school my parents had been promised to transform their pudgy little Czech boy into a proto Englishman, whatever that might prove to look like or to be. George, perhaps because he was four years older, seemed to be surviving its oddities and rigours well enough, despite being thrown in at the deep end without English as his working language. I would join him aged just six and a half.

There was, however, a complication to overcome. George had been sent to St Faith's School on the Trumpington Road in Cambridge, some sixty miles from Horndon-on-the-Hill. Because of the dangers of Luftwaffe bombing in south-east England, St Faith's boarders had been evacuated to safer, more distant parts of England (day boys had to take their chances in Cambridge – an odd decision). Sending your children to boarding school was one thing, but discovering that the school was to be evacuated to Ashburton, a South Devon market town on the edge of Dartmoor, was another. In those days that seemed remote to the point of exile. What did I think of that? I do not remember protesting or complaining. These distances and long journeys in 1942 would have to be endured, if not understood.

Preparing for school was intense and complicated. Harrods' school outfitters department was visited, armed with a list of specified clothing that filled a densely printed page. Grey flannel jackets and shorts, grey shirts, grey pullovers, long woollen socks, and the school tie with its red, thin white and black horizontal stripes, made of a shiny synthetic material which meant the knot invariably slipped. But which schoolboy's tie ever stayed in place? The traditional English school cap with red, thin white and black circles and a crescent shaped peak was the defining headpiece. Once bought, in the prescribed quantities – two of this, six of that, and woe betide omissions or oversights – school clothes were clearly labelled with Cash's name tapes and recorded on the school clothing form before being packed into a trunk which would be secured with rope and handed over to the Great Western Railway several days ahead of the journey to school. Thanks to the wondrous and universal system of PLA (Passengers' Luggage in Advance), this trunk and others like it were delivered in their hordes to the designated school on time. It sounds complicated, but it worked even in wartime.

The only items of clothing not packed in the school trunk were those worn on the day of departure. Everything was new. Much of it felt uncomfortable, stiff, hot, bristly, with badly fitting new shoes that managed to combine discomfort with actual peril as the shiny leather soles slipped without warning, especially on carpet. They needed scuffing to make them usable, but at least small boys loved scuffing new shoes.

By the time the entire school uniform had been put on, I felt thoroughly trussed. There I stood, a new entity designed to answer the demands of an alien institution whose unexplained values were contained in the important outward show of the school uniform. At six and a half, you do not protest; you accept and hope the consequences will be benign rather than unpleasant. But peering in front of a supposedly reassuring mirror accompanied by encouraging sounds of pride from both parents, the short, tubby, uncertain, uncomfortable little Czech boy only dimly understood how much life was about to change.

In September 1942, with term due to start, we drove from Horndon-on-the-Hill to Barking in East London to take the underground for Paddington. What wonders! The noise of the underground in its tunnels, the walls flashing past, clearly indicated speed – were we not travelling at sixty miles an hour? That's what it felt like! In some parts of the Metropolitan and District Line, the east and west tracks briefly run side by side where the retaining wall opens up for a potential crossing point. Trains miraculously never colliding, offering brief glimpses of strange intimacy with the lives of passengers travelling in the opposite direction.

The windows of the carriages were densely criss-crossed with brown safety tape to prevent lethal shards of flying glass if a train received a direct hit from German bombs. A helpful sign in the carriage explained what the safety tape was for. An anonymous wit had added: 'Thank you for the information / I can't see the bloody station!' Such little curiosities of life interrupted but could not delay the arrival at Paddington to join the school train and say goodbye to my parents.

I do not know if I imagined in advance how miserable parting from them would be. I do not recall suffering sleepless nights beforehand. For sure, waiting to say 'goodbye' on the platform at Paddington in September 1942 was awful. Boys, parents and staff mingled confusingly. Who were these people? How would I ever get to know them? Why should I bother? I did not think such thoughts consciously; I felt them strongly. And above all, I wanted the parting to be over quickly so I could be spared the sight of my parents' tears. A child can just about handle his or her own sadness, but lacks the equipment to accommodate let alone ease the pain of adults. I did not resent being sent away from home, I knew too little about it. I wanted to get on with whatever the new situation involved.

We boarded our reserved compartments. There were choked tears, difficult to control because such emotions had never previously been part of a six-year-old's experience. What were they choked about? Whistles blew, carriage doors slammed, steam clouds gushed and it was a relief to be off and away from that confusing, incomprehensible grief on the platform. I have often wondered if this tableau of misery at Paddington put me off dealing with partings for the rest of my life or if my tendency to invest them with perhaps excessive intensity is a reaction to the inhibition of such feelings early on.

Four and a half hours later, the train reached Newton Abbot. To this day, according to Annie, I cannot pass through that station without turning pale. The boredom of the journey was occasionally alleviated by hanging out of the window – forbidden because smuts from the engine would fly into your eye – or trailing hankies out of the window – forbidden because hankies might slip from your hand and get lost (they did; much to Matron's displeasure). From Newton Abbot, a local train took us to Totnes; a still more local train, the Ashburton Express, a grand name for a simple branch-line chuffer, completed the final leg. Some terms a coach met us at Newton Abbott to wind interminably through Devon's rolling red-soil hills and valleys. It was very different from the estuarial flatlands of south-east Essex.

St Faith's School, Cambridge, had been transplanted to the

Golden Lion Hotel in Ashburton, Devon. Distinguished by a flaking statue of a golden lion over the columned entrance on the town's high street, the hotel was just large enough to hold thirty-six evacuated boys from age six to thirteen, four teachers, Connie, a kind of all-purpose factotum and quasi-matron, the headmaster, always referred to as W. G. Butler, his wife, and their ageing, slobbering golden Labrador, Winnie. Mr Butler's study was the hotel bar; the lounge was the Butlers' sitting room; the dining room was just about big enough to hold all thirty-six boys; the capacious hotel ballroom was the 'Big Dormitory'. Smaller hotel rooms were pressed into service as four-bed dormitories. The beds were inherited from the hotel, some of them with huge pre-war box mattresses. Bedclothes would not tuck around and beneath them, so slipped off regularly in a nightmare tangle in winter nights. With its creaking stairs, rattling doors, draughts and general chill, many nights at the Golden Lion Hotel took on an almost gothic quality.

Outside the hotel, facing south, beyond a small formal garden with box hedges and flower beds, threaded by narrow asphalt paths, stood the hotel's former event venue, always called 'the Den'. This hall became the school's main play and free-time area. The asphalt paths, twisting and winding on a slight slope, proved the downfall of many a schoolboy. Ignoring adults' admonitions to 'walk, don't run', we took off down the paths with our laces trailing, our shoes so worn down that the soles and heels could gain no purchase, and inevitably came to grief on the asphalt. Skinned knees and elbows were so common as to be part of the school uniform; Matron would dress our wounds with stinging, iodine-soaked bandages whose pain was only compensated for by the subsequent pleasure of picking off and chewing the tasty, salty scabs.

Further on, beyond the Den, on a slope running away to a small dip to the south of Ashburton, were the concrete sunbathing terraces of the swimming pool, their Spartan appearance marginally softened by clustering nasturtiums. Sucking the honey at the bottom of the nasturtium flower was a brief moment of delight. We were very lucky to have the Den and the pool as part of our domain.

But I was not happy. And not because of the experience of boarding. It was wartime; food was rationed; food must not be wasted; therefore everything put on the plate must be eaten up – *everything*. There was no room for 'faddy eaters'. The gristle surrounding the chewy beef was dealt with by covertly transferring it from masticating mouth via a pretend cough and clenched fist into my trouser pocket. After the meal, I would flush it down the lavatory. For years my trouser pockets reeked of stale beef fat. This crude ruse must have been obvious but it was never rigidly policed or indeed policed at all. The Butlers must have decided that so long as every plate ended empty, the principle was observed, honours were even.

The greater problem for a 'faddy eater' – which I probably was – came with supper, which often consisted of cold milk and particularly stale cheddar. I had never much liked dairy products – a consequence perhaps of being over-enthusiastically kissed by my dairy-loving and dairy-smelling Danish godmother – so these monotonous exiguous suppers were difficult to take. Hungry as I was, cold milk and reeking stale cheddar killed my appetite. I love cheese in all its glorious varieties today; cold milk has always repelled me.

Early on, probably in the first summer term of 1943, we were to learn to swim. Everyone else, as I recall, found no difficulty. I did. The staff decided that the best way to teach me was to throw me into the pool to sink or swim. Was it at the deep end? There would have been no point in throwing me in at the shallow end and, besides, there were real swimmers in attendance to rescue me. Later I managed a few breast strokes while buoyed up by an inflated rubber tyre. I was officially judged to have learned to swim. The whole school lined up and applauded. It did not feel like an achievement so much as a small mitigation of humiliation. I have been a poor swimmer and hated swimming ever since.

Shortly after being forced to swim, I started to wet my bed.

It happened more than once, though how often I simply do not remember. The Butlers were very concerned but not considerate. It was obvious to them that drinking excessive quantities of fluids at supper caused my bed-wetting. The extraordinary remedy was to put me on a special supper diet of extra milk and cheese. I knew in my heart that it was the repellent milk and cheese that were the heart of my problem, but I had no way of saying or proving it. I do not recall being thrown into the swimming pool and disgusting dairy suppers as triggers for the bed-wetting.

An obvious cry of distress, it fell on deaf ears and closed minds. Mr Butler said bed-wetting had to stop, it was only a matter of self-control. I prayed for self-control, I prayed not to wet my bed yet again, I really prayed, eyes tight shut, hands tightly together, prayed to God not to let me wet myself yet again. I woke up the following morning in a dry bed. I forget if I thanked God for it. I have no idea why I stopped. The crisis was over.

Years later, I was told that Mr Butler had written to my parents saying that unless I stopped bed-wetting, I would be expelled from school. Expulsion was reserved for the very worst offences. My parents never spoke to me of this and I can hardly imagine the effect receiving Mr Butler's letter must have had on them.

St Faith's took education seriously, despite having just four teachers, one of whom, it was clear even to us boys, was a county lady coming in to help out. She seemed to know little about anything but was pleasant and calm. The best teacher by far was Eric Gibbins who taught arithmetic and English and played the piano with flair, usually 1930s musicals. Many Golden Lion evenings were filled with the sounds of Mr Gibbins playing 'Jealousy' on an old joanna with an infectious swing, filling the hotel's echoing spaces with a romantic aura they were otherwise devoid of. He organised the occasional drama event and guided and dragged some of us up and down Devon's hills on regular afternoon walks. They must have been as much of a penance for Mr Gibbins, who had danced in a Broadway chorus line, as they were for overweight me. Dragging Johnny 'up Tuley and down Cabbage' – two local lanes – as a standard afternoon walk was one of his chores, always carried out with good humour and undeserved patience. Eric Gibbins was funny, witty, could be waspish and was homosexual, though that was judged to be inconceivable in the 1940s. I owe him a huge amount and knew him as a friend for years afterwards. How much happier he would have been in a different time when he could have been open about who he was.

Latin was an important part of the syllabus. It was taught by Mr Butler. Translating Latin prose into English was bad enough, but translating English sentences into Latin was worse. Mr Butler marked our papers with a thick blue pencil and no toleration for mistakes. A slight error received a single underlining; a more severe one received two; a howler got three or even four. Each sentence was marked out of four. Often my translations got nought. Sometimes my exercise book was a mass of increasingly heavy blue pencil gashes.

Mr Butler also taught the Bible. With his handsome head, grey hair, glasses and rich voice he was an authority figure, an Old Testament prophet, a patriarch even. When he 'expounded' the Bible – the only word for it – he did so from a huge Concordance, a vast tome filled with textual explication and several times longer than the Bible itself. As we glumly observed this huge volume, we wondered if we had to get through the whole thing. In practice, Mr Butler's dense textual commentary was reserved for Genesis and Exodus, the start of the Pentateuch – the first five books of the Old Testament – then petered out during the dreary priestly instructions of the Books of Leviticus and Numbers. The rowdy goings on of the historical books – Kings and Chronicles – were always popular. Then he plunged into the New Testament, the core of his moral beliefs and teaching.

We sat in rows in the Den on the tottering remains of old

folding garden chairs. Few had all their slats intact; most had only three out of the five left; those with just two slats were uncomfortable. With our hands folded behind our backs, Mr Butler instructed us frequently to 'Look at me.' Eyes never wavered, they could not. The only respite in divinity classes was to put up a hand and ask 'to be excused', meaning to go to the lavatory. This could be a mere diversion from the prevailing boredom. Mr Butler was aware of such tricks. Sometimes he took his time before acknowledging an increasingly desperate hand. Once, a boy near me was genuinely full to bursting point. His arm strained for attention; the more it waved the more the headmaster ignored him. The boy – I can still remember his name – began to wet himself. The only sound in the Den apart from the steady tones of the headmaster expounding the books of the Old Testament was that of steady drips of urine falling through the slats of the garden chair onto a crushed dried milk tin lying below. I can hear the sound to this day. Did the boy ever recover from such humiliation?

Am I being totally unfair to a headmaster whom older boys remember as amusing, kind, concerned and helpful? After all, the Bible that I love and know reasonably well was un-questionably taught to me by Mr Butler's conviction. There was a great deal of 'smiting the Philistines', relieving them of their foreskins – what was going on? – and Elijah's taunting of the priests of the idol Baal always went down well, as did the charioteer 'driving furiously like unto Jehu son of Nimshi', which has since proved useful in criticising excessive speed on motorways.

Most Sunday evenings we gathered in Mr Butler's study where he read aloud – very well – from Conan Doyle, mainly Sherlock Holmes. Listening to *The Hound of the Baskervilles* on a stormy winter's night with its slavering beast roaming Dart-moor just yards away produced an unrepeatable frisson.

I learned a lot outside lessons. Several of the boys were nat-uralists, keen and expert butterfly collectors, and Devon was rife with the riches of England's Lepidoptera. Walking through summer meadows, the air thick with butterflies, butterfly nets waving to capture this elusive cornucopia was a vicarious joy. On such days the sun always seemed to shine in Devon, though more frequently we recited the old saying: 'Come to Sunny Devon; Out of Six Days it Rains Seven.'

Back in the Den, the afternoon catch of butterflies was carefully removed from the portable killing flask, their wings in all their loveliness spread out onto mounting boards. I watched this concentrated activity, this delicious knowledge that others had, with total absorption. And the names to match such beauty: Painted Ladies, Small Tortoise Shells, Peacocks and hordes of fritillaries culminating in talk of the legendary Camberwell Beauty. All this was an education in itself; it showed that knowledge could be gained beyond and outside the routines and categories of classroom learning. It could come from people who were not necessarily teachers.

Among the thirty-six in the school, there were some very clever boys. John Whale ('Jonah', of course), who won a scholarship to Winchester, ended up as political correspondent for Independent Television News (ITN). Michael Harper became an Orthodox ordained priest and a leader of the British Russian Orthodox community. He was exotic even at St Faith's. His father, Claude Harper, was a flamboyant one-armed racehorse owner from Ireland one of whose horses finished seventh in the Derby. One of the classrooms had a fine photo of the closing stages of that race, a reminder perhaps of the world beyond the petty cares of Ashburton. I took too little from my school companions. My own learning remained classroombound for too long.

There were moments of sweetness in boarding-school life: the day out to nearby Buckland Beacon, one of Dartmoor's rocky outcrops, presented the English summer at its beguiling best. Another culminated on the River Dart. On such days war seemed very remote.

Within the school, the prevailing atmosphere had an almost Victorian prudery. There were rules for undressing before bed at night: shorts and underpants had to be taken off first, pyjama trousers put on and only then could you 'safely' take off your shirt and vest. Removing your shirt before reaching the protection of your pyjama trousers earned a rebuke for risking exposure of what were never known as your private parts, referred to only by implication and preferably not at all. Anxiety about masturbation was reflected in the rule that 'Boys must lie still in bed after lights out.' Occasionally the evening would be interrupted by the dormitory head calling out 'Lie still!' A minor offence, but an offence nonetheless, was peeping from one swimming pool changing cubicle into another to catch sight of a naked boy. The pudeur was immense, probably reinforced by time spent studying 'divinity' with its Old Testament rules.

Every Sunday morning, the school walked in crocodile down the hill from the Golden Lion Hotel to the parish church, St Andrew's. We had to walk considerately, taking care not to bump into Ashburtonians; boys who failed to heed the rule would be punished by being 'put on silence' for the next week or two when walking in crocodile. This was a real punishment; what do schoolboys need to do but chatter? We always reached church early, half an hour before matins at 11 a.m. This allowed plenty of time to read the more esoteric parts of the Book of Common Prayer, including the Tables of Kindred and Affinity. Who would ever dream of marrying their Husband's Daughter's Cousin or some such? Would they notice? Why single it out for banning? The Service of Commination, long abandoned by the Church in practice, also offered good value, being filled with abomination – a good Old Testament word in any case – condemnation and curses. It took me years to comprehend why 'moving your neighbour's mark' might be cause for public cursing. There was still time to memorise the twelve tribes of Judah from the map at the back of my Bible. I once silenced an obstreperous Israeli taxi driver by reciting them in full.

The joy of matins was the soaring voice of 'Amy J', the

splendidly capacious and generous wife of the rather good organist, Mr Jones. On Sundays when the congregation was in thin voice, Amy J supplied the volume. Everyone joined in the hearty hymns from *Hymns Ancient and Modern*. Once learned, once sung, 'Eternal Father Strong to Save', 'Abide with Me' and 'Onward Christian Soldiers' became lifelong musical terms of reference. There was one puzzle in the hymn, 'There is a green hill far away / Without a city wall'. Why on earth should a green hill have a wall at all?

The hardest part of matins was the set canticles of the *Book of Common Prayer*. We mainly endured them, especially the 'tedium of the Te Deum', a poor joke that did not ease the longueurs. No one ever told us how or why the Saviour did not 'abhor the Virgin's womb', a phrase thick with obscurity and incomprehensibility. Once a month gloom descended when the Te Deum was replaced by the 'Benedicite Omnia Opera', 'Oh All ye Works of the Lord, Praise ye the Lord'! How they praised, how they lined up to take part! Who were 'Ananias, Azarias and Misrael', so keen to join in the praise of the Lord? If anybody knew, it was not passed on. Interminable, obscure, repetitive, yet the 'Benedicite' remains imprinted. It is one of my life's footprints, a sound, those words, that feeling, a sense, a memory, a ritual, a time, a place. I can recapture them all. I cannot regret enduring the endurance.

Mr Jones the organist also taught the piano. This involved a solitary walk around the parish churchyard to a semi-detached house beyond. It was worth the walk to receive Amy J's generous Welsh-bosomed welcome. More problematic were the occasional exchanges with boys from the local school, Ashburton College. They knew that we were 'from London' or thereabouts, probably 'toffee-nosed' as a result; we knew that they were local boys, a bit rough and rather big, who regularly thumped us at sport. Walking along the churchyard railings to Amy J's, being intercepted by three or four 'college' boys involved being teased. College boy: 'Have you got a cock?' Me, inwardly writhing: 'No, we don't keep chickens.' College boys retire laughing. As moments of class war went, they were incredibly harmless.

I started to lose the post-pneumonia weight, but there was a further cause of unease: I continued to feel oddly foreign. I was never picked on, it was just that everyone else was so obviously English. Other boys all seemed to have large extended families consisting of grandparents, uncles and aunts, cousins and suchlike with whom they spent their holidays. I had lots of relatives but they were stuck in the middle of war-torn Europe. I felt very isolated, reliant as I was on a small cellular family unit. The absence of an extended family, the loneliness in the holidays when I assumed all my schoolmates were playing in the countryside like children from an Enid Blyton or Arthur Ransome novel, was a dull ache.

And literary terms of reference sharpened the awareness of the divide. For my contemporaries, Ransome and his like were part of their everyday knowledge, language and undoubtedly their actual lives too. Beatrix Potter, A. A. Milne, Kenneth Grahame were just names to me, their work literally a closed book. What did I have instead? Lovely but weird Czech books like *The Chattertooth Eleven*, about a family football team, and an illustrated book, *Ferda and the Ants*, no explanation needed. I do not remember what language I read them in. Much as I loved both *Ferda* and *Chattertooth*, nobody else could relate to them. They were part of my culture, perhaps even evoking a distant memory of my first language. These were stereotypes from my country and they were foreign ones. I could not share them with others. I was apart.

This sense of difference continued with the 'tuck box', a robust wooden container used for carrying very personal belongings, above all cakes, jams and sweets which bolstered wartime rations. For English boys, they came as standard issue from school suppliers. For us, as George recalls quite intensely, the tuck box was made by the Bata Engineering Department, yet further evidence of our foreignness. As far as I could see, every other boy had a steady supply of fruit cake in his tuck box, a slice of which at mid-morning break re-energised the day. What did I have? A shoebox full of Mrs Cermak's chocolate éclairs. Now Mrs Cermak was a wonderful Czech pastry cook but she did not make fruit cake. Delicious as they were, éclairs could not last as long as an English fruit cake. After two to three weeks, the cream began to go off; but above all they were different, they were not English. They proclaimed the fact that neither was I. Occasionally I could swap an éclair for a slice of fruit cake – life was full of swaps. Less frequently I could cadge a slice, but cadgers, with their mid-morning cries of 'Anything going?', were not popular and were usually ignored. It was a rough-and-ready barter market. Every such market has its codes. Ours included: 'People who ask don't get!' To which the ineffectual response was: 'People who don't ask don't want!'

These mid-morning transactions reflected a market of small differences. Out of these, awareness of my identity was created and sharpened; no extended family, the reader of peculiar books, owner of an over-engineered tuck box, possessor of éclairs rather than fruit cake. Different, foreign.

We knew there was a war going on, however remote it might seem. Food rationing was a forceful reminder of it. Dried potato, 'Pom', could never disguise what the real vegetable had been through to reach its desiccated form. Dried egg was perfectly edible while never aspiring to be the real thing; it always remained 'dried egg'. Dried milk, on the other hand, could be addictive; this sweet-ish white powder heaped on a teaspoon gave instant gratification and comfort or just provided fun when blown into another boy's face.

The threat of the war, though distant, never disappeared completely. On more than one occasion, roused from our beds in the night, we put on dressing gowns and slippers, gathered up our bundles of blankets and pre-packed necessities tied with the school belt with the snake buckle and hurried down to the hotel cellars until the 'all clear' sounded. During a rare wartime mid-term visit to Ashburton by my parents we played in an amusement arcade on a wet afternoon in Torquay. Twenty minutes after we left, a solitary Luftwaffe fighter-bomber blundering its way home raked the rather handsome glass arcade with machine-gun fire.

During the holidays, living in south-east Essex, virtually on the front line of the home front, attack from the air was part of the experience of war. Late in the conflict, a V-2 rocket, a powerful unguided missile, fell in a nearby field and the detonation split part of an outside wall of the house. There was no protection from that kind of weapon. I would stand in the garden watching for the flying bombs, the V-1s, the 'Doodlebugs' as they droned across the sky on their primitive motors. When the motor sputtered to a halt on this crudest of unguided missiles, we knew it would fall to the ground and explode exactly eight seconds later. Waiting for them to appear was a diverting morning pastime not unlike, say, birdwatching. I did so as if surrounded by a veil of protective innocent curiosity rather than by any sense of acute danger. I can't explain this. Perhaps by 1944, having lived through several years of war, its duration, its weapons, its effects had made me comparatively knowing, even slightly inured.

But something was up in the spring and early summer of 1944. The hotel overlooked the Ashburton bypass, clearly visible and audible some three to four hundred yards away. All day and much of the night the bypass was filled with convoys of US Army lorries roaring their way – as we were never told – from Plymouth to the embarkation ports for the D-Day landings. Their steady drone kept us awake until gone midnight. The insomnia was made worse by the fact that Britain was on Double Summer Time, Greenwich Mean Time plus two hours, in order to extend the working day for the war effort. The imperfect blackout curtains of the Big Dorm had many pinholes in them, so dazzling bright rays of sunlight tormented us into sleeplessness for hours.

One afternoon, as we returned from the regulation walk along the bypass, a US Army jeep pulled up. In what was both a gesture of consideration and friendship and no doubt part of a hearts and minds campaign, two black GIs got out, talked to the master in charge and gave him a large square tin of biscuits. Whatever it contained, this definitely meant supper that evening would be something to look forward to. Back at school, the headmaster immediately confiscated the tin on the grounds that, given its source, it might be infected and was not safe to eat. It remained on the top shelf of Mr Butler's study, a tantalising reminder of what might have been. This was seen as mean, an offence to the schoolboys' moral code, our cherished values, the notion that 'it wasn't fair!'.

One morning in the summer of 1945, we were summoned to the Butlers' sitting room, the old hotel lounge. We sat on the ageing carpet, sticky with years of slobber from Winnie the Labrador. The radio announced the end of the war. I recall no jubilation, though there was presumably a huge sense of inner relief. Soon after, one boy received a food parcel including tinned peaches, an unimaginable luxury. Did that prove the war was over or just that we had won the U-boat war in the Atlantic? Soon it was clear that St Faith's would return to Cambridge for the autumn term. The exile in Ashburton was over.

Aged nine, I was probably a happier child than I had been three years previously. I had never suffered in the real sense of the word, no one had been unkind, but I had often been miserable. Some of that misery – a great deal? – will have been my own fault, reflecting an immature incapacity to deal with the new and unfamiliar. Given what I had experienced between the ages of three and nine, that may not be surprising. It is definitely the case that by the time we left Devon I had developed a facial tic, a twitch of the right eye and cheek, a very pronounced blink. I have it to this day. I find it impossible to believe that such a nervous spasm, a sign of tension and unease, was not caused by the discomforts of the previous years. I could not articulate that at the time. My teachers and family regarded it as a bad habit that I could stop if I really tried. My next headmaster suggested I devote thirty minutes a day to sitting quietly and concentrating on not blinking. It had no effect. The only time I have never compulsively twitched has been when appearing live on television. Is there a lesson there? After all, actors with a stammer in private life do not stammer on stage.

In this experience of being sent from home to board, was it my parents who really paid the emotional price? I boarded at prep school from the age of six and a half, continued straight to a boarding public school until I was eighteen, then spent two years in the army doing national service, moved on to university at Cambridge for four years and married immediately thereafter. My parents lost me as a full-time member of a regular functioning family group when I was six. We could only interact for a month at Christmas and Easter and for two months during the summer holiday. For eight months of the year, given geographical remoteness and wartime travel restrictions, I was part of a school community with surrogate parents and cousins, not of a family group. The habits of familial love and accommodation never had the time to take root and be practised. This was their loss; perhaps one they could not put into words. It was also mine. We were always considerate and loving towards one another, their generosity was boundless. But the gap of feeling and understanding that first opened between us on that platform at Paddington station in 1942 never fully closed.

St Faith's return to Cambridge, to four former detached family houses lining Trumpington Road, represented entry to a completely different place. Instead of 36 boys there were 140, mainly day boys. They were clever, very clever, like their parents – most of whom were Cambridge dons. Most were very nice; one in particular, Hugh Brogan, became a friend for life. The Brogan family home was on Belvoir Terrace, where Hugh's father, the great American historian Denis Brogan, and mother, the Roman archaeologist Olwen Brogan, welcomed friends and visitors. The house had books lining every wall in every room, piled on every step of every staircase. The long-suffering Miss Hellaby kept this academic establishment going. For us, Olwen Brogan in particular made this Cambridge house feel like a home from home for years to come.

A roster of specialist teachers taught the full range of subjects needed for entry into public schools. Most were very good, including the music- and art-loving Eric Gibbins and the all-purpose, sport-loving polymath, Mike Bayon. The divinity and occasional history teacher, Reverend Royce, had a limited scope, which started with Feudalism, took in the Wars of the Roses, then petered out soon after the Divine Right of Kings. Even in those days I felt strongly that history must involve something in between and beyond. But the main history teacher, J. B. McIntosh, with his magnificent battlefield blackboard presentations delivered in a swirl of arms, words and multicoloured chalks, more than made up for those shortcomings. My love of history I owe to him.

Only one teacher was distinctly odd. He played the flute mournfully, colouring my response to the instrument for years. He was fond too of gloomy aphorisms such as 'Every time I go into a library I am filled with sadness at all the books I will not read before I die!' He was rather too fond of giving small groups of boys – all of whom chose to attend – extra-curricular talks about sex education. He may have had permission from the headmaster to run these groups, but I doubt it. I have no evidence that he molested any boy. I suspect that these days he would at least have been told to stop.

Now that we were back at St Faith's, school meant playing fields and sport – lots of it. With my post-pneumonia fat now shed, I discovered a real enjoyment of most sports and a decent talent for several, especially tennis. I found that I only functioned well as a person if I took exercise regularly and quite seriously. I have done so all my life.

St Faith's at Cambridge, now without the Old Testament-like W. G. Butler, was still sexually prudish though not burdened with the fearsome prohibitions and prescriptions of

Ashburton. On a preliminary visit to the north Norfolk public school of Gresham's, Holt, where I was bound at age thirteen, I was taken aback by the sight of naked boys taking their post-gym showers. St Faith's prudery was well rooted. I had a lot of growing up to do.

3

Becoming British

1949–54

My public school was always called 'Gresham's, Holt', as if adding its geographical location might make up for the school's comparative obscurity. Gresham's was a 'minor' public school of some 333 boys, far from a big-hitter in the upper divisions of the English public school hierarchy. But at least the founder of the original grammar school, Sir Thomas Gresham, had a certain réclame in the City of London with a street and college named after him. Linking his name to a small educational establishment in a remote north Norfolk market town, however, was no guarantee of its wider recognition.

Gresham's reputation was forward-looking. A mere fifty years old as a public school – the grammar school foundation was of the sixteenth century – its reputation came from eschewing the classics, emphasising the sciences, operating a light disciplinary system, stamping down on bullying and being free of traditional public-school distortions such as 'fagging', over-mighty prefects and social snobbery. There was some beating – but only by the headmaster.

If Gresham's was small, it was clever in many ways. It was good at hockey – a clever game, not based on brute force. Its rifle team always performed well at Bisley. It encouraged music and drama, with a school play each summer and an annual play by each house. It had a clutch of famous old boys including the poet W. H. Auden and the composer Benjamin Britten. It was a nice school, with honest values.

My parents filed all my letters from school. I kept a daily

diary for my last three years there, 1951–54. My own memory retains intense images of key moments. These three elements – what I told my parents, what I told myself, what memory would not let me forget – interact, reinforce, sometimes omit; they are differently selective but rarely contradict one another. They reflect learning, sport, friendship, music and drama. They also capture some of my own route through the thickets of emerging sex and exercising authority. This is my adolescent self, occasionally embarrassing, always striving, sometimes self-pitying, often self-critical but not, I hope, unsympathetic. I cannot disown it.

A few miles inland from the north Norfolk coast, Gresham's was set in acres of playing fields on the edge of Holt and surrounded on two sides by handsome woods of deciduous trees. Boys boarded in four houses separated by a quarter of a mile or more. Each house had a dissimilar outlook and character; 'house spirit' was more important than 'school spirit'. It was a very federal structure and intensively competitive. Those of us in the physically remote Farfield saw ourselves as independent, free-thinking, laissez-faire and laid back, like the housemaster, Bruce Douglas. Old School House, even more distant in the town of Holt itself, was seen as fey, introvert and ineffective. Woodlands, under the devious and manipulative Max Parsons, was clever, confident but oddly collectivist in its thinking. The headmaster's house, Howson's, was self-assured, opaque, cynical and heartily disliked. But then so was the headmaster, Martin Olivier. These rivalries mainly played themselves out on the sports fields.

Gresham's was run on a tight schedule. The day started at 7 a.m., with boys out of the dormitory, cold-showered and dressed by 7.25. Why the compulsory cold shower? Nothing moral or improving about it, just practicality. The housemaster, Bruce Douglas, always said, 'If boys don't shower, the house smells!' Breakfast, from 7.30 to 7.45, was followed by free time until 8.30. The school gathered in chapel for a few prayers and a hearty hymn. Given that boys were expected to 'go to the toilet' in the morning – school slang for the lavs was 'tope', a corruption from *topos*, the Greek word for 'place' – I saw these morning rituals of closet and chapel as intimately connected – 'open bowels' followed by 'open vowels'.

A basic punishment on which much school discipline depended was to report, ready for the day, to a sleepy prefect at 7.10 a.m. This was inconvenient. For worse behaviour, reporting in games clothes at 8 a.m. was far more so. For really severe misconduct, a report in games clothes during mid-morning break was seriously disrupting. By and large, such 'punishments' underpinned a rule by consensus and mutual respect.

Classes ran from 9 a.m. to 12 p.m. with a fifteen-minute morning break. Lunch at 1 p.m. was followed by games afternoons, rugby in the winter, hockey in the spring, cricket in the summer. Classes from 4.40 to 6 p.m.; tea at 6 with free time until prep from 7 to 8.20. House prayers followed until 8.40, with juniors going to bed at 9 p.m. and seniors an hour later with lights out at 10. These timings were strictly kept and announced by a bell. They left plenty of free time for choir, music, drama, more sport, making, keeping or losing friends, doing nothing or getting up to mischief. If it was a tight framework, it was not relentless.

The autumn term in September 1949, my first, got off to a smooth start. 'I am quite alright and very happy here!' I wrote home, adding, 'I don't know what I would have done without [my brother] George!' The food was judged good, with 'I am not often hungry' thrown in for reassurance. That changed rapidly. Cakes, apples and pears made up an early food parcel from home, followed by thanks for more cakes: 'I have eaten them all.' A November parcel containing the legendary Swiss chocolate, a triangular bar of Toblerone, was especially appreciated. Jam was asked for.

A house dance with the local girls' school was an important milestone in my adolescent initiation. The housemaster, Bruce Douglas, and his glamorous wife, Betty Douglas, asked if I wanted to take part. Aged thirteen and a half, I did. My brother George said very firmly that I should not. Betty said, 'If he wants to, yes.' Every boy was instructed to have a bath, shave and put on their best suit. I had never shaved before. Everyone said I should; George said I didn't need to. Betty and others said, 'Definitely, yes.' I shaved. George conceded that it had been necessary. I remember nothing of the event beyond the food. I noted that we saw the female guests off the premises with relief and then 'finished off the food before bed at midnight'.

North Norfolk's weather was bracing – 'no land between us and the North Pole' was the slogan. We were rather proud of it and of our endurance. On 23 October 1949 it was 36 degrees Fahrenheit in the morning, 34 degrees in the evening. Despite the cold, all dormitory windows stayed open at night. On 26 November it rained incessantly for twenty-five hours.

Betty Douglas kept up her efforts to civilise us by holding ballroom dancing classes on Sunday evenings after house prayers, boys dancing with boys. We learned the waltz, quick waltz, quickstep, slow foxtrot, Veleta and St Bernard. I wrote home proudly: 'R and I dance the quick waltz. Betty says we do it rather well.' The sixteenth of October was marked as a red-letter day in my diary: 'Saw the Aurora Borealis. Learned the quickstep.'

The crucial first term included a taste of the headmaster's fussy approach to details of discipline. Martin John Olivier was short, dumpy, with fuzzy hair surrounding a bald crown and a blurred, spluttering speech impediment which gave him his nickname of 'Tish'. He was not a martinet but he was unpredictable. This term his wrath fell on the colour of boys' trousers. To be sure, they were grey, universally so, worn with the school blazer. Olivier decided that trousers that were too light a shade would be 'illegal'. I had to get special permission from Bruce Douglas for what I felt were my 'nice light grey trousers'. I warned my parents off any future lurch towards the fashionable. Later Olivier campaigned against green bicycles; unless they were black they would be sent home.

Saturday evenings regularly featured school debates. 'This House deplores the popularity of Dick Barton' (a wildly popular BBC radio thriller) was carried by 81 to 80. 'This House approves of the modern trend in art' (whatever that was in 1949) was another cliffhanger carried by 39 votes to 38. 'The return of Labour at the next election would be a national disaster' delivered a landslide (101 to 28) in favour, showing how unaware boys were of living through a beneficial social revolution in the creation of the Welfare State. When Gresham's debated the topic 'Co-education is the only true education' with neighbouring girls at Runton Hill, it was lost by 48 votes. I kept no record of how the respective schools' votes split or whether those particular girls and those boys simply decided they wanted no more of one another. Later the debates would prove my nemesis.

If shaving, dancing, debating and seeing the Aurora Borealis in Norfolk's noble, wide, night skies were highlights of that first term, I experienced what felt like two bitter disappointments. I was not picked for the Colts rugby XV to play the Leys' School, Cambridge. I stared despairingly at the team list on the school noticeboard without my name on it. The other was my own academic performance. As a scholarship holder, I expected to top the form order, which was read out to the whole school every quarter. In the third quarter I dropped from first to fourth. I knew that I had not been working well. I had to improve.

Learning and teaching seemed to play a bigger part in school life the following term. 'Latin', I reported home, 'is always easy.' Maths, however, was 'always hard'. I struggled with the abstractions of the concepts in mechanics. Geography was a delight because the loquacious, brilliant ornithologist and naturalist Dick Bagnall-Oakeley was easily sidetracked onto one of the many subjects on which he was expert. If there was a formal geography syllabus, Bagnall-Oakeley never bothered to teach it. Dick was handsome, drove a sleek Bristol saloon car, far from a schoolmaster's battered Morris, married an heiress and founded the Norfolk Naturalists' Trust, which exists to this day.

Biology offered smaller delights such as growing broad beans. 'It is great fun watching them,' I enthused, 'since we keep them in a jam jar and see them grow.' Well, yes. Double biology was even better. 'We had great fun pulling a cockroach to bits and examining it.' I have no record of learning anything from this examination.

The event of this year must have been my letter which announced 'important news': 'I was hit on the jaw by a hockey stick which broke two front teeth and cut my lip.' I needed three stitches in the wound but reassured my parents, 'I am alright now. It nearly knocked me out – I retired from the field spitting blood.' I quickly saw a possible advantage from the accident: 'I don't mind which dentist I go to as long as he will do them well. If necessary I don't mind coming home.' Mending the teeth well was to cost hundreds of pounds over a decade of dentistry and several dentists.

Mine was not the only health problem. 'R who has a large part in the house play went to the San with boils.' He made it to the first night. In the summer term, there was a house blitz on health. Athlete's foot was judged a problem. It probably was. Everybody was inspected. 'Believe it or not,' I wrote, '31 out of 55 boys have it!' Then the clincher: 'I have not got it but George has.' My rather mean-spirited triumph was short-lived. The athlete's foot fungus migrated to a highly embarrassing zone – the groin. Here it was known as 'tinea cruris'. Those like me who caught it were not only put 'off games' but suffered the indignity of having Matron paint the infected groin with purple tincture. Extreme stratagems were devised to avoid officially admitting to having tinea. Relief came with a remedial cream clandestinely acquired from outside school; it circulated widely among those anxious to avoid Matron's shameful ministrations.

May 1950 began cold and bitter. Without heating, we shivered in our studies. But awareness of nature was breaking in.

After reporting to a house prefect, showered and fully dressed at 7.10 a.m., I walked in the woods before breakfast relishing 'the trees in bud in their beautiful light green colour'. The woods were often a solace. By June it was hot. On General Inspection Day of the Cadet Force, two boys fainted. When German measles broke out, Holt was put out of bounds. Could things get any worse? Oh yes they could! On 2 July 1950, England lost 1-0 to the lowly United States in the World Cup; Australia's tennis great, Frank Sedgman, beat Britain's finest, Tony Mottram, at Wimbledon; and England lost the Test match to the West Indies. 'A Black Day for English Sport,' I lamented.

In September 1950, my second year, I moved from the fourth to the third table for meals in Farfield and into the Sixth Form. Food became an issue. Breakfast usually consisted of two courses, porridge, then bacon or scrambled egg. 'Lately, once a week, no second course, instead, stale hard toast. Once, fried potatoes on fried bread.' I might have added a clear memory of the pre-buttered slices of bread coming out of the serving tin tasting rancid. Cries for support from home grew insistent: 'Thanks for apples', then: 'Thanks for chocolates from Berlin, much appreciated!' Finally, 'I have eaten all my cakes and most of my chocolate.' Then a moment of awareness: 'What would we do without you?' I wrote. 'I sometimes think your time must be fully spent in sending off parcels to Czecho, to George and to me.'

Austerity appeared in places beyond the house kitchen. Laundry prices rose. 'We change sheets and pyjamas once a fortnight, a perfect scandal.' (And a nasty thought.) Wouldn't the house smell? Routines became established – rugger (three times a week), hot bath (shared with another boy) and into Holt (for an ice cream). Work too: 'I wrote an English essay of thirteen sides and was told it was very good.' All against the background of Norfolk weather. By the end of October 1950, we had endured twenty-eight consecutive days of rain.

The event of the term was the General Election in October

1950. A house election was held in parallel. Some of us decided that aping the political parties and spouting mini-versions of their party lines was too boring. We founded the Farfield Liberty Party (FLP), probably affecting independent – but not too shocking – shades of opinion. At a house hustings, while the Conservative candidate was considered 'pathetic', the Socialist 'very witty', the FLP organised a mass parade draped in yellow around the dining room. In the end the FLP got 23, the Conservatives 21, the Socialists just 7. We stayed glued to the radio for the national election results the following day. I breathed a sigh of relief to my parents: 'Churchill got in and that is all that matters!' Adolescent neurosis was never far away: 'I still have dandruff.'

The noisy and dangerous world outside kept breaking into the cloistered life of school. In my newly started diary, I recorded the New Year's Day 1951 offensive by Chinese forces in Korea; their advance to within twenty miles of Seoul the following day; and the Security Council decision to 'brand China an aggressor' on 31 January. On 10 April, Budget Day, a huge (sixpence) increase in income tax and a doubling of the tax on motor cars drew my attention and no doubt that of my parents. A week later 'Schumann Plan signed by Six European countries' scraped in at the bottom of an otherwise routine diary entry. Something must have told me that it was significant but how or why would have been beyond me. Besides, getting 4 out of 15 in divinity and being told to 'pull my socks up' by the chaplain, the Rev. 'Archie' Andrews, took my mind off the world, as did twelve boys being sick in the house and everyone 'feeling rotten'.

The public event of summer 1951, the Festival of Britain, was created on the previously derelict south bank of the Thames. It was an eye-opener and heart-lifter. This was what the world could look like, could feel like, should be like. It wasn't just that we were living in the bombed-out, neglected and semi-derelict surroundings of the nineteenth and early twentieth century. They felt and appeared exhausted, backward-looking, devoid of promise for the future. The Festival showed that bold colours, new materials, new shapes, new vistas were possible. Buildings could look different, glass and plastic were elbowing out brick as our everyday materials. The spirit they exuded was optimistic, forward-looking, filled with hope, not bound by tradition or formula. Nobody had told me that such a world was waiting to arrive. Now, surrounded by it on the Festival site in a glittering clamour of impressions and surfaces, of bustle, fun and vitality, I knew the world I wanted could be like this, had to be.

The only trouble that summer was that I thought I had polio. Or I feared I had polio. There was evidence for my fear. The summer was hot, an incubator for the virus. Polio was rampant. My joints ached in a classic early symptom. I dragged my puzzled limbs around the house in a misery of uncertainty. I did not contract polio; I did have adolescent growing pains, real enough but not serious.

I became junior captain of the house, the main benefit of which was not having to leave the junior dormitory before 7.25 a.m. Bruce Douglas must have judged me worthy of taking on such responsibility – a decision he later came to regret.

For the moment, the Farfield house play in March 1951, R. C. Sherriff's First World War drama, *Journey's End*, was a kind of turning point. Casting me, a fifteen-year-old, in the linchpin psychological role of the middle-aged, wise, calm Lieutenant Osborne was an unfathomable risk even for a school play. I was performing with a future actor, Robert Tunstall, whose portrayal of the histrionic, brittle, alcoholic Captain Stanhope was searingly painful. For my part, something must have happened in the performance that I did not need to control and did not understand. My diary merely records that I found performing 'pretty good' and 'enjoyable'. The review in *The Gresham*, the school magazine, spotted something very different. My performance had provided 'the most vivid experience' of the evening. It went on: 'To say he understood the part is to give no idea of the quality of the sincerity he showed. It was as if he was not acting at all but had really achieved the philosophy on which the play was certainly based.'

I cannot explain the sense that I conveyed. Clearly the producer – the English master, Hoult Taylor – saw potential in me that I did not recognise. After the performances of *Journey's End*, the headmaster preached his Sunday sermon about the pathos of the First World War experience. It was sincere enough but undermined when he burst into tears. This was not the only occasion when he wept while preaching. The school hated it and saw it as emotional self-indulgence. Bruce Douglas, by contrast, had been an infantry officer during the First World War, a position with a huge casualty toll. His own mechanism for dealing with it was to treat it lightly. 'When I joined my company in the trenches,' he explained, 'I was the most junior officer. By the end of the day I was the most senior. The others were all dead.'

House food deteriorated badly in mid-summer. The old cook, regarded as 'jolly good', retired because she felt too old. The new cook, we alleged, put no sugar in the custard, poured salt on to the hare generously provided by a parent, and made the toast under scrambled egg so soggy that 'we refused to eat it and passed it back to the kitchen'. I warned my parents ominously: 'We will soon hear more about this!' They undoubtedly felt properly sceptical about these catalogues of culinary woe.

And adolescent sex emerged. Some was real. Two house prefects, W and T, were demoted for having sex with the maids. Shrewd Betty Douglas had noted a 'change in their behaviour'. Their demotion mattered less than the fact that the two maids were sacked. When Bruce Douglas accused three boys of 'making eyes at the maids through the serving hatch into the kitchen', I snapped in my newsletter: 'The accusations were quite unfounded, unfair and unnecessarily suspicious.' The housemaster's solution was to allow privet hedges to grow unrestricted, thus obstructing the view of the kitchens from three of the studies.

For my part, homo-erotic crushes began to feature in my

diary. P was in another house. Visits were made. My diary records with feeling that we 'sat together' at a lantern lecture on Roman life, an occasion that drew two exclamation marks. During the final school service, I made up my mind to stop being silly.

There were good days that school summer of 1951. One Saturday, not untypical, involved cricket in the afternoon, a rehearsal of Shakespeare's *A Midsummer Night's Dream* before supper, tennis after that and kickabout football following house prayers. 'Felt really tired,' I wrote, but I remember also being very happy. I loved games, their endless variety, their physicality, the feeling of mind and body being wholly alive. Gresham's wide meadows were places of fulfilment. The school kept sport in balance with other activities. Those in the First Rugger XV were not put down as 'rugger-buggers'. Equally, the captain of rugger was not seen as the de facto head of the school.

The great world was not far off. On 23 September, 'The King was operated on for lung re-section.' We believed the official reassurance that his condition was 'satisfactory'. Those were different days when it came to official statements. The next year, 1952 – weight 11 st 6 lbs, height 5 ft 10 ¼ ins – had no time for boredom. Norfolk's weather opened in true style: 25 and 26 January saw heavy snow, cancelled games and a bitter 17 degrees of frost. 'The wooden cubicle walls in the dormitory were cracking loudly at night and kept us awake.' A week later a howling, snow-filled northerly gale – 'straight from the North Pole' – was so severe that dormitory windows were, uniquely, kept closed.

I sat in my study during mid-morning break on Wednesday, 6 February 1952 eating a triangle of processed Kraft cheese spread on two cream crackers. This mid-morning luxury 're-charge' included listening to music on the wireless. That morning there was something odd about the music, very slow and grave. Then silence, a lengthy pause and finally the solemn announcement of King George VI 's death. The school went into full mourning. Black ties were worn; flags flown at half-mast; the headmaster gave permission to listen to Mr Churchill's 'fine tribute' at 9 p.m. that evening. On Friday, Proclamation Day of the new Queen, flags went back to full mast and we sang the National Anthem at house prayers 'with great vigour and feeling'. The chaplain appealed for a strong turnout for Holy Communion on Sunday and sixty-four boys and staff attended.

In the second week of February 1952 I changed the way I communicated with my parents. Instead of the regular but dutiful letter with its predictable litany of endless if varied sporting activity, I started a newsletter. 'The Farfield Weekly' was laid out on two sides of A4 paper with headlines, comment and a broader range of subjects. I wrote to my parents: 'I hope you like this idea. I will be able to tell you more local gossip.' The death of the King gave a strong first headline.

From now on, there was a real contrast between what I wrote in my diary and the 'local gossip' I offered my parents. I did not confide that I found 'Tudor economic history very interesting' or Milton's *Areopagitica* excellent and stimulating. Nor did I explain that I followed 'the serenity of Brahms's Second Symphony' by relishing the knockabout of Jimmy Edwards and Dick Bentley in the BBC's *Take It From Here*. This increasingly serious, orthodox, biddable person offered a different persona in the shape of 'editor' of the 'Farfield Weekly'. There was an element of Jekyll and Hyde to it. It was as if I had deliberately if subconsciously created a necessary vehicle for the repressed 'Hyde-like' anti-authority feelings seething inside me. When Bruce Douglas thundered that no food was to be received from home in food parcels, that six dining-room knives had been found in one study and that this must stop, I commented defiantly: 'Opinion was that if no parcels were received, we would starve. So carry on please and continue your fine parcels.' At Whitsun, I protested that we were working 'while all the workers of England are enjoying themselves in the sun or perhaps the rain at elegant resorts such as Southend, Clacton or Cromer!'. I had to concede that school Speech Day with its built-in holiday was only a fortnight away, which left the sense of grievance feeling rather manufactured.

The headmaster, of course, provided fertile ground for complaint. He beat six Farfield boys who had been caught returning from unauthorised swimming in the sea. I opined that the house captain had 'unnecessarily' told Bruce Douglas about them. Yet didn't the school need rules about the possible dangers of sea bathing? Olivier beat another six who had smoked during the Field Day of the Combined Cadet Corps. There was glee over the way the headmaster 'lectured' each of the guilty smokers. 'Headmaster: "For me (pause) smoking is bad. For you (pause) smoking is worse for it stops you growing." Boy (six feet tall already aged sixteen): "Well, sir, I hope I don't grow any taller."'

My now fully developed editorial indignation reached new heights after the headmaster conducted a secret inquiry into boys smoking at the summer cadet camp. He forbade any discussion of the matter. My newsletter editorial scalded in red ink: 'The case of the HM's recent interviews brings up a point of public morality. Is it proper for the HM to run what is in fact a spy ring and to have eyes prying into our every private action? In any other society it would be indefensible.'

My journalistic indignation found another vehicle when my best friend, Willy Simpson, and I were made joint editors of the termly school magazine, *The Gresham*. I raged against 'Masters who are too old and stuck in the mud' to write interestingly or at all. I was 'sick of re-writing other people's almost intolerable tripe'. When we took our first issue to Olivier in December 1952 he condemned it and me in particular as 'arrogant'. Even my strongest ally, the English master, Hoult Taylor, warned, 'The first requisite of an editorial is taste and style.' Taylor was hugely influential. A brilliant English master, he directed the annual school play and two house plays. A fine keyboard player, he cheered up chapel services with lively organ voluntaries. As pianist he played movements from Beethoven, Mozart and Schumann piano concertos in the school concert.

He wore suede shoes, tweed suits, walked with a slight limp and had a deep, rich laugh.

Something had to break. At the end of November 1952, Bruce Douglas came to my study during late prep around 9 p.m. 'He had a feeling that I was against authority. He had expected a reaction from me once my brother George had left but this was too much. Until he was certain, he could not make me a House prefect.' A fortnight later, when house prefects were made, I was not one of them. I was very shaken but should not have been. Yet two days later, to make matters worse, I told Douglas that 'I didn't think much of his choice for next term's house play'. A good friend reported that Douglas 'was furious, said I was conceited, he didn't want me as prefect let alone as captain, said I had better mind out'. When I talked over my school problems with my father, I said, 'really they made me sick'. I had no idea what to do about them.

That autumn casualties on the rugby field were high – five broken collarbones, one broken leg and four badly twisted knees represented a serious tally. Bruce Douglas's announcement that the house of some fifty-five boys would have to subsist on one large tin of boot polish per week rather than two increased my sense of being unfairly treated. What of the saga of hard toast at breakfast? 'One boy's knife broke in two when cutting his toast.' Gossip, of which I was a part, secretly accused the Douglases of taking the choicest pieces of the hare provided by a parent, leaving the boys with the bones, the scrag and the skin.

Douglas greeted me coolly when term started in January 1953. I didn't make things easier for him. On the night of 31 January, gales and a huge North Sea surge flooded the towns and villages of the North Norfolk coast. Thirty houses were smashed in Salthouse; 160 homes flooded in Cley; nine trees were blown down on the edge of the cricket field. On Sunday afternoon, 1 February, many of us cycled down in the teeth of the gale to see if we could help. Each house sent fifteen boys. The Farfield contingent, typically, distinguished itself with a

diversity of clothes and illegal berets, hats and caps. Sometimes the headwind was so strong that we had to get off our
bikes.

The coast road was inundated and impassable. From the
lip of the Holt-Cromer Ridge, the coastline had vanished; all
around was the broad expanse of sea. Once there, we were
sent to help recovery in the local hotel. We found a thick layer
of sludge on all floors, fireplaces torn out, windows smashed,
the water still very high. The kitchen was a pitiful sight – soggy
cornflakes, bags of sugar, flour, trays, teapots and spoons all
lurking in the sludge. Furniture was heaved upstairs to protect
it from the next high tide. In an article I commissioned for
the school magazine, Jan Day, the chemistry master, observed
how glad we were to be useful. 'Only thus could we show
practically the sympathy we felt for their distress, a sympathy
which, until they gave us a chance to manifest it, nearly choked
us with frustration.'

What should have been a day of healing and generosity soon
became something else. As I was battling the gale northwards
to reach the floods at Salthouse, the headmaster passed me on
his way back to school in his small Baby Austin. His glare at
me through the windscreen was not a routine one. He meant
it directly for me.

The previous evening the Debating Society had met. Many
of us felt angry that the master in charge, the chaplain, Rev.
'Archie' Andrews, had organised only two debates that term
instead of the usual three. I persuaded two younger boys to
move a motion of no confidence in Andrews and wrote the
(aggressive) words of the motion for them. Andrews was furious and after chapel on Sunday evening, in the dark on the lawn
outside in the remnants of the gale, Olivier tore several strips
off me. 'Cheeking' the chaplain was one thing (he probably
deserved it); getting juniors to do it on my behalf was quite
another. The next day, I recorded a 'black, despairing morning'.
The house captain advised me to apologise all round, and do it
quickly. I was only too glad to try to get it over. Bruce Douglas

did not seem to take it too seriously. Olivier dismissed it as a 'gauche attempt at humour which he would let off'. But it was not a good start to the year. The editor of the 'Farfield Weekly' was silent on the subject.

The house's technical ingenuity kept us diverted. Two boys linked four studies into a local radio station. Programming was either directly pirated off the BBC – *Sports Report*, the *Eight O'Clock News* – or was 'original' from the FBC (Farfield Broadcasting Company). The programmes were judged by listeners to be original in content if based on well-tried formats – 'Schoolboys' Choice', 'Listen with Betty', 'Matron's Hour', and 'How to Cook in Studies without Setting Fire to Them'. 'Sponsorship' for programmes included Horlicks – obvious – and Veet, a well-known depilatory much used by pubescents struck with pudeur at sprouting hairs on their chests.

Farfield was awash with individualism and skill. One boy built a detailed, life-size suit of medieval armour – out of flexible materials. Another constructed a cathode ray receiver in his study before television signals and programmes existed. A third made entire clocks. Yet another built a complete electronic organ. Two others set up a study-to-study – two connections only! – telephone system. Bruce Douglas took it all in his 'laissez-faire' stride – in fact he quietly encouraged it. He enjoyed the individualism, the sheer practicality on display.

Studies in house were idiosyncratically varied. I noted someone 'who suffered from bad feet decorated his study with pictures of people who can and do excel in sport'. The tidiest room belonged to an avid birdwatcher, the walls covered with bird drawings. The most striking, in decor and because of what it said about its owner, belonged to my best friend, Willy Simpson. 'He has raised a large dais by the window where he sits in majesty screened from the prying world by handmade curtains. Beneath his dais is the "library", a very dangerous and precarious room. His walls are decorated with images of Sir Walter Raleigh, Sir Walter Scott and Hogarth.'

Willy, carrot-haired, a year older than me, was perhaps the

cleverest boy in the school. We spent a lot of time together in his study, reading poetry, creating political utopias, ranting our way through the witches in *Macbeth*. Where Willy led, I was happy to follow, Sancho Panza to his Don Quixote. He was inclined to the subversive. On Speech Day 1952 we decided to challenge the boring predictability of the classroom exhibitions of chemistry and physics experiments. From year to year, they never varied. We created an exhibition advertised by posters asking, 'Do You Want to See Something You Didn't See Last Year?' No one challenged our modest act of subversion.

I owe Willy Simpson a lot; his idealism, his intellectual irreverence, his blazing sense of fun, his restless cleverness. In an editorial in *The Gresham* in December 1951, he mused on what the next fifty years might hold for us, the joint editors. 'While one is serving his sentence in a house of correction, the other, serving his country in the House of Commons, will give away the prizes.' He was tragically prescient. Many years later, I did present the prizes at Speech Day. Long before that, Willy Simpson had put his head in a gas oven in a dingy flat in Rome aged thirty.

That spring, episodes of depression started, not of the full-blown clinical variety but a despairing adolescent self-awareness, where painful, intensely clear self-consciousness flooded my whole sense of being. The world was all around me in perfect, perhaps excessive, clarity. Life took place everywhere but I seemed detached from it or unaware of how to reconnect with it. By the end of April, I wrote that I was 'bloody depressed. Is it love or what, though none is in sight. I am not going to have my summer term wrecked with depression!' There was too much to do – all-important A-levels and the part of Antony in the school play, *Antony and Cleopatra*.

Confusion about sex there was abundantly. An old Farfield boy, 'M', visited school. I had always liked him. I noted that he talked a lot about 'homosexuality in London – it appals and revolts me especially his defence of it'. It was way beyond my emotional capacity of understanding.

My self-esteem took further blows. I spoke to Bruce Douglas 'about my prospects'. He was admirably if painfully honest. 'He was doubtful as to whether I would carry out his mandate (as prefect) if contrary to my opinion. I was certain that I could.' I had nothing to demonstrate that I would. George told me bluntly that 'I was cynical and annoying. Perhaps I am, I don't know'.

Depression struck again; 'vile mood', first migraine. Seeking solace from despair in the calm beauty of the woods, I saw a magnificent array of clouds and sun shafts above me. I wrote in my mind: 'There was a day when / Arrowing through the mountained clouds / The sun's firelight irradiated red / Through down, deep-quarried canyons.' I don't know where those words came from, what amalgam of half-remembered quotations fathered the images. I never went further with it but I have forgotten neither the moment nor the words. It was hardly an epiphany, but it was vivid, healing and welcome.

I had applied to go to St John's College, Cambridge. In June, the college rejected me. Olivier explained: 'Much depends on his recommendation. He cannot recommend me unless he is certain of my character which he proceeded to analyse.' A lot turned on that disastrous editorial in *The Gresham*, which I thought was fatuous of him. But I conceded: 'Most of the rest is pretty sound.' I did not record what it was. Yet within a fortnight, Olivier was recommending me for interview at Trinity College, Cambridge. 'All is going well with Trinity,' he reported. What had changed? I cannot have transformed myself and would not have known how to.

Circumstances were different; life had to go on. The exam load was punishing. Exams to win school prizes involved writing seven essays spread over thirty-one pages in two days in late May. The A-levels loomed in a flurry of apprehension and a feeling of not being fully prepared. 'Beginning on June 22, I have 2 exams a day for 7 days, a gruelling lot of work,' I wrote. They included four papers each in History, English, History with Foreign Texts and a General Paper. Most were three-hour papers. Ten days later I looked back on thirty-one and a half hours of work committed to 170 sides of paper: 'Fortunately, I never suffered from writer's cramp.' Much of the time it was true exam weather – hot sun, blue skies, stifling exam halls. Inter-house cricket matches were crammed between exams, with some exam sessions beginning at 7 p.m. after close of play in cricket.

Farfield was enduring a new cook. I described her approach as 'experiment without innovation, a bad mixture . . . The porridge has varied in its lumpiness, the stew has lacked gravy, the custard has lacked sugar and the pastry has lacked lightness.' A fortnight later 'the semolina was made with sour milk and erupted and smelled badly'. These were not idle complaints. That night thirty-four boys, two-thirds of the house, had diarrhoea. So did Matron.

The punishing schedule of games and exams was enlivened by the arrival of a visitor teacher from Nigeria. He immediately endeared himself. I reported: 'Rumour has it that when he was presented to the biology master, he said: 'My name is Mr Oyejago but if you can't pronounce that you can just call me "Rabbits!"''

The two events of a packed summer term were the school play and the Coronation. When Olivier told a guest that no public school had ever performed *Antony and Cleopatra* previously, they muttered darkly, 'I'm not surprised.' The review in *The Gresham* on my performance as Antony was subtly critical and entirely fair: 'The beauty of Tusa's "I am dying Egypt, dying" while moving us to admiration may well have induced a wistful review of some earlier restrictions.' Hoult Taylor did me no favours in casting me as Antony, though in the context of the school it was a considerable honour. I had neither the psychological maturity nor the physical ease to begin to capture anything of the part. I was uncomfortable and must have been uncomfortable to watch. I have always had to learn things, from sight-reading music, to playing games, to moving on stage. Few things have come naturally or instinctively.

The Coronation of Queen Elizabeth on 2 June 1953 brought out the depth of my internal contradictions. As editor of the school magazine, I was the height of conventional loyalty: 'All of us, as representatives of that generation on which so much depends in the future and which is so aptly called "The Queen's Generation" must offer our vows, however insignificant, of allegiance.' How the headmaster must have approved. My true – or manufactured? – feelings emerged in my Editor's Notice written in red ink in the 'Farfield Weekly'. The paper, I asserted stridently, was 'well known for its anarchist tendencies and affiliation to the Society for the Prevention of Mob Hysteria over the Royal Family'. There would be, I promised, no souvenir articles on 'the mystery (for us unfathomable) of mob worship of the Royal Family or any special series by Garter (or Suspender) King of Arms!'.

Such contrary responses were parts of the struggling, emerging me. I felt that I should be responsible, reasonable, considerate, well behaved. But I had laboured for years under the burden of being considered 'a nice boy'. I needed to break out from that straitjacket of politeness and good behaviour.

By the autumn term of September 1953, both the headmaster and Bruce Douglas must have decided that they had no choice but to take a risk. They gave me responsibility as house captain and school prefect. This was clever; it jolted me into a different awareness of authority: 'I am now as high as I will ever be at school,' I noted in my diary. 'Nor is this pinnacle particularly exhilarating. There's a feeling that the House belongs to you and that everything that goes wrong is a reflection of your character. This is rather an uneasy feeling.' After a prefects' meeting with the headmaster about boys drinking at cadet camp in the summer, myself included, I uncomfortably compared my past record with my exalted, responsible new status. 'Really the things I have done in my time – pubbing at Bodham with C and C, drinking in my study with N and wine at Cromer with C and P.' I would soon find out how difficult it would be to exercise authority properly.

This was 'scholarship term' for those hoping to win an Oxbridge award. 'Work is the priority,' I told my parents, 'A school's routine does not allow for much excitement nor is it intended to do so.' Eric Kelly, the history master, certainly piled it on. The time had come, he declared, for thinking, for understanding abstractions, for flights of intellectual fancy, for daring beyond the routine. Kelly would point to a free-standing bookcase on one side of his history classroom: 'That is where scholarships are won!' I read books on democracy, Eric Newton on art, E. H. Carr on revolution. I wrote a nineteen-page essay on 'Progress', another of unrecorded length on 'Morality'. By mid-October I felt 'singularly depressed', a week later, 'a really low day', two days later I complained of 'feeling dizzy'. In letters home, I enthused about the pleasure of a late-night get-together with house prefects. 'We ate a whole loaf of bread, two tins of sardines and drank orangeade staying up until after midnight eating and talking.'

In mid-November, I found out that three boys were drinking in their study. I reprimanded them; they agreed not to go further. Yet the following day, two of them left school to smoke and drink, taking a younger boy with them. I did not face them directly this time but reported straight to Bruce Douglas. He said he had to tell the headmaster. One of the accused was demoted, another received a 'gloriously rude' letter, a third was 'in despair'. The mood in the house turned. Almost everyone hated me. One of those involved started calling me 'the greasy Czech' and circulated a petition, 'the Anti-Czech'. It was awful and I was wretched at what I called 'the tragic peak of a hate campaign'.

I turned for advice and solace to Hoult Taylor, visiting him in his lodgings in Holt one evening. I knew I had handled the business badly, probably lacking courage in not facing my colleagues directly. I was shattered by the enveloping atmosphere of hate. I broke down and wept. Taylor did not try to defend what I had done or how I had acted. He listened, he sympathised. As I stood to leave some hours later, he put his arms round me and his face against mine. I can still feel his bristly eyebrows on my cheek. I was startled. It was not a sexual embrace but one of comfort and acceptance. Nothing was solved but my recovery could begin.

It needed to because the Cambridge scholarship exams were a fortnight away. The run-up to them was worrying. My practice papers with a week to go were 'condemned as rather sub-standard. They lacked mental precision and dissection.' On the eve of departure for Cambridge, Eric Kelly, the gentlest of teachers, said I 'might scrape an exhibition if I was lucky'. Amazingly, I set off by train for Cambridge in positive mood. I was tensed up but 'waiting for the exams to start'. With the winter mists rising off the Cam, the college lamps wreathed in dark and fog, the outlines of Trinity's courts emerging through the atmospheric murk, Cambridge was romantically, intoxicatingly attractive. This had to be the place for me.

I judged my English History paper on the morning of 7 December to be 'adequate'; General History in the afternoon 'had frightened me considerably but three questions were comfortable'. The following day I wrote European History 'well enough'. A note arrived in my college rooms later that day inviting me for an oral interview with Trinity history dons the day after next. A General Paper let me show my knowledge of literature and music.

The interview in George Kitson Clark's magnificent rooms over Trinity Great Gate – Byron's old rooms – was probing but not intimidating, despite Kitson Clark's authority and reputation. I recall only one exchange, about Gustavus Adolphus's lines of communication during the Thirty Years War, but that is all. It was over. I caught the train back to Holt. A taxi picked me up at Melton Mowbray station. Bruce and Betty Douglas fed me. I felt curiously complete. The anguish of the previous term had vanished.

The scholarship results were due a week later on Saturday, 19 December after the end of term. I took off to London to see the Royal Shakespeare Company's production of *Antony and*

Cleopatra at the Aldwych Theatre. It was starry, with Peggy Ashcroft as Cleopatra, Michael Redgrave as Antony and Harry Andrews as Enobarbus. This seemed an ideal way of 'escaping from a home tensed by expectation of the scholarship result'. That plan blew up in my face when the first person I met in the theatre foyer was Alan Carr from Gresham's, who had played Enobarbus to my Antony. He had already heard from King's College; he had a scholarship. It didn't ruin the performance for me but it certainly ratcheted up the tension.

I returned home to south-east Essex 'in considerable trepidation' around 7 p.m. As I came in the back door, Dora, our occasional help, shouted, 'Quick, go into the lounge!' My father handed me the telegram, delivered by taxi at his request from the local post office at nearby Grays. It read: 'Congratulations Stop Major Scholarship Trinity stop.' I threw my coat into the air with joy. I wrote in my diary: 'I was tremendously excited not only for its general value but because of all the emotions and tensions I had experienced. The long vigils in Trinity, the feeling of impending doom before I left; everything would have been incomplete without this success.'

I cannot explain how I changed from writing 'sub-standard' practice papers, from being regarded as having only an outside chance of 'scraping' an award, to being the winner of a major scholarship at Cambridge. Something inside me must have clicked into place, some of the contradictions must have eased, some of the undoubted concentrated work paid off. Or perhaps Eric Kelly had been a shrewd psychologist and applied the necessary goad at the right moment.

I have often felt guilty about staying at Gresham's for a further term after winning the scholarship. Without a formal syllabus to study, I read avidly and set about filling 'gaps' in my knowledge. Surely I should have plunged into the obligatory two years of national service without delay. I should have got on with life. It has seemed ever since like running away from the next stage of growing up. That may indeed have suited me. But I stayed because Bruce Douglas urged me to stay on as house captain; he would not have wanted to find a successor in mid-year. His own more pressing needs, his undoubted convenience, fitted with my own evasions.

I could at least look back on almost five years at Gresham's with satisfaction and what should have been gratitude. I had played games, all games – rugger, hockey, cricket, football, tennis, squash – in almost every spare hour available. I had been well taught in history, brilliantly taught in English, patiently taught in music. I had sung in the choir, acted in plays ancient and modern, cycled the Norfolk countryside. I had been tolerated by the headmaster, finally trusted by Bruce Douglas and enriched by Hoult Taylor, who accepted my faults and saw through to qualities I did not presume to possess. I had been stupid, selfish, arrogant, conceited and puzzled, depressed and clumsy. I briefly skirted the shores of the homo-erotic, rightly sensing that there was no landing place for me there. The heterosexual world was clearly perceived, strongly desired but poorly understood and still a remote destination. I had nothing to complain about and much to be grateful for. I was five years closer to growing up. I was indistinguishable from someone British. The necessary protective colouring was in place and I hardly noticed it. The British public-school system had done its work.

4

Soldiering

1954–56

For people of my generation, two years of national service in
the armed services was a fact of life, a milestone of growing
up. Since everyone had to serve, bar a few excused on medical grounds, none could feel they were being picked on. Even
the extension of the conscription from its original eighteen
months to a full two years caused little stir. While it took two
years out of what was then the steady progression through education to full-time employment, this modern hiatus on the
road from young adulthood to maturity was accepted. We only
had to look at the world around us. A Cold War was bitterly
contested with the Soviet Union and the communist camp
in Europe. Older friends had fought in Korea in the 1950s,
near-contemporaries served in the jungles of Malaya against
Chinese communist rebels or in the upland forests of Kenya
against the indigenous Mau Mau insurgency. Others would
fight in Egypt as part of the Anglo-French invasion of the Suez
Canal in 1956. It was an actively dangerous world which could
and did take lives.

While most national servicemen expected, rightly, to spend
their time in conventional deployments, there was no glib revelling in the prospect of far-flung adventures. Such shallowness
evaporated with the occasional news of a death in action. My
good friend at Gresham's School, Tony Warnes, was one. A
talented woodworker and joiner, a dashing hockey right wing,
an only son of Cromer family builders, Tony was shot dead
in a remote forest engagement with Mau Mau. In a sensitive

exchange of letters with me expressing shock, sadness and regret, the headmaster, Martin Olivier, said that at least Tony, dying so young, would not have to endure 'the experience of failing powers'. I could not imagine then what he meant.

There were local dangers closer to home. My brother, George, serving in a sapper regiment based on Salisbury Plain, was patrolling in a scout car. The driver misread the fact that at the next junction the road ahead was several feet lower than the one on which they were approaching. The scout car rolled over. Usually the officer rode with his head out of the turret. George had sat down inside with the turret lid closed a few moments before the accident.

My enlistment in the armed forces started in spring 1954 with a day of physical and educational testing. Since school was on the Norfolk coast at Holt, the recruitment centre was in nearby Norwich and meant a nice day out. The tests were much simpler than any at school. The only jolt came at the end. A small, concealed display was headed: 'Look here to see the person most responsible for your health!' Fascinating! Who would it be? An authoritative-looking doctor plus stethoscope! Perhaps a burly khaki-clad matron! Certainly a commanding figure of some kind. I moved to the table, looked down into the display and found myself looking at my own face in a mirror. A momentary twinge of shame at my gullibility was followed by the first dawning realisation: my health was my business.

I was assigned to the Royal Artillery, heavy anti-aircraft artillery, or 'heavy ack-ack'. Clever recruits went into the engineers or field artillery; those needed good maths. Socially smart people were chosen for the cavalry (tanks and armoured cars), very smart ones for traditional county-based regiments. A posting to the gunners was very ordinary.

Three months later in July 1954, it was time to enlist. I boarded the train at Euston station carrying a very small suit-case of personal belongings. From now on, the army would provide us with everything needed for life and subsistence. Besides, becoming part of a disciplined force meant putting to one side the personal and its signs and symbols. From the station at Oswestry, the Shropshire base for two weeks' 'basic training', three-ton army lorries transported us to our barracks. In a large warehouse we were signed in and given our military identity and all the clothing and equipment demanded by army life. My number was 23037865, never forgotten over sixty years, and printed in indelible numbers on every piece of army-issue clothing and kit or hammered into the handles of metal 'eating irons' – knife, fork, spoon, mug and mess tin. Was this number hammered into the soles of our boots too? Oddly, I can't remember. From this point, I was '23037865 Gunner Tusa, sir' in response to every superior.

Those first days of basic training at Oswestry were a blur. With poorly fitting uniforms, shapeless khaki berets, unbroken army boots, and incapable of marching as a unit, our platoon was a bewildered, arm-swinging medley of clumsy shapes. As the newest intake in the barracks, derision followed us wherever we marched with cries of 'Get some in!' Confused at first, we quickly learned this was shorthand for 'Get some service in', which we certainly hoped to do.

Much of the training was a question of breaking us into army ways and methods, to make us look more like soldiers even if we were not. This involved tuition in what was called 'domestic economy': folding blankets into immaculate oblong packages enveloped in an outside blanket; 'bulling your kit', polishing the brass buckles on your belt, webbing and gaiters, smearing wet green 'blanco' smoothly and generously onto all your kit; and 'bulling your boots', applying so much actual spit and polish to the toecap that it shone like a mirror. The Regimental Sergeant Major demanded that he must 'see my face in it'. It took hours. These activities filled the first weekend and much of the first week of basic training.

The barrack room, with a dozen or more men in it, was oddly convivial. From the platoon of thirty-five, just five of us had five O-levels. There was a huge social and educational gap between the public and grammar schoolboys with five

O-levels and those without. It represented a divide of class, accent, income and life experience of an almost unimaginable kind. A physical divide existed too. Those photos of a happy group of squaddies scrubbing up the barrack-room floor reveal it starkly; most of them were a good four inches shorter than me and I was not exceptionally tall. Sixty years ago, the physical difference between classes was stark. The poorer were shorter.

Yet the barrack room never divided on class lines. Rather, everyone felt bound by the clear understanding that we were all in a very strange situation together. Survival was a strong bond, shared advice too. One of my fellows observed in a friendly way as I tried to 'f— and blind' with the best of them that 'you're not used to swearing much really, are you?'. Sitting on our folding chairs of a Sunday evening, polishing brasses and boots and singing 'Please let the light that shines on me, Shine on the one I love' remains a memory of shared comradeship. Another was of a weekend spent, gladly, stripping the barrack-room walls and ceiling of old whitewash, repainting them and scrubbing the floor clean. The day was warm, the sun shone, the water and whitewash flowed, the task rounded off with a long hot communal shower. That was contentment!

Fundamentally, ex-public schoolboys found basic training easy. Some discomfort, some regimentation and communal living had been our norm for at least the previous five years. Most if not all had been in the school CCF (Combined Cadet Force). Foot drill and marching in step had been drummed into us; map-reading, elementary tactics, stripping a rifle, firing a rifle with live bullets – these had been part of normal out-of-school activities. But these were new, often painfully new experiences for our non-public-school fellow recruits. Above all, most public schoolboys had been boarding for years; was boarding in an army barrack that different? The majority of our fellow recruits had never been away from home before. For a few it was upsetting and perplexing. Recently, another Oswestry veteran reminded me of the sobbing distress felt by a young Welshman who slept in the bed between us.

Before our first Saturday evening pass out of barracks – in uniform, of course – we received a friendly lecture from the Regimental Sergeant Major cautioning us not to be carried away by 'one whiff of the barmaid's apron strings!', whatever that might mean. We returned to barracks early, sober, unscathed and still innocent.

With basic army principles and practices instilled in that first fortnight, the whole intake was parcelled out to specialist training units for the types of artillery that made up the Royal Regiment. Field artillery, twenty-five-pound howitzers still metaphorically hauled by horses, was the socially smart end of things; it also needed good maths to make the calculations needed for accurate targeting. The working assumption of anti-aircraft artillery (ack-ack) seemed to be that provided enough high explosive was fired into the sky, sooner or later it might hit an enemy plane or, if not, might at least scare them off. That was to be my military future. I did not mind; I guessed I would have felt out of place in the very social English 'county' atmosphere of a field artillery regimental mess, assuming I became a commissioned officer. Anti-aircraft gunners were trained by the sea, where they could blast off in safety with only the sheep to disturb, the gulls to annoy and the fish to alarm. A more desolate, isolated patch of coastline could not have been found for such desperate practices than Tonfanau, a very small farming hamlet between Towyn and Barmouth on the mid-Wales coast.

If Oswestry had seemed remote from London, the further journey to Tonfanau was scarring in its complexity and the sense of travelling ever further from civilisation. (Was I in truth just re-enacting the misery of the wartime Paddington to Ashburton railway trauma without quite so much platform drama?) London to Crewe was straightforward enough; then a change for Whitchurch; a second change carried us past places such as Ruabon and Gobowen – there were surely dragons here – to Machynlleth, difficult to spell, impossible to pronounce. After a further wait, the final connecting train ran on a single track due west to the sea, turned northwards on the coast to Towyn and finally to Tonfanau Halt. Any station along the route must have witnessed a score of *Brief Encounter* moments. These were places of desolation, dashed hopes and broken hearts.

My disorientation was not just the bemusement of a young man over-conditioned by living near the metropolis. Tonfanau was without doubt a long and complicated way from anywhere else. All communication was difficult. The innovation of 'subscriber trunk dialling' for long-distance calls had not arrived. A call from a Tonfanau phone box to home in south-east Essex involved being connected from one exchange to another until it reached the London base of 'trunk' – i.e. long distance – calls, an exchange identified as 'Kingsway 451'. This name became music to my ears, meaning I was just one connection away from home; at the same time it underlined how distant I really was.

Only two weeks since joining the army, there was a lot to learn. Much time was spent on the parade ground actually 'square-bashing', the air ringing with hundreds of metal-studded boots crunching into the tarmac. Somehow our efforts were never quite enough for the NCOs. Sergeant Haddock, the platoon sergeant, who sometimes didn't shave in the morning, was seen as weak, Lance Bombardier Hoeltschi clever but ineffectual. Bombardier Pierpoint was the man we relished as a good turn with a good turn of phrase: 'I'm the hangman's son!' he declared. No one dared ask if he really was. In his zeal for the highest standards of foot drill, Pierpoint, red-haired, compact with a harsh, corncrake voice, encouraged us with three trademark phrases: 'I'm going to break your arm off and hit you with the soggy end!' Or: 'I'm going to shove my prick into your ear and fuck some sense into you!' And, less threateningly: 'I want you to lift your leg up two feet and drive it into the ground three feet!' We tried. The crash of thirty young men driving their metal-studded boots into the ground to satisfy Bombardier Pierpoint became curiously satisfying.

Tonfanau camp was famous for its triple 'rat-tat-tat' halt.

Marching briskly after a day's training, lean and fit from exercise, tanned from the open air, hunger sharpened, mess tins and eating irons jangling from our belts, the platoon would come to a ringing halt at the canteen entrance with that exhilarating slam of the boots.

The remoteness and isolation, though, were wearing. The saddest sight of the day was at morning parade, timed especially, it seemed, to see the Cambrian Coast Express halt briefly at Tonfanau on its way from Aberdovey to London Euston. Oh, to be on that train, to have something to look at except sea, hills and sheep, some entertainment beyond a pub in Towyn, a film at the Army Kinema or baked beans, egg and chips in the NAAFI canteen. Could there not be something better to look forward to than more foot drill, more instruction in the monstrously cumbersome and ineffective radar system supposed to direct our equally ineffective 3.7-inch guns!

There were forty-eight-hour leaves. On one such early weekend pass to freedom I had a glimpse of a better life, going to London to meet my parents but chiefly to visit my Czech unofficial 'uncle', Mirek Vydra. A restaurateur and former night-club owner in Prague, Mirek fled from communist Czechoslovakia in the 1950s. My father helped him set up a restaurant in Baker Street, the Classic Restaurant. Famous for its authentic Czech specialities – roast duck, sauerkraut, red cabbage, dumplings, apple strudel – its back room became the meeting place for the Czechoslovak government in exile.

As an ambitious restaurateur, wanting to grow, Mirek had moved on to find a site in the middle of Wigmore Street, then a dreary neglected thoroughfare, with the exception of the legendary Debenham and Freebody's. He opened the smartly contemporary Boulevard Restaurant, which I longed to see for myself. Old Prague and Vienna oozed from every page of the menu. The intoxicating smell of cigarettes and cigars, wine and brandy, furs and perfumes, the languages of the customers – Czech and German – and the accents of the staff – Czech and German – made it a blessed oasis of '*Mitteleuropa*', not so much central London, more Central Europe. For me, to eat at the Boulevard rather than the canteen at Tonfanau was a dizzying reminder that style, fun, good living, eating and a certain kind of '*gemütlich*' sophistication still existed. Even the late-night train journey back from Euston via Crewe, Whitchurch, Ruabon, reaching Machynlleth as dawn broke, could not dampen the joy, the memory, the reassurance that a good life did exist elsewhere.

But training at Tonfanau was not supposed to last for ever. For most national servicemen, interest centred on their imminent regimental posting. For the privileged few with five O-levels, the only question was whether we were judged to have 'officer qualities', a concept never explicitly defined or identified. This judgement would be made by the War Office Selection Board ('WOSBie') on Salisbury Plain. Over two to three days, small groups of would-be officers were put through a series of tests to ferret out those elusive qualities. Was there a formal marking system? We were not told. Were specific exercises individually marked? No answer. We were assured at the outset, 'There are no trick cyclists here!' We could only guess at what a 'trick cyclist' might be. I do recall blundering incompetently through an assault course exercise, but I have never had real upper-arm strength. I tried to make up for that failure in physical leadership by giving a presentation on the 'communist threat' laced with every complex word I could think of starting with 'dialectic'. The supervising staff said they had never heard so many long words used so well – or probably not at all. With abstruse ideas like that at my disposal, I was clearly officer material. It proved not to be that simple.

Back at Tonfanau, my contemporaries were steadily called forward to officer cadet training. I received no such message. Soon their successors began receiving their summons, then those after them. Fortnight by fortnight, my name featured on none of those War Office movement orders. I was becalmed in Tonfanau, beyond training, without a future, stuck in a limbo called 'Held Strength' from which nobody showed any interest in freeing me.

The training battalion was happy to give me jobs to do – after all, I was a spare body for one of the barrack orderly teams. The first task was the daily cleaning of latrines. As this involved throwing considerable quantities of water over what were only averagely disagreeable places, the duty was far less unpleasant than it sounded. In fact, leaving the latrines clean, washed, usable and almost salubrious gave a certain job satisfaction.

My second post was as orderly in the Battery Stores, an undemanding role involving the morning issue of brooms, barrows and suchlike and signing them back six hours later. It was a considerably less satisfying than cleaning the latrines but the long dull day could be filled by reading Macaulay's *History of England*, good preparation I thought for reading History at Cambridge. This was not the army's idea of a proper use of their time. As Battery Sergeant Major 'Andy' Anderson observed when he appeared on his daily inspection: 'Can't you do something useful instead of reading a fuckin' book?' BSM Anderson was a man of few words but very direct ones. Thrusting open a latrine door, he discovered me relieving myself. He paused: 'Havin' a good shit?', but like Pontius Pilate did not stay for an answer. More distant memories of this time included the all-encompassing miasma of grease from the large roasting pans which I cleaned with primitive detergent in the canteen pan-wash; a jejune protest against army authority by lacing tomato sandwiches for the tea at the battalion cricket match with too much salt; and the rank odour of raw meat that filled the sleeping quarters of the cooks when, as Duty Night Telephonist's Orderly, I had to wake them at 0430 hours for their early-morning shift.

As the War Office still showed no interest in using my officer qualities, the battalion had to find a further duty for me beyond this repertoire of the menial. I became waiter in the Sergeant's Mess, a real advance with distinct benefits. The food was good; the cooks were kind; and the tips earned serving drinks at the NCOs' Saturday-night social came to more than my month's pay. The drawback was that at lunch and supper-time all the senior NCOs – some forty or more sergeants and above – arrived at almost the same time and expected to be served immediately. This was a challenge, for the sergeants were not notable for their patience.

There was a further drawback. While the cooks were always ready with the food, while I and one other waiter were ready to serve, our third waiter colleague, a sweet local Welsh boy, found the stress of taking orders, passing them on and serving the food altogether too much. One lunchtime, as impatience mounted at the slow service, we found our colleague cowering in a far corner of the kitchen holding a knife and muttering about 'getting anyone who tries to touch me!'. He was not violent, just sadly out of his depth.

The void into which my military career had fallen took its toll on me too. When would I ever get out of Tonfanau? Would I ever make it to officer training? I complained constantly to my fellows in Held Strength, all of whom were only briefly there before moving to officer cadet school. For six weeks I complained incessantly about the army, about life, about everything, no doubt sounding a self-pitying bore. One night, returning from a waiting shift in the Sergeants' Mess, I found a pamphlet of Christian Thoughts lying on my bunk. On it a neighbour had written: 'Read this, sonny, it may improve your outlook on life!' If anything it made it worse – leaving me ex-posed, misunderstood and patronised. I was sick to the heart, partly with the humiliation (understandable), partly with even more self-pity (less attractive), partly because I reluctantly recognised that my neighbour's observation of me was all too accurate.

Yet two nights later, walking back from the Sergeant's Mess on a balmy night with a big moon chasing billowing clouds and bright moonbeam rays lighting the landscape, I suddenly felt an extraordinary easing of spirit, as if something was lifting my gloom, my despair, my abandonment, my sense of unappeasable failure. It felt like a blessing all the more precious since I had not sought it by prayer. Let's call it an epiphany, unsought, undeserved but profoudly welcomed.

Soon after – and wholly unconnected – my future clarified. My father's company Chairman, former General Sir Edward Spears, had made enquiries about my plight with friends at the War Office. Somebody had raised security concerns about my place of birth, Czechoslovakia. The fact of my naturalisation as a British citizen in 1948 seemed of no importance and was deemed to be no guarantee of my loyalty or patriotism. However, though I know nothing of any conversations that took place, my file was unblocked and the magic summons to officer cadet training at Mons Officer Cadet School in Aldershot arrived in the autumn of 1954. For the second time in my life, Edward Spears had been my fairy godfather.

So it was farewell to the remote desolation of Tonfanau, the bleating of the sheep, the harsh calls of the drill sergeants, the little luxuries of the NAAFI canteen, the intellectual stimulus of Doris Day movies at the Army Kinema, the small balm provided by an unthreatening barrack-room life. I made no friends there; even had I done so, the vagaries of postings and deployments would soon have broken us up. Such times are no basis for real friendship, producing at best temporary alliances, associations of convenience, useful but transient. Camaraderie did exist, but surviving training was a private business negotiated by each on his own.

Now, we would all be transformed from rank-and-file soldier to the heady style of 'officer and gentleman', from '23037865 Gunner Tusa, sir' to '440939 Officer Cadet Tusa, J.'. Would a new number make a new man of me? If basic military training was about discipline, the training of an officer was about responsibility: towards your men, your unit, your entire force. I doubt if it was ever put like that, which did not seem an omission at the time but has felt like one ever since. Leadership itself was not defined beyond its exercise of a conferred authority which commanded obedience. Whether only good leadership deserved obedience, whether it had to be earned, was pushed to one side as raising too many unanswerable questions.

Much of the training at Mons Officer Cadet School at Aldershot was routine, desultory deployments with guns and radar vans through the lanes of Surrey and on to the sandy heath of the exercise areas. These were so lacklustre that when the driver of a five-ton tractor used for pulling the lumbering anti-aircraft guns was asked where the troop was to deploy that afternoon, he replied mournfully: 'Fook knows, fookin' lorries know the fookin' way!' The formal lectures about tactical deployments presented on a large floor-size sand tray were never as interesting as they should have been. They often concluded with references to the 'General Staff Solution' to a military situation. Who were the 'General Staff?' The notion of a pre-ordained solution to unfolding events in the heat of battle seemed perverse and deadening. Irrespective of how wise the 'General Staff' might be, how could battle be fought to a formula? One piece of common sense stuck: 'Time spent in reconnaissance is seldom wasted.' I did not always follow that advice, in the army or in life.

Military law, contained in a very chunky red-covered book, seemed to boil down to one coverall clause – 'Section 40 of the Army Act, Conduct Prejudicial to Good Order and Military Discipline in that . . .' followed by almost any conceivable action that might ruffle the even tenor of regimental life. The military manuals offered as a particularly heinous example of a breach of good order and military discipline that 'the accused did throw down his weapon and say "You may do what you will, I will soldier no more!"' This seemed a very stagey thing for a would-be mutineer to say, but it more or less made the point. The 'catch-all' nature of Section 40 of the Army Act was savagely parodied in the allegedly true incident of a soldier charged under that section on the grounds that, according to the accusing sergeant, 'As I was pleasuring my wife in the married quarters, the accused looked into the window and said

"Fuck harder, Sergeant, fuck harder!'" We were never troubled by the several hundred other pages of the Army Act. Section 40 did it all.

Learning how to be an 'officer and a gentleman' came rather obliquely. My platoon's officer in charge was a crusty, supercilious man who delivered two pieces of advice. The first of these, 'A gentleman pays his tailor's bills last', startled the entire group, none of whom had ever had tailors' bills to pay. On another occasion during the bitter winter of 1955, when many of us shaved last thing at night to mitigate the rigours of sub-zero washrooms in the winter dawn, he opined: 'A gentleman shaves every morning *in* the morning.'

The fortnightly parade of the entire officer cadet school at Mons marked the passage of time, of training, of our closeness to being commissioned. Starting at one end of the huge parade ground, each fortnight we moved closer and closer to the point from which the completing troop slow-marched up the steps and into commissioned military maturity. This mighty ritual, controlled by the heroic figure and resounding voice of Regimental Sergeant Major Brittain, was accompanied by full military band playfully encouraging us as we marched on to the tune 'Here we go, Here we go, Here we go again'. It had a fine swing to it, as did another favourite, 'The Old Grey Mare'. When our troop 'passed out', an official photograph shows my face rigid with tension, locked in a rictus of effort but sadly redolent with unease.

Beyond all that, we now had to dress for our new status, buying khaki service dress with that evocative cross belt known as the 'Sam Browne'; 'Blues', the mess dress for formal and official evening occasions (I inherited my brother George's); an officer's peaked cap from Herbert Johnson the Hatter's in St James's and a bowler hat and rolled umbrella for 'town dress'. We might be a very rough approximation of an officer ready to command men in battle, but at least we looked the part: young officers and gentlemen, 1955 style. Ready or not, posting to a serving military unit was now the order of the day.

The less lucky were sent to training battalions in the United Kingdom, a return to the boredom and routines they had just endured only to inflict them on the next generation. The least lucky went off to a war zone, a prospect offering thrill, excitement and interest mitigated by the distinct possibility of death. The luckiest were posted abroad but to a place not immediately threatened by or involved in actual fighting. I was one of those posted to 'Twelfth Light Anti-Aircraft Regiment, BAOR 12', a foreign posting, out of the country for sure, different enough to be interesting but hardly bizarre, exotic or life-threatening. Stationed in Celle in the West German state of Lower Saxony, the naïve numerical postcode of the British Army of the Rhine postal address was designed to keep the Red Army guessing about the actual deployment of British regiments. It cannot have taken them long to work it out.

With so much time lost in 'Held Strength' at Tonfanau, I had a mere fifteen months left of my two years' national service when I reached the regiment in the spring of 1955. The military train from Hook of Holland snaked its way through the Ruhr, northern Rhineland, middle Germany along and past as many of the main centres of Rhine Army garrisons as necessary. Station by station, the train steadily emptied its human, military cargo. Celle may well have been its final stop. What was in store?

Celle itself is a very pretty medieval town in that half-timbered, colourfully painted German style. It had a *Schloss*, a *Schloss* park, a *Rathaus*, two good churches, a pretty town square and agreeable winding streets running off it. The River Aller ran through it, the barracks themselves were a huge nineteenth-century German red-brick military building of little appeal but great solidity. The Officers' Mess, a requisitioned family villa up the slope of the hill above the river, was comfortable and friendly. A smaller villa at the bottom of the pine-filled garden housed the junior subalterns. Life was perfectly civilised, though rather dull; playing bridge after dinner was often the main pastime, dominated by regular officers and a handful of older national servicemen who were serious players.

I decided to make my own way in this new life by searching out what Celle had to offer in the arts. The court theatre in the *Schloss* was an eighteenth-century gem, a jewel box with just 130 seats. To find the Boccherini Quintet playing an evening of his quintets lifted my spirits. Some days later I experimented more boldly, plunging into a performance of Part Two of Goethe's *Faust*, blissfully ignorant of the work and without translation to help. The sound of high, poetic German in full rhetorical declamatory mode was mighty off-putting. This became an extremely long evening when sleep overcame duty to art.

A more important discovery was the State Opera in Hanover, just over an hour away by car. With the help of a glamorous, red-haired young woman assistant in the local department store, who also improved my German, I began making opera trips to Hanover only complicated by the need to get access to the 'regimental Volkswagen'. Hanover Opera is a solid second-tier house in Germany's amazing system of dispersed, federally based theatres. The productions were safe, the orchestra good, the singing variable but never poor. Where better to learn my operatic repertoire? No matter that provincial German voices didn't sit easily in Puccini's *Madame Butterfly*, no matter that I didn't realise that *Das Rheingold* runs two and a half hours straight through without interval! I discovered with delight that Verdi's *Die Macht des Schicksals*, of which I knew nothing, was merely *The Force of Destiny* in translation – and what a glorious work it was. There I heard my first *Eugene Onegin*. I learned too that German men wore dark suits and silver ties to the opera and that everyone walked in pairs anti-clockwise round the main foyer during the interval. Today I aim to be the last person keeping alive these German silver-tie traditions. It is my grateful 'hommage' to the country where I learned so much of my opera.

Operatic excursions enlivened a rather basic barrack

existence. Not that the Officers' Mess lacked characters. The Commanding Officer (CO), Lt Col. R. J. H. ('Dick') Harding-Newman, with his monocle, pencil moustache and clipped vowels, looked and sounded a figure from a previous age. He was witty, unpompous and patient with the shortcomings of national servicemen. His nickname, 'Dick Hardly-Human', was entirely affectionate. Before the daily mess lunch, he would gather with his adjutant, Major Dan Ridley, the second in command (2-i-C), Major Mervyn Lewis and the three battery commanders. Major Tony Tate was a roly-poly, genial figure whom some unwisely underestimated. A very good left-handed batsman, Tony played for exotic occasional teams such as 'I Zingari' and, more romantic-sounding still, 'Stragglers of Asia'. He handed out service cards at the regimental church on Sunday mornings with the cheerful cry, 'Card of the match'. Gin was the order of the morning in this pre-lunch circle – in the case of Major Pat Horwood, several pink gins. He invariably referred to our American allies as 'the cock suckers'. Comparatively abstemious subalterns observed these exchanges with wonder, awe and alarm.

Only two national service officers could address this senior charmed circle on anything like equal terms, both late-entry after finishing their professional qualifications. Alistair Mac-Lennan was a qualified accountant, an excellent bridge player, a crafty and skilful batsman. Alistair's apparently dry Scottish demeanour bred of a Scottish manse upbringing only briefly concealed a warm sense of humour, great tolerance of others and curiosity about almost everything, from science to opera. Given his professional qualifications, he was welcomed into the Adjutant's Office at regimental HQ. Despite a peripatetic career which took him from the oil industry to banking and life in Australia, we stayed friends with him and his wife Jenny for life.

But it was another national serviceman, the Medical Officer (MO), who in a sense ruled the roost. Captain Dr Hugh Johnson spoke his mind to everyone without fear or favour, starting with Colonel Dick. He put up with no malingering and indeed few in Twelfth Light Ack-Ack ever dared to report in sick. Hugh's cultivated brusque manner could not hide a highly professional medical mind. Faced with real sickness, he was care itself. In the Officers' Mess he was a clinical bridge player, and in regimental cricket matches an umpire who took little time in dispatching batsmen with an accusatory finger. After the army, Hugh became an authoritative Home Office forensic pathologist and lost a lung from tuberculosis for his pains, an occupational hazard. He dropped dead on the steps of the Old Bailey on his way in to give evidence. It was a huge loss to his friends and the profession.

Outside mess life, most of the time was spent in cleaning and maintaining basic equipment, the Bofors 40mm anti-aircraft gun and its three-ton tractor lorry. However often vehicles were inspected for road worthiness or however seldom they were deployed, they still broke down. At least I learned one piece of motoring common sense. Top of the army list of actions to take if a vehicle failed to start was the 'First IA (Immediate Action). Check the petrol.' Such common sense remains useful to this day.

Despite this constant maintenance regime, it seemed to me that less than two-thirds of the regiment was fit to deploy at any time. Given that 1955 was in the middle of the Cold War, that the Iron Curtain between West and East Germany was only fifty kilometres away and that only a single British regiment of fast scout cars was based closer to that dangerous border than we were, our regimental state of readiness seemed to leave a good deal to be desired. It can only be explained by the remarkably low sense of danger or impending crisis in Germany at that time.

One of the regimental duties was to patrol the East–West inter-zonal border with the Federal German border force, the BGS (BundesGrenzSchutz). I commanded one of these patrols on a lushly romantic summer day in beautiful country-side. The fields may have been lightly farmed right up to the zonal border but there was no sense of neglect or a security blight on it. Neglect was evident, rather, in the demarcation of the East–West border itself, unmaintained it seemed, reduced to a shaky line of rusting wire netting and collapsing poles. The very occasional East German observation post often stood unmanned. The BGS confirmed that what I saw on my two days of patrol was typical of the condition of the entire inter-zonal border at that time. The future horror of the Berlin Wall and the death zone surrounding the Cold War border was yet to come.

Yet the British authorities were ready for any eventuality, especially the one described as 'if the balloon goes up', a eu-phemism for 'if the East Germans, backed by the Red Army, invade'. In due course a major Rhine Army exercise was planned to anticipate such a catastrophe. Readiness would be all.

The assumption was that the 35th's Scout Cars at Wesendorf, some kilometres closer to the border than we were in Celle, would be the first to notice any invasion. What were scout cars for but reconnaissance and intelligence? With the whole of the Rhine Army alerted to the start of war, the assigned role of Twelfth Light Ack-Ack Regiment would be to up sticks and move westwards to the nearest crossing on the River Weser. Fully deployed around the Weser crossing, we would hold it until all other designated British units had safely crossed. The bridge would then be destroyed and the Red Army advance severely delayed – or so we hoped.

The regiment would then hightail it still further west-wards to the next river crossing, that of the Rhine. Here too we would hold the bridges until the slower British units had crossed. Once they were safely across, these bridges too would be blown up. At that point, the Western allies would look at the Red Army, now in control of most of West Germany, and ... We were never told what the Allies would do next. This was where the exercise stopped.

The fact that the Rhine Army appeared to be surrendering

Right Zlín,
Czechoslovakia, 1937;
myself, aged one, with
brother George

Middle Zlín, early 1939,
with George and Mother

Below Did war seem
such a possibility?
Czechoslovakia, summer
1938. I refuse the
gas mask.

Left With Babička and Dedecek Sklenář. Bystřice pod Hostýnem, 1946. Familial, loving, pastoral – one part of my background.

Middle On holiday in Crikvenica, Yugoslavia, 1939. Returning home, the Nazi border guards tried to stop us from re-entering Czechoslovakia.

Left Bystřice pod Hostýnem, Moravia. The Catholic pilgrimage shrine of the Virgin Mary. My mother's family were Hussite but suffered no discrimination.

Above I was born in Zlín on 2 March 1936. My father worked for the Bata shoe company all his life. Ordered, disciplined, modern – the other part of my background.

Right Bata Estate, East Tilbury, Essex, spring 1940. On top of an Anderson shelter.

Below Plastic helmet, wooden rifle – ready to defend, 1943.

Top Bata family Christmas Party. Whatever was in my present, I did not like it.

Middle Oswestry, Shropshire. Basic training, National Service, June 1954. Myself (far right) with fellow squaddies and brooms.

Right Gresham's school play, in the open-air theatre in Holt, Norfolk. Antonio in *The Tempest*.

Top Mons Barracks, Aldershot, Passing Out Parade, 17 March 1955. Grim determination! Five steps further and I was a fully commissioned Second Lieutenant (second from left).

Below Officers' Mess Fancy Dress Party, Herford Barracks, West Germany, June 1956. Companion unknown.

Right Leading the team for 12th Light Anti-Aircraft Regiment at the Army skiing championships, Winterberg, West Germany, February 1956.

Left As John Procter in Arthur Miller's *The Crucible* for Cambridge University Mummers, February 1957. From right: John Tydeman as Rev. Parris, Clive Swift as Judge Danforth, Fred Emery as Judge Hathorne.

Below left With Pauline Browne as Abigail in *The Crucible*.

Below right Newnham historian and fellow actor, Ann Dowson. We married when we left Cambridge in 1960.

Above The True Blue Dining Club before dinner by Great Court Fountain, Trinity College, June 1959. Affected rather than dissolute but a far cry from Oxford's Bullingdon Club.

Below On holiday with my future wife, Annie, Avignon: Provence, August 1959.

Above Fooling around, 1959.

Left Compering election night coverage on BBC World Service, 30 October 1964. With political scientist Dr Norman Hunt and veteran broadcaster Bob Reid.

Middle As BBC World Service producer, chairing a round table discussion on India with V. S. Naipaul, Malcolm Muggeridge and Philip Mason, author and former Indian civil servant. Bush House was a constant seminar on world events.

Below Filming the BBC Two series *The Unsettled Peace* in West Germany, 1974, My only 'long form' TV documentary.

most of the Federal Republic to the first major Soviet incursion was not discussed, or if so only at levels higher than that of a mere subaltern. The further fact that our regiment's Bofors 40mm gun, light artillery at best, had no armour-piercing or anti-tank capability did not seem to disqualify us from our role in holding the Weser and Rhine bridges. What mattered was that we mobilised swiftly, reached the Weser in good order, notionally saw to it that the bridges were destroyed and then pressed on to the Rhine in equally good order. This was enough for the exercise to be judged a success.

Soon after, the West German government noticed that Britain's strategic response to a communist invasion was not to stand and fight but in effect to surrender most of West Germany without a fight. Our brilliantly conducted exercise in rapid capitulation was dropped and never referred to again.

It was not long before we received very different briefings. The Rhine Army now adopted a distinctly 'forward strategy' involving the early use of tactical nuclear weapons fired from self-propelled howitzers against communist force concentrations massed across the East–West frontier. Out in the field, the magnificent Abbot self-propelled nuclear-capable howitzers were a grand sight. (As was the hospitality drummed up by their regimental mess staff in the back of a three-ton lorry.) While this was a dramatic reversal of the previous run-and-retire approach, it too suffered from serious drawbacks. It appeared that NATO was ready for first use of nuclear weapons, highly sensitive politically, militarily and strategically. Subsequent ground combat in an area polluted by nuclear fallout would be highly problematic too. Like it or not, this plan of using nuclear weapons against the attacking forces of East Germany and the Soviet Red Army involved nuclear detonations on German soil. No German politician of any political stripe could or would be indifferent to such a strategy. Perhaps it was better than 'run-and-retire', but not by much.

Such objections were not raised at any of the briefings I attended; these were information exercises intended to tell us only how we would carry out our orders if indeed 'the balloon went up'. Nobody believed that it was likely to do so. We lived in West Germany in a period of almost bucolic calm, post-war reconciliation and economic reconstruction. Within a year the world lurched into crisis as Soviet forces crushed the 1956 Hungarian Uprising and Britain and France invaded Egypt on the pretext of protecting the Suez Canal. Were we complacent? Were we ignorant? Was Europe in a strange state of complacency and inertia a mere decade after the Second World War ended?

When the regimental rugger team travelled to West Berlin on a sealed overnight military train across the Soviet Zone of Germany to play against the British Military Garrison, it was memorable twice over. Much of the first night was spent touring the strip clubs off the Kurfurstendamm before playing a passable rugger match at 11.30 the next morning. That evening, correctly dressed in uniform, we walked through the Brandenburg Gate into Soviet-occupied East Berlin, saluted senior members of the Soviet Military Mission getting into their staff car outside the Soviet Embassy and enjoyed a meal at the wonderful exchange rate of one (west) Deutschmark to five (east) Ostmarks. As we entered the restaurant on the Unter den Linden, the resident band slyly, almost subversively struck up the 'Lambeth Walk'. The evening ended some few yards further down the avenue seeing Puccini's *Tosca* at the Berlin State Opera. There was no tension in the air at any point. We were doing nothing dangerous. This was mid-Europe in 1955 before the building of the Berlin Wall, the potential Cold War flashpoint was very calm.

Army barrack life continued with its merely dreary routines. The formal Mess Night, the monthly occasion when all officers dined together in mess dress, was one of its highlights. These nights traditionally moved towards modest debauchery, including 'High Cockalorum' which involved climbing higher and higher on one another's backs to form a human pyramid before collapsing in a heap. Why more bones were not broken was never clear. On one legendary occasion during the customary post-dinner rowdyism, the unpopular acting Commanding Officer found himself bundled into a carpet, rolled up, hoisted on the shoulders of half a dozen subalterns, carried two hundred yards down the road to the bridge and thrown into the river. At this point, several of the regular officers, mindful of their prospects of promotion and the enormity of the prank, jumped in to rescue him. The acting Commanding Officer was wet, otherwise unscathed but definitely humiliated.

The fault lines between the regulars and the national servicemen dramatically exposed by that incident were clear and uneasy. The regulars were older, more experienced and certainly more professional, the essential volunteer core of a conscript army. The conscripts were far from clear why a large army was needed at all; most regarded regulars as people who could not get a job in the real world and quietly looked down on them. It was snobbish and priggishly superior without justification. But it fed growing awareness of the damage that national service was doing to regular army morale and played a part in the creation of a highly professionalised army in the years after national service dwindled away in the 1960s.

It was not as if national servicemen were particularly good officers. Colonel Dick once regaled my wife with the story of a young subaltern sent out on border patrol accompanied by a very experienced sergeant. The officer gave clear and confident instructions to his driver as they wound their way along forest tracks near the East–West border. 'I don't think this is a good idea, sir,' the sergeant began to warn. The officer pressed on: 'Right here, good, then left at the next crossing' and suchlike. They reached a barrier across the road. 'Get out and move that barrier will you, driver!' The sergeant's final warning, 'I don't think we should be here, sir,' was greeted with the immortal words: 'Thank you very much, sergeant, I can read a map!' At which point the vehicle and its three occupants vanished into East Germany.

Several hours later, so the story went, Harding-Newman

guessed that his three missing men had indeed strayed into the Soviet Zone. He called up his opposite number in the nearest border unit on the other side, not a contact I knew existed, a kind of ground-level 'hotline'. Yes, they had three British servicemen in custody. 'Will you do me a favour, please,' asked Colonel Dick. 'Keep them for three days before you send them back!' In due course a very crestfallen second lieutenant returned. As for the sergeant, he was full of beans: 'Thank you, sir, I was very well looked after, fed, watered and some nice games of cards!' Which was probably exactly what the colonel had hoped would happen.

Once Annie reminded him of the time I confusedly led my troop of three guns and vehicles in a complete circle during a night deployment along the sandy tracks of the Luneburg Heath. I too 'knew how to read a map'. Harding-Newman had his own tale to tell. When the regiment was deployed from Celle to Herford further west, the colonel and his second in command positioned themselves on a raised hillock which each unit would pass, bidding farewell to a lengthy garrison stay in Celle. As one troop drove past, officers standing at attention in their vehicles and saluting, Colonel Dick commented proudly that they looked specially well turned out. Later, the same troop passed the hillock again. Not long after, they appeared for a third time. The colonel couldn't contain himself: 'Isn't it marvellous! Even on the third time round they still look in good order!' It must have been a national serviceman in the lead.

Beyond such military incompetence, I never fully settled into the formal routines and disciplines of regimental life. I was naïvely searching for some meaning and purpose, some rationale, some intellectual core to army life. It was a vain search. There was none in the necessarily routine barrack life. My frustration erupted in instances of awful behaviour, including getting so drunk at a regimental party that I ended up in the mess garden beating my head against a tree and sweeping a tray full of wine glasses onto the ground. When confronted by a mess bill of some size for the damages, my indignation at life's unfairness was genuine because I could remember very little of the event. The chairman of the regimental mess took pity on my uncomprehending air of hurt innocence and reduced the size of the bill. It was more than I deserved. I have never got so drunk since.

The truth is that the regiment was incredibly forbearing of me and my non-military interests. Returning to Celle from the anti-aircraft firing range on the Baltic coast, we passed the outskirts of Hamburg. I badly wanted to visit Hamburg anyway and knew that good family friends were staying at the Vier Jahreszeiten, the best hotel in town. I asked my battery commander if I could hop off the convoy at a convenient moment in the suburbs of Hamburg. Although a convoy returning from exercise is on a military deployment, he let me do what I wanted. I should have been told in the roundest terms that what I did on return to Celle was my affair but that I was under military orders until then. It was another reminder of the interplay between authority, responsibility and leadership that I still had to comprehend and work out in practice. It took me years to understand that authority and leadership did not come from rank, hierarchy, uniform and a brass pip on the shoulder but must be earned by responsibility, selflessness and concern for others. It was not the army's fault that I was so slow in putting these notions together.

From an entirely selfish point of view, my time in West Germany was not wasted. I knew I was pitched into the heart of a great nation of history, architecture, culture and performing arts. I yearned to see, taste, hear, explore as much as possible with an almost physical hunger. I heard *Aida* in Hamburg, Mozart's *Idomeneo* in Essen, *Don Giovanni* and *Arabella* in Munich. I travelled north to Stockholm with Alistair MacLennan in 1955 and discovered Verdi's *Don Carlo* at the national opera, then a considerable rarity. Perhaps most wonderful of all was learning that the Kiel Opera – close to our Baltic artillery firing ranges – was performing Wagner's *Die Meistersinger von*

Nürnberg one weekend afternoon. It was a work quite new to me. The radiant glories of the third-act quintet hit me with the exhilarating joy of discovery. My evening in Kiel rounded off with a visit to a rather genteel strip bar. A twenty-year-old is riddled with inconsistency, contradictions and conflicting impulses. I am glad that I never felt guilt about the strip bar.

I discovered the German landscape too, most joyously the rolling hills and forests of Franconia and the irresistible medieval walled towns of the 'Romantische Strasse', running from Nuremberg through Rothenburg, Dinkelsbühl and Nördlingen towards Munich. It was a mere decade since the Second World War had ended, yet the towns, the countryside, the landscape were as if war had never ravaged them. In the case of heavily damaged cities such as Nuremberg, the combination of rebuilding, restoration and harmonious contemporary insertions spoke of an aesthetic confidence that England severely lacked at the time and for a good while after.

I learned cross-country skiing because it was judged to be militarily useful. Hadn't the Finns defeated the Russians in the 1940 'Winter War' by knowing how to live in the snow? During training, I discovered the hair in my nostrils froze at minus 16 degrees Celsius exactly. Once in the Harz Mountains, we inadvertently almost skied across poorly marked snowfields into East Germany. After six weeks' brutally tough training at Winterberg, running uphill on thin skis with a rifle and an army pack for several hours a day – the definition of cross-country skiing – I was so lean and fit that for the only time in my life I would leap out of bed in the morning eager for the day. On one such morning, Leroy Anderson's 'Bugler's Holiday' was playing on the radio. Ever since, it has been my anthem of uncomplicated physical joy.

My time in the army was unwinding. Friends were steadily demobbed. Newcomers predominated in the mess. By the early summer of 1956, it was my turn to return to 'civvy street'. My mother drove out to fill the car with accumulated kit and possessions. England seemed desolate. Home felt empty of friends, colleagues, activity, discovery, curiosity, energy, promise. The lack was not the fault of my parents, who were as always full of love and generosity. They did not ask about what I had experienced in Germany or through national service as a whole. I might not have known what to say, or indeed what I thought.

I asked for a party to 'welcome Johnny home'. It was a thin affair, though pleasant enough. After two years of the fierce, enforced, necessary gregariousness of military service, after occasionally quite severe explorations of myself, my feelings, my reactions when others tested me, responded to me and judged me with amazing understanding and forgiveness, I felt desperately alone, less sure of who or what I was than when I began. But I did learn something incredibly precious. Germany opened my eyes, ears and heart to the experience of the riches of the arts. Somehow or other the arts would always play a key role in my life, though I could not guess how that might work in practice. That sense was a priceless lesson for life. It was also a rich promise for the future.

5

Learning, Living, Loving

1956–60

Does Cambridge ever change? Not to my eyes, not in my experience, not over sixty years. Not physically, at least. Walk through the historic heart of the university and what did I see two generations ago? King's College Chapel rising in all its exuberant improbability dominated King's Parade. It still dominates today; the Chapel is not a reticent building. Sixty years ago, the winding, unpretentious domesticity of Trinity Street shielded the modest fronts of some of the great colleges, Caius, Trinity, St John's. No grand vistas, no formal avenues, no planned approaches. Find them if you could in their blank-walled privacy and cloistered discretion. Then as now, the colleges showed their faces in all their magnificence along the narrow, neatly banked, well-mannered stream that passes as the River Cam; buildings like palaces, curious bridges, lawns exhibitionist in their expanse, trees boasting their antiquity, and massed, generous greenery composing the sensuous landscape and scenery of the 'Backs', as they are called. Romantic and restrained, intense and understated, exclusive and available, very private and a little bit public; how very English.

How characteristically English, too, that the colleges turned their faces, their fronts, away from the actual life of the world outside and beyond. In some sense, the true 'fronts' of the colleges, their most public face, were actually the Backs. If this was perverse it was also symbolic, turning a cold shoulder to the planned, the predictable, the routine. The heart of Cambridge was and remains a series of medieval scholarly foundations reluctantly rubbing shoulders with the sleepy lives of a market town. Noble grandeur surrounded by a farmyard. So it seemed sixty years ago. So it is physically recognisable sixty years on. Yet almost everything else about university life has changed.

Britain's university world in the 1950s would be inconceivable today. There were some 45 universities in the country; today there are 156, three times as many. Sixty years ago, just 10 per cent of the age group went to university or expected to enjoy tertiary education. Today, after New Labour's brief and derided flirtation with a target of 50 per cent entering higher education, the proportion of the age group who do so has now almost reached that target. Our generation felt that we deserved to be at university, a feeling particularly strong among those from the then powerful and extensive grammar-school system. Without privileged or advantaged home background of any kind, their presence at university demonstrated 'merit', an earned personal merit. The very notion of 'meritocracy' itself was being born. Of course, it was seen as right that this merit should take them to the very top of the university pyramid.

On the summit of that small pyramid of exclusivity and privilege perched Oxford and Cambridge, united in distinctiveness and distinction, great minds in great buildings, confidently unchallengeable, each astride a modest river, twin peaks of excellence. Next, or just below, for the university world of the 1950s was rigidly stratified and judged on class and perceived reputation, were a group of science or social-science based universities such as Imperial College, London and the London School of Economics. Clearly academically excellent, distinct in their disciplines, these managed without the seductive trappings of collegiate life, idyllic surroundings and romantic illusions. A few ancient establishments such as Edinburgh, Durham and Dublin were also accorded a cautious respect and a nod of acknowledgement. The next layer of the pyramid consisted of 'red-brick' universities, nineteenth-century foundations in the new industrial cities, recognised as worthy, dubbed provincial and generally treated as second – or even third – best in the quality scale. In my years, the late 1950s, the university pyramid was acquiring a broader new base: the modern universities, radical, experimental, category-breaking, innovative in discipline, socially diverse, brashly assertive and self-confident, the 'plate-glass' institutions – Sussex, East Anglia, York, Essex. The intellectual snobbery revealed in this hierarchy of judgements was huge. These attitudes were only a mirror of the English class system itself – involving snobbery, complacency and conservatism.

I was going to Cambridge University – tick – and to Trinity College, a college with the highest possible regard for itself – bigger tick. I had won a major scholarship – biggest personal tick. I knew what this all meant. I had no doubts that I would have to work to become a deserving part of this magic place of opportunity. In the circumstances of the time, anything less would have felt like failure. After all, my brother George was at Oxford, my sister Viccy would go to Oxford later; we were only a single generation away from provincial life in southern Moravia. Our parents had left formal education in their teens. As exiles from Czechoslovakia, their commitment to getting their three children to Oxbridge demanded at least a responsible effort in return.

I was proud to walk through Trinity's Great Gate into Great Court and to feel that this was mine for the next three years. It was, we were advised, the largest enclosed space in Europe. It was also very English, wholly un-monumental, a sequence of often unpretentious domestic buildings with one grand insertion, the Hall itself. It spoke of age, continuity, adaptation, connection, a blend of forms and purpose. Typically, the centre point of Great Court, the fountain, was sited well off-centre. It expressed a harmony of sense and feeling rather than system, organisation and order. Not long ago, I walked out of Great Court on a summer moonlit night. I thought it the most beautiful place I knew. I felt that from my first moments at Trinity almost sixty years previously.

I also sensed when I arrived, when I 'went up', that Cambridge's riches would not simply fall into my hands; they would have to be earned, though I couldn't imagine how that might be done. After all, major scholar or no, many people would be cleverer than me; many people would be from richer families; most people would come from schools that had stretched them far more than mine.

What most of us had in common was the experience of two years of national service in the armed forces. We were a mature generation, going up around the age of twenty instead of eighteen, some with combat experience, many with command experience, almost all with some direct responsibility for actions, events or people. University had always been our goal, one deferred by the needs of politics and world events. No one regretted two years of national service; equally, no one looked back on it especially fondly; conscription did not invite or attract sentimentality. Some did feel that they had lost the discipline of learning. But once national service was over, once we were 'up', it was hardly spoken of. That chapter of life was firmly closed. The Fellows liked the relative maturity of national servicemen, two years of life and living tucked under our belts, eager to make up for the lost years, filled with urgent and serious commitment. Surely we would be keener to learn, more rewarding to teach. Today's Fellows see the national service substitute – the fashionable 'gap year' – as the time when their future charges go off the boil.

I walked into a place and environment draped in powerful and seductive myth. It was considered beyond question that Cambridge colleges were places of secluded beauty, scholarship and learning, peopled by dons, wise, eccentric, witty, scholarly and necessarily other-worldly, living in handsome rooms up rickety wooden staircases overlooking courts of historic aspect, dining in candlelit, hammer-beam halls, enjoying good food, fine wines, intellectual exchange and deferential college servants. It was a beguiling myth. We ourselves were not so much 'students' – very provincial that – as 'undergraduates'. As such we were essentially college guests; the dons came first, they were after all the community of 'the college' in a way that we were not.

The everyday reality of undergraduate life in the 1950s included the almost total absence of women. Confined to just three colleges – Girton, Newnham and the young and tiny New Hall – women were outnumbered by a ratio of one to eleven. An additional leavening of women for the predominantly male undergraduate community came from the teacher-training colleges such as Homerton, or somewhat 'exotic' international students at the Davies and Bell language schools, many, it seemed, Scandiwegian blondes. The gender imbalance was improved a little by the Friday-evening arrival on the London train of 'posh weekend totty'.

All colleges were single-sex. Colleges closed their gates at 10 p.m. when visitors, especially women, had to leave. Asked what a male and female undergraduate could do after 10 p.m. that they could not do before, a wise don replied, 'Nothing, but they could do it again!' Women at Newnham had to sign out if they were not attending hall, perhaps a convenience for catering but a soft kind of control too. Gowns had to be worn after dark. Women could not wear trousers with gowns. University proctors roamed the streets accompanied by two 'bulldogs' – usually college porters. The fine for not wearing a gown after dark was six shillings and eight pence, an obscure medieval fine, increasing to fifteen shillings for a repeat offence. It was however a significant sum – an Indian curry cost four shillings – which made the offence both worse and more expensive. Some undergraduates would try to avoid the fine by outrunning the 'bulldogs'.

Climbing in or out of college after 10 p.m. was an honoured and necessary activity, knowledge of the best routes over walls or gates passed from mouth to mouth. It was not dangerous, though, as one contemporary found when he impaled himself on the iron railings, painful. All this, inconceivable, even comic today, was part of accepted life sixty years ago. Restrictions and limitations on behaviour were regarded as quaint and amusing, and paled into insignificance in comparison with the richness of the opportunities before us – life surrounded by hundreds of the cleverest of our generation, fuelled with energy, driven by curiosity, taught by some of the best minds, sometimes great ones.

I expected to work diligently but not to the exclusion of other activities. At the start, I decided that my road to fame, fortune or at least recognition would involve either acting or speaking. Hoping to hone my skills in the latter, I looked to the Cambridge Union. The Union enjoyed a special cachet with its own building, rather like a Pall Mall club. Debates, it promised, would fizz with verbal wit, posturing, affectation, invention and daring repartee. The President of the Union represented a pinnacle of undergraduate prestige and achievement. The nation's great and good would and did give up evenings to pit themselves against these youthful glitterati; many national political careers started in the Union's debating chamber. This was life, perhaps this would be my life! I paid up to become a life member of the Cambridge Union. I also became a life member of the University Conservative Association.

Throughout the Michaelmas term of 1956, I attended set-piece debates and put my name down to be called to speak. I had no burning message to express; I just wanted to appear. The first debate passed without a call from the President. I put my name down for the next debate. Contemporaries got the nod to speak, but I did not. I tried a third time and was ignored or overlooked. Most of my first term had been wasted. Later a friend did some research to discover how long it took for debutant speakers to be called. In that first term, he found that approximately one third were called at their first attempt; the great majority succeeded on their second. Most remaining stragglers spoke at their third time of asking. Just one person failed to be called to speak at all – that was me. It must have been a sign. Long before, I had concluded that the glory life of the Union, of politics perhaps, was not for me.

Fortunately my other love and hoped-for path to fame, theatre, proved infinitely more rewarding. The Cambridge University Mummers included non-university members; the more prestigious ADC (Amateur Dramatic Club) was for university members only and had its own theatre. The Mummers rented the ADC Theatre for their 'nursery' productions for freshmen early in the first term of the year. On that occasion, the backdrop was the extraordinary world of 1956 when the Soviet Union invaded Hungary and the British and French invaded Egypt ostensibly to secure the Suez Canal. It was the Cold War heating up, dangerously chaotic and unpredictable. The external fire escapes of the Union and the ADC buildings abut one another. From the one at the ADC, I could hear cheers and angry shouts from the emergency debate at the Union condemning Anglo-French aggression in the Suez Canal in Egypt. Turning my head slightly, from inside the theatre I heard the anguished cry of characters from Karel Čapek's *Insect Play*: 'Ants to arms – the path between two blades of grass is in peril!' What a pity the two institutions could not compare notes.

Over three years at Cambridge, theatre provided my greatest centre of satisfaction and fulfilment. It began early with John Tydeman's ground-breaking production for the Mummers of Eugène Ionesco's *The Bald Prima Donna*. No one apart from John knew of Ionesco; he had seen the play in Paris and translated it from the French himself. It took the rest of us totally by surprise. We were unprepared for the blaze of Ionesco's assault on the banal routines of conventional human words and exchange. The sentences seemed to make sense but their connections did not. If they were absurd, they were utterly convincing. They flung open a window into our language and the way we used it. Tydeman, an exact Trinity contemporary, then and now my closest friend, found a style and stage language in his first university theatre work that captured Ionesco's torrent of ridiculous realism. There was no symbolism, no message, no metaphor – just an implicit revelation of the gaps and vacancies that existed in everyday communication.

Tydeman also found young actors to catch and play in the necessary style. One was Bill Wallis, later a stalwart of Radio 4 satire and the Bristol Old Vic. It was exhilarating. This was what theatre could do. This was what Cambridge theatre could do and often did during the next three years. Involvement in it brought me a huge moment of self-understanding and recognition. In my second term, Lent 1957, the Mummers decided to produce Arthur Miller's latest play *The Crucible*, then without a professional staging in Britain. The director, a South African postgraduate, Raymond Tunmer, cast me as the conscience-ridden, principled New England farmer John Proctor. He also cast John Tydeman as the dithering Reverend Parris and Clive Swift – of television fame – as the ruthless Judge Danforth.

During rehearsal, it was clear to us that this story of the seventeenth-century Salem witch trials, with its clear resonances of contemporary McCarthyite anti-communist 'witch-hunts' in the United States, its tussle between hysteria, guilt by association and standing on principle, would dig very deep emotionally. History it was, contemporary politics it was too; audiences might hide from one but not from both. The production sold out its week at the ADC in advance; you might say Arthur Miller's reputation did much of that. What we did not expect was the impact our performance would have on the audience. It was visceral, it was raw, it united the emotional with the intellectual. What happened when principle was undermined by a sense of moral guilt? A story from history spoke intensely to the present day.

During the week's run, word spread as far as Oxford about a remarkable production. An extra performance on a Saturday matinee was scheduled because of the demand. It too was packed. Draining as this performance was, we had just a couple of hours to recharge body and spirit for the last night at 8.15. Ray Tunmer led the cast through what I know now are yogic breathing and relaxation exercises. Our bodies glowed as they recharged. We were also unwittingly reaching into a far further understanding of the play, our parts in it, our bodies and ourselves. Not that we were out of control, but a combination of exhaustion, achievement and relaxation made us, in a profound sense, beyond control, taking us a step past the normally calculated, the usually rational.

By all accounts, that final Saturday evening performance of *The Crucible* was harrowing both on stage and in the audience. Long before the climax when Proctor, falsely accused, refuses to betray himself and his name, preferring to face death instead, I felt as if I was riding an unstoppable tide of exaltation, one based on an instinctive awareness that what I had learned, what I had rehearsed, what I was now feeling were united in a greater understanding of the play's purpose and meaning, perhaps even of myself. I was well past mere satisfaction at pulling off the necessary stage effects, the tricks of acting manipulation, the pleasant thrills of contrived pretending. Some freedom of personal expression, release from customary inhibition, was at work inside me. If the cast was drained, the audience was shattered. I felt fulfilled beyond belief or expectation. It was, too, a landmark in my Cambridge life. I never realised a stage part as completely as that of John Proctor in *The Crucible* again. That did not matter. There were many other far better actors than me around. My personal satisfaction lay in releasing expressive depths within myself that I had not known existed. That performance gave me a standing within and around the Cambridge theatre and arts scene.

The late 1950s were extraordinary theatrical times. The Romanian Eugène Ionesco was the signature playwright, everything that the 'well-made', three-act, drawing-room comedy or melodrama was not. If Terence Rattigan and his ilk were out, with what we judged as their stifling, middle-class conventions, repressed emotions and formulaic expressions, Ionesco's absurdist extravaganzas marked the start of our new era. 'Windows were being broken,' recalled John Tydeman, 'we were ahead of the times.' And these times were being made and reshaped all around us in Cambridge's theatre. Tydeman himself directed Ionesco's *Victims of Duty* with the university's finest comic actor, Michael Collings, in the lead. John Bird – of Channel 4's *Bird and Fortune* – directed *The Lesson* with David Buck, later of the Royal Shakespeare Company. The *Observer*'s legendary, radical theatre critic, Kenneth Tynan, asserted that if the names 'Tydeman, Bird and Buck weren't adorning the West End in neon lights within five years, there was something wrong with British theatre'. Tynan needn't have worried; recognition came, though David Buck sadly died in early middle age.

We were swamped in new theatre. Frank Hauser's dynamic Oxford Playhouse company visited the Cambridge Arts Theatre regularly and brought Ionesco's *Amédée*, directed by Peter Zadek, in June 1957. Feliks Topolski designed the set, which involved a huge threatening figure lying outside the luckless Amédée's home, gradually growing to take over more and more of the house and the stage. Jack McGowran played Amédée. This was drawing-room comedy all right, but one where the drawing room was physically broken up. What joy!

On one occasion, the Arts Theatre Cambridge played Ionesco one week, followed by Bernard Kops's *The Hamlet of Stepney Green* the next. The cast included the emerging talents of Harold Lang and Joss Ackland. We stood and cheered this example of the new realism, which was probably more than Kops's play deserved. But we were saluting and embracing new times, our new times. A fortnight later, in May 1958, Nigel Dennis's social comedy *Cards of Identity* was played by Ackland, Alan Dobie and the young Alan Ayckbourn.

The high point of this mood had come on 28 April 1958 with the first night and world premiere at the Arts Theatre of *The Birthday Party* by a virtually unknown playwright, Harold Pinter. Much of its full meaning, still being explored to this day, was lost on us. But we recognised that it was new, different and special. Above all, it was ours, it was for our time, of our time. If this recognition of something special on the stage before us included a good dose of puzzlement, that took nothing away from our recognition of a great moment of theatre. At the curtain, we stood and cheered. Surely, British theatre would never be the same again.

Yet the subsequent first night of *The Birthday Party* in London only days later was a disaster. Most Fleet Street critics panned it as incomprehensible, which it was to them. It closed after a week. Just one critic, Harold Hobson of the *Sunday Times*, hailed it as a masterpiece. We felt our own judgements and instincts vindicated by his verdict. The older generation was just plain wrong. They were after all 'the establishment', entrenched, comfortable, complacent, boring and wrong.

Hobson was a shrewd judge of actors too. Reviewing a production of *Henry IV,* parts 1 and 2, by the anonymous actors of the university Marlowe Society – Clive Swift was Falstaff, Derek Jacobi Prince Hal – Hobson lauded at length a slim young man playing Justice Shallow in the rural scenes. He was right to do so. It was a very early appearance by the young Ian McKellen.

Despite recognising Pinter as an original voice, we never found him easy or comprehensible. I organised a series of play readings for the Mummers of the new, mainly Royal Court playwrights, including Arnold Wesker, Keith Johnstone, Ann Jellicoe and Pinter. The common room at Peterhouse was crowded for a reading of Pinter's *The Room* and *The Dumb Waiter*. At the end, when questions from the audience were invited to the playwright, there was only a total, stunned silence. How did one react to words that sounded normal, sentences that sounded like sentences but ordered in such a way that meaning slipped away into a different meaning? Ah, meaning! What did it all mean? Pinter had not come to gloss his meticulously composed words – seeming clarity loaded with ambiguity – with glib explanations, convenient commentary. Besides, he may not have been able to explain what he had written. Why should he? The baffled silence in the room lengthened, discomfort mixed with incomprehension. Part of Pinter must have loved it. Finally, he himself broke the silence: 'A very good comment!' It was a perfect Pinteresque observation.

Exploration of the university dramatic repertoire ranged from Jean Genet's *The Maids*, the cast including Jill Daltry, later the voice-over of television's 'After Dinner Mints', to the Marlowe Society's *Edward II* with Derek Jacobi as Edward and Richard Marquand as a reptilian Gaveston. Jacobi and Swift played in Miller's *Memory of Two Mondays*, and John Bird directed David Buck and Joe Melia in Robert Penn Warren's *All the King's Men*, a big piece of Americana about a domineering, egotistical US political boss. It was very hip. 'John Bird', it was said with some awe, 'is very into "American lifestyle"!' An undergraduate with a lifestyle – a phrase, a concept never heard of before!

Future talent appeared all over the place. David Brierley was credited as business manager for many productions and went on to manage the Royal Shakespeare Company as Chief Executive for a quarter of a century. James Sargent was a formidable behind-the-scenes stage director; he too filled the same role for the RSC for some decades. Guy Woolfenden directed the music for Brecht's *Threepenny Opera* at Cambridge and then became music director at the RSC. Names such as Corin Redgrave, Eleanor Bron, Margaret Drabble and the future child-guidance guru, Penny Balchin (later Penelope Leach) appeared steadily in undergraduate cast lists.

The apotheosis of the 1950s Cambridge acting generation came in 1959 with a musical version of Shakespeare's play *Love's Labours*. The words came from Richard Cottrell, Corin Redgrave and John Wood (who turned into the John Fortune of *Bird and Fortune*). Clive Swift composed the music, Jack Thompson arranged it, John Tydeman directed. The cast was a roll call of our Cambridge acting generation – Redgrave, Jacobi, McKellen, Cottrell, Roger Hammond, Terence Hardiman and many others. The show was gentle, lyrical, witty, just sentimental enough. One of the women in the cast, the publisher Antonia Till, confirmed its intense autumnal feeling for us all, cast and audience. It made us aware of our time passing, of joy and regrets blending sweetly. It was an ending for our generation but of course a beginning as well. Years later at a misty-eyed, croaky-voiced, creaking-limbed *Love's Labour's* reunion at Antonia's home, Ian McKellen looked up at her and said simply: 'That was where it all began!' It was better than self-indulgently nostalgic; it was a generation's private farewell to itself. *Love's Labours* transferred to the Lyric, Hammersmith where it sold out.

It was not the only Cambridge show to get a London transfer. Ray Jenkins's *Clair de Lune* and Richard Cottrell's *Deutsches Haus* played as a double bill at the London Arts. Ray became a successful TV playwright, Richard Director of the Australian Theatre. One of the first from this period to get a London transfer had been Bamber Gascoigne's revue, *Share My Lettuce*. It was smart, witty, allusive. Like other parts of Cambridge theatre it was strikingly distinct in tone and subject matter from the conventions of West End revues. It broke another rule of thumb – it came from a single college, Magdalene, rather than from the wider university scene. But some humour seemed to flourish better in a college environment as David Nobbs, writer of *Reginald Perrin* and much else, showed in his sketches for St John's college revues.

For the most part it was the all-university scene that allowed talent to flourish. It was a hothouse for talent, a melting-pot for experience. These were the years when the Cambridge Footlights became a force in British humour, transmogrifying the 1930s West End formulae of revue and cabaret into the harsher, more acerbic, more bracing world of 1960s satire. Most of it was due to Peter Cook, who came up a year after us in 1957. Annie and I met him first in the St John's rooms of my prep-school friend, Hugh Brogan. Hugh said we must meet this 'very funny undergraduate' from Radley. Cook was indeed amusing, regaling us with the monologues of a Mr Boylett who stoked the boilers at Radley – a homespun philosopher who through Peter Cook's psychological ventriloquism later gave the world lines such as 'I would have been a judge but I didn't have the Latin.' Peter adopted Mr Boylett's persona and musings as an alter ego into whose mouth he could put devastating pieces of banal or contradictory common sense. An engaging act over an undergraduate tea, it was also curiously distancing.

I always found Peter elusive as a person, as if he was more at home in his various performing personae than in the more unresolved complexities of himself. He was always polite, always friendly, but I never got beyond a certain point of familiarity. In our last year he told Ann Dowson of his ambitious plans for setting up a nightclub in Soho dedicated to political cabaret satire, to be called 'The Establishment'. He would also start a satirical magazine. This all sounded to her like typical final-year undergraduate fantasy; there was a lot of it around. Peter turned both satirical club and the satirical magazine – *Private Eye* – into reality. He was an original and a genius.

Long before that, Cook was the creative mainstay of Cambridge satire and of informal Footlights evenings called 'Smokers'. Others included Joe Melia, a brilliant mime as well as actor, and Timothy Birdsall, a gifted performer, wonderful cartoonist whose work appeared regularly in the new *Private Eye*. Tim died tragically young of cancer. His single book of cartoons is a classic including the morally savage *Eating People Is Wrong*, originally from *Private Eye*, a savage depiction of the press magnate, Lord Beaverbrook, stuffing his greedy jaws with human beings.

These were people of extraordinary brilliance and originality. One ubiquitous contemporary was neither – David Frost. His exact contribution to Footlights of ideas, scripts or sketches was limited to the point of non-existence. Yet 'Frostie' had an insinuating persuasiveness, implying that other people's material would work better, sound better, if he either voiced it, introduced it or otherwise mediated between author and audience. To have 'Frostie' involved became a kind of validation that, in truth, the material did not need. It was appropriation of the highest order. This was precisely the position Frost won for himself in television, starting with *That Was the Week That Was*, the reassuring, bland middle man in the midst of often dangerous material from others. It served a purpose for sure, a protective shield against criticism, but his contribution was a lesser one than that of his peers. Frost was an entertainment entrepreneur – but he was the main beneficiary of his own entrepreneurship.

Cambridge musical theatrical life included Stravinsky's *The Rake's Progress* and Carl Orff's *Carmina Burana*, crudely energetic, brassy, falsely radical and pleasantly rude. It was a blessed time of discovery and daring. Who then thought that Berlioz's dramatic oratorio *The Damnation of Faust* might be successfully staged? It was the work and inspiration of an eccentric Hungarian former Ballet Jooss dancer turned antique shop owner, Gabor Cossa. The fully staged *Damnation* was a huge success. Later, Gabor directed the original four-act version of Oscar Wilde's *The Importance of Being Ernest*. All his shows had style and lots of his own antique jewellery. Even his commitment and festoons of necklaces, brooches and 'colliers' could not make a convincing case for the superiority of Wilde's original four-act version of his masterpiece. *The Times* reviewer thought little of it or of most of the actors, including myself as Jack Worthing. Only Rachel Herbert as Gwendolen – herself a mature student – was judged to have a 'stylised idiom apparently beyond the range of other principal players'.

Two things, I believe, explain the extraordinary creativity of those Cambridge years. First, almost all Cambridge theatre was made on a university-wide scale – the Amateur Dramatic Club (ADC), the Mummers, Marlowe Society, University Actors, Footlights were all university groups. Colleges performed very little and very occasionally. As a result, the best actors – Jacobi, Marquand, Swift, Buck, McKellen, Nunn, Eleanor Bron, Margaret Drabble – worked often and together in the best productions by the best directors – John Tydeman, John Bird, Richard Cottrell, Clive Perry (later Leicester Theatre), Waris

Habibullah (later the film director, Waris Hussein). They learned and got huge experience together.

A few university academics were directly involved in undergraduate theatre, principally George 'Dadie' Rylands, who oversaw the super-elite Marlowe Society and its super-perfect Shakespearian diction, and John Barton of King's College, later a leading influence in the RSC. Overwhelmingly, undergraduate theatre was self-starting and independently run. Accepting full responsibility for the creative, performing and business side of theatre was greatly maturing. Cambridge actors and directors were not taught, dragooned or beset with theory – they learned from and among themselves.

Secondly, perhaps a heretical thought: Cambridge had no Drama Faculty – an English Faculty, of course, but nowhere for acting and the world of theatre to be subjected to theories, ideologies, dogmatic interpretations or sociological straitjackets. Pragmatism, intelligence, passion, adventure, curiosity were the unacknowledged watchwords of Cambridge theatre in the 1950s. The result was a remarkable flowering which enriched and defined Britain's theatre scene for two generations.

Intensely engrossing as they were in terms of time and energy, the arts in Cambridge never elbowed out learning, living and loving. How could they? These were the centre of our time and efforts. Look at what was offered, look at what there was to be learned – this was a university after all. Monday morning on my lecture list in that first term, Michaelmas 1956, had Butterfield, Elton and Plumb on it, one after another at sixty-minute sessions in the Mill Lane Lecture Rooms. Herbert Butterfield, the political theorist, followed by G. R. Elton, the revolutionary historian of Tudor administration, followed by J. H. Plumb on the Hanoverians. Elton, the true 'inventor' of Thomas Cromwell, was saturnine and sardonic with a slight German accent, analysing Tudor government like a management consultant. Jack Plumb was calculatedly cynical about the corruptions of eighteenth-century life and politics under Sir Robert Walpole. This was history as a scandal sheet. Lectures were just that, spoken, sometimes read, without visual aids or assistance of any kind. The best, such as those of Denis Brogan, the great historian of the United States, were an extempore stream of jokes, scandalous tales and sarcastic observation on US presidents dead or living. None of Brogan's lectures would have been any help in writing an essay. All were rich in understanding of how US politics worked. Anyone seeking notes of those lectures would search in vain; there were no bullet-point summaries, digests or links to a website in those days. Even had the technology existed, it would have been considered insulting to offer such assistance. Learning consisted of listening and thinking and reading. Lecture notes were what you wrote for yourself while listening and thinking. This was your responsibility.

The greatest lecturers in the late 1950s were both exiles from Nazi Europe. Dr Nikolaus Pevsner, whose BBC Reith Lectures on the 'Englishness of English Art' had shaken up the intellectual world, gave a weekly public university lecture illustrated with black-and-white lantern slides on the history of European architecture. The great hall of the university Examination Schools was packed out every Friday evening at 5 p.m. Pevsner was an elegant figure with rimless glasses, a soft voice, precise profile, slightly foreign inflected English accent. There I saw for the first time images of the Byzantine masterpiece, the basilica of Hagya Sofia in Istanbul, its vast soaring dome pierced by pinpoints of light from scores of tiny windows, its grand buttresses, glittering mosaics, vast volumes. Gothic architecture we knew – it was all around us, after all, it was our culture. But this was another architectural language, a different approach to spirituality, a different civilisation. Hagya Sofia had to be seen. Years later we saw it. Dr Pevsner, in those dark winter Cambridge evenings, with scratchy images and quiet, insistent passion, had not peddled a fantasy.

Dr Walter Ullmann, an Austrian exile, lectured on medieval European history. On the face of it, he studied an almost wilfully obscure corner of that glorious Continent-wide tapestry:

not kings and queens, battles and bastards, plots and plagues, pomp and poverty, but relations between the two greatest European institutions of those centuries – the papacy and the Holy Roman Empire. Whose was the greater authority: the emperor's, springing from worldly power and possessions, or the pope's, springing from God? And where was the epic contest for power, the so-called 'Investiture Contest', fought? Not on battlefields but in and on the pages of the most obscure, most legalistic of Latin documents, especially those issued by the papacy. Ullmann, it seemed, had read them all, his mind and eye alert to the tiniest shift of phrasing that signalled a strategic shift in papal thinking.

Ullmann's lectures were packed, and not just by those reading medieval European history. Speaking freely from notes, he was urgent, cogent and with a fine sense of storytelling. Most lectures ended in a medieval cliff-hanger. On one occasion, Ullmann reached the point when the pope was about to crown the Emperor Charlemagne in AD 800. This act would signal the papacy's pre-eminence over the empire, the religious over the secular, the spiritual over the political. Then he stunned the lecture theatre with a question: 'But where did they get the crown?' No one had ever asked such a damningly common-sense, practical, essential and political question before. No wonder we rushed back the following week.

Ullmann once claimed that he had been asked to appear during the television coverage of the Queen's Coronation in 1953. He insisted to BBC producers that he could only truly convey the symbolism of coronation by handling the Crown Jewels themselves. The request was turned down; the TV audience was denied what might have been one of the great occasions of royal coverage.

Years later, as a BBC radio journalist covering the Sino-Soviet split during the 1960s period of the Cold War, I found that Ullmann's micro-textual reading of papal documents was an invaluable discipline for teasing out the nuances of the ideological struggles between the Soviet Union and Mao's

China. Words mattered when it came to ideology and theoretical orthodoxy. Communists watched their words. Often they provided the only accurate indication of what was happening politically. Reading medieval history opened the way to the conflicts of our own times.

Truth to tell, the standard of lecturers was very variable. Some were downright dull, a few obviously clever but incomprehensible, unable to translate their knowledge and understanding into communicable form. There was no monitoring, no feedback, no consumer surveys about the quality of lectures and lecturers. You took what was on offer and made of it what you could. This was a grown-up environment. The best on offer was treasurable. Spoon-feeding was not on the syllabus, you took something from even the least impressive.

Year by year, my attendance at lectures declined. That was normal; lectures were not compulsory. They were only one part of learning. The greater part was the classic Oxbridge one-to-one weekly supervision based around a pre-written essay. Of my three key supervisors at Trinity, the seventeenth-century political theorist and later sociologist, Peter Laslett, was profoundly influential but not because I understood much of what he said. He spoke with a considerable splutter, his voice rose and fell unpredictably and his mind was curious and unclassifiable. His handwriting was so bad – worse even than mine – that we were never quite sure if we had correctly noted the subject of the next essay pinned to his room door. Yet being in his presence made certain things very clear; thinking was hard work; thinking was serious; thinking involved thought. We were not there to be taught; it was our business to learn.

He was an example in other ways. Dons could be influential beyond their immediate disciplines. Besides being a radical reinterpreter of John Locke, he was a mover and shaker in the creation of the new universities such as East Anglia, and then in adapting the French idea of the 'University of the Third Age' (U3A) to British circumstances. Peter once told me how useful it was to be in Trinity with its sizeable contingent of ancient dons who needed looking after. It was a study in and test bed for managing the kingdom of the old. His greatest achievement, an educational revolution, was to devise the idea of an 'Open University' with the sociologist Michael Young and successfully lobby the Labour government to fund it.

Peter's radicalism extended to architecture. He and his wife commissioned the young Trevor Dannatt to build them a house at the far end of Barrow Road in West Cambridge. It was a confidently elegant modernist structure of wood, glass and brick. But these were the 1950s. It could not have been more different from Cambridge's prevailing conventional, red-brick, leaded-windowed, semi-detached, domestic banality, streets and streets of it. Spurred on by objections from his immediate neighbour, Fred Hoyle, proponent of the 'Big Bang' theory of the creation of the universe, Trinity College Council condemned Dannatt's design as 'aesthetically abominable and structurally unsound'. Undeterred, the Lasletts ploughed on and the house was built. When Peter invited Ann, my future wife, and me to see it, we knew this was what our future should look like, such buildings should shape our world. A love of and curiosity about contemporary architecture has never left us.

It was Laslett who persuaded me to read Part II of the History Tripos in my final year rather than veering over to Moral Science, where I would have floundered. Writing in his characteristic spider hand, Laslett first 'apologised' for not getting me a Senior Scholarship at the end of my second year. 'I finally lost a pirates' engagement with the skull and crossbones of mathematics, natural sciences and such, like Barbary Coasters!' Did I really want to read Moral Science, he continued; 'History Part II is a push over! (Look at Runciman, W.G. et al). You could be "Ullmannised" under pressure, plated with it! Still no use?' The reference to my near-contemporary Garry Runciman was Laslett's little tease at the cleverest historian of the generation. The invitation to be 'Ullmannised' on a one-to-one basis proved too tempting to turn down.

Supervisions with Walter Ullmann took place in his rooms

in Laundress Lane overlooking the mill race at Silver Street. The pretty view from his windows of the churning waters was somewhat clouded by air heavy with cigarette ash and fine particles of minutely ground coffee which he drank in liqueur-size concentrations and cups. Walter's attention was total, his involvement intense. Whatever the murk in the atmosphere, full attention was needed throughout a sixty-minute supervision. If his mind was basically a legal one, his judgements were deeply political too. On one occasion he observed that my essay on France's King Henry IV and national public opinion had really made him think. I murmured my pleasure that my ideas should have engaged the great Dr Ullmann. 'No, no, no!' he waved his arms. 'I had to think so hard because it was so wrong!' His usual dismissal of some jejune undergraduate observation was the scornful: 'Bah!'

Michael Vyvyan became my third-year supervisor when reading Theories of the Modern State. He had a ruthless mind which got to work on my essays. They were probably not very good, but, worse still in the first term of my final year, there weren't many of them. I missed essay after essay, final-year exhaustion in part, falling in love, of course – who knows what else distracted me. Vyvyan spotted the weakness and finally went on the attack. It was intellectually ferocious and wholly justified in the context of my failure to deliver the required work. I had no answer, above all no explanation intellectually. He reduced me, or I reduced myself, to tears.

A few days later Vyvyan wrote an entirely reasonable letter:

I do not mind saying that unless you have some regular psychological difficulty over putting things down on paper – and in the present case it seems rather a matter of thinking things out than writing them down – your inability to bring an essay this term seems to show an unexpected lack of intellectual resource for a Scholar. I don't think supervisors expect highly finished products of 'value' at weekly intervals as they know perfectly well they could not produce anything of the kind in the circumstances themselves. But the system does demand some sort of thesis on paper to work on.

More generously still, Vyvyan then pointed me to a change of special subject if I felt inclined.

My own reading of that supervision took me in a very different direction and to a conclusion that only crystallised rather later. Why had I broken down, apart from sheer embarrassment at my failure to write? I decided that it was caused by my inability to counter the intellectual rigour of Michael Vyvyan's (quite proper) assault. He had set out to test me under pressure. Why? Not principally because he was a don with a rigorous mind, but because he was 'known' to be an MI6 recruiter, some said even a senior officer in British Intelligence. My academic failings gave him the legitimate opportunity to see what I was made of. He broke me. It did not take long. I would not be worth recruiting. I would not have done as a spy.

These men were powerful influences. Many, perhaps most, dons left little mark on us as individuals. My contemporary and fellow historian, Anil Seal, maintains that he and I were essentially 'auto-didacts' at Trinity. We assembled small groups of fellow historians for our own seminars. They usually included the Newnham historian Ann Dowson, and Amanda Goodfellow from New Hall. Most preciously, we felt that we could turn to any relevant Trinity dons for advice and enlightenment. Once when the group was stuck on some point of Marxist theory, Anil, half Indian himself, said breezily: 'Let's go to that bright Indian Fellow called Amartya Sen. He should know the answer!' The four of us turned up at his college rooms without warning, found him in, explained our puzzlement and asked for clarification. Sen enquired which edition of Marx's works we were using, identified the relevant page that was baffling us, turned it up and resolved our difficulty without hesitation in an informal, instantaneous seminar. Later Sen won a Nobel Prize in Economics.

On another occasion, Anil and I felt that the university

teaching on our chosen special subject of 'Les Philosophes' of the eighteenth century was very poor. In Dr Ralph Leigh, Trinity had the greatest authority on our period and on Voltaire. We approached him, explained what we wanted and then had a thirty-minute seminar when Ralph Leigh taught us almost everything we needed to know for the entire special subject. Neither Leigh nor Sen had needed to give up their time. To their credit, they never grudged it nor minded our approaches. It was a normal part of college life, a recognition of shared partnership in learning, enquiry and scholarship.

Such effortless and precious contacts would be impossible today. Sixty years ago, we only had to ask for help over intellectual matters. These were real contacts, not the sterile, formalised, de-personalised 'contact hours' that disfigure universities today. Sixty years ago, nobody counted or measured them; nobody feared 'grooming', sexual molestation. Such open, generous, enriching, maturing exchanges were the stuff of college life. Their loss is a heavy one, our enjoyment of them a huge benefit and privilege.

As was the pastoral care doled out by the Dean of Chapel, the theologian Harry Williams, a great deal of it coming with gin and socialising. Would these now count towards 'contact hours' or might they be interpreted as 'grooming'? On the most notorious occasion, a particularly rowdy party of undergraduates and at least two Fellows, Rev. Harry Williams included, threw empty Schweppes tonic battles at a nearby noisy and irritating air-conditioning plant on the adjoining roof of Caius College. Reprehensible though this particular event undoubtedly was, no one could challenge or dispute Harry Williams's pastoral care for some troubled and confused undergraduates. Today, our behaviour would be judged by the modern weasel word 'appropriate' and found wanting, but it reflected the close and balanced relationship between the young and our seniors, both mature and enriching.

Some of Harry Williams's most influential teaching concerned the destructive nature of a sense of guilt. Since so many in his care came from the English public-school system where a sense of guilt was deemed a requirement of belonging, Harry's teaching was liberating. He did not preach irresponsibility, but he believed personal freedom could only come when unburdened by the corrosive pangs of 'feeling guilty'. Awareness of wrong was one thing; awareness and repentance essential. Turning it into a sense of guilt, creating a lifelong burden, was quite another.

How much were we taught, how much did we learn? How did the two processes intertwine and interrelate? A huge amount. Perhaps the unifying element was our realisation that we were in the presence of learning, of scholars and of matters of the mind. These were not necessarily for us in the future, partly because of temperament and outlook, partly because we lacked a particular aptitude for scholarship. But it set an example, set a standard, acknowledged a world of special values. The offering was rich and generous. What each of us took from it was up to us.

All of these elements needed binding together in relaxed, informal human form. We were learning, but did we know how we might live? Much of the social glue to life came from and in parties. No one reached for or expected or could afford sophisticated ingredients. Cyprus Dry sherry at seven shillings a bottle was ulcer-threatening in its acidity. Cyprus Sweet came closer to headache-inducing cough mixture. Yugoslav Riesling at the standard eight shillings a bottle mark had the slightly sticky texture that was found years later to betray the improper addition of motorcar anti-freeze to the thin grape juice. Gin flowed in decent quantities at Sunday lunchtime drinks, a useful preliminary to the 2 p.m. matinee of a foreign film at the Arts Cinema. Respectable claret was available for special occasions when dinner could be ordered from the college kitchens for delivery to your rooms. Most often, parties revolved around a large zinc bath into which each new arrival poured their own bottle, regardless of its nature, taste or appropriateness. Most self-respecting witches would have gagged at such a brew. At least there was no doubt about the alcoholic content.

Really good wine was served at annual College Feasts, a separate wine for each of four or five courses. The best wine came at dinners of the True Blue Club, a 'select' gathering of twenty or so whose senior members wore eighteenth-century dress. The discrimination involved in assembling fine food and matching wine was often vitiated by the club 'tradition' of inviting members and/or their guests to end the evening by drinking a 'bumper' – an entire bottle of claret – without taking the crystal goblet from their lips. This challenge was solemnly timed by the Chairman and the result written in the Club Record. The appropriate page will show that it took me a miserable thirty seconds plus to drink my bumper. My brother George downed his in just over eight seconds, having the unusual capacity of opening his gullet without needing to swallow. Few who took the challenge were in any shape to remember much after their test. Many found they could not simply 'hold' any of their liquor.

By the standards of Oxford's Bullingdon Club, ours were sober times, restrained behaviours. If damage was done, it was self-inflicted and philosophically accepted. Something was learned perhaps about self-restraint or lack of it. Mainly it was just huge fun.

Undergraduate life offered richer lessons in social living. They were very different from what we knew from home. We learned about living with others because of close neighbourly contact with fellow undergraduates in rooms around college courts, up staircases and in buildings. These made casual contact frequent, English avoidance almost impossible.

In my first year, I found myself on the same floor of the same staircase in Trinity's Whewell's Court as a Westminster School man called James Madge. With his thin features and rather nasal voice, James appeared intimidatingly remote, superior even. He was reading Architecture. James came from intellectual 'royalty', his mother being the poet, Kathleen

Raine, his father the sociologist and founder of the sociological programme Mass-Observation, Charles Madge. Most nights a steady flow of visitors arrived at James's bedsit from 11 p.m. onwards. In due course, living on the same floor, I was asked to join in. Many had been contemporaries at James's Westminster, a very clever and sometimes cliquey school. They were not so here. James dispensed conviviality, played Haydn string quartets on his gramophone and after midnight often cooked a risotto for those still around. I learned much of the Haydn quartet oeuvre as a result, a love that has never left me. But I learned more about living, the quiet, accepting generosity and inclusiveness of a person who shared his loves and skills with friends without stint.

In another set of rooms in Whewell's Court, a slightly different approach to living was on offer. In a shared ground-floor set, two grammar-school friends from Hertford opened their establishment. John Peer and John Tydeman could hardly have been more different. Peer was lean, practical, wryly humorous, shrewd, an engineer by discipline. Tydeman was round – getting rounder – intuitive, instinctive, inclined to generous self-indulgence, warm, Falstaffian, reading English. Together they created an atmosphere where many knew they could just drop in. Being on the ground floor helped, but being open in heart and mind mattered more. It was not a centre of intellectual discussion or speculative exploration. Events in Suez or Hungary cast little shadow here. Peer's flow of fellow engineers usefully kept matters down to earth. We gathered in Room J2 Whewell's Court to sit, listen and sing along with Tom Lehrer's satirical songs; here *My Fair Lady*'s lush, sentimental romanticism became a soundtrack to life from a bootleg US copy; here Bernstein's *West Side Story* reinforced our belief and wish that old artistic forms were being overturned, reshaped and renewed.

The Tydeman-Peer sitting room was cosy, accepting and relaxing; the Madge 'salon' a tad more elevated and rarefied in its instincts. Each was about friendship, sharing, enjoyment and conviviality. There was no falsity there, to be felt or seen. Ann and I, each from comparatively isolated home backgrounds, felt lucky to be included in and accepted by both. Each offered lessons in living for life.

A further model for living came from a fellow Trinity historian, John Drummond. He was funny, clever, acerbic, and ultra-gregarious. Drummond met, or made it his business to know, everybody, observing that he needed to do so because though he was very clever, his own means were modest. He often spoke of his poverty, relying on a single pair of trousers and a single sweater for an entire term's clothing. Drummond made a point of being entertaining, to make people laugh as a way of being accepted, being included, 'singing for his supper' socially. If it was calculated, which it was, it also reflected real personal insecurities. In some ways, the 'high camp' style, then coming into fashion as an idea and a lifestyle, was very attractive. It was undoubtedly entertaining. Few could carry it off as Drummond did. It was not for me. It was his preferred style of living and he turned it to brilliant effect in the success of his later roles as Director of the Edinburgh Festival and Director of the BBC Proms.

In my last year, a fourth, I wasted a great deal of time in trying not very seriously to carry out some organised historical research, testing whether I wanted to be or could be an academic. I came across yet another model for living. With my oldest friend and fellow historian Hugh Brogan, I found accommodation in Wordsworth Grove, just behind the back entrance to Newnham College. In a large semi-detached house lived a solitary bachelor solicitor. He had three handsome sets of rooms which he let out not for the money, which he did not need, but for the company, which he sought. Warren Cairns – always 'Mr Cairns' to us – charged ridiculously low rents – just three pounds ten shillings per week, plus one important further condition. He and his lodgers would dine together at least twice a week, inviting guests to join us. Each of us would cook one course of the three-course meal, rotating the courses between us. The direct costs of our cooking and wine would then be deducted from our weekly rent. In some weeks the hospitality was so active, the dining costs so high, that Mr Cairns earned no rent at all.

Warren Cairns knew exactly what he was looking for: companionship and the stimulus of the young for a childless bachelor. We provided it. Old enough to be a parent, he was stiff, formal, reserved, but dared to show his warmth and friendship over time. But he was also play-acting, pretending that his house was a 'college' – it was certainly a community – that the dining room was 'hall', that a special annual dinner 'in hall' was the college commemoration dinner of 'Founder's Day'. We joined in enthusiastically. The menu for such an occasion in January 1960 shows that we dined off consommé, turbot, roast duck, leg of lamb, gateau millefeuille, and a savoury of 'Japanese pigeon'. These courses were accompanied by Meursault-Genevrières, Ch. Calon-Ségur, Charmes-Chambertin, Ch. Climens and sparkling hock. Such a feast was done justice by the use of Mr Cairns's handsome nineteenth-century glasses, cutlery, porcelain, candelabra and furniture. Everything contributed to a sense of innocent occasion. It may have been play-acting, but it was oddly serious too.

Hugh Brogan, Ann Dowson (by then my fiancée) and I entered into the spirit of these occasions. Under the pressure of the conditions of our lodgings, both Hugh and I learned to cook, a skill we have never foregone nor regretted acquiring. We experimented with new dishes and new wines. Our most memorable guests included the Regius Professor of History, the great medievalist Dom David Knowles. On this occasion, much of the conversation turned on the vagaries of railway timetables in provincial France.

My only regret from that year is that Hugh and I failed to keep a record of our dinner guests and the menus we cooked. What a diary that would have been. While we would not have wanted to imitate Mr Cairns's particular and peculiar style of life, it had admirable aspects. It was gentle, generous, open, discriminating, and wedded to good things in life. Perhaps the happiest moment of that year for Mr Cairns was that I married Ann Dowson from Mr Cairns's house, 2 Wordsworth Grove. It made him feel a part of the family, almost the 'father of the groom'!

I had met Ann at history lectures in our first year. We had friends in common. We acted in the Mummers and went on summer acting tours in Devon and Cornwall together. We became close in the second year. During our final year, when I had a handsome double set of rooms in Great Court, Ann was such a regular visitor that the Trinity porters greeted her almost as a member of the college. We became engaged at the end of our final year, married a year after.

Cambridge was a kind place in which to fall in love, to be in love. Who could ignore the sharply crisp winter air, the pinky-grey blue of the tinted winter sky, the frosted shapes and forms of fields and trees that exhilarated as we skipped off reading in the University Library to relish the winter cold. Who could resist the mist rising in wraith-like swirls from the Cam as if the water itself was boiling; nothing sinister lurked in these shape-forming clouds. Then the Cambridge spring erupted, the swags of blossom, the sheets of spring flowers, the opti-mistic intensity of young green leaves. One Saturday morning in March, Ann and I walked along Trinity Street and King's Parade; the sky was blue, the sun balmy, the air was perfumed, everyone we met was a friend, anyone we did not know would surely become one. Nature's backcloth for loving, for playing at 'falling in love, for being in love' was there to be used by all. It would have been awful to waste it.

Besides, Cambridge's own rhythms offered a different op-portunity, more important than the occasional, dizzying poses of being in love. The university calendar was crucial, three terms of eight weeks, with lengthy vacations in between; three terms of total intensity and commitment, of extreme feelings condensed into a brief period, when days were followed by days and nights were fitted in from time to time. Such pockets of madness were followed by a longer period of vacation to cool off in, yearn, pine, regret, blush with embarrassment, think again, decide to plunge in headlong or withdraw. Then before any firm feeling had really clarified, another term would be upon us, a further eight weeks of emotions, thoughts, experiences crammed together beyond or alongside reason. The extreme, compressed nature of each period of this relentless annual cycle gave time to feel, time to take stock, but above all to put a possible love to the test. That was part of Cambridge's learning; it was an essential part of Cambridge living. Close friendships, the first of our mature lives, could form in such a pressure cooker of living.

Many friends became Cambridge 'couples'. Many such marriages lasted, though whether the Cambridge element was significant in the durability of a marriage is beyond proof. Not that relationships were plain sailing just because of the Cambridge environment. The late-night hours were thick with mutual counselling over gas fires, analysis over Nescafé, advice over whisky, argument over wine, puzzlement or admonition and warning with blank misery. Essay crises were the rule; emotional breakdowns frequent; abortions not unknown; homosexual relations – still illegal, 'gay' had not been coined – were presumed rather than explicit.

We acted, we studied, we partied, we flirted – these were the ingredients of our Cambridge lives in the late 1950s. It wasn't easy to leave them behind. On a glowing summer afternoon in June 1959, squatting on the steps of the fountain in Great Court, the atmosphere heavy with sultry and seductive summer airs, I decided to stay on; it seemed an easy decision and besides, leaving felt too dificult. I had the cushion of a BBC General Traineeship to take up whenever I wanted. The line of least resistance was too easy. All around me contemporaries were plunging into the real world. Advertising was the profession of the era, along with broadcasting, civil service, journalism. Few entered business, or maybe I didn't know them as well.

My fourth year did establish one thing: academic research was not for me. Perhaps it was a lesson well learned. For the rest, my time was pleasantly spent but essentially wasted. If I feel rather ashamed of it now, I felt no guilt at the time. At its end, Ann and I were married, I had a job at the BBC, she at Penguin Books. We had played, learned, lived and loved, much of it together. Our time had not been wasted. We were off to London. Now life was to start.

What had Cambridge taught us? What had we learned? The preciousness of friendship; the value of serious thinking; the complications of emotional honesty; the discovery of the new; the privilege of opportunity; the challenge of disagreement; the discomfort of the disruptive; the revelation of the different; the exhilaration of the unexpected. None of these had been set out in any formal syllabus; none were the subjects of lectures or supervisions; none came from prescribed reading. All were present in the true syllabus of everyday learning, living and loving at Cambridge.

6

Becoming a Broadcaster

1960–68

As I walked down the dreary, fumy, office-lined traffic funnel that was Kingsway in central London my life goal stood dominatingly ahead of me. Bush House commanded the southern end of that blighted thoroughfare. It was bold and grand, as confident as the headquarters of the BBC External Services surely had to be. 'Nation shall speak Peace unto Nation' was the slogan carved on the walls of Broadcasting House at Portland Place. The message from Bush House was implicit but even more lofty: the BBC would speak the truth unto the nations. As the novelist Penelope Fitzgerald observed in *Human Voices*, her 1980 novel about wartime life in the BBC:

> Without prompting, the BBC had decided that truth was more important than consolation and, in the long run, would be more effective. And yet there was no guarantee of this. Truth ensures trust but not victory or even happiness. But the BBC had clung tenaciously to its first notion, droning quietly on at intervals from dawn to midnight telling, as far as possible, exactly what had happened.

I could not have summed up my feelings about the BBC with such eloquence but I did believe that the commitment to truth from the BBC External Services lay enshrined in that building at the foot of Kingsway. That was what drew me on. In September 1960, this promise seemed important, necessary and right. I marched down to the massive coffered apsidal entrance, the two huge Corinthian columns and the two heroic figures representing . . . what? Truth and Freedom, presumably? Bush House embraced the loftiest ideals; the statues seemed worthy defenders of such portals. They would represent what we took them to represent.

I approached the BBC External Services as one member of the ten-strong annual group of elite General Trainees, those supposedly destined to be future leaders of the Corporation. My intake reflected the Great Britain of 1960. Nine came from Oxbridge; one from a red-brick university – the first to leap over that barrier. One, for the first time, was a woman, not only female but a scientist to boot, the first ever. None came from an ethnic background. Each of us would undertake a series of three-month attachments – BBC-speak for 'secondments' – during our two-year traineeships. At the end we were expected to apply for and get a permanent job in the BBC. We were incredibly privileged. I hope we knew it, but I fear we felt entitled.

There were several reasons for choosing the BBC External Services as my first attachment. With the Cold War at its height the world was a dangerous place and nuclear war a real possibility. Such a world needed understanding, study and explanation, a dose of rationality that might, just might, temper the madder political impulses with fact, history and knowledge. Weren't good decisions leading to peace not war more likely to be based on such an approach? Not content with rattling their nuclear sabres at one another in Europe, the superpowers seized every opportunity to sponsor proxy wars in the remotest corners of the globe, finding and anointing unlikely and unsavoury partners as trusty and worthy allies. Trying to fathom the most knotty and recalcitrant aspects of our world seemed an eminently decent and worthwhile occupation. Bush House was the home of such endeavour.

My Cambridge history degree, too, seemed to demonstrate that even violent conflicts finally yielded to reason and reality. Yes, finally. What I overlooked was the time factor. The forces of reason mingled with exhaustion and despair become compelling only after the passage of decades. Yet we had no reason for not being hopeful in and about our own time.

Basically, I was instinctively attracted to the External Services because they were about foreigners and I was foreign. Entering the hefty brass doorways of Bush House felt like coming home because it would be filled with other foreigners. Thereafter, nothing would feel strange because I had decided I was coming home.

Yet Bush House Centre Block – the building was a complex of five huge pavilions linked by external stairways and colonnades – should have seemed intensely strange. The entrance hallways were lined with marble and brass; every landing on each of the eight floors had marble walls and floors; the broad staircases were marble too with handsome metal balustrades. Truth to tell, a building less suitable for the grubby practicalities and accommodations of journalism could not have been found. This once-grand early-twentieth-century American office block complex had been pressed into service for the BBC External Services' needs in 1941. Original grandeur had long given way to the needs and wishes of journalists and broadcasters.

The Bush House I found in November 1960 smelled of dried cardboard, evilly strong cigarettes and cheap duplicating paper. The floors were covered with wrinkled lino, the office partitions of cheap wood and glass rattled with every passing footstep. Ventilation came from historically unyielding metal windows which, rashly opened, allowed in discernible quantities of London's then smog-ridden atmosphere. Internal heating came via asbestos-lined ducts. At the core of every floor were two studios, thick-walled to guarantee sound insulation, their entrances protected by double doors to preserve the purity and integrity of the studio sound. Every detail spoke of the pre-eminent importance of the broadcast word, a place without compromise and a clear, awesome severity of purpose, outlook and principle. If truth was indeed to be broadcast to the world, it surely deserved such respect. It needed to sound good too.

I rapidly discovered that the joy of Bush House lay in its canteen. Set in the basement, it linked the lower parts of the two main broadcasting areas – Centre Block, home of the English, African, Asian and Caribbean broadcasters – with the South-East Wing, home of the newsroom and the Europeans. It was the umbilical cord, the connecting path between Bush House's varied inhabitants. Everyone walked through the canteen; everyone ate there. There was no senior dining room, no executive common room, no reserved tables or spaces determined by rank. The Bush canteen was democratic, universal, all-embracing. No architect, planner or management consultant could ever have designed and shaped such an inclusive space to bind together a wildly disparate organisation. It was the beating, feeling, smelling, tasting, talking heart of the BBC External Services. When, decades later, the canteen became depopulated, it signalled that Bush House had lost its heart and soul.

Not that everybody spoke to everybody else. Bush House's 'nations', thirty-seven of them, sometimes spoke little to one another. On one side, the Russians clad in resentment, suspicion and paranoia glowered through their clouds of cigarette smoke. The Chinese, haunted by the distant absolutism of their homeland, sought security by staying close to one another. The Africans, in all their continental diversity, clattered cheerfully. The Arabs, just as varied, disunited behind a shared religion and a common language, brooded across their differences. The Caribbeans seemed to enjoy living whatever the problems thrown up by their lives.

The staff of the thirty-seven separate broadcasting units, the language services into which Bush House was divided, communicated in almost twice that number of spoken languages. The place was gloriously international, wondrously foreign, fabulous fun. There was an element of the stereotypical, but stereotypes have their own truth. Unlike the original Tower of

Babel, there was a unifying factor: a commitment to accurate transmission of events from the world to countries, often their own homes, who had little access to reliable news of their own. If asked, many of the broadcasters would have said, perhaps with a certain English tone of apology, that they broadcast the truth. If the Bush House air was full of tongues, there was a single voice.

With this seething and highly diverting pot of foreignness brewing in the lower ground, I was sent to the seventh floor of the Centre Block to a department named Overseas Talks and Features (OTF) which produced all the non-news output of the English-language World Service. It was run by a bilingual Englishman of French origin, Gerard ('Gerry') Mansell, even though he was only Assistant Head by title. Where was the actual departmental head, Arthur Barker? He sat in his office with the curtains half closed. Lunch was brought to him on a tray by his secretary. Though his door was open to passers-by, few troubled him by entering. I do not recall him taking a single editorial decision. Gerry Mansell was the editor, the intellectual leader. The hermit in the corner office was a fixture, a fact of BBC life. How this bizarre accommodation came about was a mystery. Oddly perhaps, we never bothered to enquire.

Mansell was intellectually clever in a French kind of way yet pragmatic and cunning in an English kind of way. It was an effective combination. Around him he gathered a group of young men who sat slightly aside from the conventional BBC journalistic model. John Radcliffe had come from the Atomic Energy Authority, Raymond Barker was an academic; Brian Smale-Adams was South African, Robert Milne-Tyte came from print journalism, the *News Chronicle*. Each was intellectually questioning, disinclined or even resistant to the assumptions of the status quo. The exchange of ideas at the morning editorial meeting was competitive. Not because we scored points off one another – though that did occur – but because we believed that international listeners around the world should have access to the most searching accounts of world events. Mansell often won these early-morning exchanges with sometimes abstruse analyses. We soon twigged that his competitive advantage lay in reading *Le Monde*, composed in Paris the previous afternoon, while we lagged behind with that morning's *Times* and *Manchester Guardian*.

And Mansell had another prey in mind – the External Services' newsroom and their team of news analysts. The accuracy of Bush House News was not at issue; it was built on certainty and caution, cast in tablets of stone. The web of comment and analysis that spun off directly from these massive certainties was another matter. It was cautious to a fault, unimaginative to a degree, conventional by instinct. Mansell had set out to challenge such a leaden way of approaching the world's great events. He would not tolerate ignorance of the facts, inaccuracy or deliberate bias. He did want an additional view of the world from that presented by the granite certainties of the newsroom and their writers. Once the outlines of an event had been captured, questions crowded in. 'Mansell's Young Men' extended the range of opinions, the nature of possible interpretations, the possibility of doubt and uncertainty, giving events interpretative colour, light and shade.

The result was huge intellectual tension between the newsroom on the third floor of the South-East Wing and OTF on the seventh floor of Centre Block. I do not know if this tension was openly recognised, officially sanctioned or just tacitly permitted. On the air waves, each coexisted side by side. The huge beneficiaries were the listeners worldwide, whose intellectual diet and range was greatly extended. It was up to us in OTF to provide the grit in the oyster, to be the contrarians, the doubters of the certainties. We thought we were pretty good. Mansell was our formidable intellectual protector.

The staple output from OTF, the flagship programmes, were the four-minute *Commentary* devoted to a single item of the news, broadcast immediately after the bulletin four times a day; and *The World Today*, a daily fifteen-minute analysis of a single major topic. I was thrown into action within days of arrival in the autumn of 1960. My first edition of *The World Today*, broadcast on 8 November, on the subject of Mexico, sticks in the memory. Each of the three supposed experts I chose for interview had a speech impediment. The content may have been excellent, but the sound and comprehensibility were something else. Lesson Number One of broadcasting production: 'Even experts should be understandable.'

From September until 17 February 1961, when my attachment ended, I produced twenty-three editions of *The World Today* on subjects as obscure but important as patterns of world trade, the Central Treaty Organisation (CENTO), France's atom bomb, Laos, the UN in the Congo (twice), the Arab League, Kenya and Soviet agriculture. I don't know what these did for the listeners but they certainly educated me. In fact, it never occurred to us to doubt that, in one way or another, listeners wanted to hear about these subjects, needed to know about them. Wherever listeners might be, the sheer consistency of the treatment – accurate, expert, unprejudiced – was judged to be as valuable as the topics themselves. This was public-service broadcasting in its global dimension.

It felt really good, too, to be part of the community of knowledge that fed our broadcasting machine. Bush House producers could call in anyone to broadcast at any time, often at short notice. (Broadcasting overwhelmingly took place in the confines of the radio studio.) Few refused. The attraction of an eight-guinea fee for a four-and-a-half-minute written *Commentary* was powerful in 1960. (It soon rose to a magnificent ten guineas.) Correspondents in their scores streamed up Fleet Street, then the home of the national press, to the doors of Bush House, often setting aside newspaper leading articles to complete on return.

In his 1967 Fleet Street novel *Towards the End of the Morning*, Michael Frayn captured the sense of frustration felt by newspaper journalists at the magnetic pull of Bush House, just a quarter-mile up the road. All the journos were short of money and frustrated in their careers. 'I've got to skip along to

Bush House now to do a talk for the West African Service,' says one. 'If anyone wants me, tell them I'm on my way up to the composing room!' Not long after, with a real sense of personal validation, the journalist boasts, 'I'm getting quite a following in West Africa. The producer had a letter this week from some girl in Conakry, of all places, asking for my photograph!'

Most of the journalists in Frayn's intensely real imagined world yearned for the fame and the fees of appearances on television. 'I shall be getting twenty-five guineas for doing nothing but sit around in a television studio for half an hour instead of beating my brains out all weekend to write a script for BBC Overseas Service and getting ten guineas for it.' Their existential crisis culminated in this cri de coeur: 'I want to liberate myself from the tyranny of the BBC Overseas Service'! Frayn was spot on about the contributors. For us BBC producers and for our worldwide listeners, Fleet Street's combination of loyalty and servitude was precious.

Academics, too, crossed the road in droves from the London School of Economics to Bush House, cutting short seminars, putting off graduate students, in order to enlighten the world. Some compiled books of essays based on their broadcasts. At least one distinguished national newspaper correspondent educated his children on the steady flow of eight- and ten-guinea fees. After broadcasting, most then ate in the Bush House canteen, adding to the atmosphere of an intellectual jamboree. Sometimes the canteen was so full of LSE academics that the public address system had to ask them to finish their meals and make room for BBC staff. The External Services bought into this reservoir of experience and knowledge very cheaply, acting as a vast inclusive tent for thoughts and ideas. For my colleagues and me, it was like organising a daily, high-level seminar on the world crisis of the moment.

Just one phone call could summon the best authority on any subject. If it was the Soviet Union, a single edition of *The World Today* would feature the *Guardian*'s Kremlinologist, Victor Zorza, the *Telegraph*'s David Floyd and the BBC's fount of communist knowledge, Anatol Goldberg. Any African topic would hear Colin Legum of the *Observer*, John Hatch of the *New Statesman*, Richard Kershaw or Erskine Childers. Diplomatic topics would be covered by academics such as Professor Fred Northedge, Geoffrey Stern or Philip Windsor of the LSE, Professor John Erickson in Edinburgh. Nicholas Carroll of the *Sunday Times* often obliged, as did Richard Scott of the *Guardian*, Alastair Burnet of the *Economist* or the generously ubiquitous Patrick Keatley of the *Guardian*, occasionally found in the street completing a *Commentary* with his Olivetti perched on a Bush House windowsill while his news editor at the paper raged, 'Where's Keatley!' He knew the answer.

These people all showed huge loyalty to Bush House. It was not just the guineas; they believed in the broadcasting, the connection with audiences, the commitment to the listeners. All had, I believed, their own implicit contract of trust with their listeners. For me it was a concentrated PhD course in international relations.

It had to end in mid-February 1961. Tuesday, 14 February, I noted in my diary, was the warmest February day since 1899, 'pale blue sky, a balm in the air, mist off the river, Westminster Abbey and any building with sky behind it was elegantly silhouetted in the soft vapoury light'. I felt strangely melancholy, perhaps because my time at Bush House was over. My personnel officer told me that the report on my attachment from OTF 'was the kind of report we all ought to get but didn't'. My mood lifted slightly, as did the evening sky, 'miraculous smoky reds and purples with clouds of birds wheeling'. On 17 February I said my farewells, assuming vaguely that I might return to OTF one day. I could not have imagined how and when. On 21 February I travelled to the next attachment of my General Traineeship: BBC Bristol.

This three-month separation was never going to be easy on a personal level. Annie and I were just seven months married. We were learning to live together; now we had to learn how to be physically remote for much of the time without becoming emotionally distant. She had a job at Penguin Books in Harmondsworth earning £550 per year; my BBC salary was a princely £750, rising to £850 a year later. A close Cambridge friend would live in to give Annie company. I had a new part of the BBC to look forward to and the West Region was known to be warm, friendly, decent and good at programmes about nature. Would it be much more?

I seem to have taken against it from the beginning. Looking for digs in Clifton, a series of dun-brown rooms furnished in old oak and smelling of cooking, was depressing. At a meeting with the assistant head of programmes, a nice man called Bill Coysh, he invited me to look around and decide what interested me. This was well meaning but hardly suggested they knew what to do with me. Watching the transmission of the daily magazine programme, *Round Up*, compounded my gloom. The items were lightweight, the parochialism oppressive, its intellectual distance light years from Bush House. Sitting alone in a Bristol cinema that night watching Burt Lancaster tearing his way through *Elmer Gantry* was no help. The audience of forty-odd was largely made up of singletons like me. My isolation and feeling of detachment increased.

Relief came the following day on running into a Cambridge contemporary even more depressed about his own work and life situation than me. The first of several lengthy sessions involving Harveys Bristol Cream sherry, wine and steak was a welcome diversion but hardly good for the liver or a basis for serious involvement with work in Bristol. Sensing my frustration, my superiors dispatched me back to London on day release, supposedly to babysit a live appearance by two Westminster MPs for a Bristol broadcast. This was a thoughtful gesture but only delayed addressing and resolving my frustrations back at base.

In part, they sprang from the loss of the intellectual stimulus of Bush House. In part, they came from the shock of being parted from Annie, however temporarily. In part they reflected my failure to appreciate what I might learn from the completely different programme environment offered by BBC Bristol. I lacked the equipment to deal with such confused emotions, which provoked a bout of intense soul-searching. My diary takes me by surprise to this day.

> Over a Chinese meal, very tired, I thought fairly fundamentally. What did I want to do? Was I setting about it in the right way? If I wanted to make films, what attitude to people, to life did I have? What philosophy guided me in any of my actions? The prospect of life and life's activity seemed so repetitive and dreary unless a higher, metaphysical viewpoint informed it. David Daiches said that real life, knowledge and literature needed an element of the tragic in it; and Philip Toynbee said that Beckett appealed to him in his fairly frequent moods of depression. Alas, I am bad at cosmic depression, at lasting 'weltschmerz' – which is sad or is it self-indulgent?

With those last phrases I turned away from a fairly deep pit. But why was I standing on its brink in any case? For nineteen of my twenty-five years I had been regimented, regulated, timetabled, taught, disciplined and directed. With the exception of Cambridge, others had taken the decisions that shaped my present and determined my future. Now alone in that Chinese restaurant in Bristol, I came face to face with the need to take control of my life, an uncomfortable challenge perhaps but an essential one. If I could not meet it directly, being aware of its existence remained important and valuable. Sadly, this moment of awareness did nothing to ease the daily frustrations of life at BBC Bristol.

The first week of March was peppered with dissatisfaction. From feelings of 'general annoyance and malaise', my diary descended to the 'futile and pointless'. Others were responsible, I felt. 'Bristol is characterless and you can be left to fester in an office, which would never happen in Bush.' I marched in to Bill Coysh and demanded work of a more challenging nature, any work come to that. He was attentive, slightly embarrassed and promised to 'sort something out'. The truth was that they still did not know what to do with me. There was no immediate relief for my boredom. The high point of the week was watching *Brief Encounter* in the BBC Club, then queueing for forty-five minutes to see *The Music Man*, walking away from the expensive tickets (twelve shillings and sixpence) and finding comfort in Camus' observation in *The Plague* that time can only be felt by doing something truly pointless. Like waiting at the box office and then not buying a ticket? It was a brief moment of Bristolian existentialism.

A month after arriving at Bristol I produced my first programme – about the acclimatisation and integration of migrants. Oddly, 22 March should have been an opportunity for me – the day of the first ever experiment in local broadcasting, the brainchild of the Controller of BBC West Region, the distinguished former war correspondent Frank Gillard. His notion of extending the reach of BBC broadcasts to local communities and cities was seen as at once radical, populist and unlikely to work. How much news could there be at such micro-units of journalistic existence? Gillard used Bristol's resources to pilot a day's such broadcasting. It seemed to me worthy, plodding, decent but far from a revelation. Obsessed as I still was by the politics of, say, Vietnam, such broadcasting seemed truly and uninterestingly parochial. I failed to see its potential. Gillard did, persisted and transformed the national radio experience.

While I moped, BBC Broadcasting House at Whiteladies Road, Bristol witnessed constitutional history in the making. The local MP, Anthony Wedgwood Benn, had reluctantly inherited a peerage from his father. He insisted on standing for parliament at the by-election caused by his necessary resignation as MP. The BBC's Political Editor, Hardiman Scott, came to Bristol to do equal five-minute TV interviews with Wedgwood Benn and his Tory rival candidate, Malcolm St Clair. It was a very rudimentary form of direct political engagement on TV. St Clair was interviewed first. I noted: 'St Clair was weak and characterless – sad looking. He began weakly and lasted no more than two minutes twenty seconds! Hardiman Scott suggested they do it again and by dint of pushing St Clair got him to four minutes forty seconds.'

Benn moved into the interviewee's chair, sat down, 'relaxed, easy, friendly and gave a splendid five minutes' worth; he packed so much in that it seemed longer. He said that while every vote for him was a vote for an important constitutional issue, no one need bother to vote for St Clair as he could get in anyway.' Benn rounded off by saying that he was sure St Clair wouldn't petition to unseat Benn if he won as 'he's a very decent chap'. Poor St Clair's eyes boggled at the patronising effrontery. But he was facing a political master who became adept at altering major parts of the British constitution. None of us crowding into the studio gallery could guess at Benn's influence on British politics in the generation ahead.

April dragged itself out with a few satisfactions, such as presenting live editions of the folksy daily magazine programme *Round Up*. My broadcasting skills began to improve but the programme material was as twee and inconsequential as ever. Such was BBC regional broadcasting in the 1960s. It was summed up in *Any Questions?*, the conventional, markedly conservative audience participation programme. Presided over by the self-satisfied Freddie Grisewood – his mind intellectually clad in a mouldering tweed jacket, his languid accent replete with complacency – with audiences entirely composed of the comfortable rural middle classes, it reflected nothing of what Britain was slowly becoming and needed to become. But the programme was beyond criticism at Whiteladies Road, a flagship of the region, symptomatic of the intellectual dullness of BBC Bristol.

The Gordian knot of my frustration was well and truly cut in mid-April when Personnel rang to say that my fellow trainee, Jill Mondy, had to leave her Manchester attachment early to get married and I could take her place on 1 May if I wanted. I leapt at it. On 27 April, I wrote a fairly rude report on my time at Bristol. The following day I slipped away quietly with absolutely no regrets. Nobody had been unpleasant to me, many were kind, some had tried to be helpful. But the fit was a poor one and I hadn't known how to take advantage of what was available. And I had drunk far too much Harveys dry sherry.

There were reasons for jumping at the move to Manchester. True, it would mean some extra weeks away from Annie and home, but she was a Salford person and I would live with her parents. I knew Manchester/Salford reasonably well. It would not be cosy like Bristol; I had had enough of cosy. I wanted purpose, I wanted gritty. I got it.

I was attached to the weekly radio magazine programme *Topics North*, a clunky title for a very un-clunky programme. It was edited by a forthright, determined, challenging Lancastrian, Bryan Blake, who had assembled a brilliant team of regular freelance interviewers: Brian Redhead, later the pillar of the *Today* programme, came in from the *Manchester Guardian*; Bill Grundy, who became a mainstay of Granada Television; and John Dekker, later a leading editor at BBC Current Affairs in London. Blake chose them because they were independent-minded, questioning, blunt and unimpressed by authority. If by his own reckoning the programme did not always deliver the edginess he demanded, it never sounded complacent.

For me it was an eye-opener editorially and as a lesson in interviewing. Every item had to have an angle, a purpose, some surprise. Every interview involved challenge, the unexpected, the different angle of attack. The programme was always correct but never merely polite. Bryan gave me work, always kept me involved and sternly criticised a programme he allowed me to edit for 'sounding incredibly bourgeois'. He was right.

I learned too from listening to the Grundy, Redhead, Dekker style of attacking interview. I realised how far short my own interview technique fell below theirs. I knew I had to get better at adding attack to my technique. My broadcasting ego suffered, but that was undoubtedly necessary in the interests of career realism. Most editions of the programme on Thursday evening ended with a lengthy alcoholic post-mortem in the BBC Club. This was good for morale and for learning. I was never excluded.

In one event, I saw at first hand how close parts of the BBC could be to the authorities, especially the local police. It was not a pretty sight. A shadowy industrial story in the Trafford Park area involved police searches of workers for reasons that never became clear. When we began nosing around, the Manchester constabulary tried to stop the story by going straight to the BBC head of region. He seemed to us to be too ready to stop our enquiries at the behest of the police. Under pressure, he conceded that, provided the local press carried the story first, we could follow it up. This seemed – was – the most craven display of editorial cowardice that I could imagine. The issue disappeared but the sight of BBC vacillation in the face of authority lingered unpleasantly.

In spare evenings, I wandered around the industrial archaeology and post-industrial dereliction of Salford with my 16mm cine camera. What was I looking for, what was I reaching towards? Some social-realism response to a city in transition from its industrial heyday to what might well be terminal decline. To the south of Manor Road, the comfortable middle-class area adjoining Buile Hill Park where Annie was brought up, stretched the docks (disused), Trafford Park (virtually abandoned) and the huge area of side-by-sides and back-to-backs that constituted Hanky Park. Most had been bulldozed flat, wiping out the slum area and much else besides. It was an area razed of hope and expectation of a future. It was sad, empty, bleak and derelict, yet in the warm days of June 1961 the very ruins had a kind of beauty. I was not sentimentalising loss; I felt that something about this experience needed capturing. Did it say more about Salford or about me?

The implicit story was of waste, human, physical, environmental. I was witnessing the inevitability of loss, the absence of political will, the passivity of inaction in the face of decline. This was Britain 1961 and nobody seemed to care or have the power to act. The sun shone, children played rough cricket in the grassy borders of a school playing field or paddled in a silted-up canal. All around stretched a severed society in an impotent state. It never occurred to me that this 'state of Britain' should be part of our journalism, for we too were part of the impotence.

I completed my attachment to Manchester on 30 June. The day was hot. My talk with the head of North Region was 'frank but fair', which was probably a simple description not an evasion. The farewell from Bryan Blake and the programme team was warm. There was mutual respect on both sides. I had learned a lot and got programme-making experience I would not have got anywhere else. It was time to return to London. Five months apart from Annie had not been easy but we had survived.

And this next secondment was going to be brilliant, wasn't it? Radio Features Department in Broadcasting House was the home of programme-making originality. Its work was legendary, its staff legends in themselves. It was a place where you tripped over human landmarks, intellectual milestones. Here Douglas Cleverdon had created Dylan Thomas's *Under Milk Wood*; here Donald McWhinnie had directed Samuel Beckett's *All That Fall*; here Barbara Bray was discovering the plays of Eugène Ionesco; here the poet Louis MacNeice wrote *The Dark Tower*. What was I doing in such company? How could I possibly measure up to such achievements? I soon found out.

At least I was expected when I turned up on 12 July 1961. The medium-sized office on the Portland Place side of Broadcasting House contained a very welcoming and friendly secretary, Anita. She looked after two of the Features Department 'greats', the authority on French literature Rayner Heppenstall, and the writer David Thompson. That seemed like a crowded office. Would there be room for me? I need not have worried. Neither of them came to the office frequently, sometimes not at all for days in a row. There was also a large metal cupboard, standard BBC issue, an Aladdin's Cave of cardboard boxes containing reels of recordings on nine-inch tapes. All had been commissioned by either Thompson or Heppenstall from freelances. All were untouched from the time of their recording. It was made clear that if I edited these raw recordings into finished programmes, I would do everyone a service.

The freelance journalists involved were an odd lot. Willie Wilshaw, one of the *Guardian*'s food writers, had interviewed George Bernard Shaw's secretary, Blanche Patch, a pleasant discovery. The brilliant radio tennis commentator Max Robertson had spoken to an old sea-dog, Captain Button, though it was not clear why. The French literature scholar Joanna Richardson was to interview Tennyson's grandson, Sir Charles Tennyson, which promised some high-level literary and historical memories. Of the three freelances, Willie Wilshaw was the easiest to work with, an outgoing bon-vivant whose *Guardian* recipes shaped at least one of our own Christmas lunches and who led a major drinking session or two at The George. Max Robertson, a tense, introverted man, treated me with huge suspicion then thawed when he saw that I could be trusted with his precious material. Joanna Richardson was a lumpy broadcaster, boasted embarrassingly about her sexual exploits, but was always generous socially in introducing us to her parts of literary London. How long would their recorded tapes have mouldered at the bottom of the metal cupboard had I not turned up as keen dogsbody?

My first day at Features Department was also my first lunchtime at The George, that fabled haunt of radio creativity around the corner from Broadcasting House. It was heaving. There was the man in whose office I was camping, David Thompson, bald, with fuzzy hair at the back, thick pebble glasses, staring eyes and a hesitant manner. Later he wrote *Woodbrook*, a touching memoir of tutoring and falling in love in Ireland, and a study of myths surrounding seals. (On one occasion he proposed making a radio feature on 'Hares in Ireland' which turned out to be about 'Rats in Sweden'. It was that kind of place.) At the other end of the bar stood the great documentary maker René Cutforth, who had shocked our initial radio training course by saying that the reason he worked for the BBC was the money. There was John Davenport, the critic, Newton Blick, the actor, and there too was my Cambridge contemporary, the brilliant Anthony Firth, working for the commercial company Associated Television and talking of ambitions for an entirely new style of programme mixing political comment and satire – unheard of then. The air was thick with cigarettes, booze and brilliance. As if the normal licensed drinking hours, 11 a.m. to 3 p.m., were not enough, the hardened producers, and that meant all the male ones, continued to the nearby 'ML', the private Marie Lloyd Club, where drinking could and did continue for several hours.

The headiness came off that first experience at The George when, later in the lunchtime session, I was introduced to a true Features veteran, Francis 'Jack' Dillon. Aged, croaking and well tanked up – (when was he not?) – he spotted me as a young, uptight, conventional public-school man and therefore a legitimate target. Probing me on what I wanted to do with myself, he ruthlessly mocked everything I said in reply. I was fair game. I would have to learn to do better in such exchanges. It was a fact of life, of the BBC that was quite new. I had wanted the atmosphere of creativity; this was it.

That evening I watched and heard the still utterly conventional side of much broadcasting at a live transmission of *Monday Night at Home* presented by the *Punch* writer, Basil Boothroyd. Like Freddie Grisewood in Bristol, Boothroyd was a reactionary personality. The programme was a security blanket for the untroubled middle classes. I hated it and went to bed very tired. The day had offered me two sides of a very confused organisation. Which was the true BBC? The wildly, often self-indulgently creative side of the programme makers in The George, or the decaying, 'playing it safe', Grisewood/Boothroyd school? It could never be the latter, surely? Why would I be interested if it were?

In fact the Features Department treated me very fairly. Tidy editing of neglected programmes – not difficult – led to early broadcasts. My name was on the credits on air. They accepted my proposal to study Joan Littlewood's Theatre Workshop, which got me to most of its luminaries from Wolf Mankowitz, to Roy Kinnear, Frank Norman, Miriam Karlin, Glynn Edwards, Meier Tzelniker, John Bury and others. Daringly, I had no narrator; one voice linked naturally into the next. It was partially successful. Another commission about success and failure in top-level sport took me to giants such as the England fast bowler Frank Tyson, the grand-prix driver Stirling Moss, the first runner of the four-minute mile, Roger Bannister, and the Wimbledon champion Angela Mortimer. I was discovering that the BBC's call opened doors.

The work routine became established. Recording, planning or editing in the morning; drinking in The George at lunchtime; sleep in the office afterwards, all part of 'another slightly unreal week at Features'. It would be too easy to dismiss the rackety, alcohol-fuelled life of most of the Features producers as irresponsible. That would be to judge them, their work and their time by today's bureaucratic, managerial and puritanical standards. It would miss the point too. My exact BBC and university contemporary, John Tydeman, insists that this group of producers was individually and collectively inventive; that they pioneered the 'creative radio feature' which then heavily influenced the making of TV documentaries; and that no other country ever created such work in its broadcasting tradition.

More importantly still, Tydeman insists that fear of 'risk' was not part of the editorial outlook. If an idea was original it was bound to be risky; without risk there could be no creativity. Today producers and managers are shackled by the practice of 'risk analysis'. Risk has to be weighed – in advance – predicted – in advance – and permitted or not permitted – in advance. Nothing could be more damaging to the necessary engagement with real artistic risk in the creative process. The Third Programme had to live with a risk mentality, not as something to be wary of but as something to nourish and cherish. Yes, it was another world, but a genuinely innovative one as a result. As to the drinking? On one occasion, so I am told, the head of Radio Features, Laurence Gilliam, found me in the office. 'What are you doing sitting in your office?' he said. 'You should be in the pub with the writers and producers!' Gilliam was surely right; ideas are to be found in the world outside, not in BBC offices or along today's serried ranks of computer workstations.

The active social life in the evenings based on Features and Drama departments' endless capacity to throw parties formed part of Annie's own induction into London. A series of very squiffy, ageing radio producers, especially the notorious Bob Pocock, competed for the opportunity of pinching her bottom. She felt besmirched and irritated but coped; sexual harassment had not then been invented.

What of the BBC top brass? Two incidents demonstrated their limitations. A distinguished Edinburgh sociologist, Tom Burns, interviewed me for a book he was writing about the BBC. As we walked along a corridor to his room, a figure approached from the opposite direction and, with head oddly tilted to one side, scuttled past without any acknowledgement. I whispered to Tom: 'That's Howard Newby, Controller of the Third Programme! But he is very shy!' Tom grinned: 'You would be surprised how many senior BBC people have been described in that way!' I was shocked. How could he, a fine novelist and considerable intellect, hold a position of authority and hide behind a convenient cloak of shyness?

The second occasion was odder. On 31 August 1961, our crop of General Trainees was summoned for tea with the Controller of Personnel, J. H. Arkell, no less. This promised to be awesome. The teapot and the tray were silver, the tea service good-quality porcelain. A waitress complete with black dress, frilly pinny and headdress stood in attendance while the Controller himself poured the tea. The conversation was stiff, never better than general. He asked nothing of us, what we believed, what we hoped for, even why we were interested in the BBC.

He in turn offered nothing to improve our understanding of why the BBC might be a great institution, why public-service broadcasting was a great ideal. As he maundered, we noticed that he had offered no milk for our tea. Soon, it was too late to ask. Arkell himself noticed nothing. We stood up to go, our untouched tea cups filled with cold, unmilked, unsugared tea. Our genteel collective behaviour was too depressing, as was his own lack of awareness. Were we supposed to learn from people like him?

Apart from tidying up other producers' cast-off piles, beyond the Theatre Workshop and sports personality programmes I made a programme based on material collected by David Tutaev about a German diplomat, the local consul Gerhard Wolf, who saved the city of Florence from destruction by the retreating Wehrmacht in 1944. Wolf was a quiet, unassuming man, decency personified, who mustered the moral courage to face down German military commanders who seemed bent on razing Florence as they retreated.

In my own two programmes about the German resistance to Hitler culminating in the July 1944 Bomb Plot, moral courage unto death was there for all to see. One of the plotters, Axel von dem Bussche, a former young Wehrmacht officer, was alive to tell his story. In 1944 he was to parade a new kind of battle-field uniform for the Führer to inspect. Von dem Bussche and his resistance friends had packed the uniform with explosive. When Hitler came to inspect, von dem Bussche would clasp the Führer around the chest and blow them both up. At the last minute, Hitler cancelled the entire parade. The opportunity never repeated itself. Von dem Bussche had an intense but quiet spiritual calm of a wholly unshowy kind. He claimed no moral credit for offering to sacrifice his life. What he felt was a profound sense of personal failure that his offer of sacrifice had not shortened the war and saved millions of lives.

Such encounters were among the joys and privileges of working in BBC Radio Features. They were not small. What was missing was advice or instruction of any kind. All around me was an accumulated mass of editorial and production ex-perience. I was offered no creative father-figure, no adviser, no mentor, no one who would gently deflect me from the elemen-tary errors of my inexperience. I was after all a trainee; I did gain experience, I did learn on the job. But teaching, advice, the offer of guidance came there none.

It was not surprising that after some unfulfilling months on the fringes of the world of television (see Chapter 7) I decided that BBC External Services at Bush House was the place for my long-term career. I got a job as producer, current affairs in Overseas Talks and Features, and began my full-time, estab-lished, pensionable BBC career in the autumn of 1962.

The next three and a bit years were intense as events like the Cuban Missile Crisis of October 1962 threatened the very world we lived in. On the night of Jack Kennedy's speech warning of nuclear retaliation on the Soviet Union if a mis-sile attack came from the Soviet-installed missiles in Cuba, Annie and I clung together in the bathroom of our house in Pimlico listening horror-struck to the President. During the night, woken by the noise of traffic on the Embankment, I was convinced it was the start of the London population's exodus to avoid nuclear extinction. As dawn broke and horses' hooves echoed around the streets, the habitual morning exercise of the Royal Horse Artillery took on a more ominous militaristic sound. Were troops being deployed around London? Some of our friends did leave town in the following days and took refuge in remote Welsh cottages. The relief amounting to in-credulity as the prospect of nuclear Armageddon receded ten days later was overwhelming.

Working at Bush House from the end of 1962 brought me face to face with the great events of our time. In January 1963, France's President de Gaulle took his most loftily dismissive view of the nature of Britain's engagement with Europe. He proclaimed that Britain under Prime Minister Harold Macmil-lan was still wedded to the United States and the Atlantic. It was therefore temperamentally unfit to be part of the European

Community. Could Britain become a member? De Gaulle's answer was to the point: 'Non!' It was a tremendous blow to the British body politic.

In October I was sent to cover the Conservative Party Conference in Blackpool with a distinguished academic political pundit, Dr Norman Hunt of Exeter College, Oxford. Normally on the BBC World Service, domestic UK politics, even a governing party conference, would have been judged worthy of a daily five-minute *Commentary* and a discussion with two MPs. That was all the world audience needed to know on the subject. On the eve of this conference, events took over. As I drove to Blackpool on 8 October 1963, the BBC *Ten O'Clock News* reported that Harold Macmillan had fallen sick with a prostate condition, had been advised that his recovery would be lengthy and so would resign immediately. In effect, the Blackpool Conference would determine his successor as Prime Minister.

The politicking took place unfettered around the conference floor. The lobbies and foyers of the pastiche nineteenth-century Victorian Winter Gardens, Blackpool are unique. Exotic and ridiculous in equal measure, the Empress Ballroom was at their heart. It was a place for drama and political theatre of the highest kind. The entire Blackpool setting was endearingly fake. The main dining room at the Imperial Hotel, with its extruded plastic moulded cornices, niches and alcoves, was universally called the 'Louis Plastique'. Having a second-sitting dinner there with Norman Hunt on BBC expenses – Robin Day and his heavies had commanded the first sitting – felt like a professional milestone.

On 10 October, political fever boiled over. Lord Hailsham, the former Quintin Hogg, announced at a packed fringe meeting dripping with anticipation and emotion that he would renounce his peerage and stand as candidate for the party leadership and premiership. Blackpool erupted. These were uncharted waters. His deputy, Rab Butler, should have been the obvious successor to Macmillan, yet Rab made no attempt to woo the party, the delegates or the conference but stayed remote and aloof in his official rooms at the grandiose Imperial Hotel.

On the closing Saturday, the traditional party rally, Rab Butler finally emerged from his lair in the Imperial. He delivered not a rallying call, not a seizure of power, nor a claim to be Macmillan's heir. It was a damp squib. Whoever would head the Tory Party, it would not be him. Later, it was seized by the 'quiet man', Sir Alec Douglas-Home. But as a case study of failing to seize power when all it needed was the outstretched hand of determination, this could not have been bettered.

The greatest international drama was yet to come. One Friday evening in November I was having a drink in the BBC Club with my colleague Raymond Barker, the senior producer and authority on US politics. We had just recorded the *Commentary* for late evening as well as the early-morning *Commentary* for the next day. The atmosphere at another week's end was pleasantly relaxed. Then sensational news began to filter through to the BBC Club. In those days, there were no mobile phones, no rolling TV news. Somebody was said to have shot President Kennedy. Shot at or shot dead? It was not clear. The next scheduled broadcast of a *Commentary* was just over an hour away; it had to comment on this world-changing event.

By the time Raymond and I had rushed back to our offices, Kennedy had been pronounced dead. Any political assassination was awful; the murder of this American president was tragedy on an epic scale. We decided that Raymond and I would script four and a half minutes together and Raymond would voice it live, the first measured assessment of a unique tragedy from the BBC External Services in London. As Raymond sat at the typewriter and I crouched by his side, we were in a state of shock. Pitching the tone and substance of the commentary was almost impossible. We knew so little; there were very few facts. Who was responsible for the assassination? What were the politics? Could it be a Soviet hitman taking Moscow's revenge on Kennedy for the humiliation of Cuba? Was it a crazed right-winger? Together, tentative thought by thought, stumbling, keeping a tenuous hold on the known, avoiding the sensational, the overly speculative, we pieced the *Commentary* together. Forty-five minutes later, when the studio green light flashed for him to start, Raymond's voice was steady. It was, as I think I recall, a decent professional cut at a world-shaking event based on incredibly few known facts. We were too shattered to be proud of what we had done. I rang Annie to ask if she could stretch supper to include Raymond? Of course she did. Two small veal escalopes did service for three. We all deserved that.

As satisfying professionally as work was at the External Services, it was relentless and demanding. In the first year of our marriage, I had been away from home for five months. Life became richer and more complex with the birth of our first child, a son, Sash, on 3 July 1962. He appeared after a dramatic early-morning emergency caesarean operation at the Westminster Hospital. Everything else was normal thereafter but the nature of the operation in those days left Annie recovering in hospital for two weeks. The following year I was incorrectly advised to have an unnecessary operation on a non-acute condition. It took me three weeks to recover. Some combination of these factors which I could never explain or understand led to a recurring cycle of infections, flu-like outbreaks and general debilitation. Even my loyal boss, Gerry Mansell, enquired sympathetically if I was up to the strains of the job. I almost wondered myself.

Annie and I went to Corsica on a kind of convalescent holiday in May 1964. Surely all the debilitating dramas and niggles of the previous six months would now fade away. On our return, we rang Annie's parents for news of how they had coped with the infant Sash. It was awful. One day he had convulsed, going stiff as a ramrod. His grandmother was appalled and blamed herself. That was nonsense, but we were shocked by the inexplicable seizure. Even the academic experts at Westminster

Children's Hospital were puzzled. They offered no diagnosis, but equally no reassurance.

The year came to a journalistic climax at the British General Election in October 1964. I must have established myself as a competent studio interviewer because I was asked to chair the overnight election results programme on the World Service. It was modest by the standards of the domestic radio or television operation, but it was the most extensive live broadcast I had ever had to anchor. Not content with the political cliff-hanger unfolding with Labour edging past the Conservatives, world events erupted throughout the night. First came the sensational overthrow of the Soviet leader, Nikita Khrushchev, closely followed by news of a Chinese nuclear test explosion. Global politics, superpower relations, Britain's political future – it made a perfect Bush House brew of interconnected events. As dawn broke and LSE's professors streamed across the road to our studios, the free range of high-grade minds knitting patterns and interpreting the night's epic events was exhilarating and unforgettable. For what was judged my 'exceptional work' on a night of broadcasting I received a bonus of £30.

That weekend we took a delayed but needed holiday. It had elements of farce and anxiety; farce because going to the Costa Brava in late October was foolish; anxiety because Annie was pregnant and a holiday was the last we could take before the baby was due the following February; anxiety too because we did not know what had caused Sash's convulsions. Besides, the Costa Brava was chilly, empty, shops and restaurants were closing all around us. John Drummond joined us and his nightly trawls through the gay bars proved decreasingly successful. So, a pregnant Annie, a frustrated Drummond, an undiagnosed toddler Sash, traumatised by three weeks in a hospital cot with just two hours' visiting time each day, an exhausted me – what a prescription for a holiday. A fortnight after our return, Westminster Children's Hospital rang to say that Sash's convulsions were probably caused by occasional localised pressure between the skull and the brain but that he would grow out of it. Our relief was enormous. Life returned to its normal levels of complexity.

Our second child, Francis, was born on 7 February 1965. Two weeks later, I left on my first overseas programme-making tour. In a four-week absence I would cover the whole of the Malaysian Federation, which then included Singapore. It was a big opportunity for me, putting a huge strain on Annie. She never complained.

The Federation was suffering from Indonesia's *Konfrontasi*, 'confrontation' or general nuisance-making short of all-out war but including guerrilla engagements in the Borneo jungles bordering Sarawak and Indonesia. For President Sukarno, Malaysia was a British 'neo-colonialist' construction, a creature of what he dismissed as *oldefo* – or 'old declining forces' – which would meet their match in the ranks of *nefo* – or 'new emerging forces' – such as Indonesia. The proliferating jargon surrounding the so-called 'new internationalist world order' was as bizarre as it was nonsensical.

I flew in a BOAC jet, the de Havilland Comet. It had a worrying record of mysteriously breaking up in mid-air because of initially undiagnosed metal fatigue. This aircraft was the heavily modified model with a limited range. The route from London involved stops at Zurich, Cairo, Teheran, Delhi, Colombo and finally Kuala Lumpur. This was the best long-distance travel could do. It gave a strong sense of actually journeying, with each stop providing a direct encounter with the local climate. The wave of humidity as the aircraft doors opened in Colombo was particularly overwhelming.

I met dozens of politicians from every Malaysian community, mastered the huge number of diverse and acronymically complex political parties, travelled to the elusive line of 'confrontation' with Indonesia in the Sarawak jungles and ended up with three thoroughly competent radio documentaries. One result of the trip was that I fell in love with South-East Asia and travelled there annually for more than a decade.

Shortly after my return from the four-week absence, the

several-week-old baby produced alarming symptoms. Francis vomited his milk, not just a slurp of a vomit but a great long-distance jet. Originally, the Westminster Children's Hospital refused to diagnose a serious condition. 'Mother' was called in by the fully starched Matron to demonstrate that 'she knew how to breastfeed Baby'! (In 1965, the great Westminster Children's Hospital was both authoritarian and patronising.) Annie duly fed Francis under Matron's watchful, critical and suspicious eye. The feed seemed to go normally; Matron began to look smug. Moments later, Baby projectile-vomited several feet across the room, covering Matron's starched apron – but not her starched face – in undigested breast milk. It was the only partly funny moment in an intensely worrying period.

With the diagnosis of pyloric stenosis confirmed beyond a doubt, the hospital swung into its clinical best. A standard operation involved making a small nick in a constricted duct leading out of the stomach. Standard it might be, but the patient was an eight-week-old baby! It worked; Francis thrived. Later Annie and I reflected that NHS emergency intervention probably saved both our sons' lives.

These home dramas took place against the background of intense work at Bush House. I had become an international affairs nerd. Beyond the three Malaysia features, the customary OTF responsibilities involved making thirty editions of *The World Today*, chairing fourteen half-hour discussion programmes and half a dozen 'one-offs' including a profile of North Vietnam's Ho Chi Minh. One remarkable programme was not broadcast. Philip Whitehead, who later became a Labour MP, was a General Trainee. For his TV programme exercise, the intensely political Philip wanted to interview the British Fascist leader, Sir Oswald Mosley. There was an absolute BBC ban on broadcasting Mosley because of his politics. Philip argued that this would be a closed-circuit exercise, it would never be broadcast but the BBC would have in its archives something that might be useful after Mosley's death. Whitehead's managers agreed to the proposal but surrounded it with cast-iron restrictions.

As a training exercise with virtually no budget, Philip asked me and two other young producers to form the interviewing panel and 'give Mosley a hard time!'. In the event he made mincemeat of us, swatting away our questions with absolute aplomb. He was very clever; he knew far more than we did; he had answered such questions a hundred times. What we hadn't reckoned on was his charm! With the recording over, as we licked our journalistic wounds, Mosley was surrounded by the entire studio crew and programme team. He held court. We stood transfixed, beguiled by his easy manner. Here was the Blackshirt ogre of the 1930s who supported Adolf Hitler and Nazi Germany, who might have run a Nazi-imposed government in England. What did we see? A sophisticated man of intelligence, style and humour. Visitors to Hitler before the war often spoke of his charm too. There were many lessons to be drawn from the experience, the most important being 'never underestimate your enemy'!

Despite this intense activity, I looked at the future without interest or joy. I was a member of BBC staff, with a guarantee of a lifetime of work and a BBC pension at the end. Many envied this; in 1966 it was indeed enviable. But what I saw was a steady, slow and safe climb through an unimaginative editorial and managerial hierarchy, to what? Head of Department by, say, forty, Channel Controller by fifty, early retirement at fifty-five? Much as I loved the External Services, this was a dreary prospect. I had little time for most of those filling the hierarchical posts above me. Why hang on for years in the hope of showing that I could do better? My zest, energy and drive would have gone long before I might be in a position to make a difference. That was no sort of future.

Besides, I was enjoying studio microphone work more and more. How could I develop a career in that direction? I mentioned my frustrations and anxieties to a close colleague, the Yugoslav-born journalist, Krsto ('Chris') Cviic. He had just got a longed-for staff job in the World Service (English) and had recently turned down a post editing an American-funded,

London-based agency, Forum World Features, syndicating news features worldwide. Chris and I both knew the Chairman of the agency, a former *Economist* writer and regular Bush House contributor, Brian Crozier. Chris thought it might offer a way out of my BBC frustrations. I went to meet Crozier and we seemed to see eye to eye. I would have a decent salary; the range of work was similar in its international scope to that at Bush; it provided a solid base for developing a freelance broadcasting career. It offered a good way of jumping, so I thought, from the ultra-security of the BBC to a life of flexible working. I was to be sadly disillusioned.

When I broke the news that I was resigning from the BBC, my colleagues were aghast, my superiors slack-jawed. Wasn't I a BBC man through and through, an elite General Trainee, one of the chosen? How could I take the financial risk, the career risk, the reputational risk? In all the talk surrounding my decision, nobody tried to dissuade me by suggesting a more exciting career route through the BBC. It did not, I think, exist. The BBC was a great traditional organisation fixed in its ways without much sense of how it needed to change. At 3.30 p.m. on 28 January 1966 I had my standard farewell BBC tea party in Room 338 Centre Block, Bush House. It was a stiff affair, a couple of dozen colleagues and superiors standing uncomfortably in a circle, teacups awkwardly balanced, well-meaning and friendly formulae tripping from official lips. I felt I was breaking out. I suspected that some in the room envied my leap to freedom. I was free, would be decently paid, with the time to freelance as a broadcaster.

Yet I had at least one pair of fingers crossed behind my back as I began work at Forum World Features' offices at Kern House in Kingsway overlooking Lincoln's Inn Fields. It was public knowledge that it was funded by the US publisher of the *International Herald Tribune*, John ('Jock') Hay Whitney. It was openly part of the Congress for Cultural Freedom (CCF), an organisation devoted to campaigning intellectually against communist beliefs and ideology, especially in the nations of the developing, non-aligned Third World. Its most powerful instrument was the monthly magazine *Encounter*, recognised as a 'journal of combat', edited by the poet Stephen Spender and widely admired. Forum World Features was part of that stable. It seemed an eminently respectable home.

I was thoroughly vetted by CCF before taking over, including an interview in Paris with the Secretary General, Josef Jossellson. That was normal enough and nothing in his questioning spoke of the need to follow a particular or general ideological line. In reality, that was one of their Congress's more adept stratagems to demonstrate its political independence.

Forum was, interestingly, generously staffed. Crozier was Chairman, though absent in Madrid writing his biography of the Spanish dictator, General Franco; the Sri Lankan journalist Tarzie Vittachi was Director; I was Editor. In addition we had a business manager, a librarian-researcher and two secretary/PAs. All were on decent salaries. This staff produced four articles a fortnight and two 800-word briefings. I was busy commissioning and editing. Were the others actually fully engaged in other activity? I was too polite to ask. Matters came to a head during 1967, towards the end of my second year. Several of my commissions were criticised for being 'anti-American'. Was I 'reliable'? One morning, the American business manager came into my room, leaned on my desk in a friendly way and put what he saw as the killer question: 'John, tell me this! What do you think of NATO?' I had no difficulty replying positively but was startled at the naïvety of the question. Was it some kind of loyalty test?

Soon rumours began in the United States. The Congress for Cultural Freedom was, it turned out, actually a CIA front organisation, its funding of Forum World Features channelled through Whitney's *International Herald Tribune* as a cover. Despite the revelation, many said that they did not care how the monthly *Encounter* had been funded; it had been a first-class magazine of intellectual debate. For my part, I had the satisfaction of knowing that I had commissioned nothing that had an official 'pro-Western' line, still less a CIA line.

I felt oddly shocked by the revelation. Several of my colleagues must have been CIA officers. They had not deceived me; I had fooled myself. My calculated career-path risk had almost exploded in my face. I spoke freely to journalists who swarmed to write the story of the CIA's 'subversion' of intellectual freedom. I had nothing to hide, none of the articles suggested I had. My freelance career with the BBC was wholly undamaged, though I often thought myself fortunate to have emerged unscathed professionally.

My two years with Forum World Features proved to be an uncomfortable, ill-fitting pendant to the previous formative five years in the BBC. For the first seven years of my working life, I had devoted myself to the world outside Britain. It was time for my focus to alter, to start an intellectual integration with the country of which I was a citizen. And it was time to stop seeing myself as in any way foreign. My first period of learning, about myself, about broadcasting, about the BBC, about life, was now surely over. It was time to start delivering.

Breaking Through

The Newsnight *Years 1979–86*

As a journalist and broadcaster in the 1960s, there was only one place to be in the broadcasting firmament – in television. It was important in a way inconceivable today. There was so little television that its rarity, its exclusiveness, made it both desirable and powerful. After all, there were only two national TV channels, the BBC and ITV. BBC Two appeared only in 1964. The satellite multi-channel world was a generation away. Watching television was an important social and family experience and method of political and social communication. No matter that the sets were small, the picture often unstable and in flickering black and white – what could colour images add, it was said, to meaning and understanding? No matter that much of it looked crude and amateurish, the cardboard studio sets visibly wobbling, the news staid and conventional, the accents and appearances of the presenters coming from another era, much of the interviewing clumsy and deferential, the panel games genteel and laughably laboured. No matter! Television was new, it was different, it transformed every home. Professionally, a career in television meant fame, fortune, public recognition of a wholly new kind.

Radio by comparison seemed and sounded stodgy, complacent, burdened by a history that weighed it down with lead boots. It feared for the future, peering anxiously at new phenomena such as 'listening on the car radio', which was distrusted but could not be prevented. Editorial attitudes were defensive, backward-looking, set for inevitable decline. Yet radio was where I had started, where I learned my journalism. The only place where I had wanted to learn it had been at the General Overseas Service of the BBC (which I much later renamed 'BBC World Service'). But the forbidden fruit of television hung tantalisingly, demanding to be nibbled. I kept returning for more.

As one of the series of three-monthly secondments that were the prescribed pattern for the BBC's two-year-long General Trainee scheme, I had begged to go to television, anywhere for any purpose. I wanted work that would appear on that small and magic screen. During my two years of secondments from 1960 to 1962, I watched Allan Tyrer, the legendary film editor of the BBC's arts and culture programme *Monitor*, painstakingly assemble some of the great statements of arts television. I watched but did not make. The programme editor did not suggest that I should look for a job with them. I had observed, but what had I learned?

I watched the deputy editor of the groundbreaking nightly magazine programme *Tonight*, Tony Essex, view rough cuts of a report. He seized the 35mm film and the magnetic sound tape in both hands and tore them apart before joining the fragments with paper clips for the film editor to stick them together correctly. The visceral and exhilarating precision with which Tony Essex worked was an eye-opener, film editing at its most physical and ferocious. I made no programmes for *Tonight*. The editor, Alasdair Milne, did not encourage me to look for a job on *Tonight*. I was present during the editorial process; would I ever be part of it?

I shot some mini-drama inserts for studio-based and very worthy schools TV programmes – but was not asked to stay. Sinking to the bottom of the TV/film world, I was sent to a tiny TV film unit connected with Bush House which made minuscule news featurettes for a handful of minor foreign TV news stations. Even they did not seem to think that my future career might lie in those obscure offices and projects. They did me a kindness. I had seen television at its best and it was way above my head or existing capabilities. I should concentrate on learning my journalistic trade in radio. I began to make a decent reputation and slightly precarious living as a freelance radio journalist from 1966 onwards.

Despite this, as my experience in radio grew, the siren calls of television would not go away. In late 1968, I started reporting and co-presenting BBC Two's *The Money Programme*, a lively engagement with the then growing field of finance and business journalism. I seized the opportunity of the catastrophic fire at the newly opened Maltings concert hall at Snape in Aldeburgh to cover Benjamin Britten and Peter Pears's fundraising tour of New York and Boston. This was stretching the editorial envelope of the *Money Programme* considerably. It would not be the last time that I nudged a programme's editorial priorities. When I caught up with Britten at his home, the Red House in Aldeburgh, he was uneasy and distracted. We were after all stopping him from composing, as he made clear in so many words. He was an uncomfortable person, on edge throughout. But he answered with candour, honesty and just enough patience. On the US trip itself, Peter Pears by contrast was open, charming and welcoming. This was getting close to my ideal – television, travel, the arts – a wonderful combination.

I visited Central Java to see the first rice-producing 'green revolution' in progress. Flying in a Pilatus crop sprayer, we played catch-as-catch-can with some huge fruit bats. I profiled the legendary Indian business dynasty, the Birlas, at work and at play, early portents of the new India's fabulously moneyed middle class. The finance behind stallions at stud in Newmarket took me and my director, Sally Doganis, into different territory and the stirring sight of a stallion 'covering' a mare. For a Christmas edition, I was sent up and down Bond Street to indulge in vicarious – and mythical – 'luxury' shopping. Sad to say, stepping into a Jensen Interceptor wearing a full-length fur coat felt absurdly pleasurable. Some of the television myth was attaching itself to me. In the tail end of the Swinging Sixties, my suits were sharp, my sideburns long, my self-image unreal. Not for nothing did the programme team call me 'Trendy Tusa'.

The Money Programme was polite about my relatively substantial items. But mainly I was confined to lighter or 'novelty' items further down the programme. Finance was interpreted very broadly; I recall one item about a maker of novelty jokes in Preston, a humorous man whose most successful lines were cat and dog turds shaped in plastic ultra-realism – 'Mucky Puss' and 'Mucky Poop', he proudly called them. I addressed the riveting question of the costs of re-labelling every item in a major hotel inventory when the Carlton Tower Hotel in Sloane Square changed its name to the 'SonEsta' to satisfy the owners' personal vanity. Today we would describe it as the 'costs of rebranding'. Another examined the pile of trivial goods and objects to be acquired through Green Shield stamps by stopping for petrol at every station between London and Southend-on-Sea. It made a pretty sight in the studio.

But the main presenters, Brian Widlake and Alan Watson, carried the substance of the programme's journalism, the heavyweight interviews, the economic and business analysis. Editorially, this was sound; although I was a good interviewer, Widlake and Watson were more experienced; they knew more about the City. But playing third fiddle on a weekly programme in television was not what I had in mind.

Other, more oblique lessons were absorbed and stored for possible future use. The programme was loosely budgeted – an overspend seemed not to matter very much. Provided the audience figures were good, which they were, meeting the budget was of secondary importance. Indeed, good audiences and a hefty overspend appeared to be necessary formulae for BBC promotion.

I nagged the head of Current Affairs, John Grist, for something mainstream, something really significant – *Panorama*, no doubt! Grist said I wasn't ready for it. What about the nightly, mass-audience, popular, populist *Nationwide*? he enquired. He was right about the first, but how could he have suggested the second? My own alarm bells should have been ringing continuously! I, whose bread and butter had been the more obscure corners of South-East Asian politics, was to join a programme whose family teatime staple was skateboarding ducks. (They were in truth very funny.)

I ignored my inner alarm bells. I bade farewell to my loyal, long-term friends and producers at Broadcasting House and Bush House and indicated that, for me, fame and fortune beckoned from the television studios of West London, from the home of BBC journalism itself: Lime Grove in Shepherd's Bush. If my colleagues had doubts about the wisdom of my chosen path they kept very quiet. My diary shows Tuesday, 28 July 1970 as my first programme on *Nationwide*. Ten years from joining the BBC, I was there on the brink, the national television screen. Wasn't this what I was intended for?

The first disappointment came immediately. I was not to present the main segment of *Nationwide*, the part that united a nation over the supper table. The avuncular Michael Barratt with the warm, burry accent and voice presided over evening family viewing. No, I was to present the 'South-East Opt Out', the regional variant seen only in London and the South-East. It had a large audience to be sure, but the topics were those deemed suitable for a regional audience with local preoccupations.

My horizons and perspectives shrank by the day. Presenting an item on hairpieces because I was already losing my hair seemed a pleasant joke. Could I not raise a smile at my incipient baldness? Interviewing a baby, tame-ish cheetah from Chessington Zoo – or rather its keeper – was remote from cross-examining politicians or international statesmen. The cub's purr was reassuring, its playful claw flexing into my upper thighs less so. When I was asked to present an item from a sauna, then a fashionable element of the 'home desirable', wearing only a sauna towel, common sense prevailed, sanity broke through. I resigned with almost immediate effect. (I kept

the two sauna towels.) My diary shows Wednesday, 2 December 1970 as my last appearance on *Nationwide* – South-East
Opt Out. How did I last that long?

Not long after, when my absence from the screen began to be
noticed, a friendly local post office counter clerk asked cheerily: 'Been given the "clickety-clack", have you?' I replied rather
stiffly: 'No, I resigned.' I am sure he had his doubts as I cashed
in the children's family allowances to pay for the weekend
shopping. My regret is not negotiating at least a three-month
termination period to re-establish my ruptured journalistic
career. My editor friends would not have been unsympathetic.
Perhaps I just wanted to be shot of a disastrous error and was
ready to pay for it without knowing how I would.

Professionally, I had been well treated by the programme
team. They fondly called me their resident 'sea-green intellectual', though the journalism hardly needed one. The editor,
Michael 'Tiger' Townson, a blunt, no-nonsense news man of
a traditional kind, must have wondered how he came to be
landed with someone with my ill-matched interests. He kept
such doubts to himself. I learned a lot from Mike about lean-
ness and economy in writing scripts and editing programmes.

Why had I made such a bad decision in the first place? Part
was frustration that my substantial journalistic knowledge and
broadcasting skills were still not recognised by television. Part
was a reasonable degree of ambition. Part was lack of realism
about my readiness for television. Surprisingly, I escaped psy-
chologically and professionally unscathed from what was a
serious misjudgement. My family was incredibly supportive
and understanding. Our eight-year-old son observed thought-
fully and wisely when allowed to watch my final appearance
that *Nationwide* was a 'comic for grown-ups'. Annie, on a
part-time teacher's salary, worried about where the money
was coming from as I had no job, no contract, no guarantee of
prospects. She (blessedly and bravely) kept her fears to herself.
In fact my radio colleagues were – yet again – very ready to
commission programmes from me as if I had never been away.

And the world of radio was changing as the BBC's new blueprint for radio, 'Broadcasting in the Seventies', tore up the old traditional networks and created Radios 1, 2, 3 and 4. The Home Service found itself transformed into BBC Radio 4. Everything changed. The formulaic *Ten O'Clock* programme was replaced by the free-flowing, more imaginative, creatively organised *The World Tonight*. The old rota was thrown away. The father figure of the new evening show, Douglas Stuart, presided five nights a week for three weeks on the trot. I was offered a whole week of presenting for the fourth week in each month. My first programme came on 1 December 1970, just two nights before my final *Nationwide*. It was a huge piece of professional good fortune. I never asked for and was never offered a formal contract of any kind, but my tacit understanding with producers was that I would cover for Douglas Stuart's absences for some fifteen weeks in the year. They honoured that understanding for a decade.

Broadcasting on the BBC World Service too was caught up in the revolutionary slipstream of 'Broadcasting in the Seventies'. If the new Radio 4 presented news and current affairs in the streamlined formats of news 'sequences', so would Bush House. In October 1972, I started a weekly routine of presenting a mid-morning news and analysis programme on the World Service. A year later, I began a regular autumn schedule of reporting from the British party political and trade union conferences. This offered a further four weeks of solid, rewarding work completing a portfolio of substantial broadcasting which was personally and financially satisfying. It was to be my pattern of work for the next five years.

With new ideas breathing life into radio, a wide range of work was on offer. Was it not a good place to be for a lengthy radio career? Yet I still only played second fiddle to Douglas Stuart on *The World Tonight*. Wide as my interests and range had become, I felt marginalised, my professionalism unrecognised. I was pushing forty; most reputations in television were well established by that age. Journalists several years younger were already recognised screen personalities. Would it be too late for a major change of career? Was I missing the professional boat of television altogether?

But television too was changing and my years of contacts in radio were to pay off. In the 1970s, television and radio stood aloof from one another within the BBC. Managers, editors and journalists in television did not bother to conceal a well-nigh total feeling of superiority towards radio. Yet some editors in radio did manage to leap across from Broadcasting House at Oxford Circus to Television Centre at Shepherd's Bush in West London. One of these, Chris Capron, knew me from Radio 4. Planning a new weekly TV programme of current affairs analysis for BBC Two, he was looking for fresh presenters and reporters on the screen to suit the more analytical, studio-based format he had in mind. Capron invited me to audition and I went to TV Centre to present some dummy scripts.

My main anxiety was over my facial twitch. I do not recall worrying about it when in the studio for *The Money Programme* or *Nationwide*. I have, I think, never 'twitched' on screen. But I was worried about that studio 'screen test' at 3 p.m. on 14 September 1978 in News Studio N2 at TV Centre. Somehow this one really counted. I concentrated fiercely without turning my face into immobile wood. I used every trick of voice production, voice colour, every piece of breath control to show that the usually sterile activity of reading a script into a TV camera could be done with expression and intelligence. Immediately after the screen test, I met the future editor of *Newsweek*, Peter Ibbotson. We seemed to speak the same language about subjects, ideas, programmes and what was important in TV journalism. A few days later, Chris Capron rang to say they wanted me as one of three presenters on BBC Two's new *Newsweek* programme. I was relieved but not surprised. For the third time, the television door swung open. Would it truly open or would it only lead to another dead end?

When the new team for *Newsweek* gathered at TV Centre

on Monday, October 16, it felt congenial. The main presenter, Richard Kershaw, was clever, strikingly handsome, and stacked with years of international experience, especially in Africa. He had television glamour streaming out of him. David Jessel was a formidable radio journalist with a sharp turn of phrase, an original mind and an engagingly quirky approach to subjects. The editor, Peter Ibbotson, had a systematic mind, formidable knowledge of domestic and international news and a determination to apply clear-headed analysis to the most complex of questions. The resulting programme was, in current television argot, 'cool'; it did not carry the emotional heat that 'good' television was deemed to generate.

In truth, *Newsweek* operated at the worthy end of the broadcasting spectrum, making programmes that were useful but never revelatory. I made one on the subject of 'Federalism' which involved a pleasant trip to Switzerland, a near-fatal road accident and a virtually incomprehensible result. Other programmes followed on Italian politics, cross-border economic cooperation in Ireland, the use of referendums and the plight of refugees from Vietnam. The only one I recall with satisfaction reported on India's research into higher-yielding varieties of wheat in Hyderabad. The notion that the country might find a way out of rural famine was sufficient to justify a whole programme. Most of it was filmed in India; the studio element was very small; that may be why I remember it with affection.

It's possible that my memory of mere worthiness is selectively unfair. In its format, *Newsweek* reflected the first stirrings of unease at the way domestic BBC presented information, analysis and comment to audiences. Journalistically, the BBC was divided into two utterly separate domains. News Division, as it was invariably called, reported on what happened, who said what to whom, who did what to whom, when and why. It believed, as the US TV serial *Dragnet* parodied, in 'the facts, just the facts'. And a fact was only recognised by news when two journalistic sources reported it. Those who worked in news

were the puritans of journalism, the 'Roundheads', sniffing out
and snuffing out inaccuracy, inference, implication, innuendo
and of course any kind of bias. The process was austere, dry,
unimpeachable, and at the core of long-held BBC values. If
admirable in its way, it was increasingly detached from the
rowdy and complex world of controversy, expression and
events.

In a terrace of nineteenth-century houses in Lime Grove,
a scruffy maze of cubbyholes, rat runs and Escher-like stairs
carved out of narrow corridors, the denizens of television current affairs brooded. Driven by ideas rather than known facts,
inclined to enquiry, speculation, irreverence and hefty doses
of paranoia and conspiracy theory, they were the 'Cavaliers'
of BBC journalism. Critics said they were cavalier with the
facts. One of the most distinguished practitioners explained
effective current affairs in these words: 'You stand outside a
building; you say that inside that building something unmen-
tionable or objectionable is being plotted; you point your arm
at the building and say, "We name the guilty men!"' Half a
mile of West London back streets separated BBC News from
BBC Current Affairs. In truth they were a world apart in temperament, outlook and beliefs. It was not a healthy situation;
increasingly insiders saw that it had to change.

If *Newsweek* was an early and ultimately imperfect precursor
of such change, by the start of 1979 the younger generation of
news editors was in radical mood. For people such as George
Carey and Ron Neil, backed by the head of Current Affairs,
John Gau, the dilemma came down to this. Historically, BBC
television news was the descendant of radio news and the
printed news of Fleet Street. It was driven by the word, expressed in the word. Yet it seldom went beyond what the word
could express. Its agenda was prescribed by the predictable
formulae of the daily 'news diary' compiled at least twenty-
four hours in advance. It churned out prescribed coverage but
rarely stopped to ask the questions that followed. How I hated
its lack of curiosity, its limited view of life!

Current Affairs came from a television culture, driven by images, nurtured by ideas. Images created stories. Its practitioners were the sons and daughters of Marshall McLuhan. This was the medium of communication of the future. For good measure, Current Affairs looked down on the 'word-driven' news broadcasters, whom they regarded as irredeemably stuck in the past. Such was the gap between them.

Each had its own shortcomings. If television News was bound to events and statements but not to the surrounding narratives, Current Affairs as it then existed would indeed cover one story intensively but might do so only once before moving on. Where were the connections, the continuity of information, the ability and inclination to pursue a story as it unfolded over time? Neither News or Current Affairs as they existed addressed or answered the major issue. In George Carey's view, neither covered the story of 'how the country was run'.

In order to win support for a programme that would break known ground, Carey and Neil looked for studio presenters who were not associated with existing programme formats, who wrote their own scripts, who were authoritative journalists in their own right. They looked beyond the existing stables of known TV reporters, what Carey saw as the stereotypical 'newsreader/presenter' looking 'smooth and cool'. The programme would harness the rationality of news with the emotional immediacy of current affairs. Words and images working together would create a new synthesis in the framework of television. It would break existing moulds.

Carey's first approach was to ITN's Peter Snow, a hugely experienced, charismatic screen presence. To put a major reporter in a studio presenting role was to overturn all existing practice and expectations. At a meeting in a pub, Carey recalls that Peter saw the point immediately. The existing news and current affairs agenda in television was stuck; the new programme, to be called *Newsnight*, might launch an entirely new kind of journalism. Although it represented a considerable professional risk, Peter Snow understood the opportunity and snapped it up.

George Carey continued to look for studio presenters with something distinctive to offer. Accident then played its part, from my point of view a fortunate accident. One afternoon in the early summer of 1979 – as Carey recalls it – he switched on the TV in his office and came across a programme I was presenting. George vaguely knew my name but otherwise knew nothing of me and certainly had no idea of what I looked like on screen. What was he looking for? 'A presenter with knowledge, a presenter who would write, a presenter who had authority and expertise.' He watched for a while and decided that I was what he was looking for.

Initially I hesitated when the offer came out of the blue. I was quite comfortable on *Newsweek*. The new project was unknown and still imperfectly defined. I did not hesitate for long. Joining *Newsnight* simply changed my life. My last edition of *Newsweek* was on 21 June 1979. The first presenters' conference of *Newsnight* took place on 17 September. But when would we get on air?

The next three months saw the planned start date for the new programme (late October 1979) delayed. No new start date was given. High-level BBC politics were involved. News Division was appalled at what it rightly saw as a challenge to its conservative view of presenting what constituted 'news'. Dick Francis, the Director of News and Current Affairs, saw parts of his empire slipping away into the hands of a new entity. What benefit was there to him from backing such a new-fangled hybrid? The higher up in the BBC hierarchy, the less support there was. Brian Wenham, Controller of BBC Two, acted with his customary mixture of caution, scepticism and cynicism. Only John Gau, head of News and Current Affairs, understood the reasons for the new programme and argued strongly in its support against Brian Wenham. Faced with the opportunity to innovate in the field of public debate and information, most senior BBC managers considered their own interest first rather than taking on the big policy and philosophical questions.

As if the internal bureaucratic battle was not bad enough, union issues affected the very different terms and conditions of work in News and Current Affairs. News had its cherished and very favourable 'Spanish practices'. With their roots in Fleet Street behaviour, they centred on the time-honoured practice of regarding negotiation with management as a matter of 'selling the rule book' for as high a price as possible. Current Affairs producers had their own rather different terms and conditions. Behind these minutely defined matters of who did what, how, when, with what job title and for how much, there lay a history of arcane distinctions. Where exact agreements did not exist, 'custom and practice' would be invoked as the reason for first resisting, then demanding additional payment for anything new. The whole activity was a witches' brew of positioning, self-interest, opportunism and career ambition masquerading as action in the defence of public-service broadcasting.

Worst of all, no BBC director, least of all the Director General, Alasdair Milne, lifted a finger to help. During the frustrating weeks of deadlocked talks with the unions and an indefinitely delayed start for *Newsnight*, I ran into Milne and his cohorts in a TV Centre lift. I pressed him on the state of the negotiations? 'I don't know, old boy,' said Milne breezily ('old boy' was his universal form of address), 'it may work, it may not.' The lift stopped, the doors opened and the Director General swept out in a tidal wave of indifference. I was shocked; was not the Director General supposed to lead?

While negotiations crawled their way from entrenched position to entrenched position, the fully assembled *Newsnight* team started a series of 'dummy' programmes in a TV Centre basement conference room, the infamous B209. Sitting on normal chairs and using tables as studio desks, we drew up the topics of the day, chose the (mythical) interviewees of the day, decided what (mythical) filmed reports would be available and fashioned a fantasy running order. Scripts were written and there would be a pretend 'transmission' of this imaginary programme with the studio director calling the shots from pretend cameramen behind pretend cameras in the pretend studio. Occasionally the director would scream, 'You've just walked in front of a camera!' as a production staff member crossed the conference room, forgetting they were 'in a studio'. But simulation could only get us so far.

These pilots taught us nothing about what the programme might be. How could they? Farcically unreal as they were, they could do nothing for morale. Amazingly, no one gave up hope though all had a lot to lose from failure. Peter Snow especially never wavered. I filled in my time with a variety of commissions in radio and other parts of TV. For me, the *Newsnight* contract had already raised my broadcasting profile. I could not contemplate the possibility that it might fail.

Just before Christmas 1979, the deal with the unions was struck after a private meeting between George Carey and the chief negotiator of the ABS (Association of Broadcasting Staff). The Director of Personnel approved the deal, explaining to George that he could do so because 'Milne has changed his mind'. We were not told why he had changed. The start date would be Monday, 28 January 1980. Three weeks of real pilot programmes began on 7 January. Almost everyone outside the programme team had been waiting for it to fail. One member of the team observed, '*Newsnight* was set up to fail!' None of us on the programme, though, were prepared to let that happen.

The production photo call on 7 January 1980 attracted moderate media curiosity. In the 1980s, TV presenters were not media celebrities as they later became. This was good for the programme; it put the journalism first, where it rightly belonged. No journalist and little journalism was ever improved by celebrity.

George Carey had chosen a highly practical journalistic team as studio presenters – Peter Snow with years of authority from ITN; Charles Wheeler, a legendary foreign news correspondent for whom the newsroom had no time, no place and no longer any purpose; Peter Hobday, an expert city and business journalist and myself, an unknown from Radio 4 and the World Service. All were experienced writing broadcasters. Brian Wenham, the famously detached Controller of BBC Two, our home channel, enjoyed observing the team's determined lack of conventional television glamour. 'Well, you're none of you "frontispieces", are you?' he observed in a friendly manner, which, coming from Wenham, passed as a compliment. His later 'mot' – 'Ah, *Newsnight*, the programme presented by three bald men' – was less ambiguous. In his cynical way, Wenham was acknowledging that things were changing, that he had contributed nothing to the change, and that while he would not support it, neither could he obstruct it. This represented progress of a kind.

Editorial meetings began on 9 January; pilot programmes in real time followed in the next fortnight; *Newsnight* launched three weeks later with a signature tune by George Fenton, still running in modified form thirty-five years later, and the first of a series of studio sets designed to show the programme's intellectual shape and intentions. The original studio presentation format used no fewer than four presenters – main presenter, co-presenter, 'newsbelt' presenter and sports presenter. Each had a role, each therefore had a separate desk, placed specifically within the set. The result was slightly church-like, with the main presenter presiding from a semicircular apse at its heart. The design simplified as the journalistic style became more direct.

Other aspects soon clarified. Charles Wheeler was never comfortable with studio presentation and preferred to stick with his forte, reporting internationally from the ground. His filmed reports became a feature of the programme. Peter Hobday's particular expertise in business and economics appeared too limited for the more wide-ranging agenda of the programme. Quite rapidly, Peter Snow and I became the two main presenters, coxing and boxing our rotas to ease the pressure of days that usually ran from 10 a.m. to past midnight.

If the presenters evolved, if the studio sets were adapted, George Carey's founding vision remained consistent. Everyone on the team could have ideas; there was no hierarchy in choosing a good idea. We were not chained to the predictabilities and formulae of the 'news diary'; rather, that diary existed to be challenged, subverted and, best of all, abandoned. Carey trusted the producers, however young, to make their ideas come good. Risks were there to be taken. As the on-screen faces of the programme, Peter Snow and I were editorially involved, wrote our own studio material and planned interviews with our producers. From the outset, George saw the programme opening with a presenter-written essay on the events of the day. I may have taken this too enthusiastically; my own pieces became known as 'Tusorials'.

But Carey had a further personal mission to, as he puts it, 'find a home for the BBC's dispersed talent'. Many had in effect been 'dispensed with' by the existing production departments. *Newsnight* became a journalistic 'salon des refusés', a gathering of apparent rejects but in truth a superb pool of individualistic talent. In hiring reporters such as David Sells, David Lomax, Robert Harris, Ian Smith and Vincent Hanna, *Newsnight* liberated them from the routine activities of the BBC, allowed them to flourish as the authoritative journalists that they were. David Sells's command of the politics of freedom in Poland, David Lomax's international forays, Robert Harris's landmark exposé of the fake 'Hitler diaries' gave the journalism depth and personality. Vincent Hanna's intense, egotistical scrutiny of by-elections – part exposé, part cabaret, part human comedy sculpted with a stiletto – created an entire genre of its own, often imitated, never bettered. The programme was not just about Peter and me, never about 'idols in the studio'.

Journalistically, I jumped in at the deep end, investigating the infiltration of the Labour Party by the Trotskyite clique Militant Tendency, particularly entrenched in Merseyside, Sheffield and increasingly in London. Labour leaders and officials were in total denial about the nature of Militant, with its policy of 'entryism' aiming to take over the Labour Party or at least to manipulate its strength. This was my first experience of working with a young TV producer, Tim Gardam, irreverent, intellectually fearless and typical of the young generation Carey recruited. We met most of the leading lights of local-authority militancy, all expressing full devotion to democracy but actually implementing the Trotskyite strategy of 'democratic centralism'. This involved the 'centre' directing the ways in which democracy would be permitted to work. Its operation was made easier by the total refusal of the Labour leadership to admit that anything sinister was taking place. These were, it was said, just enthusiastic radicals, part of Labour's 'broad church', a bit leftish to be sure, but no more threatening than that.

The most unforgettable was Militant's intellectual guru, the South African Ted Grant. He was distinguished by a suit that looked unchanged over many months and seemed encrusted with grease; by heavily slicked-down, thinning, lank wisps of hair; and by his use of a particular gesture which we named the 'Militant chop'. Grant's left hand emphasised every rhetorical point by rising up and down from the elbow like a railway signal, sometimes flailing up and down in front of his face. Ted's physical appearance and condition were so revolting that sound engineers, usually very happy to thread microphone cable leads down anybody's trousers or skirts, baulked at touching him and handed the cable over to Grant to fix himself.

The Labour Party hated our report on Militant and continued its stance of denial, paying for it with years in the political wilderness. In the *New Statesman*, Mervyn Jones's TV review condemned the programme as a smear. More damagingly still for the party, as the 'entryism' row raged out of control, Labour leaders slugged out their differences live in the *Newsnight* studios night by night. Labour's two sides needed no persuading to come into the studio; they clamoured to fight over their differences. No story could have better demonstrated the soundness of Carey's editorial instincts. The journalistic break-through of our original report was news, but not as recognised by the newsroom. The follow-through in studio controversy was possible because of *Newsnight*'s role as the regular nightly programme which connected an event with its results. We were indeed covering 'how the country was run'.

On the evening of 2 April 1980 rioting and disturbances broke out in the St Paul's district of Bristol. As soon as the transmission was finished, I got into a car with the director, Paul Woolwich, another of George's 'young Turks', and drove to Bristol to report. The tension in the streets next day was brittle. As I started to record a 'piece to camera' about the events of the day, I was very aware of a sizeable group of young black youths standing close by listening. They were not threatening. I thought especially hard about what I was to say and what words I would use. After all, my listeners were not just part of the audience, they were people whose lives were being described to the outside world by an outsider in their presence. I censored nothing but I monitored myself very closely for possible unconscious bias. One young lad of about fifteen stood very close as I prepared to speak. I turned and asked lightly if he could stand back a little. I probably gestured but did not touch. His face flashed: 'Don't touch me!' and jumped back as if stung. If I needed a reminder of the brittle-ness of feelings in St Paul's, Bristol that day, it came with that instant reflex.

The on-air studio result on Friday evening was significant as the first major appearance of a future political star, the young black local politician Paul Boateng. With race relations on the streets of St Paul's Bristol fragile and nervy, Boateng's meas-ured, calm but very direct warnings in the studio showed him to have a subtle political ear.

At the end of May 1980, George Carey decided that I should go to the Soviet Union for a two-week filming trip through Moscow, Siberia and Uzbekistan in Soviet Central Asia. It was an intellectually stimulating fortnight, a battle of wits between us and the Soviet media 'fixers'. Every detail of every facility had to be agreed in advance; in theory and often in practice we could only shoot, see, visit exactly what had been agreed weeks before reaching our locations. Two words dominated the trip: usually any request to film something not exactly in the schedule was greeted with the simple *nyet*, 'no'. Just occasionally, a possible variation was greeted with a shrug and a reluctant *mozhno*, 'possibly'. Knowing the reaction, the director, Alan Scales, and I made many requests for additional opportunities just to irritate the fixers into having to say *nyet* again.

But there was an ideological war going on too. Within hours of arriving in Moscow the accompanying fixer, a bright young man in his early thirties, started a lengthy lecture on the origins of the Second World War and how only Stalin defeated Hitler. He appeared not to know that Britain had entered the war long before the Soviet Union, still less of the Nazi-Soviet pact. He was trying to gain the psychological ground over us before we began filming. We challenged it at equal length. We established that we were not a pushover for the Soviet party propaganda machine, however tight the filming restrictions in which we worked might be.

Some of these were strategic – no filming of bridges, roads, factory facilities. Others were to avoid political embarrassment such as 'tractor parks' without tractors, or clear signs of the rape of forests in Siberia. Each, of course, was 'objectively' a sign of 'socialist progress' but could not be filmed as jaundiced Western eyes would see only evidence of shortage or failure. I consoled myself with the thought that my script would work in counterpoint to the images making clear the gaps, the omissions, the outright lies or half-truths that the officially provided images showed.

The worm of frustration at the deadening hand of official permissions began to turn in Tashkent, capital of Soviet Uzbekistan. At a friendly meal with our team and accompanying fixers, they offered an 'official' toast on the lines of 'Long live Friendship and Cooperation between Radio Moscow and the

BBC.' Vodka was downed. I responded politely with 'Long Live Friendship between the British and Soviet Peoples', always a popular toast. Vodka was downed. After a further exchange of the pleasantries that protocol demanded, something got into me. Part of it was the vodka but the bigger part was the need to ease the frustration at the blocking of every opportunity for worthwhile filming. I started a series of increasingly unlikely toasts. Obligatory vodkas followed each one. The officials knew that they were being sent up rotten but could do nothing about it. It was the first in a series of small victories.

Our filming locations in Uzbekistan were the most conventional, designed to show how happy national ethnic minorities were in the embrace of the Soviet Union. Here socialism sat side by side in 'fraternal harmony' with national diversity expressed in official 'folkloristic manifestations'. Observe these traditional coffee houses! See the colourful dresses of men and women! Note how old dirty Tashkent has been swept aside and replaced by modern workers' flats! See these old mosques are now people's socialist museums! Observe superstition replaced by science! Is this a harshly regimented society you see around you? See how they smile! Look at their costumes! Watch them dance!

We were being shown the socialist version of a 1950s cinema 'happy-doc' of the 'Look at Life' kind. Very well; if that was what they fed us, that was what we would show. My script would do the rest, a destructive counterpoint to the officially bland images. It would be all the more satisfying because the first they would know of it would be on transmission.

There was a final hurdle to jump over. Tashkent Radio wanted to interview me about my impressions of the country. My antennae twitched. I was a long-time reader of the BBC Monitoring Service's *Summary of World Broadcasts*. I was not going to find myself quoted as 'BBC Newsnight Reporter Praises Soviet Agriculture' in a transcript from Radio Tashkent. That would be humiliating personally and would spark derision from former colleagues at Bush House. I prepared my thoughts. So, 'What are your impressions of the restoration of the great monuments in our country, especially Samarkand?' I replied that they were over-restored, virtually rebuilt and had lost any sense of connection with their past; this was no way to treat a great architectural heritage. The interviewer looked glum. Then, 'What are your impressions of Soviet agriculture and farming?' I replied that by comparison with Czechoslovak agriculture, which I knew from the 1960s, or Indian farming which I had seen more recently, the Soviet countryside was very backward, looking more like Central Europe in the 1930s. Constructing obstructive and honest answers proved very easy. It was hugely satisfying as the interviewer's face fell during each unhelpful but accurate response. As I left the studio I knew there was not a single sentence that could be used as approval for the Soviet Union. My guess is that the interview was judged unsuitable for broadcast. Nothing ever appeared in BBC Monitoring's reports.

Soon after, BBC Sports Department teams arrived in Moscow to prepare for the Olympics. They found very grumpy Soviet counterparts. Why? *Newsnight* had been there and 'they did not show us proper respect!'(I was very glad). Now it was BBC Sports' turn to be grumpy with me; how dare I allow my political journalism get in the way of their sports coverage? I was wholly unapologetic. Revenge is a dish best eaten cold; this one at the expense of our Soviet 'hosts' tasted wonderful.

That first year on *Newsnight* also included two signs of how I hoped my television work and private life would blend. With the filming schedule completed, I flew out of Moscow early on the morning of 4 June. I had sworn to Annie that I would not miss that evening's performance at Covent Garden of Wagner's *Tristan and Isolde*. The cast included Birgit Nilsson as Isolde, Jon Vickers as Tristan with Sir George Solti conducting Peter Hall's production. This was not missable. I arrived at the Royal Opera from Moscow just half an hour before curtain up.

In doing so I was signalling to Annie, to myself and to others that my private life and love of the arts would not readily be surrendered to the routines of journalism. Crises, yes; mere routines, no!

Three months later I put down another marker, coincidentally also connected with music. In the upcoming Covent Garden production of Wagner's Ring cycle, the part of Siegfried was to be sung by Alberto Remedios, the first British tenor to do so. This seemed the opportunity for a ten-minute *Newsnight* report. The editors agreed, probably on two grounds: it felt right for the programme and the range of its ambitions; and if the main presenter believed in it, his instincts should be backed. For myself, it was the start of a steady run of items on the arts showing that my interests were far wider than politics and international affairs. It was a public signal that paid off years later.

Newsnight was establishing itself as an essential programme with a distinct character that reflected its melding of news and current affairs into a coherent approach to events. What it lacked was support from senior television management, notably from Brian Wenham. When pressed on its future he would observe that it might indeed have another year to run – hardly a ringing vote of support. The programme's facilities in TV Centre were cramped and shoddy. The nightly studio scripts of 35–40 pages were laid out in piles along the corridor outside the main office, manually collated by production secretaries stooping from pile to pile. How did morale survive in the face of official indifference? I learned about 'management by parties'. If morale was sagging, the wonderful office administrator, Janet McCullough, would say, 'George, the boys and girls need a party!' It worked wonders.

Journalistically, we were increasingly effective. From autumn 1980, the first year of its existence, the programme's reportage from the three party conferences broke new ground. Conference reporting was traditionally centred on conference speeches, driven by the planned agenda of the individual political party. It was their political propaganda. Television coverage came from massive floor-based, fixed TV cameras, bulky and inflexible. *Newsnight* abandoned these rigid formulae. We followed the events of the day in the corridors, the fringe meetings, the conference hall itself, creating a seamless picture of the way the conference developed. We did so with the most primitive technical equipment. *Newsnight*'s daily editors, such as the New Zealander Paul Norris, and producers, such as Tim Gardam, set out to wreck this official party presentation. Gardam would sit with a 'locked-off camera' – one not covering the live debates – and direct the cameraman to the images we felt reflected the real story of the conference day. As *Newsnight*'s nightly reports increasingly reflected our understanding of the day rather than that of the parties, officials began to notice. Gardam recalls a senior Tory Minister, Willie Whitelaw, expostulating on air: 'We have our debates, we announce our policies, we have our leaders on the platform, then *Newsnight* appears and tells a very different story!' His mixture of shock and bafflement was both endearing and satisfying. As Tim Gardam observed to me: 'We wrested the agenda from the party managers, who simply did not know what to do. This at a time when the party conferences were the bloody arena of political carnage.'

In 1980, we were struggling with ancient pre-digital technology. When party conferences took place in Blackpool, 'instant' film reportage shot on the day was couriered by motorcycle to Manchester, processed, then couriered back to Blackpool for editing. Assembling an account of the events of the conference day under these circumstances was a technical miracle. Once ENG (electronic news-gathering) digital cameras arrived, the *Newsnight* team could cut loose. What mattered: not the pro forma sterility of managed debates on the conference floor but the unmanaged controversy in the corridors outside the hall. Tim Gardam's verdict was: '*Newsnight*'s anarchy, often operating at the edge of technological possibility, falling off the air as we stretched the machine to breaking point, allowed for all

sorts of experimentation and risk-taking.' This approach was
fully backed and endorsed by Carey's successors, Ron Neil,
David Dickinson, David Lloyd and Richard Tait.

Meanwhile, BBC News lumbered on with the formulaic
reports of official debates and official motions. The contrast
could not have been greater. Their bulletin coverage missed
out on much of the real political action taking place in the
corridors. Such journalism counted in *Newsnight*'s favour; we
were never threatened with closure; but we were still never
encouraged officially.

Politics then played into our hands. The Labour Party, continuing in denial over the infiltration of the Militants, split.
What came to be called the 'Gang of Four' – Roy Jenkins,
Shirley Williams, David Owen and Bill Rodgers – broke off to
form the Social Democratic Party. In mid-February 1982 they
held their first party conference; a month later, on 25 March,
Roy Jenkins broke the mould of two-party politics by winning
the Hillhead by-election for the SDP. The whole controversy
was meat and drink to our nightly studio agenda. With Vincent
Hanna running the Hillhead by-election coverage as if he were
the ringmaster directing gymnastic performers, the screen
crackled with human energy and major political issues. Vincent
was at once a monster and a brilliant political journalist. His
journalism undoubtedly stretched BBC impartiality guidelines
to the limits but was politically revelatory. His judgement des-
erted him when it came to himself. Vincent yearned to be the
studio presenter. On the few occasions that he appeared in the
studio, he was a disaster.

Despite continuing BBC managerial indifference to us, the
Falklands War cemented the programme's position for a generation. Two factors worked in our favour. The campaign was
a running story in the fullest sense, requiring intense daily reporting. In no time we were putting on weekend editions in
addition to those on weekday nights. More importantly, since
the conflict took place in a time zone five hours after London
time, much of the day's military action took place hours after

the last major BBC news bulletin at 9 p.m. That could offer at best only a preliminary account of the earlier events of the day. Transmitting well past 11 p.m., *Newsnight* had the very latest news and events from the battle in the South Atlantic.

Newsnight then unveiled three secret weapons. The first was Peter Snow himself, who appeared live in the studio on every night of the several weeks of the conflict. He gave a virtuoso performance demonstrating stamina, persistence and total mastery of the military and political issues. The second was Peter Snow's sandtray, a large studio table-size model of the Falklands on which the exact topography of the land and the engagements could be easily seen. To this day even sophisticated computer graphics cannot do better. The third secret weapon was 'Peter's Top Brass', a seemingly endless stream of recently retired British military leaders from all three services who could not wait to opine on the strategy and tactics of the campaign. The Ministry of Defence hated it, the politicians hated it. This so-called 'second-guessing' the tactics of British commanders in a conflict was 'giving succour to the enemy' and providing them with a pre-briefing on likely British tactics. The retired brass kept on appearing in the studio, well aware of the implications of their words and opinions. It was a major service to viewers.

The cool, objective contribution of BBC correspondents such as Brian Hanrahan of 'I counted them out and I counted them back' fame is deservedly well known. The more problematic task fell to the BBC reporters based in the 'enemy capital', Buenos Aires. Some commentators thought they should not have been there at all. 'Would you have had a reporter in Berlin during the Second World War?' was a frequent refrain. (My own answer would have been 'Yes, so long as they were not censored'!) Apart from the political and editorial difficulties of working in Buenos Aires, any reports had to be flown to neighbouring Montevideo before being uplinked by satellite to TV Centre. The cumulative impact of *Newsnight*'s time-zone advantage, the BBC Buenos Aires reporters and the

sandtray gave the programme a massive authority and a huge
impact.

The biggest controversy surrounding the coverage came as
a direct result of the crucial time-zone factor. One evening,
the BBC *Nine O'Clock News*, leading as it always did with the
mannered official presentation of events by Ian McDonald of
the Ministry of Defence, carried his report of casualties and
losses in the fighting. Two hours later, as *Newsnight* prepared
to transmit, a rather different account of the day was emerging from the Argentine side. Were they lying or were they just
the most up to date? Peter began his studio script by noting
the latest version of events given from Buenos Aires. Then the
fateful words: 'The Ministry of Defence in London, if they are
to be believed . . . '. To many viewers, certainly to my ears, this
was a wholly correct journalistic assessment of two conflicting positions. The following morning, the roof fell in as the
tabloids erupted, the *Sun* calling Peter a traitor. The tabloids
loved taunting the BBC for 'not being patriotic', not backing British forces as 'our boys'. Peter was wholly vindicated
later. I thought he should have sued and would have won.
Being a nice person and a fine journalist, he just got on with
the job.

Apart from giving viewers a full account of the Falklands
War, those seven weeks secured *Newsnight*'s existence. There
could be no doubt about its journalism, its essential place in the
BBC's range of programmes. I don't recall Brian Wenham ever
admitting that it had a long-term future. From the summer of
1982, it was beyond challenge.

Like any innovatory programme, *Newsnight* had its effect
on others. One of its more novel features was a nightly sports
slot. George Carey noted that BBC Sport regarded its job as
covering events and then giving the results. There was very
little journalism about sport. He hired a South African political exile, Marshall Lee, and, more importantly, a brilliant New
Zealand producer, Sean Brown.

Similarly, my own coverage of the Pope's visit to the United

Kingdom in May 1982 shook up the very conventional manner in which such occasions were usually covered by OB Events (Outside Broadcast); essentially the images were 'left to speak for themselves'! Editorial thoughts, journalistic comments, were not part of their usual coverage. I was disinclined to act as a writer of bland signposts between pretty pictures and did not believe that an event as political as the first visit of a Pope to the United Kingdom in centuries could be presented without essential context. The producers accepted the culture shock of my approach with good grace and rather enjoyed the result. (The hardened videotape editors loved it all, summing up the ecstatic welcome for the Pope by a youth audience in Newcastle as 'a teeny-boppers' Nuremberg!') For my part, I received a precious viewer's letter from two nuns in West London. They were overjoyed by my reports of the Pope's visit and concluded, 'You are not far from the Kingdom of God!' I had to take that on their faith but was rather warmed by the thought.

Newsnight's influence spread still further. We had shown that intelligent, critical journalism could be applied to news, current affairs, sport, the arts and outside events. The main BBC Two archaeological programme, *Chronicle*, was becalmed in a soft-centred approach, especially an obsession with the raising of the Tudor warship the *Mary Rose* from the depths of Portsmouth Harbour. Attractive as this project was, its TV coverage seemed intellectually content-free. Surely history deserved a more robust treatment?

In summer 1982, Tim Gardam was chosen to create a new history-based programme, *Timewatch*. I was to present in between my *Newsnight* commitments. The pleasant soft focus of *Chronicle*'s archaeological discoveries was succeeded by a much more robust agenda and approach. *Timewatch*, driven by Gardam's restless intellectual energy, took on controversial subjects such as whether General Alexander had been complicit in handing Cossack prisoners to the Red Army at the end of the war knowing they would be murdered on return.

We covered subjects as historically varied as Cleopatra, the Emperor Hadrian, Samuel Pepys and Prince Albert. The programme also launched the public TV career of an unknown but promisingly abrasive Cambridge history don, David Cannadine. His withering attack on the author of a book about Edward VIII in a pre-recorded studio discussion was so devastating that Tim invoked a non-existent technical fault and ordered a retake. Suitably warned, Cannadine then tempered his manner without diminishing the substance of the demolition.

The satisfactions of working on *Newsnight* were both journalistic and came from collaborating with the next generation of broadcasting leaders. Many of the editors of the day rose to senior positions in broadcasting: Gardam to run Channel 4; Mark Damazer to run BBC Radio 4; Jana Bennett to head BBC Television; Lorraine Heggessey to run Talkback Thames Productions; Mark Thompson and Tony Hall to become Directors General. Being a *Newsnight* editor of the day was virtually recognition of ability and guarantee of future achievement. They and their colleagues were television's 'brightest and best'. Working with them was a privilege. Given my previous frustrations, I could and did ask for no more; the stimulus of live television, immersion in a dense political scene, assessing the great events of the Cold War, covering the arts, revelling in history. But there was more to come of a wholly unexpected kind.

Annie and I travelled to India in January 1984. When we were staying in a remote hotel outside Jaipur, Rajasthan, hotel staff found us to say that there was a long-distance call from England. International communications were primitive then. Would it be a programme summons to return for a major crisis? After three attempts to make the connection back to London, the call indeed turned out to be from *Newsnight*'s then editor, David Dickinson. Over a crackly line taken on a phone in the hotel kitchen, I made him out saying I had been named Journalist of the Year by the Royal Television Society.

This was entirely unexpected. It felt a vindication of how I worked. Ann and I celebrated with a gin and soda – the Indian hotel had no Indian Tonic.

When later that year I was given the Richard Dimbleby Award by BAFTA (The British Academy of Film and Television Arts) I felt fully recognised. I thought I offered serious, intelligent and informed journalism, believing these were the qualities viewers needed to make the world more comprehensible. I believed that my broadcasting should be useful. There were many other ways of working on the TV screen, many of them more overtly exciting, some more engaging. I regarded the Labour politician, Roy Hattersley, as giving me the highest praise: 'You were like the England fast bowler, Brian Statham, whose every ball was straight and on a good length. You had to play every one.'

I had never worked with illusions about myself. I always knew, in Wenham's friendly words, that I was no 'frontispiece'; indeed, many thought I looked odd on the screen with an 'upside down' face. All these were checks against the absurd vanity that afflicted and afflicts so many TV personalities. No journalist on *Newsnight* in those days ever confused their work with being a celebrity. That came later.

Still the channel controllers and TV schedulers refused to give us a 'fixed start' for the programme. It would, they said, make earlier programme-planning impossible. This infuriated Denis Healey, who raged as he waited to appear at 11.30 p.m. one night, 'Only drunks and junkies watch *Newsnight* at this time of night.' The programme was never officially loved. Gardam recalls that 'News was deeply unfriendly and obstructive and Lime Grove sneered.' The team kept up morale with lengthy, post-transmission 'hospitality' sessions for contributors in the B209 basement room. Fuelled by gut-rotting Côte du Rhône and clammy, semi-congealed, clingfilm-wrapped sandwiches, these sessions lasted well past midnight. They kept up morale and self-belief. Contributors loved them.

*

By 1985 my appearances were running at some 120 programmes each year, which meant a strike rate of three per
week once holidays were taken. Each year, I spent three to four
weeks covering the autumn political conferences. I had taken
on the monthly commitment of *Timewatch*. It was highly satisfying but increasingly taxing.

In addition, from 1980 to 1983, I had helped Annie research
her authoritative account of the Nuremberg Trial. When it
was published in 1983 to great reviews, she launched immediately into her account of the Berlin Blockade of 1947–48.
With children grown up, these were hugely enriching personal
and intellectual endeavours involving research in archives in
London, Germany and the United States. All took time and
energy, all involved travel, all willingly offered, willingly un-
dertaken. Each book, we sometimes observed, was like having
another child.

Yet what sapped my spirit in a way that I only appreciated
later was something very personal: the illness and death of a
very close friend, a contemporary from Trinity, Cambridge. By
the end of 1984 he was clearly suffering from a then undiag-
nosable wasting disease. As we visited him through various
hospital isolation wards and clinics, there was no comfort of
explanation, still less of treatment. In a tragic evening together
in January 1985, he filled the dinner table with food, insisting
that we eat as he tried desperately but vainly to hold his own
food down to put on weight and staunch his wasting away. He
died a few weeks later and was buried in March 1985. I did not
realise how shattering it was. But my body told me.

Soon after, in May 1985, I undertook a month-long filming
trip to China. The nation was on the edge of economic revolution and tentative freedom of expression. It was possible to take
a camera onto the streets of Beijing and interview passers-by
with a possibility of getting an honest comment in reply. This
was revolutionary. Beyond that, the whole undertaking became
a game of cat and mouse where the brilliant director Kathy
O'Neil demanded increasingly ambitious location facilities

which the wholly rigid minder from the official Ministry of Information tried to resist. This was the Soviet experience mark two. We demanded changes to the supposedly fixed schedule as opportunities for filming occurred. Many we won. When we parted company in Canton, our senior Chinese minder spat at us, 'I have never known anyone as flexible as you people!' That was an accolade signifying some victory to us, satisfaction for the obstacles we had overcome to get as close to the story we wanted as we could, China on the move.

By the autumn of 1985 I was drained and wondering in an unfocused way where my professional future lay. I felt I had in many ways completed what I could on *Newsnight*. The future would be interesting enough but would I contribute to it with the raw energy of the previous five years? I had relied too much on intellectual push and adrenalin to get me through. But I had no 'second gear' in reserve, no decent way of coasting when events lapsed as they must do into comparative routine. I was in this sense an amateur, someone who found it impossible to present a mask of professional engagement to conceal emotional detachment. I was and am bad at routine. I did not say to myself in so many words that I was bored with *Newsnight* and needed a big change. I did not realise that my tiredness and unease pointed to a profound moment of transition.

In late autumn 1985, at one of the political party conferences in Blackpool, Michael Williams, an old friend and media guru from Bush House, approached me: 'I suppose you will be putting in for the job of MDXB (Managing Director External Broadcasting) next year? Everyone says you will get it!' I had no idea the post was vacant. I had never 'managed' anything in my life. But in that moment I felt that if there was one executive role at the BBC that I could do, it was running the External Services at Bush House. I had started my BBC career there, it was my spiritual broadcasting home. Four months later, in April 1986, against all the odds, I got the job.

My final *Newsnight* came on 5 June 1986. I hoped there would be some kind of final drink to mark my going. Nothing was said. Nothing appeared to have been planned. As the final credits faded, the studio seemed to empty rather quickly. Ah well, that was that, time passes, things end. I made my way down the fire-escape stairs that lead from the studio to the offices. It was very quiet. I opened the door and found the entire *Newsnight* team and programme guests crowded around the desks with glasses of wine, assorted presents and kisses and embraces. It was a riotous party. When the speeches came, David Jenkins, Bishop of Durham, that evening's studio guest, gave a hilarious impromptu quasi-sermon parodying his own highly controversial beliefs about the nature of the Resurrection. He did link it with my farewell but the connection has long vanished in the recesses of the forgotten.

At gone 2 a.m., Niven, the *Newsnight* contract car manager, sent his fastest driver to take us back to Hampstead laden with flowers and gifts. As Annie took a kitchen meat hammer to crush the stalks of her bouquets before putting them into a vase, the mighty blows on our kitchen table brought a dear and patient neighbour around to make sure we weren't being burgled. We were safe, just marking the final minutes of a very special six years in our lives.

Those years changed my life. They were rewarding and fulfilling journalistically. As importantly, we all believed in the importance of wit, satire and humour in the work, or as Gardam says, 'We allowed for a sense of the ludicrous at all times and ironic dispassion at the heart of our impartiality.' There was no *Newsnight* formula but its successful elements included irreverence, independence, originality, controversy, laughter and investigation. All six ingredients had their place. The only formula was that there was no formula; each night something different. Gardam's conclusion rings true. 'The BBC was usually a horrible, ungenerous, ego-filled place where people got rewarded for behaving badly. *Newsnight* was never like that. It was the closest I ever came to a "band of brothers" and everyone who was there when I meet them today says the same.'

For myself, *Newsnight* gave me the confidence to trust what I had to offer. I believed I could do anything, inside or beyond broadcasting. At the age of fifty, I had full confidence in my abilities. That was why I unhesitatingly applied to be Managing Director of BBC External Broadcasting despite having no managerial experience. I was a late developer, but I had developed.

8

Broadcasting to the World

1986–92

The official notice inviting applications for the post of Managing Director External Broadcasting appeared in *The Times* on 20 February 1986. It called for a CV and 'statement of purpose' by 10 March. Candidates from outside as well as inside the BBC were welcomed, a revealing move. I had already made up my mind to throw my hat into the ring and set about making my written application as persuasive as possible. I had no illusions about the gaps in my career that could disqualify me from a major managerial position. While BBC journalist friends were hugely encouraging, the BBC's hierarchy and Secretariat ('civil service') were sniffy and dismissive. One senior figure let her views be very publicly known: 'Tusa's candidacy is irrelevant!' Conceivably she meant that it was 'irrelevant' to the true needs of the External Services and the BBC. More likely she was signalling it would be inconvenient to the BBC's traditional way of allocating the highest posts in the Corporation, often just a version of 'Buggins' Turn!'. The *Daily Telegraph* rightly observed that my candidacy had 'caused considerable irritation to the management club', which suggested that insider tongues had been wagging far too openly and indiscreetly.

Strictly speaking, I was unqualified for the post. I had to show that my understanding of the needs and values of BBC External Broadcasting was so good that management shortcomings could be set to one side – this was no time for pretence. In my 'statement of purpose', I argued that the BBC's External Services (XS) were 'an international projection of a set of values which put rights and duties, majority rule and minority rights, consent and accountability into a proper balance and proportion'. I defined their approach to providing news as involving 'a full statement of facts, analysis untrammelled by ideology and a readiness to examine critically claims and statements no matter who or what their source may be'. I stated that BBCXS was a national asset 'whose aim and responsibility is to express and project British beliefs and values about political pluralism versus authoritarianism, the importance of political debate over political coercion, of reason versus dogma, of tolerance versus discrimination, of argument over assertion'. That was my big picture.

What of the job itself? By now, I wanted it very badly. I defined the role of Managing Director as being:

> to define and express the editorial basis of its broadcasts; to defend its independent voice in the interests of the British public, the listeners and existing and future governments; to argue the case for the maintenance and preferably the expansion of its services; to lead it into new areas offered by new technologies where its unique editorial authority can achieve further projection; to convince Bush House itself that a voice which is that of a giant abroad is not that of a pigmy at home.

My application and statement of purpose were posted in good time to meet the deadline of 10 March. While I waited for acknowledgement that they had arrived, I made additional notes to use in any possible interview. The inevitable question would point to my long career in journalism but the total absence of editorial and managerial experience. How could the BBC possibly appoint me? I built up the best case I could. Others, I said to myself, had made the leap from broadcasting and journalism into management – Hugh Carleton Greene (BBC Director General), David Attenborough (Controller, BBC2), Ian Trethowan (Director General), John Freeman (ITV), Peter Dimmock (head of BBC Sport). I had, I would argue, shown adaptability in successfully moving from radio to television. I had seen all three divisions of the BBC as a programme maker and journalist over many years. So much for the defence; then it was time to go on the attack. As a broadcaster, I had been at the receiving end of plenty of management decisions, many directly affecting our working lives. 'Some of them,' I wrote to myself, 'were a good deal better than others, and some were proved in practice to be as bad as we said they were at the time.' In other words, as journalists we observed BBC leadership and management critically; we were not passive slaves of management decisions. Would this approach have been persuasive in interview? I doubt it.

Far stronger, in my mind, were the words of Mrs Thatcher's head of Policy at Number 10, the businessman Sir John Hoskyns. We needed, he insisted, more 'inners and outers' to run organisations. It was not the case that those who had been in management for fifteen years managed better; they just managed in the same way! His case for using 'outers' – that is, outsiders – was that they were far more likely to manage an institution in a way the situation demanded. I liked that; I was as much of an 'outer' as you could imagine. In any case, I would add, why not give the top job to someone who knew what the end product was – journalism and broadcasting?

Arranging my thoughts was a good discipline. I almost did not have the opportunity to use them at all. On 10 March, a guardian angel tugged my sleeve. Had the BBC received my application? Surely they had, they must have! I rang up the office of Christopher Martin, Director of Personnel. They had no record of receiving anything. Was it too late to deliver a copy by hand? Of course not, they would look out for it. My blood runs cold to this day. Or had it been bureaucratically 'lost'?

The dramas were not over. At the beginning of April, Christopher Martin wrote to invite me to an interview with the full Board of Governors on 17 April at 4.55 p.m. As a keen observer of BBC 'board-ology', I liked the time for the interview.

I would be the last to be seen; this was traditionally seen as a strong position. The date, though, was a problem. I was committed to be in Moscow for BBC Television that week to cover the return to his homeland of the legendary Russian pianist, Vladimir Horowitz. It would be a great artistic and political event which I did not want to miss. I put my dilemma – if it was one – to Christopher Martin. 'That's all right,' he replied immediately, 'we will fly you back!' That was good; they were serious about my candidacy.

Objectively, prudently, I should have cancelled the Horowitz project. Instead, I flew out to Moscow on 13 April with the director, Dennis Marks, later Director of English National Opera, and his assistant, Peter Maniura, later head of BBC TV Music. After intensive days of preparatory work on the programme in Moscow, on 16 April, my passport bulging with multiple Soviet re-entry visas, I flew back to London. The following day I rehearsed my case, ordered my thoughts and set out in good time for the interview in Broadcasting House feeling very positive and optimistic. I knew it could be a life-changer but I wasn't burdened by the thought.

My analysis of how the BBC governors might vote was tentative and incomplete. Lord Harewood would probably back me because of my interest in music. Sir Curtis Keeble too, former Ambassador in Moscow, knew of my coverage of Soviet politics. Daphne Park, a former MI6 spy, was at best a swing vote as she might have regarded me as dangerously liberal-minded. I had often broadcast with William Rees-Mogg, former editor of *The Times*. Alasdair Milne, the Director General, was definitely against my candidacy. Crucially, I suspected the Chairman, Stuart Young, a radically minded businessman, was tiring of old BBC faces, old BBC ways and of Alasdair Milne himself. They had flown me back from Moscow for the interview. I had a fighting chance.

I remember little of the interview in detail. It was neither hard nor soft, though certainly not indifferent, not one of those occasions when the board just wants to go through the motions and pack up. I made a big play of my trump card: I knew Bush House, I knew its values, I knew what made them tick and why people worked there. I could change Bush House, lift it, because I knew and loved it; it was part of me, I was part of them. I insisted that you could not change an organisation unless you loved it. I am convinced that this immersion in Bush House values proved crucial in their decision. A brief frisson of tension rippled around the table when I mentioned that I was 'returning' to Moscow the following morning. I had assumed the governors knew about the Horowitz programme. At the mention of Moscow, Daphne Park, the ex-spy, reacted as if stung by a snake. Was I, her face seemed to say, 'going to Moscow' for instructions?

I left the boardroom in Broadcasting House around 6 p.m. On the floor above the governors' meeting, I went to the offices of Radio 4's *The World Tonight*, my old broadcasting stamping ground. They wanted a short pre-recorded package for the programme that night about the state of Soviet politics. Forty minutes later, as I was working on it, the phone rang. It was Christopher Martin. Could I come round to DG's office on the third floor? There, Alasdair Milne, not the Chairman, and Christopher Martin said the governors had appointed me to be Managing Director of BBC External Broadcasting. Incredibly, perhaps now reeling under the weight of jet lag, travel and overwork, I asked for the weekend to think it over. Either Alasdair or Christopher told me in so many words not to be a silly bugger. I accepted, rang Annie, who took it in her stride and, after a celebratory, very boozy supper with our son and daughter-in-law, prepared to fly back to Moscow the following morning at 6 a.m. It was all wildly improbable but it had happened. My gamble had paid off. I would not let the governors down.

There was one part of 'old' BBC politics that my surprise appointment seriously disrupted. Traditionally, Dick Francis, Managing Director of BBC Radio, 'should' have moved to Bush House at this juncture; then Brian Wenham, Director of

Programmes, Television, 'should' have moved over to run radio; Michael Grade, Controller BBC One could then have taken on the Director of Programmes, Television. That was how the BBC worked, high-level musical chairs. Not now. '*Newsnight* man spoils the plan', wrote the *Daily Telegraph*.

Two things in particular had led to the plan being spoiled. First, the new Chairman, Stuart Young, was known to dislike this cosy parcelling-out of jobs. It felt too convenient, too self-serving, too routine; he wanted fresh additions to the senior management talent pool. Second, Dick Francis, in a sense the obvious candidate, had played a dangerous game. He may not have wanted to move to Bush House from Broadcasting House at all. But when he declined to put in a formal application but told the governors he would 'pop along' from his office down the corridor if they wanted to see him on the day of the interviews, it smacked of just that sense of senior BBC entitlement of which the governors had tired. Dick, a hugely capable programme maker, left the BBC a month later and became Director General of the British Council, a job he did very well. The constant travel to Council offices around the world finally killed him some years later.

I got a very good press over my appointment. It was easy to present me as the open-minded journalist who had bypassed the 'grey' apparatchiks and bureaucrats of BBC management. Nobody had much time for them. Bush House was delighted at the appointment of a journalist steeped in its beliefs, values and practices.

Two letters from members of the public were notable. One correspondent from North Wales, signing himself 'Pro Rex', wrote: 'How does a bastard like you get the Overseas Foreign Language Service directorship? There is something disquietingly wrong at the BBC. You need the Hungarian [he meant Bulgarian] umbrella job. Hope you get it soon – or sooner. And a lot of your queer friends too!' And as an afterthought: 'Falklands swine!!!' The second came from a Mr C.G. Clayton of Coventry: 'May I congratulate you on your new appointment to what must be one of the cushiest numbers at a BBC which has so many of the kind.' He disliked, it seemed, any programming about or for foreigners. Warming to his discontents, Mr Clayton observed: 'The only alteration will be that a more Left Wing slant will be given to all offerings. IF that is possible in the light of its present Left Wing bias.'

Letters from my former *Newsnight* friends reminded me how precious the six years had been in every human and professional sense. One, from a former programme editor, David Dickinson, reflected the huge sense of achievement and high morale the team felt and enjoyed. My appointment to Bush House, he suggested 'should only be the beginning. Snow to run Television Service with electronic sandpits on all channels; Donald (McCormick) to run the radio with Scotsmen broadcasting twenty-four hours a day; Vincent (Hanna) to run (the Labour Party) at Walworth Road perhaps; and Wheeler as the next Ambassador to the US.' In short, *Newsnight* could rule the world. What fun that would have been!

Now the work had to start. In discussing my appointment, I insisted on a two-month period of briefing at Bush House. This would not mean a protracted handover period where I trod on the heels of the outgoing Managing Director, Austen Kark. It would be a chance to talk to anyone, to understand where the External Services stood, where they wanted to go and how they needed to change. I wanted to be as well prepared and briefed as possible on the actual day I took over, 1 September 1986.

As part of my own self-analysis before the job interview, I had written a two-page note headed 'What Needs Doing?', drawing on my continuous involvement with Bush House over the previous twenty-five years. Most of the main programme formats, I observed, were old: 'A little spring cleaning is overdue!' I was critical of the balance between what we broadcast to the 'expatriate' British listeners and what we said to the core of our audience, those foreign, English-speaking listeners.

Many programmes sounded 'narrow and parochial', I wrote to myself, 'neither informing the world audience about what really mattered in Britain nor providing the world audience with the knowledge about the rest of the world that they might not have'.

Next, how good was BBC world news? 'External Services may be the best for news. How often is it first?' Adding: 'If you are that good, you should be first some of the time?' Perhaps the essential disciplines of correctness and accuracy tempered by caution 'needed with advantage to be pepped up a bit'.

Then I considered the External Service's place within the BBC. This was crucial. We were funded directly by the Foreign and Commonwealth Office. It 'prescribed', that is to say set, the number of hours for which we broadcast and the foreign languages in which we broadcast. The XS could only escape being just another 'government broadcaster' because it was part of the BBC under the BBC Charter. This was the guarantee of our journalistic independence, of our freedom from Foreign Office editorial interference. I feared the XS and the BBC were drifting apart and some of that was the fault of Bush House. My conclusion: 'As its voice gets less heard in the UK, as its public profile has become less strong, so its role within the BBC as a whole has become much weaker. Bush tends to be rather exclusive, rather intolerant of the more brash, less discriminating news palette of its domestic sisters.' As the old BBC saw had it: 'You can always tell a man from Bush! But not very much!' Amusing enough but dangerous. Fences needed to be mended.

My note to myself concluded: 'Bush itself needs jolting out of its morbid isolation. External Broadcasting needs a higher public profile as part of the broader debate about Alternative Diplomacy or Value Diplomacy – that is a diplomacy where British values are actively expressed and espoused. It needs a new look at its journalism and its programmes. There is a big editorial job to be done!' Such were the outlines of a blueprint for change and it was mine.

*

During my two months of listening, talking and questioning at Bush House, I found a tired organisation, exhausted by battles with successive governments, official inquiries and cuts in budgets and services. Led by great managing directors such as Gerard Mansell (1972–80), many of the worst dangers had been fought off, such as the Callaghan government's threat of a 20 per cent reduction of funding. Mansell himself recalled with glee how he led the Number 10 think-tank inquirers up the garden path. The only way of making real cuts in External Broadcasting's costs, he once explained helpfully and disingenuously, was not to run a twenty-four-hour newsroom at all. Incredibly, their report suggested a news operation that ran four hours on followed by four hours off. They had not noticed that world news ran on a twenty-four-hour, 365 days a year cycle. The report was ridiculed and ignored. But it had taken time and effort to endure all the inquiries and fend off their conclusions. Consequently, broadcasting and programmes had been relatively ignored in the general welter of scrutiny, challenge and defence. The External Services had survived, but at a cost.

Most editors and managers thought the World Service English network – the staple stream of programming – sounded old-fashioned, stodgy and weary. It was badly in need of updating. The voices of the network reflected a nation of almost a generation previously; class-ridden, staid and stately. For many foreign listeners, if BBC World Service English sounded hopelessly out of date, then probably the nation was out of date too. Not all programme editors agreed, insisting that the carefully chosen words, the precisely placed diction, the measured delivery were necessary because of the shortcomings of the short-wave radio signal. The majority believed that change was essential precisely because of the vagaries of the signal.

When it came to the thirty-seven foreign-language services in which the External Services broadcast, there was one overriding complaint. They were not allowed to be journalists but mere translators of material prepared by the newsroom or English-speaking talks writers. They were not wholly trusted to originate their own material; would they faithfully reflect and defend BBC and British values and standards if given more editorial freedom? A 'colonial' element lurked in the structure as British 'language supervisors' – sometimes former colonial officers – oversaw the accuracy of the translations and their consistency with the 'view from the BBC in London'. If there was dissatisfaction here, a huge opportunity lurked too: to harness the latent talent and ideas of the non-British broadcasters.

A general cocktail of frustrations welled up in almost every conversation during those first two months. Its ingredients included poor pay, low standing in the BBC, little recognition in this country, and poor audibility where it was essential – around the world. What could be more ridiculous than offering what was claimed as the world's best news service but having some of the poorest reception for listeners? The frustration was intensified by the fact that while many at Bush were impatient for change, few believed that the existing leadership had either the will or the ability to provide it.

The outgoing Managing Director, Austen Kark, was delightful, witty, a fine writer, a man of principle, a good friend. Few, though, felt he could take decisions. Much as they loved him, they were intensely frustrated at his hesitations, actual and verbal. His finest hour was as the only member of senior BBC management ready to defend publicly BBC journalism on the *Today* programme in the face of Mrs Thatcher's assault on reporting of the IRA. On Austen's return to Bush House from his broadcast, he was cheered to the echo.

In the autumn of 1986, when I entered the high-ceilinged, three-windowed office overlooking the baroque architecture of St Mary le Strand in Aldwych, help was at hand in solving the audibility problem. In 1981, the government had approved a £100 million 'audibility programme' to renew and upgrade BBCXS transmitting and relay stations. This was a huge investment. Incredibly, successive governments of both parties never deviated from it. This was Gerard Mansell's finest achievement, a priceless legacy to his successors.

There was a price to pay and a reasonable question to ask. Were the External Services efficient enough to manage such an investment? In 1985, the government commissioned an inquiry under a former Treasury civil servant, Alan Perry. He was demanding in his questioning but ended up being surprisingly radical. Perry recommended that XS should be funded on a three-yearly basis – a triennial settlement – rather than the existing annual hand-to-mouth budgeting. This was a huge advance, almost certainly the result of close and harmonious working between Perry and the Bush House representative on the review team, Jim Norris, head of the Arabic Service. Long-term planning, essential for external broadcasting, would now become possible.

But Perry also set demanding conditions. Every broadcasting section and support department was to be the subject of a value-for-money review by external accountants. Savings would be expected from this scrutiny, efficiency would be delivered. More radically still, an entirely new budgeting system would be needed. This was the language and the practice of the new management world, of the efficiency drive set up by Derek Rayner in his Whitehall managerial revolution. Many at Bush House feared it; some could not understand it; most accepted it as inevitable.

The third Perry recommendation, though, struck real fear into many hearts – the BBC External Services would be subject to a major efficiency review, at a future date, by the National Audit Office (NAO). No matter that the National Audit Act excluded the BBC from its remit, the External Services were being administratively singled out, separated, it seemed, from the constitutional 'mother ship' of the BBC. Was their very independence from government interference under threat? The political and constitutional implications that lay ahead were huge. Such was the complex situation facing me on 1 September 1986.

*

By then, after two months' briefing, I felt I knew Bush House, its staff and their concerns rather well. I knew far less about the experience of listening abroad. We claimed a massive 120 million listeners per week but in our hearts of hearts we knew that they could not hear us as well as they should. My wise Deputy Managing Director, Chris Bell, said simply: 'You must get out and see the relay stations!'

I attended the Asian Broadcasting Union conference (ABU) in Istanbul in November 1986, following it up with a trip to the medium-wave relay station in Cyprus, which transmitted a strong signal into the Arab world. At an informal ABU gathering outside the main sessions, I got an early insight into the comparative reputations of ourselves and the rival Voice of America (VOA). Standing at a reception, my VOA colleague and I fell in with three representatives from Iranian Broadcasting. They were very cool, austere, rather elegant, hair en brosse, carefully trimmed beards, white collarless shirts, neat black suits, precise if accented English. They challenged the VOA man: 'You Americans, you tell such lies about Iran, about our country! We listen to your broadcasts and we have books so high' – he opened his hands to show a two-foot gap between them – 'so high, filled with your lies!' Feeling left out, I asked if the Iranians listened as closely to the BBC? How big was the book they compiled about our broadcasts, I enquired? One of the Iranians looked momentarily downcast. His hands gestured, indicating a slim volume just a few inches thick. 'Ah, you English,' he offered by way of explanation, 'you are so tricky.' I learned years later that belief in 'English trickery' – sheer cleverness and attendant duplicity – was hard-wired into Iranian perceptions.

A fortnight later, it was time for the regular liaison meeting with VOA in Washington. They were very hospitable but it was clear that VOA laboured under a huge handicap. As part of the State Department, as an arm of US foreign policy, VOA carried daily commentaries on international events signed off by saying that they reflected official US policy. For us at the BBC, this was a reputational killer, a ball and chain around VOA's credibility. Worse, while VOA colleagues complained mildly about having to carry the 'official' commentaries, they seemed comfortable operating editorially within the State Department. In any case, Congress wanted it that way. I understood why the Iranians said what they did.

Early in December, I took in two more relay stations, the huge one on Ascension Island in the South Atlantic and the smaller one on Antigua. Ascension, a volcanic island with possibly the most balmy climate in the world tempered by sea-laden equatorial breezes, was crucial for listeners throughout West Africa and much of Brazil. Flying to Ascension Island was an eight-hour leg in an RAF TriStar troop transporter en route to the Falklands. The trip from Ascension to Antigua was a further ten-hour leg in a huge USAF C-5 Galaxy. Running and maintaining remote relay stations was an isolated and lonely business. The dedication and professionalism of the engineers was admirable and deserved support. It was important to show that we, the broadcasters at Bush House, really cared that our programmes would reach the listeners.

Meanwhile, the problems were piling up at Bush House. Autumn 1986 was a baptism of fire, a complex twist of politics and diplomacy. We were a united and well-balanced management team but found ourselves blocked in almost every direction. We urged the Commons Foreign Affairs Committee to publicly endorse the notion of 'cultural diplomacy', a comparative novelty at the time. It involved recognising that British influence in the world was not just spread by the Foreign and Commonwealth Office (FCO) through formal diplomacy and embassies. The BBC External Services and our 120 million listeners and the British Council, its offices overseas and its audiences learning English and experiencing British arts and culture, were also part of the overall 'cultural diplomacy' effort. Years later it came to be known as 'soft diplomacy' but the ingredients were the same. From Bush House's standpoint, this was a plain statement of reality and an opportunity to deploy the full portfolio of British assets of persuasion internationally. I also sought endorsement of the XS's position and purposes on a stage wider than mere broadcasting. Such recognition could be useful in future resource battles, though I did not expect it to yield extra funding immediately.

The Foreign and Commonwealth Office, an embattled institution, maintained the traditional view: diplomacy, however dressed up, was for diplomats, it was their job. Besides they weren't going to risk having their budgets raided in the name of a new-fangled definition of diplomacy. The Commons Foreign Affairs Committee Report shot 'cultural diplomacy' down in flames. It was dead for a generation. I have no doubt the FCO briefed and lobbied heavily against it. Our own virtual absence from effective Whitehall lobbying was naïve. Defeat number one.

Defeat number two was worse, though in retrospect predictable. In November 1986, the BBC put in a bid to the government for an additional grant-in-aid of £7.8 million per annum to fund a television World Service. This idea had been nagging for twenty years. Successive managing directors had raised it and one, Douglas Muggeridge, had been publicly and painfully rebuffed for even daring to do so. Now a new proposal had taken shape in a joint initiative from BBC Television and External Services. It was clear from a dinner at Broadcasting House given by Alasdair Milne for the Permanent Secretary at the FCO, Sir Patrick Wright, that they would not back it. The government officially rejected it. A follow-up World Service Television scheme on a smaller scale prepared by the merchant bankers Schroder Wagg – involving a modest £3.4 million over three years – was submitted and rejected the following year (March 1988).

Much later, we learned what had really happened. First, Sir Geoffrey Howe, the Foreign Secretary, was so frightened of Mrs Thatcher that every time the BBC World Service Television file reached the top of his ministerial box for immediate attention, he promptly returned it to the bottom. He would not risk taking it across the street to Number 10. This was just as well for him. Mrs Thatcher was under siege by the head of Independent Television News (ITN), David Nicholas, and its hugely influential front man, the presenter Alastair Burnet. They argued that if public money was to go into a government-funded international TV service, then ITN should have it and not the BBC. Their lobbying and blocking tactics worked. I do not believe they wanted to do it themselves but were determined to stop the BBC gaining an international advantage. And Mrs Thatcher was temperamentally averse to doing the BBC any favours. As a result of this Whitehall wrangle, Britain had no international TV satellite presence when Gulf War One erupted in 1981, allowing CNN to sweep the field. If it was another brick wall for us at Bush House, it was also a strategic loss for the United Kingdom.

The third defeat felt even worse at the time and concerned the National Audit Office's right to review the BBC External Services' efficiency and effectiveness. If, as I pointed out, the National Audit Act specifically excluded the BBC from its inquiries – as it did – and if the XS were an integral part of the BBC – as they undoubtedly were – how could they be singled out for NAO scrutiny? To discriminate in this way risked detaching the XS by practice and by implication from the BBC, weakening our claims of editorial and managerial autonomy from the Foreign Office.

I argued the case at a meeting with BBC governors at Broadcasting House. Lord Barnett, the former Labour Chief Secretary to the Treasury, now Vice-Chairman of the BBC and actual author of the National Audit Act, told me roundly: 'If I were you I wouldn't take my stand on legal niceties.' Staring as we were at the very clause of the Act which exempted the BBC from NAO scrutiny, this struck me as breathtaking. Only Joel could have thought that standing up for a clause in his own Act was a legal nicety! But I was alone in resisting. The BBC governors conceded NAO access to our books, whatever the constitutional consequences might be. Another battle lost, but this campaign would continue later and we were to turn it to our advantage.

By rights, my colleagues and I should have been demoralised after three rejections of major strategic initiatives. Yet we were as one over major beliefs and values, sharing objectives and principles. We were resolute that broadcasting 'in the national interest' included reporting criticism of the British government; making professional programmes to attract and keep listeners; and providing a 'credible, unbiased, reliable, balanced service of national and international developments'. All three aims anchored XS's broadcasts firmly in the camp of independent journalism free from government interference.

In our tussles with the Foreign Office over funding, there were marked differences of emphasis. They believed talking to 'opinion formers' was more valuable than broadcasting to the masses; that broadcasting in English outranked that in the vernacular services (after all an opinion former would speak English, wouldn't they?); that broadcasting to friendly democratic 'open societies' was a bit of a waste of time; and that closing a service down once democracy prevailed in the country concerned was good use of resources. For our part, we insisted that we broadcast in foreign languages as well as in English; that we spoke to mass audiences as well as to elites, to friends as well as to enemies, to open as well as closed societies. Above all, if we were to be trusted, we needed to broadcast constantly and predictably – services should not be turned off like a tap as political circumstances altered. While the FCO may have believed the External Services should be independent, persuasive and credible, many officials also yearned to bend them to basic diplomatic priorities. We never wavered over our adherence to principles of independent broadcasting.

Sharing strongly held beliefs mattered in autumn 1986. My colleagues and I knew there was work to be done internally. In a very traditional organisation, many paid lip-service to the need for change but were cautious about putting it into practice. Today, 'change management' is one of the cliché mantras of management theory and practice. It was a relatively novel idea in 1986. The Perry Review and the future prospect of National Audit Office scrutiny demanded an entirely new approach to financial management. I had strong personal reasons for leading the way. Many thought I knew nothing of management, finance or administration. I would show that I understood the practices involved and had the will to implement them.

I have no doubt that the most important decision of those first months, possibly the most important of my six years at Bush House, was not editorial but financial – how we conducted our budget. If it sounds technical, even bureaucratic, it proved the key to transforming attitudes, outlook and funding better journalism within the External Services. The accountants Deloitte Haskins and Sells were appointed to implement the Perry Review's recommendations. Meeting in my Bush House office early in autumn 1986, they recommended that we introduce 'zero-based budgeting' – or 'priority-based budgeting' as some called it – without delay. This involved examining every activity in a service or department, deciding which were essential, which merely useful, which might be done differently and which could be given up altogether. Taken together these would yield financial savings. Each department could also bid for additional expenditure for specified new activities; the more unnecessary activity surrendered, the greater the resources available for new developments. The carrots and the sticks were well balanced. The Directorate team, under the wise and often wily Chief Accountant, Ernest Newhouse, would decide which savings to make and which bids to accept. Newhouse always understood that budgets existed to make programmes and broadcasts, not just to balance the numbers.

Simple enough in concept, this process would prove time-consuming in practice. Worse still, Bush House had never budgeted like this and was terrified of it. Besides, if the Treasury and a bunch of accountants advocated it, ill intent must be lurking somewhere! Many senior colleagues urged delay by a year, warning against putting Bush under intolerable strain. A significant group, led by the Controller of Resources, David Witherow, and Ernest Newhouse, advised an immediate start. Four months later, in April 1987, after requiring departments to identify and surrender savings, we had released £1.5 million (1.5 per cent of the operating budget) for new or higher-priority activities. It was a great moment. When Michael Checkland, by then Director General, asked if we had freed up £1.5 million of resources just by 'asking the question', I answered, 'Essentially, yes.' For the very first time, Bush House had created its own freedom of manoeuvre, its own flexibility. We could initiate without going – usually fruitlessly – cap in hand to the FCO for more funding. Over the next five years, much of the broadcasting and journalism was reshaped out of a fixed grant-in-aid. We had put into practice Perry's recom-mendations; we'd demonstrated that we could manage. Most in Whitehall and probably most within the BBC thought we weren't capable of such change.

At the very end of December 1986, less than four months into my time as Managing Director, I had a stroke of luck, though it did not look like it at first. On 28 December 1986, the *Sunday Telegraph* carried a lengthy article by one Frederick Whitehead, a critical listener on the Spanish Costa del Sol to the World Service in English. In a catalogue of discontent, Mr Whitehead lambasted me personally and the World Service in general for a range of offences. These included trying to set up a World Television Service, broadcasting about the 'peasant cultures of China, Vietnam and Bulgaria', being hooked on 'Continental writers' (such as Victor Hugo), condemning Brit-ish government policies as crass and our national performance as a 'matter for derision'. In summary, in two years' listening to the World Service, Frederick Whitehead had 'yet to hear a serious programme about Britain's industrial achievements, her contributions to world civilisation, her history, her sophisticated democracy or her literary, artistic and musical genius'.

This looked serious, felt inconvenient and was a rotten new-year present. What struck me, though, was how disheartened my colleagues were by the attack. While it was only what we expected from the more rabid wing of the British expat audience, it was well, even amusingly written, an effective polemic. I asked how much of it was accurate? Could it be rebutted with chapter and verse? It was not accurate, I was assured, it could be rebutted point by point. I said we would do so and do so at length and in detail immediately. Was I sure, I was asked. Wouldn't any public response only feed the controversy? Shouldn't we lie low and hope it would pass? I saw this as a prime example of the low institutional self-esteem into which the External Services had fallen, defensive and unsure.

Richard MacCarthy, the methodical head of press, assembled a detailed reply. Exactly a week later, under the headline 'Aunty Hits back at Disgusted, Malaga', the *Sunday Telegraph* carried a rebuttal of equal length to the original article. I started with some derision. Mr Whitehead's 'sweeping generalisations and confident condemnations flowed as easily as lukewarm Spanish champagne laced with Fundador, often the undoing of many a visitor to the Spanish south'. The reply then dismantled every charge he had made about the broadcasts, their subjects and their tone and approach. The 'story' was killed stone dead.

My determination to fight back publicly at media criticism sent an important signal to everybody at Bush House, the rest of the BBC and of course to the Foreign Office. We would defend our case and our record robustly and in public. It did wonders for internal morale. Crucially, throughout the 1980s, External Services could shape and control its own agenda and reputation without prior authorisation from Broadcasting House. With Richard MacCarthy's team in the press office and Michael Williams as the ever-resourceful parliamentary liaison officer, we did just that. If this reflected what some saw as the semi-detached position of the XS within the BBC, it also gave us absolute managerial responsibility for our actions, which we were happy to take. This semi-detached freedom was increasingly valuable because of the turmoil engulfing the domestic BBC.

On 28 and 29 January 1987, the patience of the BBC governors with the Director General, Alasdair Milne, finally wore out. From the previous autumn, the new Chairman, 'Dukey' Hussey, had been growing wary of Alasdair's judgement, partly over a supposedly controversial First World War drama, *The Monocled Mutineer*, more seriously over the libel case against *Panorama* brought by two Tory MPs. Most of the Board of Management would have agreed with the view of Bill Cotton, Managing Director of BBC Television: 'Al has been dead in the water for eighteen months.' The only person who was oblivious to the atmosphere was Alasdair. At a grisly official Christmas dinner, he amazed us all by saying he intended to remain as Director General until 1990.

The mood was ominous at dinner for both boards on 28 January, the eve of the governors' meeting. As we shuffled out, one governor, the trade unionist Sir John Boyd, said loudly, 'Just you wait till tomorrow – we'll see who's in charge.' Lunch the next day started late without Hussey, Joel Barnett, the Vice-Chairman, or Milne. Only Hussey and Barnett appeared, half an hour late, as we were drinking soup. Hussey tapped his glass: 'I want you to know that DG has submitted his resignation on personal grounds. That is all the Vice-Chairman and I have to say on the subject.' Then, supposedly as a joke: 'That's put a stop to the conversation.' It did. To this day, I feel ashamed that none of us spoke up to ask for an explanation.

This putsch had one advantage for us at Bush House. 'Dukey' Hussey had too much on his plate to worry about us. The incoming Director General, the shrewd Michael Checkland, reckoned my colleagues and I could be left to sort out our problems. Crucially too, had the External Services been tightly integrated into the BBC, as later they were, we would not have been able to carry out our programme of change as quickly and radically as we did.

We first turned our attention to improving the sound and nature of our programmes. From 1987 onwards, 'World Service Renewal' – starting with the main English-language network – was in the hands of the new Controller, Elisabeth Smith, a quiet revolutionary. The network had to sound less stodgy, less ponderous; programme formats needed refreshing; News and Current Affairs had to work together more creatively. It was not a matter of turning World Service into a pale version of the domestic Radio 4 with a few foreign exotic add-ons. The great majority of listeners were not British; their needs were totally different from those of a domestic listener. They deserved something that sounded like the United Kingdom of the late 1980s rather than the England of the post-war 1950s.

Elisabeth Smith faced problems of resistance, of entrenched beliefs in the old ways, the old sounds. Many on the staff of World Service English were firmly attached to the stately, measured almost funereal tones of the network. These, they insisted, radiated seriousness, gravitas, responsibility and, yes, truth. We risked throwing away our hard-earned credibility by 'tarting up' – as it was suggested – the sound, the character of the network. Elisabeth Smith and her colleagues thought this was to miss the point. It was her task to persuade and reconcile doubters. World Service Renewal came on air in October complete with new voices, fresh programmes and important symbols such as new, less pompous signature tunes.

Most daringly we changed the name of the whole organisation. For decades, 'World Service' had meant English-language programming only, the rest being clumsily lumped together in 'External Services' which many thought involved looking after gutters, drains and roofing. Most listeners internationally called the whole organisation the 'BBC World Service' anyway. It was a good name, why resist? Changing the name meant changing every single job title, not bureaucratic tidiness but plain necessity. Within the BBC, this was widely thought to be several steps too far. To change job titles meant changing the initials and acronyms by which all senior BBC staff were universally known. Many were legendary, many post holders were deeply attached to their acronyms. Even that most pragmatic of people, Mike Checkland, doubted we would pull it off. With tongue firmly in my cheek, I set up a working party with the deliberately pompous name, 'Change of Title Implementation Group' or 'COTIG' in acronym form. I put in charge a person with common sense and a shrewd sense of humour, Ian Gilham, and told him to get on with it.

A different kind of journalistic renewal was needed for each of the thirty-seven language services. My predecessor, Austen Kark, had observed to me that as editor-in-chief he could not honestly vouch for what the language services broadcast, though safeguards and supervision existed. Senior managers and editors had to take these reassurances at second hand. I felt we had to do better. It was time too to move beyond the notion of vernacular broadcasting as a formulaic, even slavish copy of the broadcasts in English. The editorial tone, the editorial substance had to be consistent throughout the External Services. But could the vernacular broadcasters become more like journalists originating some of their own material and less like mere translators? We set out to scrutinise samples of broadcasts from each language service one by one over four years. Some thought it wouldn't work; some feared what we might discover; some doubted we would have the stomach to complete it. I gave the job to the Chief Assistant, Maureen Bebb.

The first programme evaluation took place on 28 May 1987. It was of the Hausa language service, a powerful voice in Nigeria, reaching an audience of some eight million listeners. Before a dozen-strong Bush House panel, a week of Hausa broadcasts was examined, comparing a translation of what was broadcast with the English material from which it originated. Was it accurate? How could they make better programmes? How could they improve service to the listeners? Such examination from colleagues across Bush House was a huge innovation. Understandably, many in the language services were anxious, some alarmed. Was the process to be discriminatory, disciplinary even?

The task of recording, translating and comparing the texts of the broadcasts was a huge one for Maureen Bebb, who never loosened her grip on the process. There was the occasional frisson. A 'personal' commentary by the Polish Service from a Rome-based priest referred to the President, General Jaruzelski, as a 'son of Satan'. When one of the scrutinising panel, Elizabeth Wright of the Chinese Service, questioned this, one of the Poles present replied: 'Well, he is!' It was a rare aberration. The whole activity improved broadcasts, it brought Bush House together and I was the first Managing Director who could say that he knew what was being broadcast in Britain's name in languages other than English.

As we wound our journey through most of the thirty-seven language services over the next four years it became clear that it was not critical or punitive. The aim was to raise the standards and quality of our journalism to the almost 100 million listeners of our non-English language services. As increased resources were freed up through the new budgeting system, the vernacular services got more money to produce better programmes.

We learned a great deal too about the nature of the mother language English, much about the perils of translation. As part of the information pack for each evaluation, each service organiser provided a short note about the nature of their language and the problems of translating accurately from English. What in any case could 'accurately' mean? Their observations were a wake-up call for smug Anglophones.

The Hausa explained that reporting the gender of a correspondent – or anybody for that matter – was essential for their language. Just saying 'a correspondent' wouldn't do; 'Is it a man or a woman?' Hausa listeners would be shouting at their radio sets. The Polish Service wrestled with a similar gender problem but concluded with the saying: 'Translations are like women. If they are beautiful, they aren't faithful. If they are faithful, they aren't beautiful.' We were in deep water when the Senior Producer in the Russian Service warned gloomily: 'The fixed word order in English brings the semantic centre of gravity forward in the sentence, while in Russian the tendency is the opposite.' The Turks occupied similar grammatical territory: 'Syntax is totally different from and incompatible with English.' The Finns warned cheerily that while their language was short of abstract nouns, their nouns did have fifteen declensions of which thirteen were in current use. Finnish verbs possessed four infinitives and 'the present tense has to cover also future, continuous, intended or habitual action'.

We soon understood that looking for literal translation was impossible and foolish. Accurate rendering of meaning was the desired goal. More important, the language under scrutiny proved to be English itself. Our vernacular colleagues wrote politely of its shiftiness, its plethora of weasel words, its deliberate imprecision, mere hints of meaning masquerading as statements of fact. Our Hungarian colleague observed that the task of turning English into Hungarian raised 'the difficulty of rendering opacity convincingly and of providing a plausible equivalent of waffle'. His conclusion: it was all about compromise. 'Cervantes thought that a translation was inevitably the wrong side of a tapestry.' I tried to sum up the often scholarly views of our colleagues like this: 'The English language emerged as misty as its landscape, the emanation of a people who had created a language perfectly adapted to suit their own refusal to say what they mean.' We had set out to test the behaviour of thirty-seven other languages. We emerged four years later with a chastened awareness of the oddities and myriad imprecisions of our own.

I stood in Hong Kong at the end of September 1987 opening the new relay station with a powerful signal straight into China, the world's most populous nation. It was impossible to believe that I had taken over as Managing Director only a year ago. Nobody had advised me to make changes fast. They hadn't needed to; besides, Bush House as a whole and all my senior colleagues were urgent for change and transformation. A year on, the building blocks were now in place: the audibility programme from which the government never deviated; the new budgeting system; the value-for-money reviews; the sound of World Service Renewal; language-service programme evaluation.

The year 1988 started auspiciously. A year previously, on 20 January 1987, the Soviet Union had stopped jamming BBC Russian Service transmissions into the country. (It was a stroke of luck that I had called on them to cease jamming in a speech just four days previously.) The world was changing, ears were listening, minds were opening. In July, Mrs Thatcher bravely agreed to take part in a Russian Service phone-in. It was a great success.

And the relay stations kept on opening. In October, I went to the Seychelles to commission the new medium-wave relay that would boost audibility throughout East Africa; Swahili speakers in particular would benefit. Despite avoiding, as I thought, the blistering equatorial sun in the Seychelles, in Nairobi three days later to hear the improved signal for myself I fell ill with severe sunstroke and second-degree burns on my legs. Lying on my bed, tuned into World Service programmes or chatting to the Bush House newsroom, I flipped over to Kenya Television which was screening a political rally for President Daniel Arap Moi. Did our broadcasts have any effect? What followed was essential to a managing director's experience. President Moi clearly was a listener and he hated what he heard us say about his controversial rule. He then launched into a lengthy, impromptu diatribe at the BBC and 'That BBC man who is in this country now!', gesturing dramatically to my empty seat in the stand just behind him. I felt a huge well of pride and vindication at what the World Service did and promptly rang the newsroom to tell them about Moi's attack.

We were not reshaping Bush House management, broadcasting and journalism because we sensed there might soon be a special need for it. There was never a quiet period in world affairs. Yet we had become professionally ready for 1989, the year of revolutions. No one had forecast them. With general elections looming in Poland on 4 June, with Solidarność and the unlikely but charismatic figure of the shipyard plumber Lech Wałęsa in the ascendant, I took a trip to Poland to see the election for myself – the old journalist triumphed over the new manager. Just how free could elections be under a communist government? That was a fundamental question for everyone in the European communist bloc. Besides, I needed to get out of the office. I flew to Warsaw on 1 June with a huge sense of personal liberation.

In the following hours, every meeting with journalists and politicians spoke of the volatility of Polish voters' feelings. A Solidarność MP suggested his party should beware of doing too well and humiliating the Communist Party. Others interpreted the Soviet position as being that, provided communications with East Germany were not threatened, the Poles could do what they wanted politically. It might help if the Communist Party was allowed to keep its 'leading role' in the political scene as a nominal fig leaf. Two 'official' journalists acknowledged that no Communist Party candidate could credibly run on their actual record. The best they could offer was an appeal to their (hopefully) persuasive personality. We had all watched General Jaruzelski's TV address the previous evening. Incredibly, he only referred to the Communist Party once. But, he seemed to say, a coalition after the election would be welcome, somewhat less than a rallying cry for support. The nearest thing to a party 'line' was to urge the need for 'reform'. But, as I noted in my diary: 'Why trust the Communist Party to reform the hideous, demeaning mess which it has spent the last forty years creating?'

Karol Małcużyńsky, the BBC Polish Service fixer, drove me and Andrew Taussig, Controller of European Services, north to the revolutionary shipyard city of Gdansk, home of Solidarność. We passed one of the historic landmarks of the Solidarność struggle, the exact bend in the road where police first tried to murder the 'Solidarność priest', Father Jerzy Popiełuszko, by throwing a brick at his car windscreen. His quick-witted driver had swerved and avoided it. The police got the priest later though.

We joined a party for Wałęsa's 'name day' at his modest house just outside Gdansk. A large crowd outside sang the Polish birthday song, 'Sto Lat', 'May you live for a hundred years!' Wałęsa gave a conciliatory TV interview saying he would vote for the official National List and urged his supporters to do the same. Word was coming in, though, that many Solidarność committees were striking out every single name of the official National List of candidates from their ballot papers.

On polling day itself, we went to Mass in St Brygidda's in Gdansk, the Solidarność church. Lech's driver sat us in the choir, next to Father Jankowski – successor to the murdered Popieluszko – and a row in front of Wałęsa and his wife. I wrote in my diary: 'Father Jankowski moved to the lectern to deliver the homily. He began in a matter-of-fact tone of voice and I suddenly realised he was welcoming "the BBC from London". There was a long burst of applause. I caught Lech's eye. He grinned broadly and nodded.'

A team of four ladies, two men and two boys had made Wałęsa's birthday lunch of duck, pork and meat rissole. During the meal, Wałęsa praised the BBC Polish Service for being fair and balanced and avoiding what – maybe out of politeness – he called the 'bias' of Radio Free Europe and Voice of America. More confidingly, he told Andrew Taussig that he thought Jaruzelski and his prime minister, Rakowski, were isolated and lost. 'He thinks they want to be included in his [Lech's] family, so to speak, to lay their heads on his shoulder and be loved. It is a shrewd observation.'

The drive back to Warsaw seemed quick. How could it not be with the world erupting everywhere! The World Service's *1300 News* and the *24 Hours* programme burst at the seams with coverage of the death of Iran's Ayatollah Khomeini and the Tien An Men Square protests in Beijing. Millions of listeners around the world were hearing the same authoritative account of epoch-making events as I was. Warsaw was quiet, tense, exhausted. Dinner was subdued. This being election day, there was no vodka. Now it was a question of waiting for the results.

On Monday morning, Karol Małcużyńsky rang to say he had got a last-minute appointment at midday with a senior Communist Party Politburo member, Stanislas Ciosek. Andrew Taussig and I were ushered into his big office in the Central Committee building, its walls lined with brand-new, unread copies of *The Complete Works of Lenin*, many still in their cardboard boxes. I recorded in my diary what followed:

> Ciosek comes in quickly – a large man, balding, stomach bulging a bit over his waistband, sweating. He is in a hurry. 'I had not had an appointment with you in my diary but I thought I should see you to let you know what is happening. We are losing the election and I am one of those who decided we should take the risk. The architects of reform [within the Communist Party] will not be elected to parliament.'

As Ciosek let it all pour out, I counted myself lucky to be one of the first people to hear a communist leader concede defeat in an open democratic election. For more than forty years, all my adult life, all my journalistic career, communist state elections invariably resulted in communist victory, usually with 99 per cent of the votes allegedly cast in their favour. Here was a communist leader telling me they had lost the election and they accepted the result. This was history. I thought of my Czech family who had suffered under this crooked system almost all their lives. Might they too soon find freedom? The world was turning over in 1989 and Poland was one of the levers of revolution. Poland, Iran, China – was no regime safe? And the World Service was covering it all.

My second thought was that I had to let the BBC Warsaw

correspondent, Kevin Connolly, know what Ciosek had said. It was 12.30. Taussig and I found a phone, briefed Kevin in detail and he filed for the 13.00 hours *Radio Newsreel*. It led other news sources and radio stations by six hours.

As Managing Director, my authority as a news source was not always recognised by the Bush House newsroom. On a later occasion, I attended a government news conference in Moscow. In the spirit of *glasnost* ('openness') the Soviet Economics Minister told assembled journalists that all official statistics about Soviet economic performance had been made up. They were lies. In a few sentences, he undermined every single claim about the superiority, even the practical competence, of the communist way of running the economy. This struck me as a major revelation. I rang the Bush House newsroom; the news intake editor was elaborately polite: 'Thank you very much for that, John, very interesting I'm sure. We will keep an eye out for it on the wires!' It never made a news story. It was, though, a lesson too. Managing directors shouldn't try to be correspondents. It was not their job. Mine was to get World Service properly run and properly funded.

The World Service was in the middle of its second period of three-year funding introduced by the Perry Review – the Triennium. Towards the end of the Second Triennium in 1988, we agreed with the FCO that work on the Third should start early and be based on a detailed study of existing and proposed activities. In January 1989, we set up an internal Triennium Group led by Anthony Rendell, Editor World Service English, a subtle and challenging thinker, to make our case. By now, with two years' experience of managing in line with Derek Rayner's Whitehall revolution, we felt confident of mounting a case that was journalistically credible and managerially efficient. We could talk the Whitehall talk and walk the broadcasting walk at the same time.

The work took much of the year. In September 1989, World Service Directorate examined and approved our Triennium

Bid for 1991–94. The Director General, Mike Checkland, cast his sharp accountant's eye over it at three further meetings. (Later, it emerged that he was very doubtful whether such an ambitious bid would persuade Whitehall. But his view was: 'If John believes in it, then they should go ahead!') In November, I took it to the full BBC Board of Governors, who may have read and certainly approved the full document of 275 pages – the Blue Book. I asked the BBC Secretary, John McCormick, the highest BBC civil servant, how he had got Hussey to grasp much of it, any of it? 'I took him by the scenic route', he replied, grinning! Once the document was officially adopted, the Chairman submitted it to the Foreign Secretary.

In December, my colleagues and I gave the Foreign Office a day-long presentation. Never given to shows of enthusiasm, the officials asked for the 275 pages to be boiled down to a manageable 30. They did bring themselves to concede that there had never before been such a thoroughgoing analysis of World Service activities. It was far from clear that they welcomed our newly developed rigour. We believed we had absorbed the 'Whitehall managerial revolution' far more thoroughly than they had. Our bid could not simply be batted aside on the grounds that we couldn't manage money. We had seized the initiative.

Our efficiency record set out in the Triennium funding bid showed a 6 per cent increase in broadcast hours over the past four years, now totalling 777 hours per week; a 3.5 per cent decrease in staff numbers; an 8 per cent increase in staff output; transmission costs reduced by 40 per cent; and no less than £12 million reallocated to areas of greater priority under the new budgetary system. World Service had become a serious bidder for increased Whitehall funding. Anthony Rendell and his team had produced a powerful document in 1989. Now the Deputy Managing Director, David Witherow, had to negotiate it with FCO officials throughout 1990.

As Deputy Managing Director, Witherow was a huge professional and personal asset. A former head of Bush House newsroom, he knew the World Service inside out. He was highly intelligent, thorough, calm, determined and, above all, patient – qualities needed in the year-long negotiations with the FCO. I conspicuously lacked most of them some of the time and some of them much of the time. This allowed David to play a version of 'nice guy, nasty guy' in the negotiations. If the FCO was asking too much or conceding too little, David's fallback position would be: 'Of course, I might just be able to accept what you are demanding though I don't really like it! But I am very sure John Tusa won't and when I tell him, he will be very angry and will undoubtedly go public!' This tactic was a useful weapon for David.

By May 1990, the FCO agreed to put forward the substance of our bid to the Treasury in the final public spending negotiations. This was a huge achievement by David Witherow and his team. There was a price to pay: the closure of the Japanese and Malay Services. We always hated losing services, especially when doing so threatened two cardinal principles: that we broadcast to friends as well as enemies, to open as well as closed societies. No one could predict when such broadcasts might not be deemed useful or essential. Realistically, the loss of these services was a small price to pay for the increased funding the FCO would negotiate on our behalf.

The Times got a leak about the closure of the BBC Japanese Service. Douglas Hurd, the Foreign Secretary, saw it at an airport, cursed and swore and shouted at the Office. His Deputy Under Secretary, Rosemary Spencer, promptly rang me and accused me of leaking. I hadn't and managed not to lose my temper with her, which was difficult at the best of times.

With *glasnost* in the Soviet Union in full swing, and with Mrs Thatcher's public admiration for Mr Gorbachev, it was time to invite her back to answer questions live on air from listeners in the Soviet Union on the eve of her visit to Kiev. She arrived at Bush House on Sunday, 3 June in good time before the 3 p.m. broadcast. It was raining and she was pleased: 'So marvellous for the farmers, but we need more, much more!' This was Margaret Thatcher in her 'Mother of the Nation' mood. She fussed over the headphones because they would ruin her hairdo, posed for the photographers, kicked off her shoes to get comfortable and settled down to wait for the programme to start.

Bernard Ingham, her pugnacious Yorkshire press secretary, and I left her in the studio. She did not need hand-holding. We listened in an adjoining studio. She fielded questions from Russian listeners on the USSR itself, the position of Germany now that communism was collapsing and the Wall had opened. Mrs Thatcher was notably conciliatory towards Iran and their 'great religion', while standing firm on the need for freedom of speech. 'That's the story,' nodded Ingham approvingly.

For us in the World Service, the story was having her in the building and experiencing for herself the direct contact with listeners in the Soviet Union. This was too good an opportunity to miss. Since we had her presence and full attention I would brief her on things that mattered to us. I led her into the adjoining studio. She took her customary weak whisky. 'Am I the only person drinking?' she asked. I joined her.

We had prepared two maps charting the state of World Service audibility. In 1981, the map showed most of the world coloured yellow, indicating poor audibility. At the slide of a handle, the 1990 map turned most of the world blue, the sign of good audibility, the direct result, I told the Prime Minister, of the government's £100 million investment in new relay stations. Come to that, I thought, ask her to open the new transmitting station at Skelton in Cumbria in the spring? She looked blank-ish. Ingham hissed: 'It goes to the Soviet Union, Prime Minister!' 'What a marvellous idea,' she enthused – but nothing was to come of it.

Weak whiskies in hand, we moved into the studio next door. The walls were lined with photos of heads of state who listened regularly to the World Service. Margaret Thatcher's eyes lit up – these were her friends. She went lyrical: 'Lee Kuan Yew – what a marvellous man, he should be running China!

Ah, dear Kenneth [Kaunda of Zambia], such a sweet man but quite hopeless; he changes his cabinet every six months and is ruining the economy! Pérez [de Cuéllar, UN Secretary General], a marvellous person. Do you know I keep telling President Vassiliou, you've only got de Cuéllar for another two years; you've got to use him to sort out Cyprus.' On the next wall, her eyes slid over the Dalai Lama without comment then alighted on King Hussein of Jordan. The eyes went misty, the voice husky: 'So brave, so brave, such a nice boy!'

Anxious not to push our luck too far, I started to talk about audience numbers. Quite suddenly she turned to me: 'Tell me something important – how well do you do in Japan?' Dumbstruck, given the recent decision to cut the service, I hissed to Ingham: 'We've just cut it!' An evil grin lit up his folded features: 'I know, but she doesn't.' I explained as best I could why the FCO had cut the Japanese Service. She half listened. Margaret Thatcher knew her own mind: 'The Japanese are so important. They are so insulated a society and we simply have to speak to them.' (It made no difference to the final decision to cut the service.) Time was up. I had had forty-five minutes of the Prime Minister's full attention. I have little doubt that when it came to the final decisions, her Sunday afternoon at Bush House played a significant part in getting us an increase in funding.

The following morning, we let FCO officials know of Mrs Thatcher's visit and her views about broadcasting to Japan. They were aghast, dismayed even at not knowing about the Prime Minister's visit to Bush House beforehand. As the Assistant Under Secretary grimly put it, had they known, 'we would have done some pre-emptive briefing'. Which was exactly why we kept them out of the loop. Besides, her presence was our business, broadcasting business.

In November 1990, as part of the government's public spending review, the World Service received an unprecedented increase of 6 per cent in real terms to strengthen journalism and broadcasting. We knew this was a huge achievement. In one sense, it was the culmination of two years of preparation and negotiation. In another, it was the crowning point of a decade-long transformation of Bush House from the audibility programme of 1981 to triennial funding in 1985 to the efficiency organisation that followed. Everyone in Bush House had fought for it.

In the meantime, I was travelling: East Germany and Czechoslovakia to sense the spirit of newly liberated Central Europe; Delhi for the fiftieth anniversary of the Hindi Service; Poland for a political round-table seminar; Oman for the Sultan's twenty-fifth anniversary and on to the island of Masirah to visit the relay station. On 31 December, after a big family wedding, my body rebelled. My head reeling, the room going round and round, I could hardly stand, barely walk. Four days later, patched up by my GP, I struggled in to see the BBC's doctor, Ann Fingret. She prodded and tested reflexes and reactions. She found nothing pathological. Instead, she asked me to look at my schedule for the previous four months and bring it to her. This showed the travel, the jet lag, criss-crossing time zones, the meetings, the speeches, the events, the dinners, a relentless round of intense, varied, never routine activity. She considered the sick-looking figure slumped in front of her and pointed to my schedule and asked simply: 'Are you surprised?' I could not be. Then: 'You must learn to be kind to yourself.'

Apart from one standard drug for inner-ear instability, what Ann Fingret gave me was confidence that if I looked after myself more considerately, I could still carry out a punishing schedule in 1991. This was just as well. After a dozen days at home recovering, I chaired the annual budget process for the World Service; visited Lesotho and South Africa for a fortnight in February to open the new relay station; attended meetings in New Orleans and Washington; took part in three days of broadcasts from the twin cities of Minneapolis/Saint Paul; picked up the Prix Italia for World Service in Pesaro; celebrated the start of rebroadcasting of the BBC Russian Service in Moscow and gave lectures for the British Council in Nigeria. As if this was not enough for 1991, World Service was to endure a new inquiry; we faced a major international, political row about broadcasting; and my personal fortunes suffered a heavy blow.

The BBC governors' controversial decision in 1986 to give the National Audit Office access to the World Service to examine its efficiency and effectiveness hung over us. Of course, the NAO would come in to inspect us. The question was when? We had a two-pronged strategy. I took aside Lord Barnett, BBC Vice-Chairman. He frequently boasted of his closeness to Robert Sheldon MP, Chairman of the Public Accounts Committee: 'Bob is my oldest friend, we lunch together every week!' I said: 'Joel, can you have a word with Bob Sheldon? Of course the NAO will come in. But we don't want them to examine us while our own change programme isn't finished. Can Sheldon delay their inquiry for a year?' In due course, Joel returned, looking pleased: 'I've had a word with Bob Sheldon (my oldest friend!) and he agreed to schedule the NAO inquiry a year later!' This was a major concession; the NAO would look at our management systems only once we had completed their renewal.

Mike Checkland then played his part. He invited John Bourn, the Comptroller and Auditor General, head of the NAO, to a BBC Symphony Orchestra concert at the Festival Hall. Bourn observed equably that he assumed he was invited because of the impending NAO inquiry into the World Service? I made two suggestions: first, would he and his officials come in to watch some live transmissions? (Outsiders were always impressed.) Then I made our main pitch: 'The Foreign Office want you to look at our efficiency. We think the way the FCO works with us leaves a lot to be desired. If it comes to effectiveness, they could do a lot better. Will you look at how they work as well as at how we work?' John Bourn agreed without hesitation: 'We can be very helpful, you know.' It meant that the NAO inquiry would have a twin focus, on us and on the

Foreign Office. Much of 1991 was to be devoted to it. We were getting rather good at inquiries.

Early in 1991, the world erupted into war with Iraq. On 17 January 1991, the United States and its allies launched Operation Desert Storm to throw Saddam Hussein's armies out of Kuwait after their invasion the previous August. Suddenly, millions in the Arab world were tuning into foreign radio stations, BBC Arabic Service at the head of them. Those millions included Arab heads of state. They did not relish hearing detailed coverage of events from the BBC of a kind they were not providing for their own people. The political pressure on the World Service began to build. First, William Waldegrave, Minister of State at the Foreign Office, phoned David Witherow, the Deputy Managing Director: 'World Service Coverage of the Gulf War? Weren't we overdoing it? Wasn't there just too much of the stuff?' David replied that it would look very odd if we carried less coverage than other broadcasters. Besides, actual events drove the level of reporting we provided. Witherow said he would of course 'look into it', our convention for doing nothing.

Next the FCO passed on a request from Voice of America. Could they have time on our powerful medium-wave transmitters on the island of Masirah, strategically placed at the mouth of the Gulf? The BBC Arabic Service signal was powering into the target area; VOA wanted such a signal for their broadcasts. Could we oblige? We decided not to help. How would it sound, we said, if minutes after BBC Arabic went off the air, VOA popped up on the same frequencies from the same transmitters? The VOA was regarded, especially in the context of the Gulf War, as a propaganda station; we were not. Our reputation could not be risked by possible contagion from such a deal.

The political pressure really stepped up. Jonathan Aitken MP came into my office, stretched out his long legs and said in his most languid manner how unhappy 'my Saudi friends in the Eastern Province [of Saudi] are' about the BBC Arabic

Service. I soon received an identical message from Sir Patrick Wright, Permanent Secretary at the FCO, a man I liked and trusted. Clearly, the Saudi royal family, one of Britain's closest allies, was rumbling. The details of the Saudi 'charge sheet' were long and apparently damning. All the BBC Arabic Service journalists, they alleged, were Palestinian; every news bulletin, they insisted, led with news from Baghdad; there was general bias in coverage; any reference to the Kingdom of Saudi Arabia was delivered with a sneer in the voice; mistranslations distorted the journalism. These and other similar allegations would have been highly damaging to our claims and practice of impartiality and objectivity if substantiated. They had to be bottomed out.

I engaged a distinguished Arab businessman living in London for an outside opinion. He was totally bilingual with an unimpeachable academic record and lectured at an FCO briefing centre. He agreed to listen to five hours of recordings of Arabic Service transmissions every week. Once a fortnight, he would come to Bush House to tell me about what he heard. He could find no truth in a single one of the Saudi charges, not about the over-representation of Palestinian voices, not about the tone of the broadcasts, the alleged mistranslations or their inconsistency with World Service standards. After a few weeks of listening and reporting, we concluded he had done enough. There was no evidence of BBC Arabic Service pro-Saddam Hussein bias. I had the assurance I needed.

I rang the Assistant Under Secretary at the FCO to tell her of the results. 'That is of course most reassuring, John,' she replied. 'Might we have sight of the report?' I declined, pointing out that I was editor-in-chief and I was satisfied with it. We heard no more from either the Saudis or the FCO. Yet in a detailed post-mortem of our coverage after the war, the head of the newsroom, a former Cairo correspondent, Bob Jobbins, thought with all the benefits of hindsight, too many 'uncontested assertions of a very debatable kind' from Baghdad were allowed through in the interests of 'balanced and fair reporting'. That would be a warning for the future, a desk memo to our successors.

Gulf War One led to one major change for the World Service. The comparatively new, Ted Turner-financed Cable News Network (CNN) was sweeping TV screens with its coverage. It had the field to itself. Its impact was huge. This was the future. The BBC, the United Kingdom, was nowhere. A rudimentary thirty-minute BBC World Service television programme began in April 1991, followed by a twenty-four-hour service broadcast to Asia on the Star TV satellite in October. These were important steps. The big question of how to fund a fully fledged BBC global TV network was nowhere near solution. By the autumn, the head of BBC Enterprises, James Arnold-Baker, was thinking imaginatively. Why not use income from BBC Enterprises' European cable ventures to fund WSTV? As directly earned income, neither licence fee nor grant-in-aid, the BBC could use it as it thought fit. At first I could not believe the suggestion, used as I was to an endless series of obstacles and objections blocking the project. At a Board of Management awayday at Buxted Park in spring 1992, Mike Checkland characteristically seized on the idea. He said to me: 'CNN is taking us to the cleaners. This can't happen again. Let's do it.' This was Checkland at his pragmatic and also visionary best. In a session on the future internationalisation of the BBC, Mike launched the proposal to a startled Board of Management. I threw my weight behind it and him. No one had time to think up objections. The following Thursday, he used a similar shock tactic on the Board of Governors. It went through on the nod with murmurs of governors' approval at its wisdom. It was a benign putsch. BBC World Service Television was truly born.

From the first rejection of direct government funding in 1986 it had taken almost six years to devise and fund this scheme. If that was bad for us it was far worse for the British national interest, whose presence on global TV screens had been set back half a decade by Whitehall political infighting.

*

By mid-1991, however, the BBC itself was riven over one question. Who would be the successor to Michael Checkland as Director General, whose term was drawing to a close? John Birt, then Deputy Director General, was hot favourite. Hadn't he been brought in from ITV specifically to succeed Checkland? Or might Mike be extended in post for a further three years? These seemed to be the choices. What was soon clear was that there would only be a field of two. They would not even talk to me. The decision was to be taken on Monday, 1 July 1991. Mike rang me at 12.45 the following day, terse but calm: 'The Chairman has decided that he wants John Birt as DG. After a lot of hard thought I have decided to accept a one-year extension'. I promptly rang the Secretary, John McCormick, and asked for an urgent meeting with the Chairman. I walked over to Broadcasting House for 3.30 the following day, Wednesday, a warm and sunny afternoon. I told Hussey that the governors should have interviewed me both as a matter of courtesy and in order to hear what I might have to offer as DG. While he made a slight apology for not calling me over to explain the decision, he said a contested board would have been bad for the BBC. Besides, he had taken soundings and I would not have got the job. I replied that was said of me five years ago as an outsider for the World Service job. (I learned later that Joel Barnett had told Hussey not long before: 'You can't appoint John! He knows nothing about money!') With the exchanges getting nowhere, he offered me a future lunch – which fortunately never materialised – and a farewell gift, a small enamelled sweet box from Halcyon Days, the gift shop, with Broadcasting House on the front. I should have rejected it on the spot.

Two questions need answering, the personal and the institutional. Why did I not lobby to be interviewed more vociferously beforehand? Given my record at World Service, they should have wanted to hear my views. But oddly, perhaps I may not have strongly wanted the job, which I had long thought was undoable. Intellectually, of course I could do it; physically, I subconsciously feared the strain, the daily aggro of the job, a sense of once more putting my body at risk. The need, in Ann Fingret's words, 'to be kind to yourself' stirred deep inside me. I live and work on nervous energy; I have never had a slow gear. Once the media furore subsided, I put the matter behind me. (The BBC politics of the appointment are covered in Chapter 9).

My final year in post would be 1992. There was one major piece of unfinished business to tidy up, the Report of the National Audit Office into BBC World Service management. We saw a copy in January 1992 and knew we were home and dry. In May, the NAO reported that World Service had a 'sound framework' of 'resource-planning, financial management and control, internal value-for-money reviews and comprehensive procedures to assess the effectiveness of its output.' This was all very dry, very Whitehall-speak, but it was conclusively favourable. No wonder that when the Commons Public Accounts Committee examined the Report, one member, Kim Howells MP, called it a 'clean bill of health for the World Service'. This was the climax of a strenuous five-year programme of change in the way Bush House ran itself. During it, we neither risked the quality of our journalism nor gave 'managerialism' and 'systems' a higher priority than programmes. We were pragmatic, not ideological. It should have been a lesson and an example for the BBC. And the NAO did tell the FCO to lighten up, loosen up and let the World Service do what it was good at, making programmes, getting listeners, bringing credit to Britain and running itself.

Paradoxically perhaps, freed from external inquiries, we now set up one of our own. What would international broadcasting be like in 2000? What would the World Service be like? My senior colleagues and I would not be part of the show by then. We handed the 'World Service 2000' inquiry over to the 'Young Turks' of the next generation with a remit not to be hide-bound by the present but to roam freely over where we might be by the end of the decade. It proved hugely liberating. After I presented it to the governors on 9 April 1992, earning praise from all sides, I said to Mike Checkland: 'That was the interview they didn't give me last year!' He grinned: 'I thought it was something like that!' The Foreign Office was non-plussed. We presented it to officials in July 1992 as a matter of courtesy and information. They were very uncomfortable. Shouldn't we have consulted them first? As if we had to seek their permission to think independently. They still had a lot to learn.

I always got on well with the highest levels of the FCO, Permanent Secretary and ambassadors. On one occasion, in December 1991, I agreed an increase in the hours of Romanian broadcasts with the Minister of State, William Waldegrave and the Permanent Secretary, Sir Patrick Wright, at the door of an FCO reception. It was a five-minute conversation. That was how quickly business could really be done on the basis of trust. It turned out that these feelings were reciprocated in a more profound way.

On 1 July 1992, at an FCO farewell party for a distinguished ambassador, Sir Andrew Burns, the wise TV guru, Denis Foreman, launched into a huge attack on current BBC management. We jointly lamented the recent and untimely death of Dick Francis, head of the British Council. Had I, asked Foreman, thought of the British Council for myself? I demurred. But something was stirring in Whitehall. That same evening, the new Permanent Secretary at the FCO, David Gilmore, an old Cambridge friend, took me aside at a reception: 'You are a very great nuisance to us but would you like to run the British Council?' This was a novel approach to recruitment. Three weeks later, Mike Checkland rang. Was I putting in for the British Council? He explained: 'I was talking to the Chairman, who asked if I thought you would apply. He is not on the selection committee but if you did, he would throw his weight behind you!' Then Mike added with a grin in his voice: 'I don't know if you find that reassuring or not?' We laughed at Hussey's sudden conversion to open selection for major posts.

I judged this burst of support for my interests as a belated attempt to salve governors' guilty consciences over the way they had treated me over the director generalship. I noted at the time that I lacked that 'deep knowledge in the pit of my stomach' that the British Council would be the right thing for me.

Final Whitehall dramas were yet to play out. The word was that the next public spending round would be very tight. Might it be so tight that the third year of the World Service's triennial funding for 1993-94, so laboriously earned and won, might be cut back? What a disastrous way to end my term! We sought assurances; I even considered resignation if it came to it. After a huge ceremonial banquet for the Soviet leader, Boris Yeltsin, at the Painted Hall in Greenwich on 9 November, I fell in with David Gilmore on our way to the subterranean loos. He was very agitated; the spending round was awful. As we leaned by the entrance to the gents', I asked for clarity. Could I take it that the World Service's agreed funding for '93/'94 would not be touched but that thereafter we might have to take our share of the general pain? 'Yes and no,' replied David, avoiding the swinging doors. Mike and I should come to the FCO on Wednesday for more news. On the way back home from Greenwich in the car, Annie recalls I was tense and grim-faced. As if that was not enough for an evening at a public banquet, Mike Checkland also took me aside – though not by the gents' loos. He would leave his post at Christmas six months early. He had my sympathy. How much plotting could flesh, blood and spirit stand? The wonder was that he had put up with it for so long.

But work had to go on. On Wednesday morning at the FCO, after a long litany of despair about public finances, David Gilmore handed Mike and me a small slip of paper with a few numbers pencilled on it. No World Service funding cuts in '93/'94; but there would be a £5 million reduction the year after. That was that: some pencilled numbers on a small piece of paper after a get-together outside the gents' in a former royal palace. Sometimes, Whitehall business could be done in very informal ways. Essentially, the World Service had survived. 'Have you ever seen me in such a state?', asked Mike afterwards. I had not.

We celebrated the 60th Anniversary of the World Service at Guildhall on 9 December. Prince Charles presided, though the event was overshadowed by the news that day of his divorce from Princess Diana. I threw my own farewell party at the National Portrait Gallery on 16 December. I included very few governors. Surrounded by friends from all Bush House's thirty-seven language services, fascinatingly varied, maddeningly distinctive, gloriously independent, I reflected on what might be the characteristics of a typical Bush House broadcaster. 'The self-discipline of the Russian Service; the waywardness of the Hindi Service; the restraint of the Latin Americans; the predictability of the Africans; the stoicism of the South-East Europeans; the optimism of the Central Europeans, and the sense of unity of the Arabs!' The fact is I loved them all. I was one of them. One old broadcasting friend murmured as she left: 'Is that the last of the BBC that we know and love?'

What mattered was my own sense of completeness, one shared by many colleagues. It mattered that the favourable judgement of international listeners came wrapped in very proper reserve: 'In a world of lies,' said one, 'you tell fewer. Of course we know where the BBC stands; it is a British perspective. But you are more reliable!' It mattered that we straddled the great British paradox of the relationship with government: 'We pay you but we won't tell you what to say.' It mattered that our jobs were immensely satisfying to us because they mattered to others: 'During the Cold War it was always said that we kept hope alive,' said one. 'How lucky I was to have a job that was so worth doing.'

I had shown that the BBC governors' gamble in appointing me in 1986 had paid off, that I could manage, lead and give a sense of purpose. With my colleagues, we introduced change without dogma, innovation without ideology, efficiency without rigidity, management without 'managerialism'. All these lessons were available to the BBC, a blueprint for change working with the grain of humanity rather than cutting across it. For myself, I said farewell to the lovely, motley, raucous, passionate, straggly caravan that was Bush House with its sixty cultures, dozens of tongues, hundreds of personalities and millions of connections with the world. But much of my heart never left.

9

Fighting Itself

The BBC 1991–92

The intense last two years of my time as Managing Director World Service were intertwined with, confused in and occasionally distracted by the drama of high-level BBC internal politics. These involved diversions of my time and energy. Yet none of these dramas and machinations got in the way of internal reform at Bush House. This was part of the benefit of being 'managerially responsible' for the World Service. As we made Bush House an island of purpose and stability, Broadcasting House was wracked by storms.

Because of my position heading BBC World Service, I was at the heart of these events. I sat on the BBC's Board of Management, attended all meetings of the Board of Governors, knew the members of both boards well, talked to them candidly, confidentially and liked some of them personally. Yet I was inevitably, perhaps mercifully, at a distance from the political, editorial and management issues that erupted in 1991 and 1992 in the affairs of the 'domestic' BBC. If my priority had to be steering the World Service, I had a ringside seat overlooking the affairs of the BBC as a whole. I could not be a neutral or disinterested observer; the World Service could only thrive within a healthy, strong BBC. What I witnessed and what I was told was so extraordinary and disagreeable that I recorded it on paper. My account of these two years is based on what I wrote in a journal. The events described feel grubby today, a story of infighting, gossip, malice, viciousness and incompetence at the very top of the BBC.

The year 1991 began with real uncertainty about the future leadership of the BBC. The governors were edgy. The Chairman, Marmaduke ('Dukey') Hussey, would reach the end of his term in September, the Vice-Chairman, Joel Barnett, the following June. A year further on, Mike Checkland's tenure as Director General would finish in March 1992. The feeling was that the future of the chairmanship should be settled well before autumn 1991 to manage an orderly succession to the director generalship. The speculation was that Hussey would get an eighteen-month extension, leaving a new chairman to navigate the further shoals of BBC Charter Renewal in 1994. Joel Barnett, we guessed, would not be renewed as Vice-Chairman, partly because they rarely were in the BBC, and largely because he was regarded as 'too gabby and indiscreet'. Despite our many disagreements, I had a soft spot for Joel, whom I saw as a 'cheeky chappie' and usually good for political gossip. My tolerance was to cost me dearly.

On Thursday, 11 April, the governors threw a grand farewell lunch for Paul Fox, the Managing Director Television. At the end of his speech, Paul said: 'I have something serious to say to end with. The BBC is a great institution and deserves to be handled decently. It has to know what its future leadership will be as it goes into the 1990s. Continuity or change, whichever it is, the BBC needs to know and to know soon.' As Paul sat down, Joel Barnett leaned over to me grinning broadly and said: 'I bet Dukey that he'd say that!'

We got clarity more quickly than we expected. It was not what we had hoped for. The week after the Fox farewell lunch, Checkland rang me with the news: Hussey would be extended for five years, a full term in office. The word from some was that Hussey was amazed to be extended at all, let alone for five years. It may well have been more than he wanted, though others said his lobbying in advance of the decision had been intense. In addition, Joel Barnett would serve a further two years as Vice-Chairman. We had asked for stability at the top but this was taking it too far! Reappointing the Chairman and

Vice-Chairman had the effect of firing the starting gun on the succession to the director generalship. This would be their decision, their responsibility. Two questions followed immediately. Who would it be? And how would the appointment be made? My concern was that a proper selection process should be followed, involving a public trawl for candidates leading to formal interviews with a selected shortlist. The post of Director General of the BBC was, after all, one of the major appointments in the national media, culture and communications scene. It had, surely, to be conducted in line with accepted principles of good governance.

The annual joint governors/management 'awayday' took place on 1–3 May at a very upmarket venue, the Lucknam Park Hotel & Spa, near Bath in Somerset. Leafy, wooded, cushioned in lawns and countryside, comfortable to the point of luxury, it became in my experience the setting for some truly grisly scenes of internal BBC politicking. It was also the place where I got closer to 'Dukey' Hussey than at any other time.

I played table tennis with him after dinner, often a very dead period in the conference. He was physically large, a real presence. Despite his prosthetic leg, despite a damaged right hand, the fingers gnarled and twisted – both severe war wounds – he was formidable, with sharp reflexes, a quick eye, deft wrist and remarkably mobile. As a young man he had been a considerable sportsman. He often beat me. One day, I was cooling off in the pool after the afternoon session. Behind me, the door from the changing room swung open. I looked over my shoulder to see who had entered but there seemed to be nobody there. Glancing down to ground level, I saw Dukey crawling over the poolside tiles on two hands and his one whole leg before launching himself from this tripod of stability into the pool. I admired his toughness. Whatever our growing disagreements about how he ran the BBC or about myself, I never forgot that image of the man's determination and courage.

Formally, the main business of the awayday was to consider plans to reduce the size of the BBC's resource base: studios, technical facilities, equipment of all kinds. Did we have too much, or more than we generally needed? Would it be better to reduce what we had and hire in the extra at times of peak demand? Potentially, I saw it as the first theoretical and political clash between Mike Checkland, the pragmatic Director General, and his more ideologically driven deputy, John Birt. Like a sheriff in a Western marching into town to restore order, Birt had two managerial weapons bulging in his holsters: one was called 'reform', the other 'efficiency'. In the event, it seemed to me, Lucknam Park in May 1991 was no Gunfight at the OK Corral, no terminal shoot-out, more a recce in strength. On this occasion, both Checkland and Birt chose not to clash head on. Yes, some studios would be closed; but no, we shouldn't be too dogmatic about how many and where. Everyone was on their best behaviour. Significant straws in the political wind would appear later.

Light relief at the start of the awayday had come from the Home Secretary, Kenneth ('Ken') Baker. He was shallow and depressing, which made his extravagant praise of the World Service even worse. I noticed that those most hostile to the BBC as a whole often doled out praise to the World Service as a code. 'This is what the rest of the BBC should be,' they insinuated. We hated being held up as some sort of 'goody-goody' version of the true BBC. Baker then launched into a eulogy of what he called the 'great English tradition of story-telling, from people like Shakespeare, Louis Stevenson, Charles Dickens'. The BBC should be part of this tradition, and Baker kept trotting out his newly minted narrative canon, 'Shakespeare, Louis Stevenson, Dickens,' as if mere invocation of great names, a mantra of middle-brow orthodoxy, would give substance to his thoughts.

In between sessions, the Lucknam Park lawns were the setting for many private exchanges, a kind of psycho-choreography, with groups of two or three circling, pausing, pondering, breaking off when interrupted. Some plotted, some whispered, some despaired. At one of these, I prodded Jane Glover, the arts governor, about the need for clarity over the BBC's leadership: which was it to be, continuity (Checkland) or change (Birt)? She replied drily that they 'had got the point'.

On the final evening, Greg Dyke from London Weekend Television gave the after-dinner speech. He seemed to me an odd choice but – as old-style communists always said – 'Comrades, this was no accident.' Dyke, the one-time ultra-populist, now reinvented from Harvard Business School, spoke glowingly of his managerial revolution at LWT. To me it sounded strikingly similar to the approach advanced by John Birt in his presentation on BBC Resources earlier in the day. Had there been pre-planned coordination of message? Conference conspiracy theorists, myself among them, were convinced there had been. Some in the room, I observed, applauded Dyke a little too enthusiastically. Maybe they had a prophetic vision of the future or at least a personal interest in it. Or perhaps they just knew what was going on.

At the conference close the following afternoon, the Chairman chose to sum up. He was very downbeat, full of the threats facing the BBC. 'What a summing up,' said one management colleague, 'all negative!' Incredibly, Hussey did not give Mike Checkland, his Chief Executive, the chance to give his assessment. The future of the director generalship was now in play.

In the days following Lucknam Park, I mused over the choice facing the governors. How did the arguments stack up? Writing at the time, the 'case for change' looked like this:

> The BBC needed radical change in the next five years. Checkland had been a great stabiliser after the sacking of Alasdair Milne. But he was inclined to caution and he was a known quantity. Looking for change as they were, he looked an unlikely leader of the change governors were seeking. He could not be the man for the new moment.

The 'case for continuity', as I saw it, was more complex but far from unreasonable:

Checkland had laid the foundations for future evolutionary change. He should be retained to build on them. He was systematic, efficient and effective. Staff and colleagues liked him and would work for him. Besides, did the governors know what they would get if they insisted on 'radical change'? And did they truly know the person, John Birt, who said he would deliver it?

I packed away my thoughts and travelled to New Orleans and Washington for meetings of Public Radio and the Voice of America. That was followed by a week's intense preparation before anchoring an entire BBC Radio 3 weekend of programmes from the twin cities of Minneapolis/Saint Paul masterminded by the Controller, John Drummond.

On return from my travels early in June, the process of decision-making clicked into place. The governors would meet on 1 July to decide the future leadership of the BBC. Just that. Despite the pressure, despite the lobbying, there would be no public advertisement, no headhunting, no systematic selection process, no interviews. The train of good governance had never left the station, let alone been coupled to an engine. Now speculation could really start about how the governors would cast their votes in a two-horse race.

However weighed up, the outlook looked bad for Checkland. Worse for the BBC, people were leaking to the press. Hussey was known to have lunched at the *Observer* the previous week. When that paper's high-level gossip column, Pendennis, claimed to know that Hussey, Barnett and P. D. James, a loyal follower of 'Dukey', wanted Checkland out, no one had to look far for the source. Whether a Chairman should have behaved like this was quite another matter. But how might the other governors split?

Based on what we thought we knew and on past form, at least three more governors would toe the Chairman's line: Shahwar Sadeque, because she always did; Nicky Gordon-Lennox, because he was pleased to have been appointed; and

Dr John Roberts, Warden of Merton College, Oxford, who had hated the BBC ever since his major TV series on world history failed to set either audiences or ratings alight. Add in the Welsh governor, John Parry, the vet who was absurdly grateful for being appointed at all, and Jane Glover, the conductor, who had never sounded enthusiastic about Mike's renewal or extension. If these forecasts were accurate, it would be a very short meeting.

Annie and I spent the evening at the final concert at the Wigmore Hall before an eighteen-month closure period for renovation. Peter Schreier, the great German tenor, gave a performance of Schubert's song cycle *Schwanengesang* with the then emerging Hungarian pianist, András Schiff. It was radiant, intense and mesmerising, totally banishing all thought of events elsewhere, especially those unfolding just 400 yards up the road at Broadcasting House.

The following morning, news soon spread. John Birt was the Chairman's choice as the next Director General; but Mike Checkland would stay on for an extra year until March 1993. The meeting was said to have been long and bloody, with a group of three 'floaters' finally coming down on Hussey's side only because they could not imagine opposing the Chairman. This decision meant there would be a twenty-one-month 'double-banking' of a current DG with his designated successor. Inevitably, such a decision led to confusion and contention rather than offering clarity, continuity or change. The infighting of the next eighteen months was the direct result of the governors' failure to choose one direction or another for the BBC's future leadership.

I noted at the time that I found the official BBC press statement about the appointments 'stomach-turning'. Mike was said to be 'delighted', Birt was praised, Hussey called it all 'marvellous'. I wrote in my journal: 'It was like a Kremlin handout with the victims thanking Comrade Beria for the correctness of his line, praising his character and ability while looking forward urgently to the time when Beria would blow their brains out.'

Apart from wanting – and failing to get – an explanation from Hussey about the lack of process in appointing the Director General (described in Chapter 8), I had a mini-crisis entirely of my own making to resolve. Some weeks previously, Roger Bolton, a former colleague from Lime Grove Current Affairs, approached me with the invitation to give the highly prestigious MacTaggart Lecture at the Edinburgh Television Festival in the summer. Rather against my instincts, I agreed to talk further. On 1 July, Bolton and his colleague, Peter Ibbotson, my former editor at the BBC Two *Newsweek* programme, came to plan it out. They were looking for a high-level piece of what I saw as obsessive TV techno-talk, all about the scale of national industrial bases, market shares, satellites, platforms and suchlike. I knew nothing of these topics and cared less. I countered with a fanciful proposal to look at how the TV world of the year 2000 would appear by comparison with writers' predictions in novels, drama or academic theory. It was a bad idea, I had no clue how to write it but I put it forward nevertheless. I should have turned the invitation down there and then.

My mind and stomach rebelled. I could not imagine writing any kind of MacTaggart Lecture in any shape or form. I was in a state of shock, not because I had been overlooked and rejected in absentia but because of the almost unconstitutional violation of the way the BBC should be run. When I rang Roger Bolton to tell him of my withdrawal, he was, rightly, not best pleased. I was treating good colleagues very badly. The media immediately linked my withdrawal from the MacTaggart Lecture with my not becoming Director General. I protested that pressure of work was the actual reason, batting back suggestions that I was 'considering my position' in protest at my treatment by the governors. But I did let friendly journos know how I felt. When accurate reports of my views appeared, I was content that governors should know of them.

Meanwhile, John Birt was visiting BBC managing directors to 'touch base'. He made no attempt to call on me at Bush House. There would have been little to say. On the Director

General's desk, Checkland sported a wooden duck, 'to show I am not downhearted!'.

A week later, a fortuitously timed farewell party for Lime Grove Studios in Shepherd's Bush threw the BBC's future direction into strong relief. Randomly converted out of old film studios, Lime Grove had been at the heart of BBC journalistic creativity for a generation. It was not a place for the faint-hearted or the overly scrupulous. Its critics called it conspiratorial (it was), driven by machination, egotism, infighting (it was) and characterised by irresponsibility (on occasion). When times were bad, it was said of the BBC Club Bar at Lime Grove that 'people are stabbing one another in the chest'. The place needed physical renovation of course, but not necessarily the journalistic approach of its denizens. These were increasingly out of kilter with the new, formulaic ways of making programmes. At the party, I looked at giants of the screen such as Ludovic Kennedy, Robin Day, Peter Dimmock and others. My eyes skated past those of John Birt. I had no doubt where my sympathies lay: with Lime Grove practices and ethos, imperfect and flawed as they sometimes had been.

Writing in my journal soon after, I decided that Lime Grove had been 'creative, innovative, devoted to programmes, combined entertainment with commitment, made big television figures, loved the medium, saw that creativity came from the combustion of individuals working in departments with a very strong ethos'. Instead, programming was now to be driven by types and categories of format divided and subdivided into 'genres', 'sub-genres' and – incredibly, but I had heard this proposed – 'sub-genres according to national regional needs'. On this new, reductive view, making programmes was a mere subdivision of planning. For myself, I defined a 'good programme' as the result of a 'good idea, strong editors who knew their mind, a team who believed in the idea, and presenters independent enough to realise the idea on air. Such was a creative, intuitive, human activity.' This was about to be undermined by market-driven pseudo-logic and pseudo-theory, or alternatively by sheer gobbledy gook. The physical farewell to Lime Grove Studios felt like a farewell to an era of programme-making which had made the BBC great.

Soon after, I called on Bill Cotton, Managing Director BBC Television, once king of light entertainment, a person of huge decency, common sense and wisdom. I needed to share and straighten out my thoughts. Had Bill read the clearly inspired article in the *Independent* saying that 'influential leaders in the BBC did not like the institution and wanted to change it'? Had it struck him – and these were my words – that 'too many of the governors hated the BBC'? I pointed to 'Dukey' Hussey, to Joel Barnett and above all to Dr John Roberts of Merton College, who 'never opened his mouth without sneering at the BBC – in the most elaborately polite donnish way, of course'. As for John Birt, Director General designate, he had already launched a root-and-branch attack on what he called 'old-style' BBC journalism. Bill Cotton paused and turned his thoughts over. 'Of course,' he reflected, 'it all falls into place. The politicians hate the BBC. So does Birt. The politicians like him because he shares their hatred. That is why he is where he is.' This shared conclusion was no comfort to either of us.

By mid-July, only a fortnight after taking the big decision, the governors were warring with each other. Their last meeting before the summer break was filled with complaints about the number of newspaper leaks. Many thought Joel Barnett was responsible. They cannot have enjoyed the way that the appointment 'non-process' was being criticised or that interested parties such as myself had spoken openly about it. At the start of the meeting, as Hussey formally noted the board's decisions about the future leadership of the BBC, few looked up, most avoided other people's eyes, many papers were shuffled in a pretence of business. The air was heavy with bad conscience and some doubt. It was too late. One departing governor commented: 'When I joined the BBC, the governors and management were deeply divided. When I leave, the governors are deeply divided.'

The summer business break in mid-July began with the First Night of the BBC Proms at the Royal Albert Hall. This was always a big BBC occasion, one for spreading the message about BBC excellence through invitations and hospitality. The Proms Director, John Drummond, was a generous master of ceremonies, gregarious host, brilliant programme planner and instinctive and persuasive showman. 'Dukey' Hussey, as Chairman of the BBC, was to be the official host of the first-night party. Reflecting the awfulness of the atmosphere within the BBC, Hussey had told Drummond there should be no after-concert supper, especially if Mike Checkland was to be there. But how could the Director General not be?

As Annie and I came into his Proms box for pre-concert drinks, Drummond approached, straight-faced: 'Awful news!' he warned. 'Dukey's not coming. He fell and broke his wooden leg and has hurt himself.' We looked one another in the eyes and agreed that the evening would not be the same without him. Apparently, Hussey had tripped coming down the stairs at Buckingham Palace the previous evening after a state banquet. He was in considerable pain. Real sympathy proved in short supply. The word was 'Dukey hates this music anyway!' As a result, the Director General had to host the box over which the Chairman should have presided. The irony was not lost on anyone.

We parted for the summer holidays with accusation and acrimony over the appointments. John Drummond, whose ebullience and forcefulness gave him a certain licence to harangue governors, used the Proms to tell any passing governor what a bad decision they had made. The novelist P. D. James had a particularly hard time for supporting Hussey's wishes. Giving her a lift home after one concert, Drummond let fly: 'You have got a good DG now; you could have had a potentially great DG waiting at Bush House; you have got rid of them both!' Phyllis, he reported, 'got very trembly and said of course they might have made a mistake but she could hardly be unaware of how some feelings were running'. The last embers of gossip about the way the decision was taken flared briefly in late September. One governor with a business background was reliably reported as saying: 'When the vote is six to five, you know that you cannot take that decision. It is too divided.' But it had been taken.

Major decisions were now needed on the size of the BBC's resource base and how the BBC's case for renewal of the Charter in 1994 should be made. The organisation needed strong focus, clear vision and an overriding sense of unity. As if these issues weren't big enough, the fifteen months to the end of 1992 saw arguments about the size of the BBC's audience share, what it should pay in pension contributions and whether it was breaking its overdraft limits. Instead of calm, the BBC wallowed in disputes, point-scoring and bitterness. The two boards, governors and management, were at open war with one another, often among themselves.

In this situation, responsibility had to lie squarely with the person at the very top, the Chairman. Hussey took a long time to recover from his fall at Buckingham Palace. He was often said to be working at only 70 per cent of his capacity. He would return from an overseas trip exhausted, complaining at the weight of papers facing him and accusing the BBC Secretariat of swamping him with complexity. He was in no condition to guide a riven organisation through a thicket of problems during a vexed transition which was entirely of his own making. Temperamentally, he had never comprehended that a chairman's role was to conciliate as well as to set a direction.

Throughout my final fifteen months, Hussey gave no sign of trying to reconcile the gaping divisions in the BBC leadership, either within the governors, between governors and management, still less between Checkland and Birt. The fact that his Vice-Chairman, Joel Barnett, had to have an operation for stomach cancer hardly helped matters. But I detected no sign that Hussey was aware of the gravity, the almost existential threat to the BBC that followed his decisions. A year of open, internal guerrilla war followed.

This was the year in which the BBC had to make its case for the renewal of its Charter, the governing document of its existence. How should the BBC go about it? How should it consult its own staff about the future? In my view, this demanded a wide canvassing of ideas across the organisation; how could a body that existed on and dealt in ideas not have ideas about its own future? In practice, the process was to be tightly managed by a small central group who employed outside consultants to lead selected specialist groups to what were predetermined conclusions. I objected to the controlling role of the consultants. And how could proposals for the future be made without understanding how large the BBC's resource base should be? This was the scene for the next battle.

On 14 October 1991, we announced the first stage of World Service Television News, the result of five years of effort, ingenuity and determination. At the Board of Management meeting that morning, battle was joined over the size of BBC Resources – how many studios did we really need? How many stood idle for how long? How much equipment was needed? How much could be hired in when needed? These issues became a tug of war between John Birt, the self-proclaimed manager, and Mike Checkland, the sharp-eyed sceptic. Picking holes in the schematic plans as Mike did, he was greatly helped by the consultants' naïve admission that so as not to 'overestimate' the demand for one particular BBC studio centre, they had 'reduced the number for demand by 50 per cent'. This shrieked of 'cooking the books'. The conclusion was to be a joint DG/DDG paper on what resources the BBC would need in future. Those present agreed it was a triumph for Checkland, a rout for Birt. We agreed, too, that the consultants had performed miserably and should be shown the door. Fascinating as such managerial wrestling was, it also seemed wasteful for the BBC's best minds to have ended up fighting one another. That was what 'double-banking' the top job led to.

Things turned really unpleasant at the Board of Governors meeting on 28 November. It was not clear how far they were triggered by a detailed article by Maggie Brown in the *Independent* the previous Tuesday. By now we were used to her apparent role as the unofficial mouthpiece of the Birt camp. Whether or not that was the case, Brown seemed to write with inside information. The BBC's audience ratings, she wrote, were 'disastrous', the television schedule was dismissed as 'weak'. Certainly, the article acted as a provocative curtain raiser for the appearance before the Board of the Controller of BBC One, Jonathan Powell. He explained quietly and patiently that BBC One could indeed compete with ITV on ratings if he commissioned programmes for the 6–7 p.m. slot to take on ITV's hugely popular *Coronation Street* and *Emmerdale*. They commanded the schedules and audiences. One by one, governors lined up to attack him. This was not what the BBC was about! Why could he not deliver a 50 per cent share of the ratings? Jonathan explained that with the arrival of satellites, the days of a 50 per cent audience share were long gone. If governors insisted on a greatly increased audience, he could move the evening news from 9 p.m. to 10 p.m. (then regarded as vandalism), *Panorama* to 10.30 (viewed as akin to treason) and replace arts and science with early-evening quiz shows. Governors seethed; they wanted bigger audiences, but not like this.

When Checkland felt obliged to point out that Powell had set out this identical scenario at Lucknam Park in May but that the board only authorised the necessary increased spending on drama a few weeks ago, Keith Oates, a governor from Marks and Spencer normally regarded as a voice of common sense, leaned across to David Hatch, Managing Director Radio, and said sarcastically: 'I see, it's all the Board's fault!' Throughout, they never accepted responsibility for their indecisions.

Things went from bad to worse. After seventy-five minutes of pillorying Jonathan Powell, Hussey said how concerned he was at hearing nothing from the Board of Management. Dr

John Roberts taunted me and Howell James, Director of Communications: 'Now then, chaps, I do hope you feel free to speak up at any time!' The truth was that management's contribution had been dismal. We did not speak up in Powell's support. We looked and sounded weak, disunited and thoroughly unimpressive. In the gents' loo at coffee time, Bill Jordan, the trade union governor, congratulated me on the successes of the World Service, 'the only part of the organisation that has done well'. Such praise at that time in that place was galling.

Weak as management's non-contribution was, most of the responsibility for the blatant irrationality of much of the discussion must lie at the Chairman's door. It was his duty to shape a balanced debate, drawing out a full range of opinions but not shying away from conclusions. He gave the impression of encouraging the governors' onslaught, whether intentionally or through incompetence. It was impossible to tell. Any real intervention by management would have led to head-on disagreement and a blazing row.

After coffee break, the BBC's six monthly financial accounts were on the table. On the face of it, they didn't look good, the BBC's official borrowing bumping up close to the agreed limit of £250 million. The Director of Finance, Ian Phillips, explained why this was happening. At Lucknam Park, the governors had agreed that instead of a one-off, lump-sum annual payment for the TV licence fee, viewers could pay in monthly instalments. This 'easy payment' system, it had been fully explained, would inevitably cause cashflow problems in the early years. Now they had arrived. The governors seemed disinclined to listen. Hussey leapt in; BBC finances were 'out of control'; the government was warning that they were worried; this was a poor springboard for charter renewal. But management had warned the governors of the consequences of their decision. Now, they were rewriting history and they did not like having this pointed out.

Never a man to miss an opportunity for mischief, John Roberts spotted that the accounts also contained a significant overspend on programmes commissioned or made but not yet transmitted. In his most silky tone, he declared that in an industrial organisation, such an overspend would lead to 'someone being held responsible for such unauthorised action'. In other words, somebody would lose their job? He did not hint at who he might have in mind.

Lunch was stiff and grim. I don't know how we faced one another. Afterwards, I walked Nicky Gordon-Lennox down the corridor. 'That was a ghastly meeting,' I said, 'what are you up to? Are you trying to drive Mike out early?' Nicky thought it had been stimulating but not aggressive. But he conceded: 'There were a couple of ball-tightening moments. But I do assure you, there is no general intention to get rid of him.' Was there a specific one? Back at Bush House, I let off steam to my deputy, the ever-patient David Witherow. I had seen one DG fired, Alasdair Milne; to watch it happen a second time would almost certainly be too much. The next day, David said it would be a tragedy if I went early and I promised to do nothing rash. But my gorge was rising at what I was witnessing. Scrutiny and challenge were one thing; systematic malice quite another.

In December, the governors signalled their dissatisfaction with management in a tangible way. BBC salaries generally needed to become more competitive; a major comparative pay review demonstrated how out of line they were. The governors accepted the case for some necessary pay adjustments for staff. These would, they insisted, specifically exclude Board of Management. We took it as a collective slap in the face.

Throughout December, press leaks included one from a Charter Review Group recommending the hiving off of the BBC orchestras, known to be an incendiary topic. At the board meeting on 19 December, Hussey made no attempt to stem the leaks but welcomed them as evidence of the BBC's seriousness in debating its future. He was probably the only person to think so. The meeting itself featured congratulatory remarks about the 'great achievements' of the World Service.

Someone had clearly suggested I needed stroking. The BBC's overdraft passed without acrimony and John Roberts was said to have accepted that he had gone too far at the previous meeting. The eruptions of the November board were regarded as a 'ghastly miscalculation' rather than any kind of conspiracy. But the Chairman had undoubtedly lost control.

The pre-Christmas governors' lunch on 19 December provided grim relief. Traditionally, guests included broadcasters and programme makers; the BBC was after all about programmes. My lunch companion was Belinda Lang, star of a then popular sit-com, *2.4 Children*. She reported on her pre-lunch conversation with the Chairman. How long was he to be Chairman, asked Belinda. Five years. Wasn't that rather long? asked Belinda sweetly. Yes, it did seem so and it was very heavy lifting. Couldn't he resign? asked Belinda. Yes, he could resign and that would certainly be one way out. Would it be different if Labour won the next election? asked Belinda. Yes, it would be very different in that event. Seemingly, an 'innocent' starlet put questions to Hussey that management could not dream of asking or having answered.

In the car back to Bush House, Barbara Myers, who presented the World Service magazine programme *Outlook*, was puzzled by the occasion. 'Are the governors supposed to defend the BBC?' she asked worriedly. I replied that since they were the BBC constitutionally, they did defend it though not invariably. Why did she ask? Barbara had been seated next to John Roberts who, to her surprise, launched into a wholly destructive case against the continuation of the BBC after 1996. Barbara said she was shocked and fought back. I explained why nothing John Roberts said surprised me. I added: 'Now you see what our problems are with the governors.'

The grim year of 1991 ended with a moment of schadenfreude. John Parry, the Wales governor, had voted with Hussey over the Director General appointment. His reward, he hoped, would be a second term on the board. Today we learned the Home Office had declined to renew him. It was impossible to feel sorry. I was aware of a coarsening of my responses to people and events.

The first six months of the Interregnum at the BBC had been predictably unpleasant. Could 1992 be any worse? If there was a governors/management truce, it lasted just two months. The Cardiff meeting on 4–5 March 1992 saw pitched battle over how much the BBC needed to pay into the pension fund to meet its obligations. Actuaries calculated that even if the BBC stopped paying contributions altogether for eight years until the year 2000, the fund would still be overvalued; it could meet all conceivable future obligations. They recommended conservatively that staff and employers could reduce annual contributions to 3 per cent per annum. This would release several million pounds for making programmes. Ian Phillips thought the BBC should not be putting licence fee funds into areas where they were not needed. Management backed Ian Phillips and was broadly united.

Hussey returned from a trip to Hong Kong, Australia and Singapore on the eve of the Cardiff meeting jet-lagged and exhausted. BBC Secretariat immediately briefed him on what they saw as the dangers of reducing the BBC's pension contributions regardless of the actuaries' professional advice. I believe he was nobbled. All of us awaited the discussion with anxiety. I had a particular interest in the recommendation: reducing pension contributions would put more than £1 million into World Service finances. (Later I had to fight off FCO attempts to claw the money back.)

Ian Phillips presented the actuaries' case and explained why the BBC could safely reduce its pension contributions. Normally the word of the Finance Director would carry weight, but these were not normal times. John Roberts deployed classic, university-honed delaying tactics: the time wasn't right, call for more papers, take stock, wait until the summer. As usual Shahwar Sadeque played 'little Miss Echo'; so did Nicky Gordon-Lennox, the Chairman's friend. Encouragingly, the new Northern Ireland governor, the independently minded former civil servant Ken Bloomfield, had no difficulty with the proposal nor did another new governor, the Welsh businessman, Gwyn Jones. Another businessman, Keith Oates, of whom we expected more, was only cautiously supportive. Joel Barnett, in his favourite 'financial man of the world' mode, slammed the actuaries and doubted their numbers. Facing disaster, Checkland warned of the damage rejection would do to the World Service in particular and suggested a reduction of BBC contributions to a mere 4.5 per cent rather than the recommended 3 per cent. This was a pure Checkland canny tactical concession. Hussey welcomed the idea as statesman-like almost, I thought, with relief.

We were still not home and dry. Given the uncertainty over the level of the BBC's contributions, Ian Phillips had delayed paying into the pension fund the fourth-quarter sum of £9 million. Once paid in it would be irretrievable. Hussey virtually accused Phillips of improper conduct. Yet he was only acting as a prudent Finance Director should, husbanding an institution's resources as efficiently as possible. What was suddenly clear was that the governors loathed anything that might make management's life easier. They preferred resources to be locked away unproductively in an already overvalued pension fund rather than being put into programmes. Such was the depth of the chasm between non-executives and executives.

The argument had lasted ninety minutes. It had been bad-tempered, narky and fuelled by undertones of unadmitted resentment. Much of the responsibility for the confusion had to lie at the Chairman's door. Hussey could not lead that discussion and appeared – perhaps was – indifferent to the almost public humiliation delivered to the BBC's most senior executives. He was less an impartial Chairman, more a leader of the opposition, perhaps even leader of a lynch-mob! Over drinks at the Cardiff hotel, a small group of us groaned with horror at what had been a disgraceful performance, destructive at best, sheerly malicious at worst. Ian Phillips wondered why he put up with it. (He would be gone by the year end.)

The BBC's annual budget was approved fairly smoothly at the next meeting on 9 April. But discussion of the Charter Review process presaged the next major row. Work was almost complete; everyone seemed content; when should we publish? Overwhelmingly, management believed that early publication by the BBC before the government's views on the future in a consultative Green Paper would be right. It would show an organisation confident in its case, its performance and its future. The first seeds of dissent were sowed: 'Shouldn't the BBC wait to publish until the government's own thoughts came out in the autumn Green Paper? Wasn't it presumptuous for the BBC to "go first"?' These seeds came to flower on lush and fertile ground in the parkland idyll of luxurious Lucknam Park on 20 May.

The two boards spent almost the whole day agreeing the substance of the Charter Application. I thought the result adequate but uninspired. Given the top-heavy way in which ideas had been managed and directed, the result was better than might have been expected. Significantly, Hussey made no contribution of thought or time to the Charter process. Later he complained that it was a 'standstill' document. If so he had done nothing to move it forward. A month previously, governors had enthused about the vigour and creativity of the World Service's look into the future, 'World Service 2000'. That document came from freeing up Bush House colleagues at all levels to think and imagine. Sadly, the governors never reflected on whether that confident, open approach might not have been preferable to the domestic BBC's consultant-based and constipated processes. If the World Service was publicly admired within the BBC, it was never taken as a possible model of management. But would the BBC dare to publish its own proposals before the government?

The main event at Lucknam Park that day was the visit of the Secretary of State for Culture, David Mellor, with his Permanent Secretary, Hayden Phillips. Mellor's diary was tight, confused and changing constantly. He would stay for dinner.

No, there was a three-line whip on Maastricht in the Commons. He would come at six and leave at eight. No, he would come at four-thirty and leave by six. What was constant was neurosis about publicity from the event. A large van was parked across the library windows of the hotel to keep out photographers' prying lenses.

The opening exchanges were friendly enough. Mellor said he liked broadcasters and broadcasting. He had no argument with the BBC; it was his job to 'hold the ring' within which argument could take place. It should be fair and candid, not driven by rancour or personalities. There were no 'scores to settle' with the BBC though he noted that some – not him – thought the BBC was 'too many things to too many people'. So far, so bland.

Then the crunch: the timing of the BBC's own publication on its future. The government Green Paper would be in September. Mellor himself would not mind if the BBC published first! Others, though, might then take the opportunity to enter the debate early and destructively. Mellor seemed slightly unsure in his own mind as he turned to his 'mandarin', Hayden Phillips, for a steer. Phillips did not let his 'master' down. 'Well, Minister, as I might say in my best *Yes, Minister* way, a BBC decision to publish first would be seen as "very courageous". We would watch them get out of the hole with interest.' As uncomfortable laughter rippled through the room and as courage ebbed fast, Hayden Phillips moved in smoothly with the Whitehall stiletto: 'Of course, if you publish first, then the Green Paper will have to be very different.' It was a statement of the obvious and also studiedly ambiguous. But it was heard as a threat.

Hussey and Mellor had a long chat in the drive before Mellor returned to London. Governors and directors meandered gloomily around the darkling lawns. I told one of them I hated being bullied; our colleagues would hate it. I found another who seemed to back me over early publication of the BBC document. I told Mike Checkland: 'Well,' he said, 'I agree with you, there's the two of you, can you deliver ten other governors?' We knew the answer. The game was up. Later, Tim Bell, the BBC's media guru, agreed with me that the BBC's decision not to publish before the government did was a disaster. It was too late.

The only person to enjoy himself that evening was Hayden Phillips. He had not expected to speak but, with his minister absent, he was asked to fill the vacant after-dinner slot. For a practised Whitehall mandarin, this was part of the job. Swaying on the balls of his feet, Hayden Phillips told us a fable of political life: 'In my previous incarnation in the Treasury, I was involved in NHS reform. A consultant took me into a ward where Mrs X was lying plugged in with tubes and wires. "Mrs X," he said, "this is Mr Phillips from the Treasury." She leaned forward to greet me and shake my hand, not knowing that the Treasury is usually involved in switching off life-support machines.' Nervous laughter rippled around the dining room. Hayden Phillips moved towards his point: 'My minister is not in the business of switching off life-support machines such as the licence fee. I think his message was clear.' If this was intended to be modestly reassuring, it failed with that audience. The previous five hours had killed stone-dead any notion of the BBC publishing its Charter Renewal proposals before the government did.

The entire Lucknam Park conference of May 1992 had itself become a target for press ridicule. Why was the BBC leadership living it up at a five-star luxury bolt-hole for the rich? Why was the BBC spending licence-fee money on such organisational hedonism? Ask the Chairman. It did not help that the weather was warm, the sun shining, the lawns gleaming. The air was heavy with feelings of remoteness and privilege.

The assembled press failed to get hold of the story of the very wide debate about relations between the two boards – governors and management. Hussey said he had tried to make the two boards functionally unified but agreed with Joel Barnett that we had slipped back to the old atmosphere.

He overlooked his own responsibility for the situation. I pointed out that although the managing directors now sat in on the entire meeting, we did so by invitation only, not by right. This was profoundly inhibiting. I added that the length of the governors' private session before the full meeting inevitably created tension and suspicion. It could last an hour. What was going on? Mike Checkland confirmed that when he came into the Council Chamber after attending some of the governors' private meeting, the managing directors all looked at his body language to guess how awful the previous session had been. It wasn't, it appeared, disagreeable only for management. Jane Glover said that when she entered the Council Chamber after the private session, we glared at her 'as if I were going through the Green Channel carrying illegal undeclared drink'. Keith Oates observed that the BBC was the only organisation he knew of where the non-executive board was more powerful than the executive. With such dysfunctional governance at the top of the BBC, it was a miracle that it survived.

By the beginning of August the BBC's case for renewal of the Royal Charter was nearly complete. I looked back on the ups and downs of the process and found it depressing: 'No unified idea of the future; no idea of strategy; major issues of priorities ducked, realignment of radio frequencies not addressed.' Yet I could not, ever, despair of the BBC as such. There were so many contradictions, I mused: 'It's odd. Are we weak or strong? On the up or down; well directed or badly; rigid or innovative; creative or bureaucratic; cowed or rampaging? On the evidence, we might be all the positive things listed rather than the weak, declining body we are often painted as being. Yet the danger is still in the perceived strength. The cry of "The BBC is too strong" could still be the danger cry to watch in the Charter debate.'

Such was the corrosive distrust and disloyalty among the highest levels of the BBC that the substance of the Charter Renewal draft was leaked to *Broadcast* magazine at the end of

August. It undermined the entire Lucknam Park strategy – if it deserved the name – of waiting for the government's Green Paper. We had already surrendered any tactical advantage we might have had, any element of surprise from 'going first'. Whatever the motive behind the leak, the BBC was surely weakened by it.

From September, my own time as senior BBC executive was running out. My final contribution to World Service colleagues would be to get them the right leader – preferably one who shared Bush House's editorial beliefs and priorities. Time and again, I insisted that the choice had to be by open, public process; the World Service deserved no less. Centrally, the BBC seemed in no hurry to find a successor.

The two-year internal BBC war reached a kind of climax at the end of October 1992. On 20 October the Royal Television Society held a seminar about the future of the BBC. Elizabeth Smith, Controller, English Services, came rushing into my office at Bush House. 'DG has made an extraordinary attack on the Chairman. He said he was too old to guide the future of the BBC; the way John Birt had been appointed was ludicrous; and the governors interfered too much.' The press were agog; the *Evening Standard* carried five column inches on the attack. What had triggered it?

As part of the conference debate, my former colleague, Fiona Murch of *Channel Four News*, had made a twelve-minute film about the issues facing the BBC. In it she said: 'The BBC's three-headed leadership was no good; it was full of tensions and contradictions and it was ruining the BBC.' At the coffee break at the seminar, people crowded round Fiona saying how 'near the knuckle it was'. She was only saying out loud what everyone was muttering in private. But had her film, Fiona wondered, acted as a trigger for Checkland's subsequent outburst? His guard had fallen. The wonder was that he had kept it up so long.

Matters began to unravel fast. I witnessed one final tussle between governors and management. On 28 October, the

governors' Audit Committee was concerned that BBC Network Television was overspending heavily; the BBC, they
feared, was close to breaching its overdraft limit. Heads, they
said, had to roll. Amazingly, the Director of Finance, Ian Phillips, was not present. A fortnight later, he was criticised over
the same issue by another governors' sub-committee. He told
me bitterly that he had been 'thrown to the wolves'.

Ian had just two shots left. A letter to the national dailies
stated that BBC spending was in line with the agreed budget;
it was in no sense out of control. 'The governors won't like that
at all,' he told me. At the final board meeting of the year, Ian
Phillips went one stage further. He bluntly told the governors
how he saw the finances and added, 'I do not expect to read
stories to the contrary after I am gone.' It was a decent man
demanding that his record should be treated with honesty and
respect. As Annie and I flew back from a visit to Egypt at the
beginning of December, we read a newspaper on the plane
announcing Ian's resignation as Finance Director.

The governors' Christmas lunch was awful even by its own
low standards. The Chairman praised the BBC's efficiency
and its commitment to artistic activities. Considering that
both Mike Checkland and I were leaving within days, his
failure to refer to either of us spoke volumes. John Roberts
had the last word over coffee: 'We had intended you to be the
next Director General but three.' His sneering made leaving
very easy.

What had gone so disastrously, unpleasantly wrong over
the previous eighteen months when the BBC was truly at war
with itself? The first error was to reappoint 'Dukey' Hussey as
Chairman for five years. Given his age, his physical injuries and
the demands of the job, this was pushing him further than he
could go. Hussey's weaknesses as a Chairman, his prejudices,
his snobbishness, his failing ability to concentrate unfitted
him for a taxing job. The second error was to extend Joel Barnett, the Vice-Chairman, for two years. Hussey and Barnett
played off one another's prejudices and vanities. A different

Vice-Chairman might just have counterbalanced Hussey's strong mood swings.

Hussey and Barnett then jointly committed the third great, defining error of the time – 'double-banking' the BBC's executive leadership by extending Checkland for a further year while crowning John Birt as the successor. They may have thought that not to have extended Checkland would look too much like getting rid of him. Governors may have thought they were playing safe. In fact they plunged the BBC into division and confusion.

Mike Checkland was practical, pragmatic, shrewd and a decent human being, He would manage change 'with the grain' of BBC beliefs, values and skills. John Birt, his appointed successor eighteen months ahead of time, believed in systems, processes and structures. He would apply these – many said impose them – to an organisation based on beliefs, values, skills and ideas. There was little spontaneity in John Birt's world. I often sat next to him at governors' meetings. He prepared any intervention by writing it out in longhand organised in bullet points laid out in classic consultants' 'landscape' format. There was little room for the instant response driven by the sudden rush of ideas expressed in the forms of written English. Bullet points are mere assertions, expressions of dogma, unconnected by logic.

Above all Birt had no time for talk of 'BBC values'. He was critical of much BBC journalism. He was publicly dismissive of those, like my friend John Drummond, whom he considered 'tainted by experience'. He did not go out of his way to ingratiate. I once rang the Secretariat urgently before a BBC formal dinner begging that my wife should not have to sit next to John Birt; once had been enough. 'You're not the only Director to ring and ask for that,' replied a stressed secretary.

Birt and I never exchanged the most casual of social words at meetings. I do know that he wholly disapproved of what he thought I stood for. One of his senior outriders – Alan Yentob, still highly placed in the BBC – met a young producer who said he had worked with me on a project. Yentob commented: 'Oh, in that case, we must have you decontaminated!' Birt would never have got within reaching distance of understanding my conviction that 'to change an institution, you must love it first'.

BBC staff were in many ways untidy, inconvenient, unpredictable, individualistic. They could be self-indulgent, ungovernable, irreverent and bolshy. But they were often creative, frequently original and never forgot that they worked for and to an audience. So how could a person with a devotion to the tidy, the calculated, the predictable, the managed, a man so convinced of the correctness of his views, be the right person to put in charge of one of the world's great creative organisations?

It might be argued that given the challenges facing the BBC, some robust decisions by the governors were called for. After all, the BBC had a new Charter to fight for; there were indeed problems over cashflow, levels of borrowing, production overspends, the share of the audience and pension contributions. The BBC itself was trying to reorganise how it commissioned programmes, how large its resource base should be. Surely, it could be argued, the Chairman and governors had to step up the pressure if they thought management was falling down on the job? Were the bitterness and miseries of 1991–92 in truth a reflection of the shortcomings of BBC management rather than those of the BBC governors?

This does not bear examination. For a start, management was divided in theory and in practice by the chasm resulting from the governors' decision to 'double-bank' BBC leadership. This chasm had a damaging, even crippling, effect on executive decision-making and clarity of policy-making. Worse was to follow. Management no longer trusted the governors when contentious issues invariably turned into major disputes between the two boards. Consensus about how to run the BBC, even about its future, collapsed. In such a failure of governance, responsibility must lie with the Chairman and the non-executive board. They neither accepted this responsibility nor had a way of facing up to it and mitigating it. Instead they lapsed into guerrilla war against management with the Chairman looking on and then complaining about the gap between the boards. Who permitted the 'war of the BBC with itself' to flourish? Only one person, the Chairman, 'Dukey' Hussey.

If I left the BBC World Service with a light step and a sense of achievement shared with my colleagues, I left Broadcasting House with a deep sense of anxiety about a great organisation soon to be radically reshaped against its real nature. These were no longer my problems. Yet I could not wholly shrug off my concerns about where the BBC was heading. Nor could I ever forget the distasteful, destructive, undignified way in which the business of a great organisation had been conducted. Over the next two years, as part of my own farewell to the BBC, I would set out my beliefs in detail and put my thoughts to the test.

10

Breaking with the BBC

1993–94

It was difficult to leave my official position within the BBC, to give up daily involvement in its affairs, however melodramatic and bizarre they were. Intense immersion in the organisation had left me verging on the obsessive. For my own satisfaction at least, I needed to give time to examining what the BBC was becoming under the new leadership of John Birt and how substantial was my constant critique of what I called his new 'managerialist' culture. I defined this as giving priority to the routines and processes of management over the values, skills and disciplines of broadcasting itself. Had the BBC had any kind of 'exit interview' available to outgoing executives, I might have addressed these questions at the time. As it was, I had to take stock in my own way as part of a personal 'exit strategy'. But events at the BBC after my departure also made 'letting go' quietly almost impossible.

My standard response to the question 'How do you think Birt will do as Director General?' was simple: 'He has got to succeed.' I meant it. Wracked as the BBC had been over the previous three years, the failure of the Birt regime would cause intolerable damage to an institution I loved. So, whatever I thought of his theories and methods, 'Birt had to succeed'.

He almost fell at the first fence. Early in January 1993, the *Independent on Sunday* broke the story that Birt's BBC salary was being paid into a private company of which he was a self-employed employee. As it was reported that he even charged his Italian suits through the company, it was quickly branded

the 'Armani Suits' affair. There was of course nothing improper about such a tax-favourable arrangement. Hadn't the
governors approved it? This was to miss the point: perceptions
mattered. For the 18,000 BBC staff, to be directed by a person
who couldn't be bothered to serve as a BBC employee himself
mixed indifference with arrogance.

The situation was then thoroughly mishandled, as I recorded
in my journal. Birt's letter to all staff saying he would immediately move to the BBC payroll was judged insensitive in tone
and unapologetic in manner. His proffered explanation that
'he came from another world' caused paroxysms of laughter.
And there were the Sherlock Holmes-ian 'dogs that did not
bark'. Where was support from within the BBC? What did the
governors think?

Internal support finally came from six senior BBC correspondents in a letter to *The Times*. They warned with all their
accumulated journalistic authority that the BBC faced a stark
choice, that it stood at a crossroads: either staff supported
'reform' under John Birt or the corporation faced a dread 'A. N.
Other' and an inevitable return to the bad old unreconstructed
days of the 'Alasdair Milne BBC'. The letter writers quickly
became known as the 'Magnificent Six' – they included John
Simpson, Martyn Lewis, Polly Toynbee and Ian Hargreaves. It
was widely treated with contempt; in particular, Peter Jay's
pompous claim that the letter had been written 'out of a regard
for the truth' induced still more hilarity among staff.

I found myself drawn into the maelstrom. The press began
to identify me as what they called the 'Insiders' Choice' to run
the BBC if Birt did not survive (which some thought a real
possibility). The 'Sunday Indie' then claimed that the heavy-
hitting media consultants, Lowe Bell, had been hired to talk up
Birt and to rubbish me. This was highly flattering. At no stage
did I suggest to anyone that I 'might be available to serve' if the
occasion demanded. I did not yearn for one last hurrah. The
fact that some within the BBC feared that I might be 'available'
only revealed the depth of the crisis and their own paranoia.

The governors remained silent. With 'Dukey' Hussey away in the Far East, attention turned to him and his responsibility for the mess. Who after all had insisted on appointing Birt as Director General? Who had plunged the BBC into its past three years of turmoil? Who had sanctioned Birt's tax arrangements? Perhaps Hussey was the person who should resign? From that moment, when the journalistic hounds caught the scent of a more gamey prey, Birt himself was safe.

Hussey, however, still had a fight on his hands. At a governors' dinner on his return from Asia, Hussey whipped in his devoted supporters, such as the crime novelist P. D. James. He then bullied the others into a quite extraordinary set of positions. The governors accepted full collective responsibility for Birt's tax arrangements. So that was that, massive retrospective approval; Birt did not need to resign; neither did the Chairman. As Hussey observed, 'it is not in the BBC's interest that anybody should resign,' thus confusing, not for the first time, the BBC's interest with his own. Even a scorching denunciation by the *Guardian*'s Hugo Young headed 'Brazen Hussey Must Go' had no effect. The storm had been weathered.

The loose ends of my career-long relationship with the BBC kept getting farcically knotted. Early in 1993, I had returned to broadcasting, presenting the *One O'Clock News* on BBC One from Television Centre. When the BBC Annual Report for 1992 appeared later in the year, supposedly an official record of the past year, the *Financial Times* diary spotted that while everyone else who had left official and senior positions in the Corporation was acknowledged in the Report, I was not. The document is supposed to be a journal of BBC record. On the evidence of the official publication, I was not part of the record; I might not have existed. I was airbrushed out.

This caused bureaucratic panic at Broadcasting House. A hastily composed letter of apology complete with 'Dukey's' handwritten additions was chauffeured round to me in the newsroom at White City. My diary has it marked in capital letters on 3 August 1993: 'Chairman's Letter!' Hussey explained my omission from the BBC Annual Report by pleading acute time pressures during its preparation. Yet nobody else was overlooked. On this evidence, as far as the BBC officially was concerned, my six years at BBC World Service might never have been. I was struck more by the bad manners than by the incompetence.

Closer reading of the Annual Report revealed a further omission. The year under review, 1992, included the BBC World Service's appearance before the fearsome House of Commons Public Accounts Committee. On its agenda had been the National Audit Office's recent evaluation of the World Service. The NAO and the PAC had concluded without reservation that the World Service was efficiently and effectively run. It came as near to a clean bill of health as any public organisation would get from such scrutiny. Yet the BBC Annual Report for 1992 ignored this outside evaluation and made no mention of the authoritative performance under MPs' questioning of the Director General, Michael Checkland, the official 'accounting officer' for the BBC World Service.

With hindsight, I believe this omission was deliberate and decided at the highest levels of the BBC. Within two years, the World Service would be controversially 'integrated' into the domestic BBC's structures. How could this administrative coup d'état have been justified if the World Service's demonstrated efficiency and effectiveness had been formally acknowledged in the BBC's own publications? Incompetence, inefficiency or indifference will no longer do as an explanation for such a glaring omission. It was ruthless censorship and a suppression of the historical record for internal political purposes.

It is not surprising that by August 1993 I felt the need to pull my thoughts together on the BBC. I called it, unoriginally, 'Thoughts on the Present Discontents' in a piece intended for publication but never actually placed. I began by noting the quiescence within the BBC about its new administration. Many insiders spoke to me of a 'climate of fear' within the Corporation, though I noted without comment that such a 'climate of fear' had been officially declared 'not to exist'! A colleague offered me verbal codes for staying out of trouble amidst new BBC ways: 'If you are talking to someone who refers to "John", keep your mouth shut. If they talk of "John Birt", it is still best to be careful. But if they call him "Birt", you know you're talking to a friend!'

I challenged the context and environment in which the BBC internal debate was taking place, one of 'false simplicities, blunt antitheses, of Manichean dichotomies'. These assertions were: 'Either the BBC "reforms" or it returns to the "ancien regime"; there is only one road to efficiency; either you are wholly committed to every detail of reform or you cannot be interested in reform at all.' These sounded too much like the mantras of the Thatcher years: 'Are you one of us?' and 'There is no alternative.'

I suggested that, rather than parade such directed certainties, questions should be asked about 'the nature of the changes; the manner of their implementation; their suitability and relevance to an institution of a very particular kind'. I defended my belief that the BBC was indeed a particular kind of institution. This was not special pleading:

> It is not to urge that change is inevitable for others but inconvenient for us. It is to insist that blueprints for change must, when imposed on a mature organisation, have due regard for the nature of the organisation if they are to stand a decent chance of succeeding. It is not good management to ride rough shod over what exists because you cannot bother to understand it or will not differentiate between the good to be saved and the bad to be discarded.

For good measure, I restated my conclusion from a 1992 speech about the philosophy and practice of managing change: 'An institution must be loved and respected if it is to be changed. Provided that such love and respect exist and their existence is recognised, then the process of change itself can be fairly brisk, not least because there will be people who wish to be part of it because it meets their own wishes. Without love and respect, a clamorous programme of change can only run into resistance and never gain full intellectual legitimacy.' Which is exactly what happened in the Birtian BBC.

I noted that one of the tactics of the new regime was to portray itself as founder of 'Year Zero'. Everything new and worthy, on this view, began with them; naturally, everything that existed before 'Year Zero' was worthless. I knew from my colleagues in the television newsroom that new managers were busily rewriting the BBC's past practices and fantastically distorting its characteristics:

> That there was no management worth speaking of; that there were no financial controls worth the name; that producers were selfish egotists who had to be checked by the threat that an independent might take over their ideas and output; that journalists were unprincipled scavengers who had to have responsibility institutionalised into them in order to control their excesses; that those who worked in the BBC did so more out of personal gratification than a sense of public responsibility.

If I slightly exaggerated the criticisms levelled by Birtists at what they presented as previous BBC behaviour, it was impossible to exaggerate the tone of Puritanical superiority and dogmatic certainty with which they were delivered. But then those possessed of a new truth know that they must tell it as they see it. It was neither a pretty sight nor a pretty sound.

I then challenged key areas of so-called 'new thinking' shortly to become entrenched as BBC administrative orthodoxy. The Charter Renewal process had not dared to enlist new thinking from within the BBC; management consultants acted as perimeter guards on any possible outbreak of originality or invention. Those consultants remained in place even after Charter Renewal was completed; 'their presence', I was told, 'felt like an occupying army complete with thought police whose zealous aim was to introduce correct management thinking.' As one colleague said: 'BBC morale could be improved at a stroke if the whole set of management consultants was sent packing tomorrow!' The essence of the obsession with management consultants was that the Birtian regime did not trust the staff. In which case, why should staff trust the bosses? Of course they didn't.

Writing in August 1993, I insisted that the use of external consultants needed 'a sense of proportion. If change can only be mediated through outsiders, then it signals all too clearly that the organisation and its people cannot be trusted to manage change themselves. This downgrades the staff within, devalues their ideas and diminishes their experience.' I added: 'It reduces them to management objects, to units who will have change imposed upon them because they will not produce change themselves. It tells staff that their ideas are worthless, that they cannot contribute to the new direction, that the ideas of outsiders are intrinsically more valuable.'

This was my personal credo: people are not 'management objects', they are not just part of a solution, they must be the solution. I could and did cast doubt on the 'great' management innovations of the time such as Producer Choice, Specialist Units, or the semi-literate neologism of 'bi-medialism' (the edict that every correspondent must be equally proficient in radio and television). Some of these innovations lasted longer than others. Some were better than others. None deserved to be regarded as 'the only way'. What I could see with increasing clarity was that management styles came and went, management nostrums waxed and waned, fads and fashions jostled one another. None of them was 'the truth', none even came close to being 'a truth'. An organisation like the BBC deserved to be treated not just with trust but with understanding of the worth of its own accumulated wisdom. Rejecting this was arrogant and would ultimately be self-defeating.

I used this approach in examining those essential tools of

modern management, objectives and performance indicators. To put it in plain English (which the 'managerialists' never did): 'What will you do and how will you know if you have done it?' Good questions, all the better when simply put. I insisted that the use of objectives would be more effective if they helped staff to do their jobs better rather than be used as instruments of correction when targets were not met. We had used objectives and performance indicators fully at the World Service for years past and were very specific about how they should be applied:

> They should help to reinforce positive activities rather than create new ones. They should derive from existing measures of activity codified in a systematic way if needed. The process should not lead to extra costs and should not spawn a huge new sub-industry of factitious indicators whose purpose served neither programme makers nor audiences.

Many of my newsroom colleagues in the 1993 BBC told me that performance indicators had become just the 'sub-industry' that I had predicted, with rival sets of indicators brandished by bureaucrats seeking managerial advantage. At the World Service, I was told, there were already three competing sets of indicators, each claiming the truth about World Service performance.

Working in the television newsroom, as I did for three days a week in mid-1993, I was well placed to witness an organisation troubled in spirit and doubtful in mind about the ways of the new regime. My conclusion was that the new intensive one-day 'training sessions' – dismissively labelled 'Ground Hog Days' – felt more like an attempt to tell staff that they were wrong than that new systems were right. My colleagues stubbornly withheld their consent. I summed up their views like this: they doubted that greater efficiency would flow from the changes, or at least not in the quantities promised; they were concerned about the growth of independent productions; and they saw the BBC's resource base of people, skill, equipment and facilities being undermined. Just to be told that all the new systems were right, true and necessary was mere assertion, a blunt instrument of management which neither persuaded nor gained consent. I have no doubt that I caught the mood of many in the BBC in August 1993 accurately.

I did not try to publish these thoughts. The time did not feel right; my motives would have been rubbished. I was principally writing for myself, testing my own critique of the new regime. I became convinced that my approach to leadership through people, with people, for programmes, for audiences, informed by thoughtful management could have worked in the BBC. I had long since ceased worrying about the fact that the governors did not consider me for the post of Director General. My 'Thoughts on the Present Discontents' reassured me strongly that they had been wrong not to do so. I no longer regretted it.

Then an opportunity came that I could not refuse. Hugh Stephenson, Professor of Journalism at City University, London, rang in late spring 1994 with an invitation to give that year's James Cameron Memorial Lecture. Cameron had been a journalistic giant of his time, fearless, opinionated, fluent, daring, unique. To stand in his shadow was to be in a place of honour. Previous lecturers had been Michael Grade, Tom Bower, Godfrey Hodgson, Liz Forgan, Louis Blom-Cooper, Denis Forman and Ben Bradlee. This was good company. I accepted. What would I talk about? I had no interest in a routine piece of BBC-baiting spiced with juicy tidbits of life at the top management table. I would tell no tales out of school, spill no confidences, settle no old scores. What might be worth saying?

I cannot remember where the theme for my lecture came from: 'Programmes or Products: The Management Ethos and Creative Values'. What emerged on 14 June 1994 was later aptly summed up by Hugh Stephenson: 'A scarcely coded attack on Birt's management consultant approach to his mission (which) reflected widespread internal distrust at what Birt was doing.'

My coding was indeed thorough and deliberate. I made no mention of the Director General at all, by name or by title; there were very few references to the BBC as such. I spoke a good deal about the origins of the Whitehall managerial revolution from 1982 onwards. This was the world in which the BBC World Service had demonstrated its efficiency and effectiveness. I analysed how the new management disciplines could be used and when they were used wrongly. I noted that when Whitehall examined its own practices, it warned against 'the pitfalls of radical change poorly handled, roughly introduced and crudely imposed'. That sounded familiar. It warned of 'the damaging side effects ... of introducing institutional change in the name of management efficiency and effectiveness'. That sounded familiar too.

I added further cautionary evidence from the press. The *Observer* had quoted a senior civil servant as saying: 'All the very naïve management theories that have been chucked at us in the last ten to fifteen years have had a corrosive effect. They have not been thought through, they have not been applied by people who believe in them, and because the civil service is not used to this sort of thing, it has probably accepted fads and fashions too easily.'

It was time to stop throwing mere darts at the new ways. I closed in on the whole practice of management by numbers. 'In a management culture where only numbers count, the uncountable is not only illegitimate, it is insignificant as well. Professional judgement is dismissed as subjective hunch; professional experience is written off as disabling prejudice; those who have it are dismissed as tainted with experience; professional claims are rejected as mere special pleading or self-serving protectionism.' This was pure Thatcherite managerialism. I recalled a five-year-old report from the World Service pointing out that every organisation had its own 'ethos' – what it was – but almost as importantly, its own 'pathos' – how it felt. Sounds of distress from the 'pathos' of an organisation might warn that its fundamental 'ethos' was being violated.

My only reference to the BBC from the entire lecture came almost at the end: 'Most in the BBC are extremely loyal to the institution and the idea behind it. Whoever heard of anyone being loyal to a business unit or cost centre?' There it was, coded but clear.

What strike me now are the echoes of authoritarian systems of behaviour in the new BBC management prescriptions. The root-and-branch radicalism of the notion of 'Year Zero'; the staff re-education, more like a kind of brainwashing to instil correct thinking through insistence and repetition; the Puritan knowledge of the only road to salvation. All these added up to an oppressive ideologue's certainty about the necessary truth of the defined way. It was totally inimical to the liberal, humanist, pluralist values of the BBC. How could it be expected to work?

I gave an advance copy of the lecture to the *Guardian*, which carried a 600-word digest the following morning. Coded the lecture may have been, but the BBC Secretariat at Broadcasting House was up to the task of decoding it. When I arrived at TV Centre, I was called into the office of the Editor of News, an old *Newsnight* colleague, Peter Bell. The bosses at BH, he told me, were up in arms at what I had said. There was talk of sacking me for breaking my contract. I denied that I had but recognised that, in strict legal terms, I probably had. As a trained lawyer, Peter thought I had too. We both doubted that they would be stupid enough to throw me out but this era of BBC apparatchik was something new. Peter hit the phones to BH to save them from their own worst instincts. For my part, I lobbied no one, no one rang me. Wisely for the apparatchiks, common sense prevailed. The threats to my employment vanished. Peter Bell behaved like a good manager, a decent person and a brave man.

Looking back at this period, I am struck by the intellectual absolutism of the Birt regime, the dogmatic certainty, the moral superiority, the lack of self-awareness, the lack of generosity, the intolerance, the ruthlessness. They would never have understood Oliver Cromwell's plea to his opponents: 'I beseech you in the bowels of Christ, consider that you may be mistaken!' Error was something that other people fell into.

What I wrote in 1993 and 1994 was not a complete account of how I would have run the BBC. I did not have that in mind. But in my emphasis on putting people, programmes and values above systems, process and numbers, I am as comfortable now as I was insistent then.

I had had my last word on the BBC in public and with myself. It seems that 'Dukey' Hussey wanted the last word to be his. In his 2001 autobiography, *Chance Governs All*, he asserted that the row over Birt's private company arrangements and Armani suits was entirely factitious. Others, such as myself, he asserted, had similar financial arrangements. I had not read the book. My old friend, Fred Emery, former diplomatic editor of *The Times*, had. Did I know that Hussey was alleging that I used a private company to pay my salary and buy my suits? I assured Fred that what Hussey had written was wholly untrue; I had never set up a private company for taxation purposes. Why Hussey wrote what he did will never be known. I knew he disliked me but had not realised how much! I can only describe what he wrote as a vendetta carried to his grave.

11

Leaping Free

The Wolfson Year: January to October 1993

As departure from the World Service on 31 December 1992 drew closer, I was planning my return to active television journalism. I needed to earn a living, I was only fifty-six. Where should I go? Much as I had loved *Newsnight*, a return to late-evening TV would have been a backward step. What satisfaction could there be in retracing old ground? Those days were over, I had given them my all. Semi-retirement with my sixtieth birthday on the horizon? Impossible. I wanted to do things. I was looking for serious executive involvement which left time for other activities and interests. I was more than a journalist and broadcaster; I was a manager too. I had shown that I could run things, lead people. It would be a shame to allow six years of experience to go to waste.

In the final three months at Bush House, I found that my record as Managing Director had not gone unnoticed beyond the world of broadcasting. Approaches from the world of academia appeared; first inviting me to consider becoming Vice-Chancellor at Reading University then a similar position at York. I had seen the inner workings of a university when sitting on the governing council of Imperial College, London. I had no illusions about the complexities of university finances or organisation. But if outsiders judged that my record at the World Service made me a potential Vice-Chancellor, why should I reject their approaches?

My interest in Reading University was the first to wane. It was ambitious, adventurous and progressive. But I had little

feel for the place or for the range of disciplines in which it spec-
ialised. With my arts, humanities and journalism background,
I could not see myself representing the university's interests
and values persuasively or effectively. It would be a poor fit for
both of us. We agreed not to pursue talks any further.

Annie and I felt it was time to visit York to get a whiff of the
city, the campus, the atmosphere. As these approaches were
confidential on both sides, we made what we intended to be a
secret trip to York in early October. Our hoped-for cover was
almost blown at the first moment as we stepped off the train
at York station and ran straight into our nephew's wife, Ro,
returning from a concert engagement with The Sixteen. We
mumbled some plausible reason for being in York and went
on to explore the city and university. We loved the city (who
could not?), admired the university campus and were attracted
by the friendly nature of the contacts. Whether a post at York
was compatible with my basic plan of a resumed career in television, presenting the *One O'Clock News* on BBC One, was
very doubtful. Those talks were well advanced, but nothing
was firmly decided and it was best to keep every possibility in
play.

At this point, a new direction seemed to open. My old colleague Bill Kirkman, former Africa correspondent of *The Times*,
ran the journalism programme at Wolfson College, Cambridge.
Would I, he asked, be interested in becoming President of the
college? At first glance, this looked as if it would be a good fit
with TV news-presenting. Heading a Cambridge 'house' was
not a full-time job or anything like it. This combination – television and academia – was worth taking seriously. It satisfied
my interests; both played to my strengths. Wolfson paid very
little but my TV work would provide enough for our needs.

For the moment, though, the York option did not go away. I
travelled there for further interviews with just three members
of the University Court in mid-October. I liked them; we got
on well. Later that week they rang to say I was on a shortlist
of three for the vice-chancellorship. This was getting serious;

decision time was looming. Annie however was at the Eisen-
hower Library in Abilene, Kansas – a small town, remote even
by Kansas standards – researching her book on the building of
the Berlin Wall. I rang to tell her the latest development from
York. She listened, then said briefly: 'I'm on my way,' or words
to that effect. It would not be the only time that my career got
in the way of her research and writing. She never complained. I
met Annie off the overnight flight at Heathrow on 26 November. It was time for hard talking.

We did not expect to disagree. Yet now that York was more
of a possibility, we were slightly surprised to discover the
depth of our reservations. I was concerned at the complexity
of university finances; I was unclear about the real nature of
a vice-chancellor's executive authority and responsibilities; I
knew how to manage journalists and broadcasters. How would
a university be led, how was it managed or indeed was it managed at all?

We shared unease about the personal upheaval involved in
a move to York after living in the heart of London for more
than thirty years. To shift from the international variety and
intensity of a global city to one based on cathedral, county and
university would be tricky. We would have a formal, almost
official, place and standing in that society which threatened
to be restrictive, even claustrophobic. Neither of us wanted to
become becalmed and isolated in a perceived 'position' within
local society. There was nothing wrong with this but neither of
us had ever lived in this way and neither of us felt we would be
any good at it. We both felt these anxieties strongly.

And there was a further worry. Discussing with friends the
possibility of a move to York, too many observed reassuringly
that the train to London was 'very fast'. A place whose attraction appeared defined by its lack of distance from London was
missing something else, self-confidence perhaps? Annie and I
were at one: wonderful as York undoubtedly was, fascinating
as the university position might be, it was not for us. I gave
my apologies to the members of the Court of Governors, with

whom I had enjoyed very friendly meetings. They took my withdrawal generously and we parted with warm feelings on both sides.

My negotiations with BBC Television were promising – presenting the *One O'Clock News* on BBC One three days a week would leave plenty of time for other activities. In this context, what might Wolfson College, Cambridge have to offer? Heading a Cambridge college, after all, had a good ring to it, offering a post, an address, a place in the university. Were we in part still seeing Cambridge through the radiant prism of happy remembered undergraduate years? For myself, one of my motivations was, albeit unconsciously, a high degree of personal vanity. This did not serve me well.

First reconaissances were encouraging. Wolfson, the youngest of the Cambridge collegiate institutions, was set in pleasant grounds at the city's western edge on the Barton Road. The architecture was tidy and diluted modern-ish, essentially undistinguished, incorporating two Cambridge professional family homes into its fabric. If there was nothing to alarm in the look of the place, neither was there anything to thrill. In conversations with some senior members, it was clear that the college had thought seriously about what kind of community it wanted to be. Wolfson was, by its own definition, modern, outward-looking, with connections to business and journalism. It was not garlanded with history, not festooned in tradition, not imprisoned by a glorious past, not encumbered by memories. It had no 'high table' where dons sat removed from undergraduates or resident dons. In part, it was an address for academics with no collegiate home. It was a settled adult college based on postgraduates and mature undergraduates. Wolfson felt open-minded and eager to carve a distinctive role for itself. I believed I could identify with its sense of purpose and could contribute a lot.

Annie and I accepted that for most of the week and much of term time – twenty-four weeks a year – Cambridge would be our principal dwelling. But it was only a sixty-minute drive

back home to Hampstead. We would strip our house of furniture for Cambridge but we never considered selling. This
proved wise. For her part, Annie bore without complaint the
disruption to her research that all the numerous toings and
froings connected with Wolfson involved. By mid-December, I
was on a shortlist of three for the position of President. Election
would take place at a College Council on 20 January 1993.

I was in Moscow that week for the launch of one of my final
initiatives at Bush House, a bold radio outreach project for the
Soviet Union called the 'Marshall Plan of the Mind' (MPM).
It used conventional broadcasting formats to introduce Soviet
radio audiences to the law, economics and other aspects of
the open society they were hopefully about to enter in the
post-communist world. MPM also pioneered a daily radio
soap opera, *Dom Syem Podhest Ctery* ('House Seven, Staircase
Four'), based on everyday life in a typical Moscow block of
flats. Once the Russian scriptwriters had been weaned off
giving the characters long, philosophical speeches, this became
a hugely effective form of entertainment and information.

Incredibly, these innovative, pluralistic programmes were
not part of BBC Russian Service broadcasts; they would be
carried on the domestic frequencies of Moscow Radio itself
under a special agreement. This made them part of the fabric
of everyday Russian listening. The programmes became very
popular, sometimes attracting the biggest audience of the day.
Reaching the agreement represented a huge breakthrough in
post-communist attitudes and relationships. Listeners were
hungry to know how their new non-communist world worked.
Minds were opening intellectually in the former Soviet Union.

I could not help recalling that I had been in Moscow in 1986
in the week of my interview to become MD of the World Service. Could the city be some kind of lucky talisman for me?
In January 1993 I stayed in the Arbat area of Moscow, with
Francis Richards, the British Minister, and his journalist wife,
Gill. On 20 January I dined with Bridget Kendall, the Moscow
correspondent, in the BBC flat. At 10 p.m. Bill Kirkman rang

from Cambridge with the news that I had been elected President of Wolfson College by a large majority. By midnight I was back with Francis and Gill in the Arbat to down a bottle of champagne. As this was the day that my appointment to front the TV *One O'Clock News* was also announced, celebration was in order. Was my 'luck of Moscow' really at work? The only sadness was that I could not share my happiness with Annie in London. There was a fault on one of the phone receivers in Hampstead and she was left sitting forlorn, without news. We finally spoke late the next morning. We agreed that it was good news – President of Wolfson College, presenter of the BBC *One O'Clock News*, surely the 'dream double'?

I learned rapidly that the decisive vote in my favour and the big attendance at the college vote on the presidency was a surprise to most and a major inconvenience to some. The lengthy candidacy period had produced a huge amount of preliminary politicking, settling of old scores, stoking of personal ambitions, blocking of other candidates and stirring up all the malice traditionally said to characterise academic life. Setting up a search committee to canvass external candidates had been an attempt to calm the febrile internal atmosphere.

Even so, there had been uncertainty and unease during the contest. How many Fellows would turn up to vote? Would there even be a quorum? Might the vote be deadlocked? Here neurosis took over. In case of a deadlock, would the college's governing body have to be recalled? Fantasy then boiled over. Suppose the governing body itself was deadlocked, might 'The Visitor' – the supreme external authority over college matters – have to be called in? Throughout, Fellows regarded the possible intervention of 'The Visitor' – spoken in hushed tones, complete with inverted commas and capital letters – as an inconceivable disaster, a 'visitation' in the worst sense. Such was the unease enveloping the college on the night of the election.

The division among the Fellows was indeed profound, all the more so for not being admitted. The 'insiders', I was told later, those with a particularly proprietary feeling about how the college should work, were confident that attendance at the vote would be small and an insider candidate would be chosen. This group did not want me at all and my presence on the list of three was purely to show that correct forms had been observed. I was, at best, a colourful decoy duck for them to display.

From their point of view, the evening had been a disaster. Many Fellows turned up to vote, far more than expected. They voted for me overwhelmingly on the first ballot. It was, one Fellow later told me, a triumph for 'the peasants', for the 'non-insiders', those whose voices were usually disregarded, the outer core of the college who played little part in its affairs. Another told me, 'It was the revolt of the excluded.' When the result was announced at the meeting there was a stunned silence, as if the college was wondering what it had done. We would all soon find out. I now believe that many of the events of the next six months sprang directly from the night of the vote. The result was not what the 'insiders' wanted at all. Not so deep down, some of them never accepted it.

We were soon surrounded by friendly warnings about the future. I returned from Moscow on 21 January. The following evening, Annie and I were in Oxford for a farewell dinner given by the Reuter Foundation for an old friend, their outgoing Director, Neville Maxwell, one-time India correspondent for *The Times*. We stayed with the President of Trinity College and former Director of the British Council, John Burgh and his wife Ann. At the Reuter dinner, other heads of house such as the Crispin Tickells from Green College and the John Robertses from Merton all wished us well at Wolfson. All without exception then asked: 'What is the Master's Lodge like?' At first we thought this sounded very materialistic; it had not occurred to us to ask to see the President's accommodation before accepting the appointment. Then it dawned on us that all three heads were speaking from long practical experience. The 'lodge' was a key part of college life, the main instrument for the head's ability to entertain, to bring the college together, to keep university-wide contacts, to represent college interests. If it was not suitable for the role, being 'head of house' would become very difficult. One added: 'Do get it right before you move in! Make sure they do it up as you want!' We failed on both counts and paid the price.

Over a late-night drink at Trinity after the dinner, John Burgh, a shrewd observer of life, born in Vienna, a former senior Treasury civil servant, counselled: 'Being head of a college is a very pleasant backcloth to life. But it is a fairly tin-pot activity. Don't take it too seriously, it can't stand the strain.' We didn't hear it as a warning. There was nothing we could have done about it even if we had really heard.

Wolfson College in the meantime was in a hurry. The former president, David Williams, a gregarious, shrewd Welsh lawyer, had combined that position with the role of University Vice-Chancellor. That was how Cambridge was run at the time. Now the college wished, reasonably, to get back to ordered life. Having elected me on 20 January 1993, the college wanted me 'inducted' in haste on 10 February. The Senior Fellow, Jack King, cooked up a short ceremony to fit the occasion.

King had been one of the founders of the college. A large, rotund, expansive figure, at best only a moderate academic, King's beaming face and inclusive manner, his love of good wines and fishing, spoke of satisfaction with things as they were. He was not ready to let go of his cosy vision of the college. His first act was one of co-option of the new President and his wife. On the day of the Induction we were called to lunch at the Kings' house in Great Shelford, just outside Cambridge. We were in a small group but, as it turned out, an important one. Apart from us and Jack King and his wife, Ruth, the only other person present was the Bursar, John Seagrave. Most Oxbridge colleges are run by the bursar; most heads of house have rows with their bursars; we were to be no exception. Lunch was served by Rita. Who was Rita? Why, she was the head of the 'bedders', the college's domestic staff. Here was the triumvirate of power and authority at Wolfson. Rita – by far the nicest of the three – ran the staff; Seagrave, withdrawn and suspicious, ran the money; King, outward bonhomie personified, believed he ran the Fellows.

This show of hospitality was also an act of ownership. They owned us; we owed them; we were appropriated by them. The gesture signalled that we were less independent actors on the college scene, more people holding a position defined and circumscribed by the ruling group. We took the lunch as a piece of pleasant manners; had we read its meaning more clearly, we would not have accepted its implied message.

Induction took place at 6 p.m. the same day. It involved a great deal of marching in and out of Hall in gowned procession led by the Head Porter; resounding stamping of feet on the floor; doffing of mortar boards and bowler hats to all corners of the room; swearing an oath of office; and signing a book which meant something to the college. It was flummery of course, harmless enough and mercifully brief. Even new institutions need traditions. If they don't exist, they make them up. Time then sanctifies all.

Pre-dinner drinks with almost a hundred Fellows present was oddly uneasy. Given that a large majority had voted for me, they seemed to know little about us. Annie and I were regularly asked, politely but anxiously, whether we 'knew Cambridge'. She would explain that she had been at the neighbouring college of Newnham for three years. For good measure, two sons and a daughter-in-law had also been at Cambridge. For my part, I explained that I had been at a Cambridge prep school for three years, Trinity College for four. We did indeed 'know Cambridge'! Their search for reassurance was almost painful to witness, the underlying unease simmered.

What was wholly absent was any curiosity about Annie and me as people. Nobody asked her what she did or if she had a job. Nobody had registered her books on the Nuremberg Trial and the Berlin Blockade. Nobody asked about her current book – the building of the Berlin Wall – or whether moving to Cambridge was disrupting her research. (It was!) As she remarked caustically: 'I wouldn't have minded if a Fellow had enquired if I was looking for work at a Sainsbury's checkout! That would have shown some human interest!'

The nearest any Fellow came to showing interest was a distinguished veterinarian who, several weeks later, enquired: 'And what do you do, Mrs Tusa, to keep yourself out of mischief?!' This was an attempt, no doubt, at donnish humour. Annie slapped him down with a lengthy account of all the research institutes and libraries she had been visiting for her Berlin Wall book. That shut him up.

There was, however, worse to come on Induction evening. Making a short speech after dinner, I drew the links between my own profession of journalism and their academic disciplines. They were dedicated to truth and accuracy; but so, I pointed out, were journalists. At which the hall burst into loud laughter. I knew journalists were not held in high regard, but given that the college ran a journalism programme, this sneer was above all rude. I wondered later if the laughter did not reveal nervous academic unease at association not just with a non-academic but with a journalist? But who did they think they had voted for?

At the time, I brushed the incident aside. Dinner over, Annie and I returned to the 'President's Flat', a minuscule one-bedroom plus sitting room and kitchenette affair. There was no President's Lodge available for us to do our job in. With its cheap three-piece suite from a Wolfson Great Universal Stores catalogue, its nylon moquette upholstery, cheap brown curtains and air of faded gentility, the President's Flat was unusable for any of the functions the college expected us to carry out. At least enduring a night there counted as 'being in residence', a matter of some importance in the months ahead. We called it our 'sheltered accommodation'. Comparing notes on the evening, Annie and I judged it to have been odd but perhaps not much odder than we expected. In any case, this was where we were, we would make the best of it. In fact, we would do a better job than they were entitled to expect.

In the middle of the night, I woke up in a muck sweat, drenched. My body was telling me in the most unmistakable terms that the whole Wolfson involvement was a ghastly error. I could not ignore this violent psychosomatic reaction. I could tell my mind that it would all work; I could not argue with my body. Next morning, I said nothing to Annie of my intense nocturnal physical reaction. We would have to make the best of it. The presidency of Wolfson College, Cambridge was our decision, our future and our lot, even without any kind of President's Lodge to work from.

Originally I had wanted a three-month break between the intensity of the World Service and my new pattern of life. The college wanted me at once, with or without the necessary accommodation. I obliged, plunging straight into a full round of college meetings, Formal Halls, Guest Nights and all the dates in a college calendar. But we needed to know where we were going to live and work in the college. This, apparently, was to be our problem, not the college's.

Annie visited the two possible future President's Lodges with the Bursar. The college's pride and joy, its 'crown jewels', was No. 78 Barton Road, a dour, grey-brick, graceless house of indeterminate style bought from the Antarctic explorer Sir Vivian Fuchs as a residence for David Williams when he became full-time University Vice-Chancellor. The price was £500,000 and the word, never contradicted, was that a badly managed conversion had cost a further £500,000. Given that the college's endowment was a mere £5 million, such expenditure seemed reckless, indeed feckless.

Annie was invariably accompanied by the Bursar on these visits, never allowed to visit by herself. She found the house lugubrious, with inconvenient rooms, a weird-shaped kitchen, no privacy to the garden, and yet more furnishing straight from the Great Universal Store catalogue. With its heavily drawn curtains, she thought of Miss Havisham in *Great Expectations* draped in disappointed hopes, psychological cobwebs and outdated wedding dress. By contrast, loyal members of the college saw it more as Snow White's Castle, a place of wonder and dreams which of course they were not entitled to enter. When I came into its virtually windowless hall for the first time and saw eight closed doors radiating off it, I knew where I was: Bartók's *Duke Bluebeard's Castle*, where each closed door concealed some increasingly ghastly horror.

Annie said she would go stir-crazy there. The college took offence at the strength of her reaction, but after all they didn't want us to use the house anyway. We could, however, have as much of the GUS furniture and re-cut carpeting as we wanted. We should have spotted that Wolfson wanted a new head, they wanted one fast, but also wanted one on the cheap. The college had 'willed the ends' – a serving President – but they would not 'will the means' – the premises from which to represent the college.

On the other side of the grounds stood No. 5 Barton Close, a decent, 1930s Cambridge solicitor's family house. The David Williamses had lived and entertained there successfully. Since then, much of the garden had been lost to the new Singapore-Chinese-funded library which overlooked the garden and much of the house. The college set aside a paltry £20,000 for a long-overdue refurbishment but pointed out that since the house was in use as student accommodation and tutorial rooms, work could not commence until after summer exams at the end of July. Given a prompt start thereafter, we might have a usable 'President's Lodge' by September, a leisurely eight months after being inducted in haste. The college said it had wanted speed, but not apparently at any price.

The summer term – the Trinity Term in university parlance – started in April, as did my stint presenting the *One O'Clock News* on BBC One three times a week. Though the door-to-door journey from Hampstead to Wolfson was just an hour, a regular commute for many, the time pressures were real. On some days, I left the TV studio at Shepherd's Bush at 1.30, snatched a sandwich at home, packed and left, avoiding the rush-hour traffic, to take a committee meeting or preside over

Formal Hall or a Guest Night. On other days, I attended a college committee at 5 p.m., drove home for a late supper to make an early start at TV Centre the following morning. Often this schedule was a stretch, but it was not dull.

I decided that being President must mean more than being a figurehead at formal events. What, I asked myself, did the college want to do? I learned soon enough that colleges are not there to 'do' very much; they are there to 'be', a crucial difference. Still, I set out to talk to as many Fellows as I could and see them in their laboratory, library or office, their places of real work. The great majority welcomed the opportunity to talk about the college, not an experience they had had before. They enjoyed Wolfson's informal, inclusive ethos, populated by a shifting body of visiting scholars mingling in a rather pleasingly diverse way at Formal Halls. They felt excluded from the way the college was run by the clique of 'insiders'. Almost all wanted a more distinct academic profile for the college, specifically raising some element of a teaching role for the college going beyond the pleasures of collegiate communal living. I sensed that such enquiring conversations were not what the 'insiders' wanted or welcomed. I continued meeting with and talking to the Fellows.

Several asked questions about the costly, brooding, curtained, locked-up folly of No. 78. Could it not be used for something useful, a centre of research or learning, perhaps an institute? After conversations with Fellows in a wide variety of faculties, I came up with a radical proposal. What many pointed to was what I self-consciously labelled an 'International Institute for the Study of Ethics in Business, Medicine and the Professions'. It would be multi-disciplinary; it would be cross-disciplinary; it would trespass on no other existing faculty's patch. The composite, portmanteau title was deliberately modish, stringing together the buzz-words of the time.

It was also a huge tease on my part. No institute was ever set up from scratch like this; it would take two years to agree definitions, purposes and structures; perhaps another two years to find the funding. It might see the light of day in five to six years. Why did I do it at all? I needed to have some activity to fill the time; it was a form of games-playing, creating a fantasy institute out of probably fantasy needs. I also wanted to jolt Wolfson into thinking about what it might be beyond a pleasant gathering of fairly academic folk. My teasing had an unexpected effect.

The Global Security Programme, run by a former academic acquaintance, Gwyn Prinz, was part of the Social and Political Sciences Faculty. They wanted their own physical home; No. 78 would be a good fit, Wolfson a good home. The college would get an academic profile, might earn £30,000 annual rent – a useful sum which could fund three research fellowships. I was pleased; to my surprise, something practical had been achieved.

The rest of the summer term was filled with a cat-and-mouse game with the Bursar, John Seagrave, over the President's Lodge. He was determined to turn it into a place worthy, as he saw it, of the college's self-image. It was a major effort for us to prise architectural or garden planting plans from college staff, difficult to meet or talk to architects or garden designers. When we did, we found that this sensible 1930s brick-built house was to be tricked out with a porte-cochère complete with tiled roof at the front door; an arch over the beech-hedged drive and fake flat classical columns stuck on the garden side of the house. All this apparently would make The Lodge suitably 'grand'. None of the plans provided a kitchen suitable for large-scale entertaining or an adequate cloakroom.

As for the garden, which had vestiges of nice old fruit trees and attractive planting, it was bulldozed overnight, flattened for easy maintenance and cheap upkeep; a wooden pergola would run its full length along the wall of the new library. We were consulted about none of this. There was a difficult site meeting when we struck out the much-loved porte-cochère, the equally loved pergola and the fake classical columns. It was too late to save any of the old planting. The landscape designer, a reasonable man, looked into the college secretary's office after that meeting and said: 'It's going rather well! The Tusas are cutting out all the right things!' They were some of the few words of approval we ever got.

For ourselves, we said, 'Keep it simple, paint the place white, we will bring the furniture and organise the pictures, let us get on with the job.' But the house was still filled with students; we remained in the 'sheltered accommodation'. Annie and I knew how much time and effort we were putting in; research on her Berlin book had ground to a halt. We judged the Trinity Term to have been a decent success; we had certainly put our all into it. Did the college notice?

Internally, the atmosphere remained wary. I decoded that Fellows who spoke most loudly about the 'Authority of the President' – there was much talk in capital letters! – were the most hostile. Those Fellows who loudly invoked the 'Interests of the College' were usually hawking a matter of personal interest. And a gap of curiosity yawned about the real world outside and beyond. The night of the great Commons vote on the Maastricht Treaty was a Formal Hall dinner. Annie and I rose a few minutes early before 10 p.m., explaining that we wanted to hear the result of a vote that would shape Britain's future in Europe. This was greeted with looks of blank astonishment that a Commons vote might be of such importance to us. We were in a different world.

Any complacency Annie and I had about the effort we had put into Wolfson under the least promising circumstances was shattered at the end of June. Term had just ended. The Senior Fellow, Jack King, heaved himself massively into my office, settled into the sofa and announced that I was not doing the job as they wanted. I was, he asserted, 'never there'; I needed to be 'seen around more'; the college needed to 'feel my presence'. He brushed aside the fact that I had no President's Lodge to work from. He warned that 'my absence' was being 'commented on'.

I knew none of this was true. When he lumbered off, I

checked the diary for the term just ended. I set out the facts in a letter to him on 2 July. In the previous eight weeks, I had presided over seven Formal Halls, two Guest Nights, one Spouse's night, a Fellows' Night and a graduands' dinner. Annie and I had given four parties – two for Fellows, two for students. I attended fourteen other college events, including the College Garden Party and the Press Fellows' seminar, and chaired every single one of the scheduled eleven college committee meetings. Jack King neither acknowledged nor replied to my letter. Later I was told by a journalist that a very senior Fellow had alleged that I had spent no nights in college that term. He must have known that was untrue. I had in fact spent twenty nights in residence, more than required, and given no fewer than thirty-five working days to the college.

I never speculated about the motivation for what can only be called malice. I accepted that King and colleagues would never be won over. I knew that the thirty-five Fellows I had visited were overwhelmingly on the side of a new era for Wolfson. They wanted more involvement but felt excluded; they wanted to contribute but were prevented from doing so; they wanted a lively and curious college, not the staid replica of a conventional college. Most fundamentally, these Fellows wanted the college's own self-definition as a place engaged with the outside world to be turned into reality. My contacts with these Fellows, my direct knowledge of their thoughts and feelings, were seen as a challenge by the tight, conservative oligarchy of 'insiders'. They scorned the wider Fellowship and would sabotage me in my efforts to include them.

Whether it was sabotage, obstructionism or mere incompetence, the Lodge was not ready for occupation by 1 September as promised. Annie and I decided to take matters into our own hands. Our own furniture would come up from Hampstead on 10 September. We had bought new living-room furniture at our own expense, organised first-class picture loans from friends at the Fitzwilliam Museum and Kettle's Yard, spent days over choosing the right curtains on a very tight budget. The college's contribution was second-hand carpets, second-hand furniture from No. 78, a leaking second-hand fridge and an old dishwasher. The Bursar agreed to repaint the ancient kitchen units. With the flattened and bulldozed garden churned like a First World War battlefield, the front unpaved and caked in mud, Annie and I decided that we would get the Lodge ready for use even if the college wouldn't.

For two whole weekends in September, we attacked the accumulated filth of a year of student living and builders' dust. John Seagrave never offered to send in the college cleaners. Instead, while Annie scrubbed the kitchen floor, washed down shelves and cupboards, I repeatedly swept and vacuumed the living and dining rooms until the dust settled. During the second weekend of house-cleaning, I remembered a remark of our old friend, John Drummond, when he was Director of the Edinburgh Festival. As he scrubbed the kitchen floor of his London basement flat, he mused: 'I bet George Harewood never washed the kitchen floor at Harewood House when he was Director. I bet Ian Hunter didn't. I bet Peter Diamand never got down on his knees to scrub the kitchen. Why do I have to do it?' We thought him very funny at the time. Now, as I vacuumed builders' dust from the floor for the third time, I found myself voicing a similar litany: 'I bet David Williams didn't have to vacuum the Lodge before he moved in as President! I bet the Master of Trinity didn't clean the Lodge by hand! Why should I?'

The next day, we took Seagrave over the uncompleted dirty Lodge and itemised everything wrong with it. By now this included eccentricities such as lavatories which flushed very hot water, and no connection with the university phone system, which the college did not see as a priority. He took it badly. The college's failure to provide a decent usable Lodge seemed to be of less importance than the fact that we complained about it. At a face-to-face meeting in the Bursar's office to discuss the long schedule of incompletion, he told me that I did not understand the nature of authority in a college. Seagrave added:

'There's a lot of poison around. Some Fellows are asking if we have made a mistake.' It was easy to reply to that: 'Do you know, I am beginning to ask myself the same question.' He recoiled in shock as if that possibility had not occurred to him. Though I did not realise it at the time, I had loosened the psychological bolts on the door of resignation.

The whole of that September was ridiculous. In retrospect, faced with the college's total failure to provide a house from where we could do the job it wanted done, we should have said that we would live in London until the Lodge was fit for purpose. I would have attended a skeleton of formal events and committees. Annie and I would not have spent the greater part of our time at Wolfson as we had done during the previous six months. We should have done this – it might have jolted the college into facing up to its behaviour. For us, it was a matter of our own self-respect. We were set on doing the job we had agreed and would do it better than they deserved.

Events were driving rapidly to a denouement. The college meeting on 4 October was due to consider a report by a retired Fellow, Hugh Bevan, into my suspension of the Senior Tutor, John Cathie. He had blatantly ignored two college instructions about spending money and at first agreed to resign on decent terms. Cathie then backtracked and refused to go. I saw this defiance of college instructions and flouting of the President's authority as grounds for suspending him as Senior Tutor. On 19 July, the College Council had backed the suspension by eight votes to none, with two abstentions. Jack King then forced through the idea of an 'independent' report on the affair, hoping no doubt that it would find me at fault. Hugh Bevan, a scrupulous lawyer, was commissioned to interview all the parties involved and prepare a report for the next Council meeting. By mid-September, I knew that the report backed what I had done.

On the evening of 4 October, Council had the Bevan Report before them. Jack King struck as the meeting began. Since what he called the 'non-involved' members of the Council had not had the chance to discuss the Report, would those directly involved in the affair – myself, the Vice-President, the Bursar – care to withdraw? Twenty minutes later, a Fellow ushered us back into the meeting saying, 'We think that nobody comes out of the Bevan Report smelling of roses!' This was so outrageous that its author, Hugh Bevan, present as an observer, asked for his opinion to be placed on the record that 'the Senior Tutor has a weak case'. Despite this, the Council spent time not discussing how to get Cathie out of the college but rather how he could be kept 'within the 'Society of the College'. (Once again, the air was thick with abstracts and capital letters.) The Council's reluctance to make a decision was laughable.

Since that day, I have always regretted not saying to the Council: 'Ladies and gentlemen, if you insist on my leaving the room, please understand that I will never return!' How we got through the rest of the business I cannot remember. They had little choice but to back me and sack Cathie. As it was, when I phoned Annie at 11 p.m. from a service station outside Baldock on my way home, she asked anxiously how the meeting had gone. 'Not too bad,' I replied. 'I got my way on both issues. Let's talk in the morning.'

At 4 a.m. my body once again became my best counsellor. It rebelled. I woke in a muck sweat. What could I see ahead? More unpleasant Council meetings, a full-scale, contentious governing body and the knowledge that there was 'a lot of poison in the air!'. Beyond the immediate unpleasantness, some Fellows would feel that they had the President where they wanted him – as a permanent plaything to be toyed with, obstructed and never forgiven. That was how Fellows behaved – in their faculty, laboratory or research institute they were deadly serious. Colleges were their playground. What better toy to have to pull apart than the head of house?

I made no decision over early breakfast on 5 October before driving to TV Centre. In a pause after the morning editorial meeting, I started my calls to the Vice-President, the Senior Fellow and another Council member. I told them that last night's meeting had been a disgrace; that offering the Senior Tutor another position was unacceptable; getting me to leave the meeting was intolerable and that I was very angry. Jack King got all pathetic: why was I attacking him? He would resign! I replied that the college was his creation and my resignation would be in before his. Something crystallised at that moment. I rang home and told Annie that I was thinking of resigning. How did she feel? 'That's just fine by me,' she replied immediately, and said later that months-long accumulated knots of suppressed tension in her neck and shoulders suddenly eased.

That afternoon, we weighed up the pros and cons of resignation. For eight months we had behaved like good troupers, our stiff upper lips concealing our growing doubts from one another, each boosting the other when down. There had of course been laughs when the college behaviour was too ridiculous, pompous or incompetent. In truth, both of us had found the time deeply unpleasant: rude of course, obstructive often, but above all astonishingly ungenerous. Resignation would be easy. Annie could get back to her research and writing. And the choice that coming Thursday offered us alternative paths to life and living. 'The Cambridge Way' involved another dreary Formal Hall in college; 'The London Way', a private view of the latest show at the National Portrait Gallery with much champagne and dinner with friends. There was no contest.

The process of resignation then became positively enjoyable. One Fellow said aghast: 'President, most people couldn't take a decision like this!' That made it especially easy. When the Bursar protested that I should give three months' notice, I replied that I was leaving the day after next. Earlier in the affair, a Fellow had lamented: 'Heaven forbid, President, that we should appear in the columns of *The Times*!' Later, my resignation letter to the governing body was leaked to the *Guardian*. The key phrase was 'I suddenly realised that I had better things to do with my time.' It was true. I did. But the college did not understand it.

They remained mean to the end, arguing about reimbursing us for the costs we incurred in trying to kit out the Lodge. Worst of all, in the following weeks several Fellows said, 'Of course, Cathie should have been got rid of ages ago!' A bit late in the day, it spoke poorly of the strength of academics' spines. The 'bedders' were the only part of the college who seemed sorry to see us go. When Annie went to say farewell and thank Rita and her team, she thought them the nicest people in the entire place.

Soon after leaving, I observed to a Hampstead neighbour that one of the frustrations of the experience was that I could see no lesson to be learned from it. He paused: 'Sometimes, there is no lesson to be learned; perhaps that is the lesson!' It was a bleak observation but a realistic one. As we consoled ourselves in Venice as an antidote to the pettinesses of Wolfson, Annie and I reflected that if the worst decision we took had been to accept the presidency of the college, the best was to resign and walk away immediately. As the Fellow had said: 'Most people couldn't take a decision like this!' We had and with one bound we were free. We never looked back. But we had wasted a year.

Top Interviewing Margaret Thatcher in Number 10 Downing Street live for *Newsnight*, 27 July 1984.

Middle As Managing Director, BBC World Service. Facing Taliban on the Pakistan/Afghan frontier, up the Khyber Pass, August 1989, with Annie.

Left The Communist Party loses the election in Poland, 4 June 1989. With Lech Wałęsa, Solidarnoć leader, at his birthday celebrations in Gdansk. With Karol Małcużyńsky, BBC Producer, Andrew Taussig, Head of BBC Central European Services.

Left With former West German Chancellor Willy Brandt at a BBC 'English by Radio' conference, West Berlin, 10 June 1992.

Middle Filming in Samarkand, Soviet Central Asia for *Newsnight*, 1 June 1980.

Right With Archbishop Desmond Tutu, for 'Believing: 20/20 – A View of the Century', 13 March 1995.

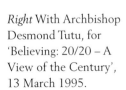

Above and *right* The
Fall of the Wall, 1989.
I contemplate it; Annie
takes a hammer to it.

Left With John
Drummond, Controller,
BBC Radio 3, at a Wall
fragment, BBC Berlin
Weekend, 5–6 April 1990.

To John Tusa
With appreciation and best wishes,

Above As Chairman of the Advisory Committee to the
Government Art Collection with the Director Penny Johnson.
President George Bush and First Lady Laura Bush acknowledge
the loan to the Oval Office of the GAC's Epstein bust of Winston
Churchill, January 2002.

Below Interviewing György Ligeti in Hamburg for the Radio 3
'John Tusa Interview', 21 January 2001, with my producer
Tony Cheevers.

Right With Sir William Glock, legend of BBC classical music, and Nicholas Snowman, former director, South Bank Centre.

Middle Post-LSO concert backstage at the Barbican, 2000, Annie with a sweaty Slava Rostropovich.

Left Kabul, Afghanistan. At Rory Stewart's Turquoise Mountain Foundation project in Murat Khane, 28 September 2014.

Top Kabul, Afghanistan, with engineer Hedayatullah Ahmadzai and master woodworker Ustad Abdul Hadi Khan.

Middle After interviewing David Hockney, 16 April 2004.

Right Chairman of University of the Arts London, Degree Day, with Grayson Perry, University President, and Nigel Carrington, University Vice-Chancellor, July 2013.

Right Taken by Richard Hamilton after our Radio 3 interview, April 2002.

Below Snapped by Gilbert and George after interviewing them for Radio 3, March 2002.

Above At Clore Leadership Programme farewell party, 4 July 2014.

12

Softening the Concrete

The Barbican Years 1995–2007

Free of the manipulations of Cambridge dons and their spiders' webs of gossip and malice, Annie put our Hampstead house in order and got back to writing. She had lost almost a year's research effort on her next Berlin book, something that Cambridge dons ought to have understood. I settled down to a life based on presenting the *One O'Clock News* and a variety of other activities. It was pleasant enough, though a very far cry from the dazzling, innovative years of *Newsnight*. That was television journalism at its most ambitious and demanding, where Peter Snow, Donald McCormick and I were directly involved in the daily shaping, creation and writing of the programme. By contrast, newscasting was a trammelled, restricted activity, difficult to put an individual stamp on. I was not stretched, personally or journalistically. I knew I was in a career holding pattern with no long-term prospect. Grateful as I was for employment, it was activity without a future. Besides, pushing sixty years old, I had no assured place on the increasingly youth-driven screens and programming of the day. It was only a matter of time before a programme editor took me aside and whispered 'Time's up!' in my ear. I would not want that to happen. I bided my time with little sense of what might come next. Max Hastings once observed that he and I had already enjoyed the best job of our lives; he as editor of the *Daily Telegraph*, myself as Managing Director of the BBC World Service. Was Max right? Could I expect anything better?

I had no complaints about the broadcasting opportunities

that came my way around the basic newscasting rotas. I had made friends over the years with the BBC Outside Broadcast teams at the party political conferences and thanks to them anchored two days of live broadcasts from the Normandy beaches for the fiftieth anniversary of the D-Day landings in June 1944. A year later, I played the same role in Japan for the fiftieth anniversary of the dropping of the atomic bomb on Hiroshima, then reported for the news on the anniversary of the second bomb dropped on Nagasaki a few days later. I missed anchoring the fiftieth anniversary of VJ Day in Hyde Park only because I returned from Japan with a severe throat infection and my voice turned into a soundless croak on the morning of the broadcast. John Humphrys valiantly stood in as presenter of the whole day at a few hours' notice.

The most satisfying commission came in late 1994. All editors were gearing up competitively for the forthcoming millennium, albeit six long years away. Given the length of television lead times, plans had to be made early; in any case, people like getting their anniversaries in early! In addition, radio did not want to play second fiddle to the inevitable heavyweight TV commemorations. It decided to get in first by broadcasting its own millennium programmes as early as 1995. Brian Redhead was commissioned to write the twenty programmes, titled *20/20: A View of the Century*, as personal essays. On his unexpected death, the producers had to look elsewhere and came to me. They liked my background in politics from *Newsnight* and in history from *Timewatch*. The young producer, Philip Sellars, had taken some key decisions. The programmes would be thematic, not historical and chronological. Each would start from a universal aspect of human behaviour with its own distinct radio form. We entered what Philip and I informally called 'the Days of the Gerund', since the programme titles ran from 'Dreaming' to 'Controlling', 'Enjoying', 'Exploring', 'Living', 'Believing', 'Killing', 'Loving', 'Talking' and 'Belonging'. They might not cover every detail of the twentieth century but they could illuminate aspects that more conventional approaches would overlook or ignore. In some respects relying on decades, politics, landmarks, events and chronology would have been easier. Meeting the challenge we set ourselves was very taxing but proved more rewarding.

Philip Sellars, the executive producer Suzanne Levy and I spent weeks travelling from Tokyo to Los Angeles and many points in between. We tested the extremes of contemporary experience, from chatting up Snow White, a nice American girl, in California Disneyland to mingling with fans at Arsenal FC at Highbury Stadium; we faced the brutality of the Berlin Wall and the gas chambers of Auschwitz. It was intense, compressed, bewilderingly varied and complex. The twentieth century was not going to yield to a few slick formulations. What did we find out about the century? 'Silence had become a rare commodity,' I observed in one programme, but 'was anyone listening?' The century made dreams come true, I suggested in another, but then we had to learn to live with the consequences of those dreams. 'Genocide and Holocaust were the century's unlovely calling cards,' I concluded another. There were moments of hope, beauty and wonder throughout our travels and the programmes. One voice above all, that of Archbishop Desmond Tutu, spoke with its message of calm, offering balm to the spirit, a reminder and reassurance, not a reproach: 'I am because I belong.' Yet even here doubt and uncertainty lingered; to what did we belong?

Making those programmes was highly satisfying; they broke conventional categories. They owed nothing to other forms, they were a real stretch, intellectually and physically. I was working with the new generation of BBC producers. Spanning the world for location interviews and scene-painting was glamorous and privileged. But the wear and tear mounted up. Not for the first time, I found I had over-committed myself. Restricting or even programming my workload was not a lesson that I have ever wholly learned. I dropped out after making the first ten programmes in August 1995. The first of the series, 'Dreaming', was broadcast on 13 September 1995. Fortunately,

Michael Ignatieff was ready to take on the second decade of 'gerunds for the twentieth century'. The rest of life returned to its pleasant, unremarkable routine. Was that all it was going to be? In fact, I already had a good idea of what it might be.

One morning in early 1995, scanning the press in the TV newsroom, a news story leapt out of the arts pages of *The Times*. Detta O'Cathain, the Managing Director of the decade-old Barbican Centre, had fallen out with her City of London Corporation employers and resigned. It sounded like a huge row; later I learned that it was. I should have recognised a can of worms when I saw one. After all, I knew the Barbican, had been to the concert hall and theatre, attended post-concert dinners. I shared the prevailing view that it was difficult to find, confusing to navigate and austere in its welcome. But as a fully paid-up architectural modernist, brought up by university friends to revere Le Corbusier and applaud the severity of Peter and Alison Smithson, I was not put off by concrete grandeur. The Barbican was ambitious and bold; I would not run away from it because it was a troubled institution. Perhaps the architecture and the art it housed were simply not gelling spiritually or practically. A sense of opportunity stirred. I might be the person to solve its problems.

I had always led a kind of double life, a journalist and editor by day, an arts lover by night, attending concerts, theatres and galleries on a regular basis. Many, perhaps most, of our closest friends worked in the arts. Very few business trips or journalistic assignments passed without going to a museum or finding an opera house. I had seen Verdi's *Aida* in Tashkent, Indonesian shadow plays in Java, discovered American abstract expressionism in New York. I had led and managed journalists and broadcasters; why could I not lead those who worked in the arts? The Barbican with its multiple art forms and venues was so big, so varied, so complex that it needed leadership to allow the arts to flourish. I had no doubt I could provide that. It was time to make enquiries.

I phoned Cecile Latham-Koenig, the Barbican's imminently departing Artistic Director. Was it, I asked her, worth taking my interest in the Barbican position further? Cecile had no doubt that it was. She had, after all, been engaged by the Town Clerk, Bernard Harty, the Chief Executive of the City of London Corporation, to find a new leadership team. She had already netted Graham Sheffield, seasoned BBC Radio 3 music producer and latterly Arts Director at the South Bank Centre, to take on the more wide-ranging arts role at the Barbican. Now Cecile had to net her other prey, the Managing Director; it just happened to be me.

Unaware of these internal machinations, I had been taking my own soundings, consulting Adrian Noble, Director of the Royal Shakespeare Company, and Clive Gillinson, Managing Director of the LSO (London Symphony Orchestra). They were the Barbican's chief artistic resident companies and had led the revolt against Detta O'Cathain. Each was decently encouraging. On 4 April 1995, Cecile brought me and Bernard Harty together for dinner at The Ivy. It went well. At further meetings at Guildhall in the City of London, Harty and I explored possibilities and practicalities. He was very positive about my candidacy but the decision would be one for the Barbican Centre Committee. I took the precaution of raising the age question. 'Look, Bernard,' I said on one occasion, 'I don't want to go through the whole selection process and find that someone says, "Tusa is the man for us but isn't he too old, rising sixty?"' Bernard assured me that my age would not be a problem.

Interviews took place in a committee room at Guildhall over dinner with members of the Barbican Centre Committee and Bernard Harty. Five candidates were interviewed over five consecutive dinners. Mine was on Thursday, 20 July 1995 at six-thirty. The unfortunate committee endured the same meal on each occasion. Harty had not thought to vary the menu.

Events moved fast. I was their preferred candidate. First, would I bring Annie to dinner the following Monday with

Harty and the Chairman of the Finance Committee, Richard
Scriven. This was social 'vetting' time! A pleasant occasion at
the Café du Marché in Smithfield turned into a raging success
when Scriven, a jovial man and an inveterate chain smoker,
found that Annie was a fellow smoker. That settled it; a chap
whose wife smoked must be a good chap too. 'We're having
HIM!' beamed Richard. 'SHE smokes!'

The formalities took place the following Thursday; the interviewing panel recommended me at 11.15; the full Barbican
Committee approved me as Managing Director at midday. A
good lunch had to follow, that was the City's way. (I was to be
part of the 'City lunch' regime for the next twelve years!) I
met the press at 2 p.m., Barbican Centre staff at 3.15 p.m. and
was interviewed live on Radio 3's *In Tune* at 7.15. I would work
out my broadcasting commitments by the end of September
and start work at the Barbican on 13 November. My hiatus was
healed, a new direction set. Three years after leaving the BBC
World Service, two years after walking out of Wolfson College,
I had a new and proper challenge.

There was one oddity about the selection process: the Arts
Director, Graham Sheffield, had been appointed before the
Managing Director. Not knowing Graham personally, I made
mild objections that surely the Chief Executive should have
been left to choose his senior staff? This was explained by the
timing of Cecile Latham-Koenig's own departure from the arts
post. Without a chief executive, the Barbican needed somebody
in post with clout and authority. For his part, too, Graham had
sought assurances that whoever became Managing Director
would be someone he could work with. Ultimately, we both
suspected that a shared BBC background meant we would
have a great deal in common. At our first meeting, we decided
we would get on very well. We did for the next twelve years
and do so to this day.

This was just as well, for the Barbican's problems were
stacked very high. The prevailing view was that the architecture was off-putting, its hammered concrete redolent of

wartime submarine pens. Getting to the Barbican through the labyrinthine, medieval alleys of the City of London had even, it was whispered, baffled Royal chauffeurs and bemused Her Majesty. Once inside this hermetic temple to the arts, the bewildering arrays of varying levels, staircases stretching skywards, balconies and ledges, a brass-trimmed web of Piranesi bridges and connections that never connected, frustrated the best endeavours of barely patient visitors and audiences to get where they wanted.

Worse still, in 1995 the Barbican sat marooned in a cultural desert, without bars and restaurants, little footfall, a morgue at night, amid a belief held by many in the City of London Corporation that visitors and tourists should not be encouraged to intrude into the Square Mile. Adjacent Shoreditch consisted of declining small craftsmen's shops, slightly more distant Hoxton was not yet modishly derelict, never mind ragingly trendy. The Barbican perched precariously on the eastern edge of London, a city which still habitually looked west.

As Graham Sheffield and I mulled over ways to make the building work physically, we found a miserable, dysfunctional organisation inside it. Departments were stuck in their own silos believing that, provided they did their own jobs, being helpful to colleagues was not expected or called for. At the top, the directors were at war with one another, fighting bitterly over scraps of turf. The Commercial department wanted to use the venues for money-making conferences and events; naturally the Arts department wanted them for the arts. Finance stood haplessly aside, wringing its hands at the lack of resources and poor box-office returns. Engineering kept the building running but never asked if it did so in a way that others found useful. Press and Publicity tried desperately to put a decent gloss on misery and confusion.

And what of the arts for whose sake the Barbican existed? The City of London Corporation paid large and annually growing sums of money to the RSC to programme the theatre (custom-built to their specification) and the underground experimental Pit theatre. The Corporation paid a direct annual grant to the LSO for some seventy main concerts in the hall. Neither 'resident' company showed any inclination to become artistic partners of the Barbican. They behaved like indifferent tenants, turning their backs on any offer to cooperate. This left the Barbican's own artistic offer meagre to the point of mediocrity; a few 'own promotion' concerts in the hall; a decent but limited cinema programme; no theatre promotions whatever. True, there was a sizeable art gallery, but that fell outside our control under a rival Corporation committee. Where would we have been without the stalwart business support of the ever-popular music impresario, Raymond Gubbay, with his eighty concerts per year?

This was no arts powerhouse but a chaotic, warring assembly of disconnected, non-communicating, incoherent, independent entities. The resident companies existed within the Barbican; they were funded by the City of London; they cared not a fig for either. It was a prescription for failure, conflict and disaster. Welcome to the Barbican 1995! Against all the evidence, both Graham Sheffield and I sensed there was huge artistic potential lurking behind the concrete pillars. Could we entice it out of the shadows to face the public?

A united management team had to be the first priority. The arts could not work if management was a mess. Within weeks, I steeled myself to persuade the Corporation that I must 'part company' with two of the directors. But first, my prostate 'blew up' during an LSO concert. Colin Davis was conducting Bruckner. I wondered occasionally if the prostate was making its own artistic judgement on the composer (I think differently about his music now). But it was just a case of full, total bladder retention. Three days later I had the standard operation and a standard, if quite lengthy, recovery followed.

During my convalescence, one of the 'difficult' directors became totally obstructive. I was fielding phone calls at home about rows at the Barbican when I least felt like it. I rang my Chairman on his holidays and insisted that on my return from convalescence I must have a free hand to reshape my directorate. He agreed and I immediately felt better. A month later, the 'exits' had been completed. Worried staff asked if this was the start of a general clearout? I could say in all honesty that it was not. Within two months, by June 1996, I had the new directors that I needed in Finance, Commercial and Communications. I never regretted that early purge. Delay would have been damaging. Now we could get down to business.

The first task was to rebuild the Corporation's trust in the Barbican in any shape or form. The public row over the departure of the former Managing Director, Detta O'Cathain, had upset the Corporation, an organisation highly sensitive about and protective of its reputation. The public notoriety that followed, the press coverage of her departure, made them feel foolish. The Town Clerk had stepped in to manage the Barbican for a few months and briefly considered the possibility of closing it down or turning it into a pure conference centre. Either option would have made matters worse and the Corporation knew it. Reluctantly, in the minds of some, an arts centre it had to remain; for good measure, Bernard Harty decided it needed an extra million pounds to improve arts programming. Graham Sheffield and I now had to prove that the money would be well spent, that the Barbican would be taken seriously, nationally and internationally, as a dynamic innovator in the arts. It was a tall order.

For many in the Corporation, the odds remained stacked against us. The first decade of the Barbican's existence was seen as underwhelming. Few appreciated that its creation under the tireless Canadian-born arts administrator Henry Wrong was little short of miraculous. Nobody ever thanked the Corporation for pouring millions into what was seen as a remote venue for which there was small public demand. Theatre consultants assured the Barbican Committee that if the RSC were absent, nobody else would want to work in a large 1,100-seat, lyric-dramatic space remote from the theatrical West End. Besides, did the RSC, now under the direction of Adrian Noble, even want to remain at the Barbican? 'Adrian has stars in his eyes,' I was warned, 'he dreams of the West End, the neon lights of Shaftesbury Avenue billboards. He isn't interested in being locked in the Barbican Theatre's windowless concrete walls!' Others warned: 'Adrian loves the "wandering player" image of theatre, especially if they play in "distressed spaces"!' Suddenly, the RSC announced its decision: from 1997 they would play at the Barbican for just six months a year; thereafter they would pull out completely. It was a huge blow.

I did not handle the RSC's departure well. Faced with growing rumours about Adrian Noble's intentions, I went into denial. 'They wouldn't walk away from the Corporation's multi-million annual subvention.' (They did.) 'The RSC couldn't risk losing that part of their Arts Council grant which related specifically to performing at the Barbican.' (They knew what they were doing.) 'The Arts Council couldn't continue to pay the RSC for performing at the Barbican if they were not doing so!' (Oh yes, they could.) Rational as these calculations might have been, and they were shared by my colleagues, they missed the point. The RSC were determined to go and did so without any formal consultation, warning or indication. I had been imprudent in failing to anticipate how they would act. The RSC were at least massively discourteous in not taking us into their confidence, ungrateful to the Corporation which had bailed them out financially for years past. The truth was that they did not care if the Barbican Theatre stayed open or fell dark. They had after all only ever been tenants, never partners, let alone stakeholders. The parting was disputed and quarrelsome, with raised voices and accusations of bad faith. RSC leaders, it turned out, had not read the terms of their residency agreement with the Corporation or understood their residual financial obligations. But their departure, first for six months, later in 2002 a total one, gave us artistic control of our main theatrical spaces. That turned one of the keys on the locks restricting our artistic freedom, though the RSC had not sought to do us any favours.

The behaviour of the Arts Council was even worse. Throughout the 1990s, the RSC had been running annual deficits on their overall budget. The Corporation, terrified that a bankrupt RSC might abandon the Barbican, duly filled the increasing annual budgetary gap; they felt they had no choice. In effect the City of London Corporation saved the RSC from bankruptcy and the Arts Council from a major reconstruction job. Yet the Arts Council was indifferent to any damage that the RSC departure might cause the Barbican. It cynically allowed the 'Barbican subsidy' to depart with the RSC. Throughout my twelve years at the Barbican, the Arts Council never raised a finger or offered a single pound towards our buildings or arts programming. They knew that we would not bend the knee to their intrusive 'managerialist' regimes. No matter that we were reshaping the London arts scene, we would have made inconvenient clients for them, too independent by half. There was no love lost between us. I was told that the Arts Council Chairman, Christopher Frayling, usually referred to me as 'that f***er Tusa'. I felt honoured.

The City of London Corporation stood by us, transferring some of their previous RSC subsidy money to Barbican arts. They funded the renovation of the theatre in 1997, opening up a disused orchestra pit, improving the acoustics, adding a dance floor, and reconfiguring the stage so that more ambitious productions could be mounted.

Graham Sheffield's achievement in the next four years was extraordinary. With his senior team of Louise Jeffreys in theatre and Robert van Leer in classical music, he built a programme that connected the art forms, explored the continents, and broke down traditional divisions. Graham observed that London was poorly served by the best international theatre. LIFT – the London International Festival of Theatre – ran only every other year, and then for just a fortnight. Students of international theatre had to catch it at the Edinburgh Festival or not at all.

The Brooklyn Academy of Music – BAM – pioneered the kind of programming that London lacked. Graham seized it as the Barbican's opportunity, spotting a cultural gap in the London artistic scene. 'Inventing America' in 1998 was a wildly ambitious year-long festival of American culture a little more than two years since we took over. Starting with the Robert Wilson/Philip Glass 3D epic *Monsters of Grace*, it amounted to the ultimate calling card. This is what the Barbican was uniquely going to present as an innovative arts organisation. The 'new guard' of American innovation and creativity, Philip Glass, John Adams, Steve Reich, Peter Sellars made unforgettable showcase appearances. *Paris sur Scène* brought new European dimensions to London. A distinct artistic character was emerging, though our resident companies had wanted no part of it. During earlier conversations about artistic plans, Adrian Noble once told Graham and me to our faces that 'Only artists can talk with artists.' In fact, he was terrified that Graham wanted to take over the RSC's programming at the Barbican, a sad misunderstanding. The LSO still behaved as if any enhancement of our own concert promotions might undermine rather than boost their own standing.

Within two years, Graham and Louise Jeffreys filled the theatre with BITE – 'Barbican International Theatre Event' – an eclectic, cross-cultural, cross-art form programme which brought us younger, more diverse, more open-minded, more experimentally inclined audiences. We opened with Thelma Holt's presentation of the legendary Japanese director Yukio Ninagawa. The Royal Opera, then temporarily out of their Covent Garden home, brought in three productions, extending still further the audience's view of what the Barbican theatre could do.

As the RSC withdrew its increasingly safe and predictable productions from the Barbican, their audience – white, middle-class, conventional and declining – migrated with them. This was their loss, not ours. The new Barbican audience – younger, more curious – matched our artistic ambitions. We had not found them through targeted marketing. The audiences found us because of our new artistic programming. This was the greatest achievement of the Barbican's artistic triumvirate, Graham Sheffield, Louise Jeffreys and Robert van Leer: understanding that audiences follow programmes, that marketing does not shape the public. Vision, knowledge and belief have always topped marketing segmentation.

There were times in my first three-year term, though, when I wondered if it was worth continuing. Progress on any front was heavy going, negotiations with the Corporation's committees wearing and I was obviously wavering. When a senior Barbican Committee member urged me to 'give us another chance!' the hint was too friendly to reject. Besides, my next Committee Chairman was to be Michael Cassidy, former Chairman of the senior City committee, Policy and Resources. I liked Michael; he was a doer, a City heavy hitter. Together we would get things done. I renewed my contract for a further three years in 1998.

Being Managing Director of a large arts organisation brought interesting personal opportunities. Every year in late January, BBC Radio 3 devoted an entire weekend at the Barbican to the music of a single composer. Ann McKay, the BBC Symphony Orchestra's senior producer, put two and two together and invited me to present all eleven broadcasts from Friday evening to Sunday night during the weekend. There I was, she reasoned, identified with running the Barbican, an experienced broadcaster, I knew my music, it was a natural fit. Varied strands from my life were coming together in a rewarding way. It would also be a massive learning experience.

For a decade from January 1998, I researched, wrote and presented weekends of saturation coverage of the music of Bohuslav Martinů, Olivier Messiaen, Kurt Weill, Alfred Schnittke, John Adams, Mark-Anthony Turnage, John Cage, James MacMillan, Elliott Carter and Sofia Gubaidulina. I knew some of the work of all of them; I learned a vast amount more. How undervalued Martinů was as a symphonist; how wondrous, engrossing and magic was Messiaen's unique sound world; how bitingly savage was Kurt Weill, reeking of the decadent cabarets and politics of Weimar-era Berlin; how spiky and raucously anarchic was Schnittke; how John Adams grew beyond the easy formulae of early minimalism. Mark-Anthony Turnage incorporated jazz into his own modernism; John Cage still surprised and shocked even in his familiarity, James Mac-Millan reinvented an unashamed Catholic devotion in music, Elliott Carter burnished austerity and discipline into the most demanding lines and patterns while Sofia Gubaidulina confirmed the lasting power of Russian Orthodox ecstasy. My own journey of discovery through these lesser-known peaks of twentieth-century musical creativity was mind-opening.

And the performers and performances! Messiaen's sounds and huge forces filling the echoing spaces of Westminster Cathedral; Pierre-Laurent Aimard mastering the two hours of Messiaen's *Vingt Regards sur L'Enfant Jésus* from 11 a.m. one Sunday morning; the great German chanteuse, Ute Lemper, rehearsing a set of Weill songs and demanding that her accompanist should be 'more situational!'; the planned disruptions as musicians marched and counter-marched through the Barbican Hall in a Schnittke symphony; a top-hatted Stephen Montague masterminding the three-ring circus of John Cage's *MusiCircus* through many levels of the Barbican's layered foyers; the stony-faced respect that greeted Cage's *4'33"* of orchestral silence, the audience torn between embarrassment and bemusement; the lasting radicalism and originality of Turnage's opera *Greek*; the brutal, intellectual demands of Carter's music on the BBC Symphony Orchestra's musicians.

Perhaps such intense concentration on what was music of our time should have had more immediate impact on regular concert programming. Some of it did. Messiaen is a more regular main-concert fixture than previously; James MacMillan and John Adams have become close to staples of concert-planning. Mark-Anthony Turnage features as a modern classic, Martinů inches towards a balanced recognition of his sound-world, Cage is seen as more than a mere musical provocateur. But musical fashions take two generations to change, public musical tastes move at a glacial pace. Perhaps the greatest shift in my own appreciation was finding that the string-quartet repertoire was far richer, far more adventurous than the prevailing world of the classics plus Shostakovich and Bartók. One day, perhaps, one day.

Being at the Barbican threw me unexpectedly into politics and the arts. The year 1995 saw the start of the Arts Council lottery, releasing large sums of money for much-needed capital schemes – John Major, the former Prime Minister, had given the arts their greatest boost in a generation. While a multi-million-pound feeding frenzy of major capital projects broke out, the political world changed with the election of Tony Blair's glossily rebranded 'New Labour'. Determined to show that New Labour was as tough on finance as the outgoing Tories, Blair and the Chancellor of the Exchequer, Gordon Brown, adopted the plans of their Tory predecessors involving reductions in spending of 2 per cent. Not only did such cuts hurt an already straitened arts world, the Arts Council supinely accepted them. Worst of all, it became clear that New Labour had no interest in the arts whatever.

Within weeks of arriving at Number 10, Tony Blair showed where his heart truly lay, his indifference to the arts revealed by his lists of guests to his new abode. Bedazzled by belief in his own version of the glamour of power, heady on the intoxicating ingredients of the cocktail that was 'Brand Blair', a fully believing member of the supposed new dawn breaking over Britain, he threw open the doors of Downing Street to the new royalty of the worlds of pop and fashion. This was 'Cool Britannia', this was 'Creative Britain', both cornerstones of Blair's 'New Labour, New Britain'. It was the rebirth of 'Swinging London' thirty years on. Somehow, the arts were omitted, overlooked or actively ignored. Somehow artists, singers, composers, painters, playwrights, actors, directors, sculptors, poets and novelists were missed out. There was a reason for these omissions, never publicly stated but quietly whispered by Blairite outriders: 'The arts were elitist, artists laid claim to special creativity when it belonged to everyone, the arts were rather, well, "heritage".' In this brave new glittering, cool, creative world, few words were more damning than 'heritage'. Of course, Blairite apparatchiks conceded, the arts might have a value. But they had to be useful: improving lives, creating jobs, renewing towns and cities. Otherwise what was their point?

Outside the self-satisfied fun palace that Number 10 had become, the arts and artists noticed the change of mood. Short of funding, undefended by their own Arts Council, dismissed by the government, 'luvvies' did what they are often derided as doing – they became 'revolting'. I played my part in creating the 'Shadow Arts Council' with Peter Hall, Norman Rosenthal and Clive Bradley. We put two fingers up at the timid leaders and bureaucrats of the real Arts Council and irritated the hell out of them by calling for a fight, arguing for increased funding, speaking up for the arts as arts, and daring to laud their intrinsic value. The politicians noticed. We were asked to meet the Culture Secretary, Chris Smith, to explain exactly why we were revolting. Chris understood well enough. He advised us to be patient. We were happy to give him plenty of ammunition to use in Downing Street and with the Treasury – which he did.

I still felt provoked by the limitations of the modish Blairite view of the arts. On 11 March 1998 *The Times* carried an article by me headed: 'I'm Worried About Tony'. I set out how the arts world felt about the way Blair ignored them, his love of the world of pop, the modish, his love of the famous, the fashionable, the febrile. Anything else was too difficult to fit into his lifestyle. The arts were, I concluded in my piece, 'lumbered in the Prime Minister's mind with a heap of pejorative associations. We can expect little sympathy, minimal understanding and feeble support for the financial crisis in which the performing arts now find themselves.' Hence my 'worries about Tony'. The article was accompanied by a half-length photo of me in an over-formal double-breasted suit.

The following morning, it was clear that Whitehall had noticed. A call came from the Permanent Secretary at the Culture Ministry, Sir Hayden Phillips. I knew Hayden and was amused by him. He affected a high-camp parody of the *Yes, Minister* mandarin as his standard operating manner. 'Dear boy,' he began, 'saw your piece in *The Times*, very interesting! That picture, your suit! The buttons seem to be pulling a bit tight! I'd see your tailor if I were you.' Then Hayden got smoothly to the point as if the thought had just come to him. Would I be interested in becoming Chairman of the Victoria and Albert Museum? The transition was effortless, the manipulative shimmy deft and elegant, the Whitehall mandarin at his most accomplished. It struck me they were paying an unnecessarily heavy price for one slightly troublesome piece in *The Times* but that was their business. I declined politely. But Hayden's call, mischief apart, suggested something was brewing in Whitehall even if it wasn't clear what it might be. We were soon to find out.

On 29 June 1998, some twenty leaders of major arts institutions were invited for talks with the Prime Minister at Number 10. They included Simon Rattle, Neil MacGregor, Genista McIntosh, Trevor Phillips and their peers. The young gofer doing the legwork was one James Purnell, destined for much higher things. He explained that we would each have a set time to make our points at the meeting. When it came to my turn, I insisted that the government's preoccupation with 'usefulness' – or 'instrumentalism' as it had come to be known – was driving a disruptive wedge between the subsidised arts and the newly emerging creative industries. They were in practice a continuum. Each relied on the other; if the continuum were to succeed, the arts had first to be excellent in their own terms. Beyond that, the twenty arts leaders called for a four-part 'Blair Settlement': restoring the cash value of the arts grant to its level four years back; fixing the grant with an annual inflation uplift; making it a three-year settlement; and telling the arts that that was that, we would be on our own thereafter. It was practical, it was cheap, it was doable.

Tony Blair encouraged us all by promising 'to write the arts into our core script'. The beauty of this assurance faded over the months as very different lobbying groups left Number 10 with an identical promise ringing in their ears. New Labour's 'core script' got very full. But within a fortnight, Gordon Brown's comprehensive spending review put an extra £290 million into the arts over the next three years. Why had it come so easily? A political adviser explained that no one in the government was remotely interested in the arts. 'But they don't like the fuss, they see it will not go away and if a few million will buy it off, then it's worth paying.' The Shadow Arts Council had done its job.

Yet the arts were never written into Tony Blair's core personal script while he remained at Number 10. The continuing debate over the 'instrumental value' of the arts versus their 'intrinsic value' – art for society's sake versus art for art's sake – raged for years to come. The Downing Street seminar settled nothing in this respect though it quietened the arts down. As Andrew Rawnsley observed in his biography, Tony Blair listened but he did not hear. But Blair's 'listening act' was very persuasive in the flesh.

My *Times* article had another effect. On the day after it appeared, 12 March 1998, Michael Earley, the publisher at Methuen, rang. We knew one another slightly from the BBC. He had liked the Blair article; what about a book of essays about the state of the arts today? I planned the book by the end of July, wrote and adapted previously written speeches during the autumn, added others and handed the text to Michael in February 1999. He suggested the title *Art Matters*, which had an attractive resonance for the times. A print of Catherine Yass's striking light-box image of the fly-tower of the Barbican

Theatre made an apt cover. It was published in the summer with a launch party in the Barbican Conservatory.

I thought my position as arts controversialist was good for the Barbican's standing. The Corporation did not see it that way and the Town Clerk and Chamberlain, Bernard Harty, instructed one of his staff to comb the book to see if there were sufficient complimentary references to the City of London. The scrutinised copy of the book was presented to me with yellow stickers at pages flagging each such mention. There were not, in Harty's estimation, enough. I was told to repay half the cost of the book launch. Perhaps he was minding the Corporation's value for money.

What emerged from the essays was a collection of my feelings and thoughts about the arts that had accumulated over the previous fifty years. Collectively they made up a personal arts credo: the arts had to be excellent if they were to be useful; the notion of creativity was no substitute for imagination and originality; marketing was an instrument for the arts rather than a driver; the arts must offer joy as well as enjoyment; language about the arts must be clear and honest, not managerial and obfuscating. Above all, I insisted that excellence and inclusiveness, often presented as contradictions, marched hand in hand: 'The best for the best is the best for all.'

While I handled the politics, Graham Sheffield and his team could be left to continue innovating the arts programme. All of us accepted that the Barbican must be well run if City of London support was to continue. In addition to the pressures on local-government funding – and in the end the Corporation was just another local authority – we had to find new ways of expanding the Centre's earnings and impact. Between 1998 and 2002, particularly under the chairmanship of Michael Cassidy, we tried every approach to find new or additional forms of support. The City expected no less.

For instance, could the Barbican's capital programme be funded through the then fashionable Private Finance Initiative

(PFI)? Alastair Ross Goobey, a true City gent and decent man, explained that PFI funding was (a) unlikely to be forthcoming, and (b) if it were available, it would prove to be ruinously expensive. He advised against it. (Tragically, the public sector seems not to have received the same advice!) Cassidy and I then visited major City firms to ask if they might be interested in an 'equity stake' in the Barbican? I was never sure what that meant, given that we ran at a permanent loss – the reason for arts subsidy – but the City wanted the question put. The answer from powerful City institutions to the invitation to invest in permanent subsidy was invariably a slightly incredulous 'of course not'!

In an attempt to silence the boring but damaging litany of 'we can't find the Barbican', I created the notion of 'CitySide – London's new Cultural Quarter' to give some identity and cohesion to the area. Our partners were Sadler's Wells theatre, City University and the Museum of London, though the last was never wholehearted in its involvement. Today, new 'urban quarters' in London are three-a-penny. CitySide was a decade ahead of its time, far too far. It never caught on and died a quiet, unnoticed death. Audiences told us they still found the Barbican 'hard to find'. We still existed in a cultural desert.

I made another attempt to break out of what we felt was physical and psychological encirclement. I called it 'Barbican without Walls'. Working with the LSO and RSC, our residents in the role of partners, we would reach out to the largely culturally deprived outer London boroughs. For an entire week, I proposed, the Barbican and its partners would descend on a particular borough with every conceivable arts offering – open-air events, school appearances, workshops in acting, singing, dancing and performance. Schools and libraries would host lectures, discussions, question times. At the final weekend, each Barbican partner would present two days of continuous informal and formal performances. By the end, I hoped and believed, a fuse of curiosity, excitement and involvement in the arts would have been lit. The Barbican would be extending its reach out dramatically, the arts would have been spread broadly and generously. There was no funding for such an idea but both Graham and I thought it had real potential. The LSO and RSC were extremely uninterested. 'Barbican without Walls' just crumbled into the ground like the walls of Jericho without a single LSO trumpet blast.

The idea of reaching out eastwards in London did not vanish altogether. From the very start in 1995, Graham Sheffield observed that the Barbican was the only major cultural institution without an education department. He funded one from the arts division's own budget and appointed the dynamic Jillian Barker as its head. Jillian's outreach into East London schools, culminating in week-long residencies, proved that going beyond the Barbican's walls could be a reality. My successor, Nicholas Kenyon, has turned working in and with neighbours to the east into an active reality.

Within the Centre itself, one fact stared us in the face. None of our venues or spaces was fit for purpose; arts promoters were reluctant to hire them; at best we were seen as a venue for commercial hire. At the time, Arts Council lottery funds were the first port of call for any building needing multi-million-pound capital injections – why should we be left out? The Barbican's £30 million Lottery Capital Fund bid was thorough and professional, we thought, the 'going rate' for a centre such as ours. Given our artistic record, we would, surely, receive some support? But the Arts Council was in no mood to do us a favour of any kind. Curiously, we were only slightly surprised and even less disappointed.

Rejection had one benefit: we had to think harder about finding funds for capital renewal. With Michael Cassidy as Chairman, we decided it was wrong to ask the City of London for a one-shot, lottery-size lump sum. Such mega-developments were disruptive of the arts and a brute to manage. The time had come for piecemeal development, or what we later called 'strategic pragmatism'. The urgency to renew the concert hall, the art gallery, the cinemas and the entrances and public spaces was not in doubt. It helped that refurbishing the theatre in 1997 had proved a success in the work we could present there. It helped, too, that my insistence on removing the ridiculous, gilded statues of the 'Nine Graces' from the Silk Street entrance was greeted with cheers, that painting out the measles-rash-like 'pointilliste' spots from the concert hall walls drew cries of relief. The Corporation knew by now that the Barbican team could be trusted artistically and professionally.

Bit by bit, from 2001 to 2006, the Barbican's places and spaces were renewed and transformed. Each project had to make its specific case without any guarantee that other projects would follow. The concert hall came first in 2001, a new acoustic lending a glow to the sound; the intrusive air ventilation noise was gone. it would never rival the world's best, but it was worth playing in and listening to. When our great acoustician, Larry Kierkegaard, led me into the renovated hall, we stood for a moment before he said: 'Listen, I've given you a quiet room!' That was the proudest claim an acoustician could make.

The art gallery followed in 2003, transformed by filling in a void at its very centre and creating a fully integrated and enclosed space. Between 2004 and 2006, the foyers were given clarity by removing three redundant or just confusing staircases and introducing a clear direction and line of entry into the public spaces. The internal signage and wayfinding was renewed, but now that the architecture was clear, the signage could follow where the architecture pointed. Finally, the Centre's street entrances were made to look like, well, entrances for the first time in a quarter of a century. All told, the City of London invested £35 million in the Barbican over the whole decade carefully, purposefully but effectively.

The architecture critic Hugh Pearman adopted our own phrase of 'strategic pragmatism' and wrote approvingly of the approach: 'Instead of wishing for the moon and waiting for decades, the Barbican just gets on and does what is necessary

. . . In its quiet way it is the best of the lot.' Writing in the Annual Report soon after, I said it was nice to be recognised but added: 'We haven't got to where we are by accident or chance.'

Choosing the right architects for the extraordinarily varied tasks at the Barbican had been enlightening for us, challenging for them. After all, it was the polar opposite to a new build on a brownfield site. Each project – theatre, gallery, concert hall, entrances and foyers – was specific and different. Each involved working with and around a strong, resistant and listed building which it had been from the outset. It needed serious but subtle adaptation and improvement. At the front of my mind was the foolish attempt by the renowned Theo Crosby of Pentagram to 'lighten up' the Barbican's severity in the early 1990s by installing the 'Golden Graces' over the entrance, covering the external walls of the concert hall with those 'pointilliste spots' and other would-be 'jokey' interventions. The attempt to 'jolly up' the building was a dismal failure, widely ridiculed. I always maintained there was no point shouting at the Barbican and ordering it to be what it could never be; it deserved to be listened to. At the front of my mind was the remark of the philosopher Sir Isaiah Berlin, some years previously: 'You will not make the Barbican loved! But you can make it respected!' That seemed a decent ambition.

After lengthy searches, we choose Caruso St John to adapt the concert hall, and Allford Hall Monaghan and Morris to reshape the art gallery and transform the entrances and foyers. Each practice realised their task brilliantly; each went on to win the Stirling Prize and become leaders in their profession; each was barely four years into professional practice life when chosen by the Barbican. Youth had not been a consideration in choosing them; simply, their solutions had been the best on offer. But it certainly helped that younger architects have found the Barbican easier to admire than others.

As the spaces and places were renewed, as navigating the building became more pleasant, as the venues revealed their

new authority, the Barbican finally came into its own artistically. The RSC's final exit in 2002, once feared as a body blow
to our artistic programming, had proved to be a liberation. For
the first time, we had full responsibility for two theatres; we
had taken over programming of the art gallery after its renovation. Robert van Leer was filling the concert hall with events
that matched the world-class quality of the LSO. With one
concert hall, two theatres, two art galleries and three cinemas
to manage and programme, the Barbican was in full control
of its offer to audiences for the first time in its near-quarter-
century history. I could claim without exaggeration that 'the
Barbican's programming across all the art forms constitutes
an essential element in the national and European arts scene'.
With country-based weekend festivals from Cuba and Mexico,
with the heady, mega-arts salute to Brazil in 'Tropicalia', we
were driving the arts agenda. We might still be hemmed in by
physical walls, but as the world leapt over them, we stopped
feeling claustrophobically restricted. If there was work still to
be done, our sense was of huge potential in the future.

Publishing my essays, *Art Matters*, in 1999 had some unexpected consequences. A former Radio 3 colleague, Tony Cheevers, commissioned me to adapt some of the chapters to make
twenty-minute interval talks during concerts. He followed
with a more ambitious proposal. He judged the network to
be failing to create a sound archive of influential artists of our
times. He was critical of the fact that the only time that many
major or creative figures were heard was in brief snippets of
publicity interviews preceding a gallery opening, a first night
or a book launch. They were, in Tony's view, shallow, narrow
and limited. He argued now for forty-five-minute, in-depth
interviews with leading artists of our times free from the limitations of the routine publicity interview. Choosing the artists
would not be driven by an event, solely by their reputation as
an artist. Would I be interested in doing these interviews on a
monthly basis at the rate of ten per year? It was an unbelievable

invitation, happily blending once more my personal delights with my professional past as a broadcaster and my present as an arts leader.

From April 2000, starting with the sculptor Anthony Caro, I conducted more than fifty such interviews. They included composers such as Elliott Carter, Harrison Birtwistle and György Ligeti; artists such as Howard Hodgkin, Paula Rego, Bridget Riley and Michael Craig-Martin; architects like Renzo Piano, Frank Gehry and Santiago Calatrava. Writers included Muriel Spark, Michael Frayn, Tom Stoppard and Ivan Klima; film directors, Bernardo Bertolucci and Miloš Forman; choreographers, Merce Cunningham and William Forsythe. It was an extraordinary chance to meet the creative and intellectual giants of my time.

Two books followed with printed texts of thirteen of the interviews in each. The first, *On Creativity* in 2003, showed that most artists avoided the very thought of being 'creative', let alone of 'inspiration'; their activity was work, the continuity of one piece of work after another, the relentless pursuit of what seemed 'right', the ruthless rejection of solutions that felt too easy. We found Muriel Spark cloistered in her Tuscan farmhouse, running a streaming cold, a dog yapping incessantly in the background. She was working on her latest novel, in longhand of course. She remained clear-headed, explaining that when she 'got into a tangle' in the narrative, her way out was to 'complicate it again, even more, and then get out of it'. She used to have three novels in her mind queuing up to get written, but in her old age there was just the one. The painter Frank Auerbach recognised the existence of personal aggressiveness in the act of painting because 'life's a battle'. This extended to his response to his own work: 'If one feels a slight unease, even if the thing seems plausible and presentable and nobody else might notice that it is no good, one's got to destroy it. Destroy your darlings.' In his garden studio in Wiltshire, Harry Birtwistle gazed at a huge manuscript sheet almost three feet high and sighed at the absence of big gestures available to a composer: 'You build it up, pebble by pebble by pebble. Look at that piece of page there – it takes about ten seconds to play and two days to write!' And like many of the others, Birtwistle veered away from seemingly easy solutions: 'If I get to a point in my work where I think I know where I am going and I go away and leave it, when I come back I very rarely continue in the way that I thought I was going to continue.' After, Harry cooked us a delicious onion quiche. Tony Cheevers noted a minimalist artwork on the wall. He wondered why, given Harry's clearly stated dislike of minimalist music?

The discoveries continued. Paula Rego spoke of painting as 'opening a corridor into the darkness' and the danger faced during the process of discovery: 'There's a thrill that you might go over the edge into some area which is so fraught with danger and risk of total embarrassment, something that is going to reveal unspeakable things. I don't quite know what, but that's the risk of it.' She was warm and lovely, with few obvious hints of the dangerous borderlands she inhabited and often crossed. The great art critic David Sylvester spoke of the need to 'be patient with Matisse' in order to understand him, whereas his response to Picasso was immediate: 'Picasso hits you immediately in the solar plexus and then often fades.' And Sylvester's description of the critical act of looking at paintings? 'The experience is instinctive. It's somewhere between prayer and sex. When I say "sex", I mean responses that one feels in one's body.'

The second collection of thirteen interviews, *The Janus Aspect*, followed in 2005, with a title too clever by half. The theme though was strong: how even the most seemingly modern artists found connections to and inspiration from the distant past. The video artist Bill Viola rooted his reinterpretations of Christian imagery and mythology in his early love of the fifteenth-century Siennese masters. The sculptor of vast steel sheets, Richard Serra, owned that his massive Corten-steel-torqued ellipses were inspired by Borromini's church in Rome, the Quattro Fontane. The architect of some of the most arresting shapes in contemporary architecture, Frank Gehry, rooted his visual sensibility in the Romanesque churches of France and what he called the 'Baroque extravaganzas' of southern Germany. Perhaps my original notion of the 'two-faced deity' looking backwards and forwards wasn't such a bad idea after all to capture the extraordinary sources of artists' imagination.

In the five years spent criss-crossing the disciplines and the art forms, my mind jangling with intellectual surprise, certain images stood out. A very old Merce Cunningham, sitting slumped, head down in his wheelchair in a London hotel room. Would anything come from this interview, I wondered. The moment I put my first question, the head lifted, the eyes shone, the mind engaged, and Merce was in full, articulate, wise flow. David Hockney's room was thick with cigarette fug, waving his lighted fag around as we talked. 'Smoking will kill you but you're going to die anyway.'

After interviewing Richard Hamilton, I took his photograph on my small camera. It is perfectly adequate, a likeness of Richard Hamilton. Would he take one of me? He agreed. The result was something different, a composition of a person in a radio studio. An artist with an eye composes images totally differently from the rest of us. Other subjects, it seemed to me, came to resemble their own art. My own two photos of Gilbert and George look just like, well, Gilbert and George, their deadpan features, their immaculate suits, their controlled gaze somewhere between calculation and a pretence of the natural. Tony Cheevers thought they were playing the part of being outsiders, which of course they weren't. My own snaps of them lack surprise or insight. More puzzling is that when I asked each to photograph me in turn, in an identical position standing before a studio screen, each image looks totally different. What was different of course was the eye of each photographer.

Two interviews left me feeling personally dissatisfied. I became irritated with the playwright Edward Bond's wild generalisations about totalitarianism linking Adolf Hitler, Jesus

Christ and great names through the ages. Anyone who invokes Hitler is usually sporting a weak and lazy case. We had an argument, it sounded amusing enough on air but I basically hated it. I had lost control of the exchanges. Tony Cheevers, though, recalled Bond being friendship itself as he left the studio. The other failure was of a very different kind. Talking to Tom Stoppard at the National Theatre, I opened by saying he and I might have a lot in common. I was born in the medical clinic of the Bata Shoe Company town in Zlín, southern Moravia. Tom's dad was one of the clinic's two doctors. There had to be a 50/50 chance that I was delivered by Tom's father. I thought that, without warning, this 'revelation' would break the ice at the start of the interview. Quite the reverse. Stoppard froze and the interview limped its way onward in discomfort. But my post-interview photo shows us smilingly arm in arm. Perhaps it wasn't as icy as I feared, or does the camera lie?

As the sixth series of interviews got under way in 2005, I made a major mistake. Feeling tired with accumulated overwork, I found it increasingly difficult to think of artists to talk to. The interviews had been an important part of the Radio 3 schedules; we had created a huge archive of more than fifty artistic figures of our time in extended conversation, amounting to a rich and intense sound canvas of the arts world around us. Tony Cheevers's ambition had been realised. I rang Roger Wright, Controller of Radio 3, and said that it had been a great experience, but after being on air regularly for five years perhaps the time had come to bring it to a close. Roger understood and agreed. Yet, within a few weeks, my mind had filled with the names of artists I was desperate to speak to. I rang Roger to say I had changed my mind! It was too late, the schedules had altered; the waters had closed. There was a lesson: never offer to stop an activity or project. Wait for others to take the decision for you.

In the meantime, I had had a wonderful surprise with the offer of a knighthood from Number 10. It was both unexpected and unsought. In the closing months of my time at the BBC World Service in 1992, I had been offered a CBE. I turned it down without a qualm; I would not accept anything that came through 'Dukey' Hussey and the official processes of the BBC. This offer was different, appearing quite out of the blue. Later, it appeared that the City of London Corporation was even more surprised than I was. They had a precise pecking order for their recommendations for honours; the Managing Director of the Barbican Centre would certainly not have been in line for a 'K'. Only the Chairman of Policy and Resources and the Lord Mayor got that. The slight element of mystery only added to my pleasure.

By 2005, I had been in post for ten years. I would stay until the Barbican celebrated twenty-five years in February 2007. It was possible to take stock in a slightly valedictory mood, to offer some perspective. On my arrival, the Barbican was known as a rather stroppy and gawky teenager, who scowled at others, had its personality defined by others, had just gone through an acute institutional breakdown and was searching for a role. A decade later, it had become a confident, outward-looking adult with links around the world with its artistic peers, mature relationships with its closest domestic partners. It had a well-defined and distinctive artistic personality that embraced innovation, internationalism, radicalism and diversity in all its forms, and was underpinned in every art form by an absolute commitment to quality. The City of London had been constant in its backing, demanding in its scrutiny, shrewd in its investment. The Arts Council and the Department for Culture, Media and Sport remained aloof to the very end, indifferent to the Barbican's welfare, hostile even, but content enough to include the Barbican's artistic contribution to the flourishing national arts scene.

It is impossible to exaggerate the way that Graham Sheffield and his closest colleagues fashioned an arts programme whose base lay in cooperation between and among the art forms. By 2005, the Barbican's regular artistic partners, virtually 'resident' visiting companies, included Merce Cunningham's Dance, the Michael Clark Company, Simon McBurney's 'Complicité', Declan Donnellan's 'Cheek by Jowl', Robert Lepage, Deborah Warner, Peter Sellars, Thelma Holt and Yukio Ninagawa, William Christie's 'Les Arts Florissants', the London Symphony Orchestra, the BBC Symphony Orchestra, Valery Gergiev's Maryinsky Company, the great orchestras of the world and scores of specific projects. It was impossible to forget Deborah Warner's *Julius Caesar* with its locally recruited crowd of Roman citizens, or Robert Lepage's *Hans Christian Andersen*; Slava Rostropovich's conducting of the Shostakovich symphonies, Colin Davis's complete cycle of Berlioz or Valery Gergiev's epic performances with his Maryinsky forces of Shostakovich's *Lady Macbeth of Mtsensk* followed by Tchaikovsky's *Queen of Spades* on successive nights. The Barbican's venues had become a destination of choice and preference for the world's finest companies and artists.

I wanted to capture this cavalcade of the arts in tangible form beyond faithfully keeping the programmes of every event I attended. I took my camera backstage for more than a decade. The results form a visual canvas of the time. One image stands out for its power and glamour. In July 1999, Jessye Norman came to sing an evening of spirituals. Some weeks before the event, her agent said Miss Norman wanted Tony and Cherie Blair to attend; they had met recently at the White House. It was a kind of 'royal command'! The Barbican Theatre team were flummoxed; what should they do? I told them to ring Number 10 with the invitation; they could only say no! The Blairs, it turned out, were happy to accept; it would, explained Number 10, be a private visit. My photos of the three of them outside Jessye Norman's dressing room are a reminder of their happier days. All three glow with pleasure at who they are, who they are with. They seemed to have it all at that moment. A small crowd waited to greet the Blairs outside the stage door. Those were their glory days.

I caught some striking pairings. Here is Simon Rattle talking to the then head chef of our Searcy's restaurant, Richard Corrigan, great conductor, soon-to-be great chef. Jon Vickers, one of the finest dramatic tenors of my life with one of his closest collaborators, the conductor Edward Downes. And the composers: a golden-locked John Taverner sitting by an amused-looking Louis Andriessen; a reassuringly massive Ollie Knussen seated while his mentor, the ninety-year-old Elliott Carter, stands by his side, leaning lightly on his stick; the precisely elegant Pierre Boulez chatting to the impresario Lilian Hochhauser; there the ultimate opera power couple, the silver-locked Dmitri Hvorostovsky in conversation with the golden-voiced Renée Fleming. A shining, gleaming, badly shaved Rostropovich embraces Annie warmly and wetly. Goodness, how conductors sweat.

Many of the strongest images of my 800 are of individuals. Theatre directors by their craft and nature give little of themselves away; Lev Dodin of St Petersburg's Maly Theatre is massive but opaque; Yukio Ninagawa implies a stored energy; Deborah Warner invites collusive confidences. None should be misread, still less underestimated. The pianist Mikhail Pletnev offers the blankest of Russian deadpan faces. The Romanian, Radu Lupu, stares bleakly into a glass of water waiting for his painkiller to work. The conductor Andrew Davis sits, his shirt open to his waist, drained but exhilarated after a concert. Over a decade of capturing artists after work, Maxim Vengerov grows up, Yo Yo Ma bulks up, Peter Sellars becomes less imp-like, Michael Tilson Thomas retains his boyish winsomeness.

One person totally eluded me on camera – the principal conductor of the London Symphony Orchestra, Colin Davis. I keep my memory of him without the help of the image. In the green room after a concert, Colin would sit at a table with a double Scotch in hand. On one occasion only, he was on his feet when we came in, almost dancing with glee. He had just conducted the most exhilarating performance of Verdi's *Falstaff*.

*

In 2007, the Barbican's twenty-fifth birthday fell. It was celebrated in style artistically, a showcase of the arts that Graham
Sheffield had brought in over the preceding decade. The former
Lord Mayor, Sir Robert Finch, hosted the first-ever 'City's
Lunch for the Arts' at Mansion House; Ian Bostridge and Valery
Gergiev spoke. It meant that the City of London finally felt it
owned the Barbican in every sense. The Queen came to the
anniversary concert. Buckingham Palace courtiers advised us
that it didn't matter what the actual music was, Her Majesty
would sit and take it. In fact as we left the Hall afterwards, she
said she had been 'exhilarated' by Colin Davis's performance
of Tchaikovsky's Fourth Symphony with the LSO. Why, I
wondered, didn't her courtiers play her Tchaikovsky every
morning with her coffee to keep her 'exhilarated'? Shouldn't
they have known her better as a human being?

I published a second book of essays, *Engaged with the Arts*.
I knew the arts still needed publicly defending and fighting
for. I hated complaisant collusion with the political establishment and arts bureaucrats. In a lecture for Martin Randall's
cultural travel organisation at the Royal Geographical Society,
something began to boil over as I started a riff on the theme
of 'I'm sick to death of . . . ' because I was. I was sick to death
of arguments over arts funding because so little money was
involved, argument was a waste of time. I was sick to death of
justifying support for the arts as if it was especially difficult to
do so. I was sick to death of government officials finally realis-
ing that the arts were a success story, that they helped people
and society by being excellent. I was sick to death of the arts
being seen as a personal indulgence, of local authorities falling
down on their job. Later *The Times* gave it a big spread. I felt a
little better afterwards.

The last weeks at the Barbican were spent in a glow of
laudatory press coverage and a round of champagne-fuelled
parties and events. At a final press gathering, I tried to prick
the growing bubble of praise by listing the areas where I had
made little or no progress. Relations with the Arts Council had

been a disaster; all attempts to build a serious development function, to attract private or corporate sponsorship had failed. The press ignored my self-flagellation. They knew their story – 'Barbican pronounced success!' Why should I worry?

As to the quantities of champagne consumed! After routine blood tests, I asked my GP if he was worried about my liver function. Why did I ask, he enquired. Because I had been afloat on a river of champagne for the past few weeks! 'It's perfectly normal,' he replied, 'your liver is obviously doing its job!'

I thought of Max Hastings's observation. The Barbican had been a wonderful time for me, in its different way quite as satisfying as the years at the BBC World Service. I reflected that at the institutional level, there was little generosity in the arts world; when it had been in dire straits, the Barbican was left to sink or swim by its peers and competitors. I observed the Arts Council growing ever narrower in its perspectives and devising ever more particular ways of justifying funding in the name of accountability. It had adopted grant-giving through micro-management at its most intrusive. Most such schemes fizzled out, only to be replaced by another complex and usually ineffective wheeze. I grew ever more grateful for the sheer common sense of the City of London Corporation. In my dozen years as Managing Director, they never set objectives nor required us to set any (we set our own). Colleagues in the arts world were amazed at this flouting of what some regarded as basic management orthodoxy. I explained that I did have objectives to work by: first, to produce great art; second, to be efficient and manage well; third, perhaps most importantly, to bring credit to the City of London Corporation; last, not to insult the Lord Mayor! These objectives may have been unwritten but were none the weaker for being implied and not prescribed. The Corporation, perhaps unconsciously, operated 'strategic laissez-faire-ism'. Some in the City no doubt regarded me as stroppy. Most understood that the person running the Barbican had to fight its corner; a degree of 'bolshyness' came with the job description. But the Corporation recognised success when they saw it.

Little would have worked without one person sustaining me during the whole twelve years: my wife Annie. She was the uncomplaining recipient of emotional accounts of the trials of Barbican life – of which there were many – and the most trenchant but appreciative critic of the hundreds of events at which she had been present – of which there were many. She stood for what the Barbican stood for, she was a part of the team. It would all have been far less fun without her commitment. It probably would not have been worth doing.

13

Teaching and Learning

*University of the Arts and the Clore Leadership
Programme 2007–14*

I started planning my future life post-Barbican during the final hectic months there. Although I was seventy-one, I did not want to retire; I believed I had a lot still to offer and inactivity held no appeal. Scouting the scene, I became aware of a slightly off-centre academic organisation with an old-fashioned name, The London Institute. Seven independent, small art colleges, once directly funded by the Inner London Education Authority (ILEA), had been pushed into a single administrative unit in preparation for the ILEA's abolition in 1986. Interestingly, they included some of the legendary names of the national arts scene: Chelsea School of Art, Central Saint Martins, Camberwell, London College of Fashion, London College of Communication and Wimbledon. In 2004, it became University of the Arts London (UAL).

I knew the Chairman of the Court of Governors, Will Wyatt, former MD of BBC Television. I got to know the Rector – a vice-chancellor in university parlance – Sir Michael Bichard, a heavyweight former civil servant. I liked and admired both; this was a serious outfit, clearly evolving with huge potential. Based in and around London, it was not an all-purpose, multi-faculty university; it was about the arts. It felt like a good fit for what I had learned, what I could do and the stage I was at. After preliminary chats, both sides agreed to take things further and I went for formal interviews. In November 2006 I was offered the post of Chairman of the Court of Governors, University of the Arts London and took up the position in March 2007. It felt like a good start to a big personal transition.

In those dying months of the Barbican years, I had found myself in demand. After all, my twelve years there were regarded as successful; media coverage and political controversy had given me a public profile. Opportunities appeared, almost bewilderingly. I was shortlisted for the chairmanship of English Heritage and interviewed by officials from the DCMS (Department of Culture Media and Sport) on 25 April. A fortnight later, on 9 May, some of the same DCMS officials considered me for the Chair of the Victoria and Albert Museum. (I looked back with amusement to the circumstances in which I was previously offered the post in 1998.) I am not sure what I thought I was doing in applying for what would have been a 'triple-crown' of arts bodies – university, heritage, museum. Was I terrified of being idle, of having time on my hands, or was I just overplaying my hand? Surfing as I was on waves of approval, regarded as a doer, known to be independent-minded, I was happy to be taken seriously at such levels. I doubt if I expected to be offered both posts and decided to face that problem were it to occur. I started attending meetings at UAL as part of a smooth handover from the outgoing Chair, Will Wyatt.

I wasn't hanging onto my mobile for calls from the DCMS when Annie and I set off for Afghanistan in mid-May to see the work of Rory Stewart's Turquoise Mountain Foundation in Kabul (TMF), of which I was a trustee. On 25 May, we travelled an hour and a half north from Kabul to the mountain village of Istalif, which had a centuries-old tradition of making pottery. Surrounded by the snow-capped peaks of the Hindu Kush, we looked down on the vast sandy plains through which had swept the great armies of history, from Genghis Khan to Timur and Babur. That great lover of gardens, the Emperor Babur, had created one in Kabul, a haven for Afghan families to this day. He laid out another in Istalif, its lines of old huge plane trees still showing the original layout of the garden. Babur had gazed at this vast view reaching to a distant horizon; we were able to share it.

Looking down on the village from high up on the mountain-side, we sat in the mud-built house of the master potter. Sitting at his wheel, he would always say a brief prayer before starting to throw a new bowl. Pottery was harder for him now, he said, his knees stiffened from years at the potters' wheel. We drank coffee and exchanged social pleasantries through Rory's fluent Dari. Annie sat in the adjoining rooms for the women. They laughed, they taught one another to count in their respective tongues. Why didn't we stay the night, they asked? Their house was our house; the quiet, the balm of the place, the stillness of time, the people and the moment were beguiling.

Suddenly Rory's mobile rang. This was not unusual; what was unusual was that it was a call for me. Not bothering to ask how they had traced my location down to Rory's phone, I found myself speaking to a very polite civil servant from the DCMS. They were very grateful for my interest in the chairmanship of English Heritage, they appreciated the time and effort I had given to thinking about it but they regretted that I was not being offered the position. I looked around at the mountains and plains of Afghanistan, drew a breath, expressed my gratitude for their courtesy in contacting me and, feeling very calm, replied: 'Just at the moment, I am six thousand feet high in the Hindu Kush in Afghanistan. That rather puts anything else into perspective.' It did. We did not stay the night with the master potter and his family – definitely our loss.

On my return to London, I had time to wonder what was happening about the V&A chairmanship. It would, surely, make a good, natural fit with that of the UAL? As I emerged from a university awayday at Hartwell House in Herefordshire on 6 June, Alan Davey, a senior civil servant from the DCMS, rang. Ministers had cleared my appointment to the V&A chairmanship, so would I accept? This all seemed too good to be true.

Rounding off my Barbican years I took every opportunity possible to catch live arts. Over to Brussels for the regular conference of ISPA (International Society for the Performing Arts) which Graham Sheffield had revived. En route to Amsterdam to Netherlands Opera for the first night of John Adams's opera *Dr Atomic* about J. Robert Oppenheimer, the creator of the atom bomb, I visited the joyous Franz Hals Museum in Haarlem, a wonderful collection in a harmonious old brick-built hospital. A week later, Annie and I travelled to Russia with the London Symphony Orchestra and Valery Gergiev for concerts in Moscow and St Petersburg, our last chance to tour with the company, many of whom had become good friends. The second concert took place in Gergiev's new Maryinsky concert hall, oddly shaped we thought but with fine acoustics.

We learned a lot about the orchestral musician's life. The overnight train sleeper from Moscow to St Petersburg was followed by a late-night, post-concert charter flight for the players back to Stansted, before flying out for another trip the following day. We learned even more about Valery Gergiev's own work schedule, about which we had few illusions to start with. His concert with the LSO ended around 9 p.m. As the LSO players climbed into buses for the airport, members of his own Maryinsky Orchestra were drifting in for another Gergiev concert starting at 10 p.m. Backstage in the green room, Gergiev stood calm, collected, perfectly mannered, thanking sponsors, oligarchs no doubt, surrounded by flowers and flunkeys, fresh for his next spell of making music.

Starting my new life and activities, I got to know governors, directors and staff at the UAL's colleges. I liked what and whom I saw and sensed there was a great deal that could be done. The highpoint of this fevered period, leaving the Barbican, soaking up great musical events, came on 26 June 2007 at the V&A's annual party. I was attending for the first time as 'Chairman designate' of the trustees. With the main foyer crammed with guests under Dale Chihuly's astonishing glass spiral ceiling-suspended sculpture, my welcome from trustees, future colleagues and friends was extraordinary. It took almost half an hour, it seemed, champagne in hand, to get from the museum entrance to the fresh air of the Madejski Garden courtyard. I felt buoyed by a sea of goodwill. If this was anything to go by, life ahead would be very enjoyable. My post-Barbican transition had fallen into place. I would be at the heart of two major institutions in the arts world. Or so it seemed.

A few days later, I had a message from the Deputy Chair of the UAL Court of Governors, Stephen Barter. I knew Stephen, a high-level property man from the City of London, and respected his work. 'Could I', said the message, 'drop by UAL head office in Davies Street on Monday for a "natter"?' It was an odd choice of word but I read nothing into it. I turned up at 5.30 on 9 July. Stephen was there, so was Clara Freeman, the governor who had recruited me, as was the Rector, Michael Bichard. He looked downcast; they looked grim; there was an atmosphere.

Stephen began: they wanted a 'natter', because a worrying number of people were saying that my holding the two chairmanships, UAL and V&A, could become a real conflict of interest. Who would I really represent? Which would I give more time to? In fund-raising in particular – for whom would I really be seen to speak?

Now that these concerns were expressed, I recognised them as valid. We talked openly and cleared the ground on basics. We agreed that bad faith was not involved, there had been no lack of candour. Both sides had known about the possibility of my having a dual role; nothing had been held back. In principle, there ought not to be a clash because a museum and a university were quite different. But once a possible conflict of interest had been perceived, it could not be wished away. After quite a long and friendly discussion, I said it looked as if I had to make a choice. They agreed. I promised to make it with an open mind. Clara Freeman replied they were very grateful for that. I think all three assumed I would choose the 'glamorous' museum rather than the emerging university, but they had risked speaking out knowingly. That was why they looked so glum.

I rang Annie before I got on the tube at Bond Street, and explained that we needed a good long think. Before we sat down to eat, after a drink in the sitting room on a typically wet July evening, we had decided that the best/right thing to do was for me to 'pass' on the V&A and to stay at the university. I had liked the idea from the start; I liked the people, the flexibility, the sense of fun, the potential. I admired what they had achieved in a short period of time. I had said 'yes' to them first. I would not go back on that.

The next day, Tuesday, I rang Michael Bichard with a question: 'Were I to throw in my lot with UAL, would any governors vote against me?' After all, I wasn't going to go through this turmoil if some remained unreconciled. He assured me that everyone would be absolutely behind me. I thought for a while longer, then rang Clara Freeman, Stephen Barter and Michael again to say that I had decided to step aside from the V&A; I would stay with UAL. They were quietly relieved and very positive. Their responses suggested that I had taken the correct decision. I never regretted doing so.

The painful part came next. I called Alan Davey at DCMS first, explaining as briefly as possible my reasons for taking my decision. A good civil servant, he was efficiency personified. 'Right, pity; let me get it sorted out.' The outgoing Chair of Trustees, Paula Ridley, was stunned, the Director of the Museum, Mark Jones, shocked. Both took it with calm, style, utter decency and without recrimination. It made my decision a lot easier. No one ever made me feel foolish for getting into this position. The nuts and bolts of my abrupt departure, including finding a successor for the Chair of V&A Trustees, was managed in just a fortnight. Remarkably, there was no leak. More remarkably, I think, once a fairly detailed statement was issued about my change of mind, once it became clear that there was 'no story', no scandal, it was reported but not stirred.

Personal reactions from friends were more interesting. Some saw the point immediately; if there was a danger of conflict of interest, they said, better to get it over at once. The possible alternative would have been to tough it out, to prove over a period of time that there could be no conflict. That route risked a clash which could damage one or both institutions. Others were puzzled. Where was the conflict of interest? Why was the UAL being so defensive? What a shame for me, how much the V&A needed me and so on.

A third group put into words something that had escaped me. 'Ah yes,' they observed, 'it's quite clear. You have chosen the future, you have chosen possibilities. The V&A, great institution that it is, is the past!' Once I heard that, and it came from more than one person, it clarified a lot and made my decision feel particularly right. A final group insisted on a political conspiracy. A minister or ministers, unnamed and unknowable, had – they asserted – plotted to get rid of me. No amount of assurance that this was not the case would ever convince them to the contrary. The bone of conspiracy was too tasty to put down.

With my position as Chairman of the Governors at UAL now settled, I faced a sizeable agenda. A new Rector had to be found since Michael Bichard was standing down. This was the way that leadership succession at UAL had been planned. A final decision about developing a new campus to replace the dispersed buildings of Central Saint Martins was drawing nearer. And UAL was rightly concerned about how good a university it was, or indeed whether it was good at all. Was it capable of answering its own questions? It was going to be an intensive twelve months.

Headhunters had produced a strong longlist for the post of Rector, a helpful mix of academics, international art-world administrators and outsiders. All candidates had proven records of achievement, major administrative experience, strong personality, real energy. The quality of the list itself was a tribute to UAL's standing and attractiveness. After extensive and repeated interviews, Clara Freeman and I were increasingly taken by the two non-academic 'outsiders'. Each was a high-class professional in his own world. Each was interested in the visual arts well beyond the dilettante 'I love watercolours' stage. Neither outsider had ever run an academic institution. After further formal and informal interviews, Clara and I recommended Nigel Carrington, former managing partner of a huge law firm, Baker & McKenzie. Since you can't boss law firm partners around, we reckoned that Nigel would well understand that academics, too, couldn't be dragooned or directed.

Appointing a Chief Executive in the world of arts or academia was one of the hardest decisions to be made. I had previously made a couple of bad appointments in other organisations from which I suffered for years afterwards. Making no decision, delaying an appointment, was infinitely preferable to making the wrong one. Clara Freeman and I had spent weeks considering the candidates for the rectorship. We had no doubts in appointing Nigel Carrington. He proved a brilliant Rector from September 2008.

Before he arrived, Michael Bichard, the governors and I had to take an important decision about UAL's next property development, a major consolidated campus for Central Saint Martins at King's Cross. I admired the UAL's sense of purpose. It had moved away from its historic origins in crafts, trades and skills when it became a university, meeting rigorous external standards to do so. Previously, it had sold seven scattered premises throughout Chelsea and created a handsome single campus for Chelsea College of Art next door to Tate Britain on the Embankment. Now it was on the verge of selling existing historic buildings in Charing Cross Road and Southampton Row and investing the money and a sizeable lump of bank borrowing into the great Thomas Cubitt Granary Building at the heart of the still-emerging King's Cross redevelopment. It was incredibly ambitious. What price would we get for our key properties as the banking crisis enveloped the Western economies? Even if the bank was ready to lend a great deal of money, were UAL finances sufficiently robust to bear the burden of repaying capital and interest as they fell due? This great scheme had been developed by the Wyatt/Bichard team.

It gave UAL a sense of delivering continuity. If it was both risky and finely balanced, it was not reckless.

The property deal with Argent, the visionary King's Cross developers, had been negotiated by the university's deputy Chairman, Stephen Barter. Throughout 2008, as the world economy, international banks and property values lurched and often collapsed, Stephen chaired regular, internal reviews of the total cost of the King's Cross Granary Square campus and its affordability. If this was 'Plan A' – the realisation of a magnificent campus by the architects Stanton Williams – did we have a viable 'Plan B', or indeed a plan of any kind? We could spend tens of millions of pounds on refitting two ancient and entirely unsuitable premises, Charing Cross Road and Southampton Row. Academics and past students insisted that the old Saint Martins building in Charing Cross Road was the temple of historic arts creativity. But no amount of money would turn it into a twenty-first-century art college. In short, the university had no workable 'Plan B'. Doing nothing was worse than perilous; it was unacceptable.

The university's Estates Committee approved the numbers in June 2008, the governors endorsed them on 14 July. Lehmann Brothers was folding, property prices were falling, the risks of proceeding were recognised, weighed and balanced. Some contracts were renegotiated, HEFCE, the higher-education funding body, was approached for a bridging loan. None of us judged the overall package endangered the finances of the university. It was a risk but we did everything to mitigate the worst consequences. The vision realised, Michael Bichard retired as Rector on 30 July 2008. It would be Nigel Carrington's task to deliver the vision in practice.

In between finding a new rector and betting the shop on the King's Cross campus, I found the university ready to take a searching look at itself. Everyone had their ideas of what the university's aims should be. The late Rodney Fitch, a lion of the design business and long-standing governor, said it came down to three words – Talent, Geography and Technology.

Did we have sufficient talent? Did we realise how huge the global challenge was? Were we facing up to the technology sea-change? There would never be conclusive answers to such questions. But they had to be addressed.

With another approach, Ben Evans of the London Design Festival and Mathew Slotover of Frieze questioned whether UAL was truly innovative, was it creative enough? Had London lost its creative burn since the YBAs (Young British Artists) had grown up? For these two, the ideal for nurturing creativity was the European model of a score of staff working with a hundred students, everyone an artist. This was the classic art college, run by a few, teaching a few, answerable only to their own genius. Successful as it once had been, beguiling as it might be, it was remote from the direction on which UAL was irrevocably set. How excellent could we make our much larger and more complex model?

At his final awayday in June, Michael Bichard warned against complacency and conservatism. We had a long way to go, he said, to become a 'great' institution. University IT was in a mess, internal communications poor, 'student satisfaction' scores stubbornly low. In addition, UAL had no brand identity, or, come to that, no identity as an institution. An outsider had described it as 'a bit like British Leyland', a cobbling-together of obsolete models. This healthy realism was tempered with internal caution and anxiety: 'Don't forget how far we have come in five years,' some academics warned, as if getting to where we were was all that could reasonably be expected. Nigel Carrington and I knew such attitudes were wholly inadequate. The progress of the 'last five years' could only be the first steps on a long path of university reform.

As part of its public face, UAL hosted discussion dinners about arts topics. The best of these – 'Is Public Art a Waste of Space?' – allowed us to vent our dislike of the seemingly uncontrollable rash of new public monuments, called 'oppressive memorialisation'. The War Memorial to Animals in London's Park Lane had no friends that evening. A positive torrent of contempt poured out for *Boy with Dolphin* on Thames Embankment, *Boy Meets Girl* at St Pancras and *Industry and Genius* in Birmingham's City Square. I weighed in with what I called the cutesy kitsch of the Queen Elizabeth the Queen Mother Gates in Hyde Park and the railed-off yet intrusive banality, 'sentimentality set in stone', of the Princess Diana Fountain, once again in long-suffering Hyde Park. Michael Craig-Martin warned: 'Space is undifferentiated. When you introduce a statue into space it then makes us look at the whole in space in a totally new and different way.' How many commissioners – or makers – of public memorials considered their impact on the space surrounding them? When the sculptor Anish Kapoor, a former student, opened the remodelled Rootstein Hopkins Parade Ground at the heart of Chelsea College, he spoke of the importance of seriousness in public art, warning against indulgence in whimsy. 'It is a kind of English default position – when embarrassed by the proximity of seriousness, try the whimsical!' The effectively solemn, he might have added, is far more of a challenge to achieve.

From my first meetings with Nigel Carrington in September 2008, I knew that we were united by a sense of purpose. He wanted to streamline the university's executive board, which was large, unwieldy and poorly attended; I wanted to reduce those attending the Court of Governors from a clumsy group of thirty-three, dominated by the heads of college, to a little over twenty where externally appointed governors would predominate. How could I attract busy professionals to be involved in the University Court if they sat there being lectured at by senior staff? That item was high on my to-do list.

Nigel and I agreed my other task. I would lead two-hour sessions in every college and central department about what the university was, what each college was, how they connected and how they might evolve, separately and within a single entity. I saw it as an essential part of moving the university forward. Armed with the results, we could take on the unaddressed question of university identity. What exactly was the University of the Arts London? What should it be? Each college was set questions to discuss; I insisted the gatherings be open, amusing and playful; I led them all, employing no moderators or consultants, and summarised the conclusions. In agreeing that Nigel would not be present at these gatherings, we sent a signal to the university: 'The Chairman and Rector trust one another!' We were not to be played off against one other, and we never were.

Just as my UAL agenda was filling up satisfactorily, Liz Amos, the headhunter, rang in September 2008. Would I be interested in applying for the position of Executive Chairman of the Clore Leadership Programme (CLP)? Five years previously, the arts philanthropist and well-known force of nature, Dame Vivien Duffield, diagnosed a crisis in national arts leadership. Sitting as she did on numerous major arts boards, such as the Royal Opera and the South Bank Centre, she tired of seeing what she regarded as a merry-go-round of the same old candidates chasing the same old jobs. In her laser eyes, none were right for the positions and responsibilities facing them. Where were the arts leaders of the future?

Dame Vivien had commissioned the consultants John Holden and Robert Hewison to draw up a programme for developing the new generations of arts leaders. They recommended a two-year fellowship, to be based on practice, experience and self-awareness, and avoiding academic-style learning modules. The proposal turned most available training schemes on their head. Arts leadership would be learned not taught, would develop self-knowledge as well as skills, understanding as well as mere cleverness. It would value experience before routines, emphasise purpose over process, put the heart in balance with the head. There was no mystery in the recipe apart from its contrariness. Why did others never steal or copy it? Academics would fight shy because it was not what academics demanded – replicability, verifiability, measurability, system, theory. All admirable, some necessary, but in an activity such as arts leadership, they risked squeezing the life out of things, people, ideas. Holden and Hewison were unorthodox and Dame Vivien recognised their originality. Chris Smith, the former Labour Culture Secretary, had been the first Director of the Clore Leadership Programme; now, after five years, Chris was moving elsewhere. His deputy, Sue Hoyle, would move up to become Director. Dame Vivien was looking for a part-time, paid, Executive Chairman to work in tandem with Sue Hoyle. Would I, enquired Liz Amos, be interested?

Initially, I was cautious. Suddenly, my UAL commitments looked involving and interesting. Was I risking another 'conflict of interest' career clash? I knew of the CLP's work, had met several Fellows and mentored four of them. I liked Chris Smith, with our clashes over New Labour arts policies well behind us. (A friend of us both, a notorious gossip, once claimed that while Culture Secretary, Chris Smith was known to refer to me as 'the anti-Christ Tusa'!) A few warned me against Dame Vivien Duffield herself, characterised as 'opinionated' (she was), 'hectoring' (but she accepted counter-arguments) and 'judgemental' (she did not suffer fools). I choose to see her as decisive, visionary, generous and independent of mind and spirit. I applied for the job.

My interview for the chairmanship of the Clore Leadership Programme took place on 22 October 2008 in an office at Tate Britain. Sitting with Dame Vivien were the Director of Tate, Nicholas Serota, the Director of the Clore Duffield Foundation, Sally Bacon, Nicola Johnson, the existing CLP Chair and Dame Vivien's lawyer, David Harrell. I felt very relaxed and spoke very openly. Were they right to 'dilute the brand' of the extended fellowships by also doing two-week 'short courses'? Wasn't Clore's uniqueness based on the one-to-two-year fellowship programme? I was open about myself. How big was their risk in making me, an out-and-out executive by nature and instinct, the Chairman? Would I be able to adapt my style, to rein in my executive instincts? I was not set to provoke but preferred to lay everything on the table. The atmosphere was friendly but not cosy. As Nick Serota showed me out, he murmured, 'Thank you for interviewing like that!' By mid-afternoon, Liz Amos, the headhunter, rang my mobile to say that, if I accepted, the interviewing panel would stand down the other planned interviewees. I did so without hesitation. 'You knocked their socks off,' she said. It was a good moment.

It was highly satisfying that in my new portfolio of activities, both Nigel Carrington and Sue Hoyle were bent on change. They needed no urging from my side. Sue Hoyle, with four years' experience of actually running CLP fellowships, moved quickly and decisively. At one of the first Clore Strategy Boards in March 2009, she recommended focusing the fellowship programme from a rather baggy two years to a highly concentrated eight months. The time was right for a radical rethink. It proved a total success.

Clore, like the university, I found open to ideas and fun. In June 2009, we held an Open Day to allow the first five Clore 'cohorts' to bond, to renew and to be astonished by ideas. The theme was 'It's the Art, Stupid', a deliberate echo of Bill Clinton's campaign slogan, 'It's the Economy, Stupid'. At it, Kwame Kwei-Armah, the theatre director and later UAL Chancellor, warned Fellows: 'Don't be burdened by inspiration! Do be burdened by a desire to be original.' Kwame urged them to 'draw from the past because the present is not strong enough to sustain a human being'. And he offered this challenge to the Fellows: 'What are you going to do to create the environment to engage with talent?'

The choreographer Siobhan (Sue) Davies, who never uttered a dull thought in her life, urged: 'The artist must aim to be a destabiliser. You must reorganise your thinking – dismantle your previous learning to free yourself up for the next stage.' Sue explained that though she had a new building for her work in Lambeth, it was not an answer to making art. That came from somewhere else. 'I don't want a home!' she protested. 'I want a windy corner, a place of waking, constant transfer.' Sue was anxious that art forms should not merge into one another; there should be a natural gap between them. Why? 'The gap is where the creation takes place!' And a final warning: 'Creativity and innovation are lazy buzz words. They pull you off like Elastoplast!'

Grayson Perry, the potter, admitted to having a hangover that morning. He was provocative, as always, and occasionally contradictory: 'I don't want to be creative! Creativity is mistakes.' Then a series of one-liners: 'Beware the cult of youth. You can't be creative when young; it happens much later in life.' Or, why psychotherapy was dangerous for an artist: 'It cleans up your tool shed!' A swipe at the art world followed: 'I don't want failed artists to be curators. I don't want to be a rung on their career!' His best insights came about how originality emerges: 'New ideas are like furry creatures at the edge of a forest. Don't frighten them away by paying too much attention to them!' And Grayson ended with a warning: 'The process of making art is a war of attrition – there is no Zen moment!' He was not in his transvestite-costumed 'Clare' manifestation; 'It tends to stop people listening,' he said. The event was generally voted the 'best Clore open day' yet. I felt exhilarated by the freshness of the thinking.

At another Clore event, the pianist Joanna MacGregor gave this advice about fighting your corner in the arts: you should employ 'the expedient and the pragmatic fuelled by bad temper'. Anger had its place, she insisted: 'Rage comes back, get crazy, don't apologise.' Jatinder Verma from Tara Arts offered wise advice in dark times: 'Lack of funding is not a judgement on your work!' Joining Clore had been a wise decision.

By summer 2009, Nigel Carrington was driving change at UAL. He cut out an entire top-level layer of management. This saved a lot of money; it freed up a previously repressed middle management to take decisions; and it disarmed the university unions, who could not accuse the Rector of cutting staff at the bottom but not at the top; he had shot their fox. Within colleges, the ramshackle collection of taught courses, randomly accumulated without rigour over years, was being culled. The six-month appraisal of Nigel's performance, with finances under control, senior staff on side and problems being addressed rather than avoided, was positively enjoyable.

On my side, I set about revitalising the Court of Governors, recruiting rigorously, emphasising professional skills and regular attendance, promoting gender and ethnic diversity, encouraging the contributions of external governors. Most tricky was taking on and neutralising an obstreperous union representative. He refused to accept that, as a governor, his responsibility lay to the university and to the court rather than principally to his not very numerous members. He could not see that his members' legitimate concerns might best be served by taking a university-wide view; he and they thought only of their short-term, particular interests. His form of communication was to harangue the court as if they were hapless attenders at a union branch meeting. It was intolerable and he and I got into several shouting matches. In general, the unions' contribution to any innovation at UAL was consistently negative. Delay, regardless of the resulting cost, was their only tactic when faced with proposals for change. They revelled, too, in impossibilist demands: 'No course closures! No redundancies! Full reinstatement!' It reeked of Militant Tendency in the Labour Party in the early 1980s. Such tactics had destroyed the Labour Party; they would not destroy the university.

Far and away the most unpleasant agitation occurred at the London College of Communication at Elephant and Castle, formerly the London College of Printing. We saw this as the last gasp of the old printing unions such as SOGAT who had brought the Fleet Street national press to its knees with their famed 'Spanish practices'. Just how far they were prepared to go in defence of their territory was revealed when the head of college, introducing essential restructuring, was faced with death threats and advised to have a police escort. Sit-ins, verbal abuse, sustained intimidation were standard union tactics; reasoned argument played little part. Nigel and his managers, backed by the governors, stood firm; none of the necessary university reforms was obstructed though time was certainly wasted. By then, UAL's sense of purpose and determination should surely have been obvious to all.

In September 2009, we held a development party at the Granary Building in King's Cross, future heart of the new Central Saint Martins, still a building site but clearly an urban landmark in the making. The scale would be grand, the location on the Regent's Canal dramatic. Distinguished former students such as Peter Blake and Stella McCartney spoke in support. The atmospherics were great. While it may have started to put UAL on the map of creative London, it was a dismal failure as a major fund-raising launch pad. No one opened their wallets to support us.

Money was not the issue at an intoxicating celebration of the Clore Leadership Programme's first five years on 21 October. Dame Vivien – or DVD as we usually referred to her – revelled in her creative offspring. Wherever she went, people would announce themselves as former Clore Fellows and tell her how it had transformed their lives. This was powerfully reinforcing for the benefactor. It was, she said, the best thing she funded – and we knew how generously she did. On a high now, DVD cried out: 'Go out and run British arts!' Then, pointing directly to Nick Serota of the Tate and Sandy Nairne of the National Portrait Gallery, she told the assembled Fellows to be their successors. Nick and Sandy demurred; they weren't quite ready to go yet. When CLP had begun, the expectation was that it might run for three or four years. That would be sufficient to mould the next generation of arts leaders. Now, it had demonstrated both its success and the scale of the continuing need. It was here for the duration. Vivien, incidentally, always somewhat disingenuously deflected questions about her own leadership style: 'I chair my foundation, I sit on boards, I am not a leader.' She was, in truth, in a category of her own.

For me, there was a pleasing harmony to the concerns of both UAL and CLP. Both were about teaching and learning and the connection between them. In neither case was there a simple, one-way connection between information, originating from the teacher, and understanding, the responsibility of the student. At CLP, we refused to 'teach' the practice of leadership; each Fellow must choose what he or she decided to 'learn' about his or her own form of leadership. In the university too, the exchange between teacher and student was an equal one, with the student's own responsibility to learn being at least as important as the teacher's role to offer ideas and to question.

At UAL, asking about good teaching produced rich anecdotes but nothing approaching formal theory. The late and legendary Professor Louise Wilson, who taught the entire generation of British fashion designers from Alexander McQueen to Stella McCartney, was notoriously foul-mouthed, demanding and almost destructively critical. Yet all her students believed she had shaped them decisively. No other teacher could adopt her approach. By contrast, former students at Saint Martins in Charing Cross Road also spoke warmly of 'the lovely Freddy Gore. What a teacher! He had this office on a half landing and used to play the ukulele! And he was a wonderful pantomime dame in the Christmas panto!' Something about him made him judged to be a good teacher, though what that quality might be was impossible to fathom.

A lot of myth surrounded teaching. When the Pro-Vice-Chancellor for academic standards assembled all the university's deans for the first ever joint seminar on approaches to teaching, everyone arrived convinced that their own college's approach was unique and quite distinct from that of the other five colleges. By the end of the afternoon, they began to realise that there was more in common between their methods than there were differences. It was a great moment of binding UAL together.

After repeated questioning on my part, one college dean gave me this description of how he taught: 'At the end of the year, say, I look at the student's work. I ask them, "Was this what you intended to do?" If they say "yes", I ask, "Do you want to continue or will you take a different direction?" If they reply "no" to my original question, I ask them why they think that. "Was it the wrong idea to start with, or was it the right idea imperfectly realised?" At each stage, I ask open questions, allowing them to frame their own answers.' I found such a set of exchanges very satisfying; teaching and learning blended into a series of enquiries without any sense of the correct or incorrect, and students reaching a personal understanding of what they had chosen to do and what they might do next.

At the Clore Leadership Programme there was no formal teaching about 'how to lead in the arts'. Charlatans, management theorists, self-improvement gurus might offer gilded paths to the top. Books abounded filled with nostrums, magic potions, wizard spells advising how to act, how to behave, how to see yourself, how to make yourself seen as you wished to be seen – as the 'great leader'. Since most such authors, most lecturers, most course leaders had never led anything or anyone in their lives, I regarded their utterances as worse than useless at best and often downright misleading. Even when closer to the practical, they were too prescriptive, too falsely systematic, incapable of capturing the plasticity, the human complexity of arts leadership in practice.

From the start of the Clore Leadership Programme, Fellows were exposed to most of the major arts leaders in the United Kingdom. None refused an invitation to speak. None luxuriated in tales of their achievements, their brilliance, their extraordinary judgement and superior wisdom. None offered 'the way' to lead; all spoke of the elements in their experience, good and bad, which had allowed or helped them to lead. All placed their experiences at the disposal of the Fellows. All the speakers had found their own path to leadership. So would the Fellows.

Since my role as Executive Chairman involved me in frequent discussions with Fellows and short-course participants, I attempted to organise my own thoughts and experiences. I offered them as my learning process on the job, certainly not as definitive lessons cast in tablets of stone. They were compressed into the notion of the 'Six Omissions', the 'Six Senses' and the 'Four Antitheses'.

The 'Six Omissions' warned what happened to an organisation where the leader gave no lead. What would be lost, I asked. Instead of movement, there would be stasis; instead of activity, passivity; instead of dynamism, caution. Consolidation would replace purpose, assumption would drive out reflection, the status quo would block the way forward. Too many organisations had leaders who were fearful of leading, which should have disqualified them from the outset.

In identifying the 'Six Senses', I tried to catch the qualities of awareness that the active leader needed to possess: a sense of vision, a sense of direction, a sense of purpose, a sense of cohesion, a sense of identity, a sense of feeling. Paying attention to all these parts of an institution had to be essential to leading it.

I emphasised, too, what I labelled the 'Four Antitheses' facing the leader, a tricky notion at first glance, paradoxical certainly. Leaders must have authority but should not be authoritarian; they must listen but must also decide; they should know what they believed but accept that others might influence that belief; they must take risks but should not be foolhardy. To those who judged these to be contradictions, my advice would be that they too should avoid trying to lead.

As I worked out my own thoughts, it dawned on me that the two best books on leadership and management were not ponderous tomes from so-called 'advanced schools of business management' but two children's classics: A A. Milne's *Winnie the Pooh* and Lewis Carroll's *Alice's Adventures in Wonderland*. I had long been aware that the executive team at the Barbican closely matched the eight characters of Milne's stories. As Managing Director, I was clearly Christopher Robin. I had my much-loved, 'snackerel-loving' Pooh Bear (the Arts Director?), an eager Rabbit type (Finance), a furiously bustling Tigger

(Commercial), a pessimistic Eeyore the melancholic donkey (Operations), a slightly abstracted Owl (Media), a motherly Kanga (Human Relations) and a devoted Piglet (personal assistant), who was seldom in need of care and protection. I did not recruit my colleagues on the basis of these stereotypes; nor did I share my wholly affectionate observations. I realised later that the effectiveness of the Barbican team came from the sharpness of the characterisation of each individual.

The management lessons I drew from *Alice's Adventures in Wonderland* were relevant as a cautionary account of management chaos. When I arrived at the Barbican in 1995, the Arts and Commercial Directors behaved like Tweedledum and Tweedledee, who agreed to have a battle and did so every day. The hapless Finance Director was stuffed into a teapot like the dormouse and ignored. My observations to Clore Fellows sprang from direct experience of arts leadership. They could take them, leave them, judge them irrelevant, adapt them or be amused by them. I finally developed them more fully in my 2014 book *Pain in the Arts*, which came as close to a book on arts leadership as I would ever want to go.

What the Fellows truly valued from all speakers was honesty about setbacks and failures. All spoke on condition of confidentiality, which so far as I know was never broken. One warned of the importance of being able to 'live with uncertainty', personal and professional. Another probed deeply into their experience, naming what they called the 'trinity of danger' facing any arts leader – 'ambition, vanity, resilience'. How realistic was your ambition to advance? How far was that ambition driven by vanity? Would your resilience be sufficient to carry the weight of your ambition and your vanity? Without good answers to these questions, the would-be leader could be unseated in a moment.

The two Clore residential courses, each of a fortnight, took place at a country retreat south-east of Sevenoaks on an ecologically managed farm called Bore Place. Remote and surrounded by woods and fields, reachable along winding one-track roads, with a very poor mobile phone signal, no TV, and farm-grown, home-cooked produce for nourishment, Bore Place had set the tone of the fellowship from the start: sensuously beguiling, caressingly silent, healing in its calm, it invited, almost demanded, honesty in personal exchanges.

In September 2010, it was my turn to talk of my setbacks and failures. Taking for granted the scores of routine errors and everyday mistakes I had made, four career setbacks seemed especially worth talking about. The Fellows settled back in their pre-dinner sofas and armchairs and waited. I did not know then where this session would lead. I plotted the chronology of my career on a flipchart against the satisfaction that I got from various jobs. There were plenty of those. Then came the 'downs' in the satisfaction rating, starting with my time at Forum World Features in 1966 which turned out to be a CIA front. Howls of glee! Next, my short national TV stint on *Nationwide* 'South-East Opt Out', including interviewing a baby cheetah from Chessington Zoo. More howls of delight! What of my few months as President of Wolfson College, Cambridge in 1993, just sad and pointless. Or most recently, my strategic error in thinking I could reasonably be both Chairman of University of the Arts London and Chairman of the Trustees of the Victoria and Albert Museum at the same time.

As the Fellows mulled over these troughs in my career, it dawned on me that the best things had come when someone else sparked the opportunity for me. I had been invited to join *Newsnight* by the editor; a friend had drawn my attention to the vacant BBC World Service job; a newspaper story had alerted me to the opportunity at the Barbican; a phone call opened the door to the Clore Leadership Programme. Was there an explanation for this pattern? Was it essential to be ready for something new, to be open to a change of direction. Was I creating my own luck, benefiting from the workings of chance? I suggested to the Fellows that it was readiness and openness to opportunity that was important, not passivity. It was essential, too, not to let others assume who you were, what your life path should be or place you in a career slot defined by them.

As we talked and the light fell on Bore Place's meadows and trees, I understood something else, for the first time. On each occasion that I had positively sought something for myself – Forum World Features, *Nationwide*, Wolfson College, the V&A chairmanship – every one had come unstuck, each had ended in failure and disappointment. Was I so bad at judging what was in my best interests? This was quite a shock, a fresh moment of self-understanding. Was there a moral, beyond the blunt reminder that ambition fed by vanity was a bad counsellor? On the evidence of this profound learning in the gloaming of Bore Place, in an environment where self-deception was almost unacceptable, who was teaching whom? I knew whose was the learning that evening.

I understood something else about the instincts involved in making decisions. Of course rational analysis was essential when choosing between paths. Was it only or primarily up to the brain to take decisions? Didn't feelings have a place, or sheer animal instincts? Thinking back, I finally appreciated how truly complex the process was. It involved, in my case at least, three distinct parts of the body; head, heart, stomach. My conclusion was: 'You think with your head; you feel with your heart; but you know with your stomach.' All three parts of your body had to be aligned over a major decision, with the stomach often uttering dire warnings. That was another result of sylvan soul-searching at Bore Place, another piece of my personal learning.

By contrast, life at UAL in the new head offices in High Holborn in the centre of London was severely practical. We knew by mid-summer 2010 how effective Nigel Carrington was as Rector. The governors were active and involved, they intervened but did not interfere, contributed but did not pester. The committee chairmen were capable, committed and gave generously of their time and expertise. Nigel had an executive

team to whom he could turn and with whom he could work.
The King's Cross project was on time and on budget; the current year's budget would deliver a decent surplus; next year's
finances were solid, leaving us able to face any further central
government funding cuts. Union disruption had been faced
down, discontents were fizzling out and Nigel's grip on events
was beyond question.

Yet at the governors' September awayday that year, we
looked squarely at areas of university failure, a salutary reminder of how much still had to be done. It was proving to be
a struggle to get an effective development programme under
way, let alone raise significant sums of cash. UAL had no media
profile and enjoyed no regular media interest or coverage.
UAL had no brand identity – was it six separate colleges or
one university? It hadn't even a shared logo, the expression
of a common identity. Internal resistance to both a university
brand and a logo remained strong. Internal communications
were poor despite Nigel's regular open staff meetings at every
college. Colleges declared full support for the idea of 'one university', but did very little to make it happen. These were all
classic academic delaying tactics.

Matters came to a head in 2011, at the end of which the 'University of the Arts Campus at King's Cross for Central Saint
Martins' was to open. I used that deliberately long-winded
title to emphasise that without the iniversity there would have
been no King's Cross campus at all and Central Saint Martins
would have been condemned to obsolescence in its decaying
premises in Charing Cross Road and Southampton Row.

First and foremost, Stanton Williams's realisation of the
building appeared ever more remarkable as it approached
completion. In mid-July 2011 at fit-out stage, even with 650
workers on site day and night, the ambition of the project
was clearly visible. Based on the great Thomas Cubitt Granary Building, Paul Williams's design united that core with
the 100-yard-long block of former railway receiving sheds
stretching behind. Linked under a translucent roof and across

an open avenue, the campus was large but not bombastically monumental. The spaces were grand but obviously designed in the service of students. The design was also about the history of the buildings, using their old fittings, exposing patched-up brickwork, keeping old loading-bay numbers as the new building's historic memory, an essential part of the modern fabric. The old signs and symbols were not smoothed over or painted out, the history was living, not suppressed.

Second, the King's Cross campus was intended for students to use as students do, with exposed services and ducting works and nothing posh about it. Elegant in concept, it was also rough and ready. Some walls, covered with the cheapest board, were labelled 'sacrificial walls'. Students could paint on them, fool around on them, make a mess, knowing that they would be cheaply replaced or painted over so that their successors could be equally messy and creative. It was collegiate not corporate.

Above all, there were acres of open, public space waiting to be used, colonised, made to live. To start with, this was not easy for students and teachers to fully appreciate, still less value. Coming from small, dirty spaces and moving into large, open areas where different departments would be aware of the work of others, these invited a new, different, more complex response to work and learning. It would take years to learn to use such spaces but the rewards when they did would be huge. As I took in the vast new building, I knew it would succeed. It all pointed to the fact, existence and effectiveness of UAL as a living institution. University of the Arts London had arrived.

Yet nothing was ever straightforward. Soon after, at a 'soft launch' for the King's Cross campus in June 2011, I was made rudely aware of how far we still had to go to create a shared consciousness within the university itself. The invitations and publicity material came from Central Saint Martin's with no reference to UAL whatever. The university might just as well not have existed. I was furious and exploded in my journal: 'Without UAL there would be no King's Cross campus at all; whatsoever; no time; no way; wake up, boys and girls. To cap it all, we are in the middle of a university identity exercise! Is no one listening?' Nigel duly read the riot act to the college: the primacy of the UAL and its role in creating King's Cross was made clear for all to see.

The best moment during the 'soft launch' came in a conversation with Roger Madelin, the CEO of Argent, developers of the entire site. Argent had always understood that an important part of the value and character of the King's Cross site was thirty-six buildings and structures dating from Victorian times. Argent did not want a 'brown-mud' site to work in. Integrating the historic structures of the industrial past would define its look, its feel, its character. At a very early stage, when the vast site was little more than mud and derelict-looking old brick and metal, Roger took Ken Livingstone, then Mayor of London over it. Ken viewed it with some puzzlement. Then offered helpfully: 'You know, Roger, if you need any help in getting rid of some of these dirty old buildings, just let me know!'

The official launch of the King's Cross Campus for Central Saint Martins in November 2011 was everything we hoped for. Admiration, awe even, at the whole complex, an adaptation of the old into the persuasively modern; a place for study and students, for creation and creativity; a landmark for UAL and for the entire King's Cross development, a triumph for the imagination of the architect, Paul Williams and the vision of the developer, Argent. The evening had almost been ruined when Nigel and I arrived an hour ahead of guests to check that everything was in order. Instead of gazing at the long lines of the buildings, the uncluttered spaces and elegant vistas, we found entrances blocked by metal crowd barriers festooned with black-and-yellow security tape. It looked more like preparation for a rowdy rock festival than an academic opening. What, we exploded, was going on? The event managers said that 'ElfinSafety' had insisted on the barriers because of the expected numbers. The notion that crash barriers were needed to control the arts world establishment was too absurd. UAL staff were told in the plainest terms to dismantle every barrier, to remove them from site and to detach every inch of security tape. 'Or,' I added, 'I will tear it down myself!' It was a dispiriting sign of how deep-rooted box-ticking instincts and conformist habits could override common sense.

Meanwhile, much of July was spent on the unfinished business of university identity. Nigel and I agreed that a shared identity was essential if UAL was to move ahead. Just saying that it was 'a gathering of six historic colleges' each going their own way ducked the issue. From matters such as shared academic standards, student admissions, recruitment, an international presence, capital projects, libraries, to research and the creative industries, the university centre was the engine for advancing the interests of the colleges. They were nothing by themselves, they would not survive alone. I told them that I had seen identical resistance in the BBC and at the Barbican when the identities of various divisions were harmonised into the larger whole. The objections had been identical, the hurt feelings too, the general puzzlement! Did I look like a crazed, dogmatic centraliser? Well then! Both organisations, I told university colleagues, emerged stronger when they acted in a united way. Would colleges please stop playing the 'zero-sum' game where the centre's supposed 'gain' must be the colleges' 'loss' and recognise it as a 'zero-plus' game where a benefit to one accrued to all?

It took another six months to get an agreed UAL brand and identity. I thought the process a huge waste of time and often urged Nigel to push harder and faster. He shared my impatience but always promised that he would get the result we needed in his own time and his own way. It came finally in March 2012 with all the elements of a university visual and communications identity finally agreed. The slowness of the process did not show academics at their best.

By then I knew my future as Executive Chairman of the Clore Leadership Programme. Gratifyingly, Sally Bacon, Director of the Clore Duffield Foundation, had already invited me to stay on for a couple of years. Dame Vivien wanted it, Sue Hoyle wanted it and I certainly wanted it. The CLP was an immensely fulfilling activity to be involved in. We agreed that I would see the tenth cohort of Fellows through and leave in August 2014.

Armed with this vote of confidence from Clore, I then over-played my hand at the university. I enjoyed being Chairman, I loved working with Nigel Carrington, the place was work-ing together. Why not stay on for a further two years until 2015? Everyone at UAL welcomed the prospect of stability and continuity for a while longer. It took Annie to bring me to my senses in June 2012. Once she had recovered from the shock of finding out that I had discussed my future with the university before talking it over with her, she delivered a measured but wise judgement: 'You are getting increasingly tired and overwrought; you are picking up minor ailments like food poisoning and taking longer to get over them; you are not sleeping; you are not recovering as you once did – and are you surprised? You must start to learn to do less, even to do nothing and to enjoy having time at your disposal.'

I could not disagree with her diagnosis. I recognised most of the symptoms she described. There were dangers in having business as a displacement activity for real life, in flaunting the vanity of exercising responsibility in my mid-seventies, in pushing aside retirement as something other people did, in bol-stering the self-image of my capacity to endure, to stay alert, to make a contribution. Yes, it was vanity increasingly bought at the price of irritability, poor judgement and other unattractive traits. I did not want to relapse into inertia, boredom, futility and emptiness. But doing less, doing things differently must itself be another skill to be learned. We agreed that I would end the chairmanship of the university at the agreed date in 2013. I had to reassure my UAL colleagues that this rather abrupt change of heart had nothing dramatic or sinister attached to it. Generously they took it in good part and got on with the job of finding a successor.

Nigel Carrington and I agreed a programme of actions for the UAL team before I left. The finances were healthy, surpluses were being earned, efficiency was officially approved, the new student fees regime would play in our favour, international recruitment was buoyant, the King's Cross campus was a success, the university had an identity and profile. He had been practical, persuasive and determined. I hoped that within a few years, the initials UAL would be as instantly recognisable as LSE. That was a reasonable ambition.

By mid-2012, with the recruitment of the tenth cohort of Clore Fellows approaching, the Strategic Committee thought a root-and-branch look at the entire fellowship programme was in order. This was no time for complacency. Was such a programme still needed? Was its approach still valid? DVD's lawyer, David Harrell, considered the suggestion and observed tightly: 'That sounds rather expensive!' Dame Vivien herself was typically practical. Take stock by all means, she said, but: 'I don't think we need all this Jewish angst about whether we are doing the right thing!' She clearly thought we were. I observed that the suggestion for a review was more 'an excess of Protestant conscience at work'. DVD responded: 'You all got it from the Jews in the first place!'

We commissioned a limited review to keep ourselves, our programmes, our speakers fresh. In truth, there was little danger of becoming stale. Each cohort of Fellows brought their own energy, curiosity and vigour with them. Their ideas poured out. 'If I don't take risks, I hide under a rock saying can I come out and play,' said one. 'Bring together those parts (of an organisation) that are wounded with those parts that have learned,' said another who seemed well on the road to understanding leadership. The Fellow who observed, 'Leadership is both a privilege and an affliction, it burdens you with solitude' must have been speaking from a well of experience and understanding, as did the one who declared: 'The states of leadership include reluctance, fear, bravery and more bravery.'

Others reflected on the world in which they existed: 'A great performance is as good as food, it fills you. It tells you something you didn't know before.' Or even more daringly: 'Art is a mystery; without mystery we are not human; it's why we wake up in the morning.' I cherished these observations, hundreds of them, as Fellows poured out their experiences and took the risk of putting them on full public display before their colleagues. Some were pleasantly down to earth, such as: 'We want minds on seats not bums on seats.' Or the very simple-sounding thought from a Hong Kong Fellow: 'We spend too much time doing, not enough time being.'

For my part, I increasingly tried to encourage them to value, use and appreciate the words they used in their professional lives. They should not be imprisoned by professional jargon and cant. All those 'quasi-managerialist' usages restricted meaning, narrowed the full potential of words. Words, I argued, needed to be rich, open-ended, ambiguous, open to interpretation. They needed simplicity and directness too, to call a spade a spade. What was 'policy', which every organisation had to have, but a statement of 'what you want to do'? What was the much-lauded notion of 'vision' but the idea that drove you and the organisation? What was the (dreaded) concept of 'process' but the simple question 'how are you going to do it'? What were 'objectives', on which hours and days were spent, but 'how will you know when you have done what you want'? What was 'risk analysis' but a dressing for 'a sense of danger'? 'Outcomes' were a posh way of tarting up simple old 'results'. If language was allowed to confuse rather than clarify, the results would be deadly.

At one evening session at Bore Place, the Fellows and I wallowed in the sea of 'official-sounding' verbiage that we all, it turned out, loathed. We joined in creating a Lexicon of Abomination. Among the several score of words most hated as oppressive, obstructive or intrusive, some lurid and inelegant neologisms stood out: access, additionality, benchmark, baseline, connectivity, coopetition, driver, discourse, direction of travel, edutainment, experiential, going forward, glocal, holistic, narrative, indicators, push back, transformational. It was a dismal list, worse for still being in current use. These words were rejected because they came from disciplines beyond the world of the arts, they were not meant to be useful, they were usually deployed as instruments of control over the arts. Worst of all, they were ugly and too often used in craven capitulation to bureaucratic demands. Would you be taken seriously if you didn't use them?

Of all the sessions conducted by distinguished outside speakers at Bore Place, that by the Poet Laureate, Andrew Motion, was perhaps the most intense. He would read his own poetry, simply, quietly and beautifully. Then he would invite each of us to write a poem. Most had never written one before. He offered suggestions about what a good poem might be about, not about how it might be written: 'Write about a strong feeling; be simple; strip out unnecessary words; avoid repetition; be short, not more than ten lines.' We all drifted off to our favourite corner of the Bore Place grounds for the next forty-five minutes. In all the four years that I witnessed these sessions, the merest handful of Fellows decided it was not for them.

Taking it in turns to read our fledgling lines, Andrew listened to each intently and offered thoughts on each, generously, wisely, warmly. 'Good, the feeling is strong,' to one. 'It feels as if you cut the last verse, that's often a very good thing!' to another. 'I like the way the poem turns in the middle,' to someone else. The actual poems were remarkable, ingenious, moving, surprising, some terse and witty. The afternoon spoke volumes for the way Andrew Motion set the tone. One Fellow noted that Andrew's approach to the occasion demonstrated good leadership in all its aspects – it involved 'guidance, example, listening, assessing, praising, encouraging, no pretending'. And, I might have added, 'no preening egotism'.

I had not thought of writing a poem since school days. Surrounded by this intoxicating collective rush of passionate openness, how could I sit back and not join in? I did.

One of the Fellows said: 'I love it when you join in with us!' I replied: 'I am learning how to play,' though I might have added 'You are teaching me how to play!'

Those years had a fine coherence to them – the necessary business, the practicality of helping to shape a university; the imagination, the energy, the creative self-discovery of working with the Clore Fellows. Annie always maintained that time with them was my equivalent of having a rejuvenating shot of monkey-gland serum, the treatment reportedly used by the great post-war Federal German Chancellor, Konrad Adenauer. To over-simplify, in my role at the university I applied all my near-twenty-year experience of running and shaping institutions. This was my teaching role. Among Clore Fellows, I discovered things about myself that I had not known, sometimes only half understood: how I led, how I managed, what I believed about working in the arts. This was me in my learning role. Each played off the other.

They were also years of intense activity beyond the university and Clore Leadership. At the start of 2013, I took detailed stock in my current journal of the events of the previous year, 2012. How were Annie and I using our time, seizing the opportunities that offered themselves? This was the summary of our year 2012 that I wrote at the time:

> Our most numerous activity turned out to be 34 exhibitions – including Hockney, Freud, Hirst, Grayson Perry, Picasso, Joan Miró at Yorkshire Sculpture Park, Naum Gabo, 'Documenta' in Kassel, Frieze Masters. (We like the parties.) Less surprisingly there were 21 visits to the Wigmore – only 21? – Christian Blackshaw, Alice Coote, Stephen Hough, Joyce DiDonato, Stephen Kovacevich, Paul Lewis, Christian Gerhaher, Belcea Quartet (several), 'wot no Bostridge'? There were 17 orchestral concerts, but how many were memorable? Yes, Petrenko and the RLPO, Jansons and the Concertgebouw, Rattle and the Vienna Phil, Ades and the LSO but no pleasure

from Gergiev except in the Russian repertoire – and an aching hole that Colin Davis's illness now leaves in the London orchestral scene. Only 16 operas but many were memorable – Thielemann's *Parsifal* in Vienna, Jurowski's *Vixen* at Glyndebourne, Gardner's *Billy Budd*, Pappano's *Otello* at ROH, his *Siegfried* (twice) and *Götterdämmerung* at ROH, *Vixen* in Brno, three rarities (good) at Wexford, Knussen's magical double bill at the Barbican, and how can I forget Pappano's Prom version of the *Trojans?* A good haul overall. We have been neglectful, wary of theatre, too often finding ourselves marginally let down by the experience. So what did thirteen visits yield? McBurney's extraordinary *Master and Margarita*, the RNT's exuberant *Two Guvnors*, the odd – strange – Botho Strauss with Cate Blanchett (boy, does she ACT!!!), *The Browning Version*, Simon Russell Beale in the modern-dress *Timon*, Mnouchkine's epic *Les Naufrages* at Edinburgh, KneeHigh in *Steptoe*, Chakrabarti's *Red Velvet* about the first black Othello, Russell Beale camping it up in *Privates on Parade*, altogether an eclectic, unstructured, disorganised but oddly enjoyable list reinforcing the axiom that selection (or luck) is vital. How are we doing? Well, 27 parties and 16 events or lectures. We gave 38 dinner parties and received 39 a pleasing social symmetry. And the travel! In chronological order: Lyon, Hong Kong, Laax, Vienna (twice), Moscow, Edinburgh (twice), Kassel, Wakefield, Cornwall, Armenia, Brno, Wexford and Tunis racking up some 64 days and nights away, en route or otherwise involved. Adding in a few miscellaneous category activities and we get a grand total of 298 days/evenings out, engaged, involved etc. It leaves just one day a week in toto that is wholly or principally unoccupied. We are incredibly lucky. Very few of these events were a waste of time, none really. And for our next trick? We have just had to cancel 4 days in Berlin because Annie developed a stinker of a cold. So the year starts off slowly but who is competing?

Only ourselves with ourselves perhaps? Yet it was not competition of any kind; we never went to anything because we felt a duty, intellectual or social, to do so. We attended because we were interested in the works, the artists or the people. We felt lucky to be able to do so; it would have been foolish to throw away the opportunities that came our way. We were surrounded by the worlds of the arts; we revelled in them.

I left UAL in the summer of 2013 clutching a superb Grayson Perry print, *The Island of Bad Art*, savagely satirising the international world of 'big art'. It repays a closer look every time I pass. I finished with the Clore Fellows a year later, showered with messages, gifts, love and shared experiences. Would I miss either or both, I was asked. Of course, I replied, I would miss them but I had no regrets about leaving, at finishing with either. I had a sense of completion from both, a feeling of personal fulfilment. Perhaps I had taught from time to time; I had certainly learned. I could not have hoped for more.

14

Envoi

Regretting and Remembering

Memories come in at least two forms: the organised, tidily remembered ones that make up the flesh and bones of my story. And those that emerge, unbidden, isolated, crystal-clear, vivid in themselves and in their own terms. They do not form part of the story, their absence is not an omission from it. They have their own validity, a particular moment, a flash of illuminated memory that does not contradict but adds an unexpected intensity. A few nudged themselves forward for my attention, the whole activity of writing having stirred the silts and depths of more formal recollections. I started collecting them since they had an additional quality beyond those that I had already written. They do not represent an alternative account of my life but perhaps throw a further light on key events not part of the more organised narrative. I had not previously denied or repressed them and offer them now as a mosaic, a patchwork of more inner memories.

I set them out below under the overall heading of 'I Remember . . . '. It would have been tiresome to start each of the hundred or so moments with those words. They are not tidy, not chronological (though some are dated), not themed, deliberately not organised; they appear largely in the pleasingly random manner in which they popped up from my mind. Perhaps they were demanding not to be overlooked. I am glad they spoke up.

I start with two shorter sections called 'I Regret . . . ' and 'I Do Not Regret . . . ', each being a far cry from the cris de coeur of either Frank Sinatra or Edith Piaf.

I regret

Not learning to speak Czech
Not making a major TV documentary series
Not having lived and worked abroad
Not presenting *The World's Strongest Man* TV programmes
Not continuing to broadcast actively
Not presenting the News Year's Day Concert from Vienna
Being considered a 'bastard', 'the Anti-Christ', 'a contaminant'
   by some people.

I do not regret

Being a generalist
Being interested in so many aspects of arts and the creative
   world
Not becoming an academic
Being called a 'bastard', 'the anti-Christ', 'a contaminant' by
   those who used those words
Changing my job direction and reinventing myself every six
   years
Sitting on so many boards
Being British, speaking English and feeling European.

I remember

Standing at the top of a ski run in Tignes, putting my skis together and deciding, 'Down to the bottom of the mountain,
no stopping, no pauses for breath' – and doing so, turning,
bending, keeping the downhill line, anorak flying, snow crystals
tingling my cheeks, fast, straight, exhilarating.

Walking along the Bayswater Road in 1960 high on the overnight news that JFK had been elected President of the United
States.

How quickly my father's body got cold in the moments after he died.

Catching my first sea trout on a fly, night fishing on the Clifden River in Connemara instructed by my teenage son, Sash.

Going into Nuremberg Gaol when Annie was researching her book on the Nuremberg Trial and standing in the cell where Hermann Göring committed suicide in October 1946.

Sitting in Archbishop Desmond Tutu's waiting room in Cape Town, hearing gales of laughter as he talked to a group of ordinands next door, then starting our meeting with a prayer and a blessing.

Hearing Mikhail Gorbachev tell a Moscow news conference that he knew what was happening during his detention in the Crimea in 1961 because 'I heard it on the BBC'.

Driving along the north coast of Sicily on our honeymoon in 1960 and coming across the town of Castel di Tusa. Yes, it is a Sicilian name.

After interviewing Margaret Thatcher at Downing Street for *Newsnight* in 1986, I drew her attention to a large piece of walnut veneer missing from a Chippendale chest in the drawing room. She threw herself on her knees to scrabble for it on the carpet before finding it hidden in one of the drawers.

Lighting candles in Ferrara Cathedral for our brother-in-law, Peter, on hearing of his death.

Driving to West Berlin along the autobahn through communist East Germany, starting the cassette of Beethoven's *Fidelio* as we cleared the Helmstedt checkpoint, winding down the windows so that the Prisoners' Chorus cries of '*Freiheit, Freiheit*'

('Freedom' Freedom!) sounded across the fields and finding that *Fidelio* lasted exactly the length of the journey to Berlin.

Finding nine glorious churches in Venice open on a single day in November 2013.

Watching the shadow of the total eclipse of the sun come racing towards us across St Ives bay and hearing the silence it brought with it.

Talking to the chief government vet in the loos at Number 10 and being assured that they had foot and mouth 'under control' just a few days before it really erupted.

My *Newsnight* colleague, David Sells, observing during the Yugoslav war: 'Just because the Serbs are bastards doesn't mean they don't have a case.'

Going up and down the Grand Canal in Venice in a vaporetto in the pearly cool of dawn with the cafés not yet open and us, poor students, without money to buy breakfast.

Giving a dinner party as young marrieds, taking a beef casserole out of the oven and when the handle broke spilling the meat onto the kitchen floor, Annie and I scooping it back and serving it without a second's hesitation.

Hearing the Hungarian String Quartet play Beethoven's *Grosse Fuge* for the first time in the early 1960s.

Burning down our garden fence during a joyful neighbours' fireworks party. When one neighbour said it was dangerous, a friend replied: 'All children love fire! Let them learn!'

Nearly freezing to death in a Moscow street in deepest winter when a taxi took me to the wrong address, leaving me wandering clueless in a light overcoat feeling the body heat ebbing from me.

Asking our guide in Isfahan why he wouldn't come into the Armenian church with us. 'Their paintings have too much cruelty, suffering and killing. When I go to our mosques, I see only flowers and patterns and beauty.'

Meeting our Minneapolis friends, Ken and Judy Dayton, in Venice where we escaped after resigning from Wolfson College. After listening to our painful experience, Ken, a shrewd businessman, said: 'John, the first markdown is always the hardest.'

Seeing possibly the most beautiful brick building in the world, the Mausoleum of Ismail Samani in Bukhara.

Sitting in the concentrated calm of the writing room in the Public Record Office at Kew, a researcher one desk away started whooping with joy out loud! The rest of us smiled in sympathy and curiosity.

Seeing the Milky Way spread over the entire sky at Arniston, in South Africa.

Diana Burnett, my PA at Bush House, ringing me at a Washington conference with the news of the birth of our grandson, Felix.

Three years later, walking up the path to our son and daughter-in-law's house, Felix leaned from the window to announce the arrival of his sister: 'The baby is born!'

Listening to monks chanting the service in the Coptic monastery of Wadi Latrun.

Buying a glass of hot mint tea from a street seller in the Tunis Medina. He offered another glass; we made to hurry on. '*Doucement!*' he said. '*Doucement!*'

Sitting in the rooftop verandah of an old mansion in Jeddah, the Mayor explained: 'Soon you will hear the evening call to prayer and thirty-six muezzins all within one square mile will make their calls! Listen!' They did so for almost three and a half ecstatic, soaring, united, polychromatic minutes. We floated on the waves of sound.

An old Irish friend, Judge Barra O'Brien, talked of a recent illness in hospital: 'I thought, if I die tonight, at least I won't have to shave in the morning!'

Catching the final chairlift down from the freezing mountain top in Mayrhofen with Annie and knowing that if it were to stop accidentally, we would freeze to death and our sons would be orphans.

The Queen and the President of Finland opened a big Finland festival at the Barbican. The Lord Mayor was nowhere to be seen. I asked Prince Philip what I should do? 'Get on with it,' he barked.

At my grim farewell tea party at Bush House in 1966, one senior figure commented: 'I can't understand why you are leaving. You've got a BBC pension?'

At a dinner party in Singapore in 1965, Fred Emery, *The Times*' South-East Asia correspondent, leaned over and said: 'Everyone else around this table is a spy. I'm not! You're not, are you?'

Five of us stood in thick cloud at 6,000 feet in the middle of a very long ski run in Tignes, the tips of our skis barely visible. 'Our combined ages are pushing four hundred years!' I said.

'No one else is on the mountain! Shouldn't we have known better?'

Alasdair Milne, Director General of the BBC, sweeping into my office at Bush House shortly after my appointment as Managing Director. 'Contrary to what you may have heard, I was not against your appointment!'

On the German-Czechoslovak border in the Cold War days of 1961, the border-post captain tore into my mother: 'Madame, I must warn you against provocations. Your daughters have been trying to bribe my guards with knitting wool!'

An Israeli friend: '"No" is already a good answer!'

At a Conservative Party Conference in Blackpool, Sir Keith Joseph, anguished at length over the difference between the 'common ground' and the 'middle ground' in politics. In the briefing room afterwards, a journalist asked him exactly what he meant? Sir Keith's eyes swivelled, his veins bulged as he smote his forehead: 'I've failed, I've failed!'

The advice given me by a colleague in Hong Kong: 'Never break another man's rice bowl'.

At a Labour Party Conference, Tony Benn protested: 'Typical BBC only to talk of "personalities" rather than the "ishoos". It's the "ishoos" that matter.'

In the south Indian town of Madurai, we resisted pestering by a young cycle pedishaw rider. 'If you don't ride,' he said, 'I don't eat.' We climbed on.

Over Sunday lunches at my parents', my father often waxed eloquent over the nationalist rivalries of East and Central Europe. One day, Sash and Francis decided to enquire innocently: 'Grandpa, is there any nation in East and Central Europe that you have nothing against?' Father pondered seriously: 'Personally, I have nothing against the Bulgarians!' My mother stormed out of the kitchen: 'Well I do!' They may, it seems, have been useful itinerant vegetable and fruit sellers, but they stole chickens.

A former Oxford head of college recalled traditional rivalries between Fellows and Master. 'My father was a Balliol Fellow. Once a month on the day of the College Council he would go in extra early. When we asked why, he said, "To find out what the Master is planning and to stop him!"'

Our Berber guide in Libya lamented bitterly the destruction that Ghaddafi was wreaking on his country: 'Once in 728 years, Allah sends a madman from the desert to destroy us!'

Ilya Repin's shatteringly honest but poignant portrait of Mussorgsky just days before he died of alcoholism.

Transferring planes at Istanbul airport after holidaying in Turkey, we scanned the British newspaper headlines. The face of our friend Austen Kark leapt off a front page, killed in the Potters Bar train crash.

Nina Bawden, Austen's wife, was asked why she pursued the railway companies so vigorously for compensation for all the victims of the crash? 'Because the company needs to learn that it is more expensive to kill people than to carry them safely.'

Finding that, however cunningly I tried to play, I would never beat my younger son Francis at squash.

Arriving at Blackpool station for the Conservative Conference the year after the Brighton bomb, the taxi driver asserted: 'There'll be another IRA bomb this year; the Council has drained the Stanley Baths so that they can be used as an emergency morgue!'

On the anniversary of the Brighton bomb, we danced to Billy Joel's 'Uptown Girl' until the exact time of the explosion was past.

John Gielgud as Prospero in *The Tempest*. 'Our revels now are ended' – time stood still.

A British policeman at London City airport thumbing through the heavily visa-stamped pages of my passport: 'Pakistan, Afghanistan, Iran, Syria – nice places for a holiday would you say, *sir?*'

Witnessing evening puja at the Hindu temple of Madurai where acolytes, priests and elephants processed around the massive stone corridors three times before anointing Khrishna's image with flowers, honey and yoghurt. Our guide whispered: 'The Lord Khrishna is present.'

Graham Greene, Chairman of the British Museum Trustees, invited me to join the board. 'Some colleagues advised against it,' he said 'because "the government doesn't like him!" I replied, "That's an excellent reason for inviting him!" Huge grin!

Hearing the opening bars of Wagner's *The Mastersingers* conducted by Reginald Goodall at Sadler's Wells.

We took refuge on the Irish west-coast island of Inishbofin on the day of Charles and Diana's wedding. Dolphins played, leaping out of the water in the harbour for our benefit.

The road in the high Chitral Valley in north Pakistan runs down a steep mountainside in a series of tight zigzags with no turning circle. We faced the cliff edge as the driver paused before reversing to make the turn. 'At this moment,' observed our guide, 'it is very important to engage the correct gear.'

Waking up at 4 a.m. to the news that the United Kingdom had voted to leave the European Union.

Denis Healey walking past me at a party conference as I sat writing a script: 'Scribble, scribble, scribble, Mr Gibbon,' he chortled.

Getting into our car in Carrickmore, a known IRA hotbed, after dinner, our host advised 'Drive very steadily, keep an eye on the rear mirror and do not stop.'

Taking our young sons to their first *Macbeth*. Sash, the elder, said: 'That man didn't have a chance right from the beginning.'

Taking our sons to Prokofiev's *War and Peace*. At the end, Francis, the younger, shouted: 'Play it again, Sam!'

At Termes, the crossing post between Uzbekistan and Afghanistan, the Uzbek officer challenged me: 'What do English people write on postcards when they are abroad?' None of my answers, such as 'Wish you were here' satisfied him. 'Come, I search you,' he said, and led me into a white-tiled room.

Walking around a remote headland at Dog's Bay in Connemara with Francis and finding a carefully arranged spiral of white stones. Years later, we discovered it was a work by the sculptor Richard Long.

Dozing on a wooden daybed under trees laden with pomegranates in a garden in Yazd, Iran.

Visiting the Bauhaus building in Dessau, shabby and neglected, but Annie and I deciding that it was simply glorious.

Listening to nightingales in Hertfordshire with Sash and Francis.

Before lunches in New York with my old friend, Marti Segal: 'John, have a cocktail with me!'

Annie rang me at the Barbican: 'There's a letter here from Number 10. Do you want me to open it?' She does. Then: 'Are you sitting down?' It was the offer of a 'K'.

Hitting the sweet spot of the tennis racquet with a full swing.

I tried to impress my Soviet minder by learning some words of Russian: 'Excuse me, can you tell me the way to the toilets?' He frowned: 'You sound like a Pole.'

At a roadblock in Uganda manned by Kalashnikov-armed teenagers I resolved not to have my head blown off to protect £3,000 of BBC expenses. It wasn't necessary.

Annie reading 'Fear no more the heat of the sun' at her mother's funeral.

Sunday afternoons in the shared lane behind our house in Hampstead, children lighting a bonfire, baking potatoes, neighbours emerging with tea, later wine.

JT 31 October 2016

Acknowledgements and Thanks

I am very aware of those who have given their time and ransacked their memories or archives to help me in shaping my own recollections. I am deeply grateful for the generosity and openness with which those I have mentioned spoke to me. What they said was important in the final stage of what I wrote. I hope they will feel that I have done justice to the experiences we shared.

In Chapter 1 ('Being Czech') my elder brother George Tusa was crucial in his detailed account of our three pre-war years in Czechoslovakia, especially the traumatic events on the Czech-Yugoslav border crossing. I trust his memory without hesitation. My younger sister, Vicky Bocock, provided vivid details of life and Czech customs on the Bata Estate at East Tilbury. She was incredibly thorough in checking spellings and precise meanings of our rather earthy Moravian family sayings. Karl Svoboda gave me valuable information about life under communism. Rhys Jones and Mike Tabard of the Bata Resource Centre in East Tilbury provided accurate dates about the foundation of the Bata factory and community, and found valuable archive photographs of Zlín.

For Chapter 2 ('Distance Learning') George provided important details about my double pneumonia in 1941, life during the Blitz and conditions in the evacuated school in Ashburton, Devon. Hugh Brogan gave me impressions of St Faith's on its return to peacetime Cambridge.

Chapter 3 ('Becoming British') draws largely on my assorted

diaries and letters and newsletters home which my parents faithfully kept. Jeremy Tunstall gave me the details of the tragic death of our contemporary Tony Simpsons. Liz Larby, the Gresham's archivist, dug out reviews and editorials from the school magazine. Robin Whittle and George Tusa gave me their impressions of school life and atmosphere.

Chapter 4 ('Soldiering') relies on my own quite thorough diaries. Certain oddly inaccurate memories were corrected by my fellow national serviceman, Alistair MacLennan, who also showed me his own memoir of our time in West Germany. Hugh Brogan, whom I ran into disconsolately working in the blanket store in Tonfanau, recognised my account of conditions during national service life.

Chapter 5 ('Learning, Living, Loving') is informed by John Tydeman's account of the brilliant flowering of Cambridge theatre life in the mid-1950s. Adrian Slade shared his experience of the eruption on to the Cambridge scene of Peter Cook. Anil Seal reminisced about our privileged involvement with Trinity's historians. Antonia Clapham showed me her account of life at Newnham College. David Hargreaves, a fellow historian and participant in communal living in Whewell's Court, read and commented on the entire chapter.

Chapter 6 ('Becoming a Broadcaster') includes John Radcliffe's account of journalism and broadcasting at Bush House in the early 1960s. No one knows more about the life, personality and characters of the legendary BBC radio Features and Drama Department in the 1960s than John Tydeman. I was delighted to find in my files the studio script and my own preparatory notes for Philip Whitehead's bizarre TV 'training' programme with Oswald Mosley. It must be in the BBC vaults somewhere – if not, some archive should want to have it!

Chapter 7 ('Breaking Through') relies importantly on the memories of George Carey, *Newsnight*'s creator and first editor, and Tim Gardam, my first producer. Tim gave me an eloquent memoir of his own of that time. Both read and commented on the chapter.

Chapter 8 ('Broadcasting to the World') involved conversations with many of my senior colleagues at BBC World Service – Graham Mytton, Maureen Bebb, Ernest Newhouse, Mary Raine and Elisabeth Wright. Ian Richardson is the custodian of the often misrepresented origins of BBC World Service Television. Richard MacCarthy's compilation of press coverage from my Bush House years is an invaluable resource.

Elizabeth Smith made available her rich cache of World Service documents and let me see a personal memoir written by the late Anthony Rendell in his final weeks. I relied absolutely – then and now – on the judgement and observations on the chapter of my former Deputy Managing Director at World Service, David Witherow.

Chapter 9 ('Fighting Itself'), is based on the detailed, contemporaneous journal I kept on the politics and plotting inside the BBC from 1986 to 1992.

Chapter 10 ('Breaking with the BBC') draws on one unpublished article written at the time and on one public speech, my City University Cameron Lecture of 1994. Fred Emery confirmed my judgement on a key event.

Chapter 11 ('Leaping Free'), on the fiasco of our time at Wolfson College, Cambridge, is based on my contemporaneous account of every event of those bizarre few months.

Chapter 12 ('Softening the Concrete') involved conversations with one of my former Chairmen, Michael Cassidy, my Arts Director, Graham Sheffield – who also read it – my essential PA, Leah Nicholls, Dianne Lennan and Ernest Newhouse. Tony Cheevers and Philip Sellars recalled important moments from my BBC Radio 3 interviews and in Philip's case from *Twenty Twenty – A View of the Century*. Ann McKay gave me her detailed recollections of our work together on the BBC Radio 3 Composer weekends. Nick Kenyon kindly allowed me to glean reports from the Barbican archive. Maddeningly, I kept no diary account from those years. But I did take several hundred photos of artists and musicians of every kind at the Barbican. Those images speak eloquently of those years.

Chapter 13 ('Teaching and Learning') involved conversations with Will Wyatt, my predecessor as Chairman of University of the Arts London, and my first Rector, Michael Bichard. My Vice-Chairman, Clara Freeman, was an invaluable witness to events not least the appointment of Nigel Carrington as Rector, later Vice-Chancellor. Happily but not surprisingly, Nigel's verdict on our five years in harness together are in full harmony with my own.

Sue Hoyle was my anchor during the time with the Clore Leadership Programme and read Chapter 13. Graham Devlin gave me his account of the national arts environment at the time and set me on the road to thinking up a title for the book. During the UAL/Clore years I kept a very detailed daily journal, totalling some 500,000 words. They proved an essential resource when it came to writing and occasionally took me by surprise.

Chapter 14 ('Envoi') wrote itself with frequent prompts from Annie Tusa.

The entire process of book production has been facilitated by Lucinda McNeile, editorial director at Orion. She has been wonderfully patient, constantly encouraging and, of course, efficient.

Two people above all have been intimately involved in the two-year process of writing. My publisher and friend, Alan Samson, devoted time and patience to reading each chapter as it emerged. This was an act of faith and trust; he cannot have known whether his wise oversight might not be wasted. Alan's reassurances at crucial stages of writing were invaluable. Thirty years ago, Alan edited Annie's book *The Nuremberg Trial*. Of such constancy, friendship is made.

I cannot adequately thank my wife Annie for her contribution to the memoir. She read and commented on each chapter as it was written. Many were reshaped or altered in tone as a result. When a complete text was available, she read and edited it from start to finish. She is a fine writer and rigorous editor. If the process was sometimes painful for me, it was also essential. Nobody could be more professional and demanding. I could not be more grateful or more aware of the commitment, judgement and honesty she brought to the process. For in writing of my life, I am also very aware that I have written of hers too. I hope she feels I have not trespassed on what is hers. Mere thanks are inadequate. Love must do.

Permissions

I am very grateful to the following for permission to quote from their books:

Michael Frayn and Faber & Faber for extracts from *Towards the End of the Morning* (Faber & Faber, 1967).

Harper Collins Publishers Ltd for an extract from Penelope Fitzgerald's *Human Voices* (Collins, 1980).

Professor Howard Tumber and the James Cameron Lecture Trust for extracts from my 1994 Cameron Lecture 'Programmes or Products: the management ethos and creative values' (Politico's 2001).

Index